Personal Identity and Applied Ethics

G000059461

'Soul', 'self', 'substance', and 'person' are just four of the terms often used to refer to the human individual. Cutting across metaphysics, ethics and religion, the nature of personal identity and the self is a fundamental and long-standing puzzle in philosophy.

Personal Identity and Applied Ethics introduces and examines different conceptions of the self, our nature, and personal identity and considers the implications of these for applied ethics. A key feature of the book is that it considers a range of different approaches to personal identity: philosophical, religious and cross-cultural, including perspectives from non-Western traditions. Within this comparative framework, Andrea Sauchelli examines the following topics:

- Early views of the soul in Plato, Christianity, and Descartes;
- The Buddhist 'no-self' views and the self as a fiction;
- Confucian ideas of our nature and the importance of self-cultivation as constitutive of the self;
- Locke's theory of personal identity as continuity of consciousness and memory and objections by Butler and Reid as well as contemporary critics;
- The theory of 'animalism' and arguments concerning embodied concepts of personal identity;
- Practical and narrative theories of personal identity and moral agency;
- Personal identity and issues in applied ethics, including abortion, organ transplantation, and the idea of life after death;
- Implications of life-extending technologies for personal identity.

Throughout the book Sauchelli also considers the views of important recent philosophers such as Sydney Shoemaker, Bernard Williams, Derek Parfit, Marya Schechtman, and Christine Korsgaard, placing these in helpful historical context.

Chapter summaries, a glossary of key terms, and suggestions for further reading make this a refreshing, approachable introduction to personal identity and applied ethics. It is an ideal text for courses on personal identity that consider both Western and non-Western approaches and that apply theories of personal identity to ethical problems. It will also be of interest to those in related subjects such as religious studies and history of ideas.

Andrea Sauchelli is an Associate Professor of Philosophy at Lingnan University, Hong Kong.

Personal Identity and Applied Ethics

A Historical and Philosophical Introduction

Andrea Sauchelli

Routledge
Taylor & Francis Group

LONDON AND NEW YORK

First published 2018
by Routledge
2 Park Square, Milton Park, Abingdon, Oxon OX14 4RN

and by Routledge
711 Third Avenue, New York, NY 10017

Routledge is an imprint of the Taylor & Francis Group, an informa business

British Library Cataloguing-in-Publication Data
A catalogue record for this book is available from the British Library

Library of Congress Cataloguing-in-Publication Data
Names: Sauchelli, Andrea, author.
Title: Personal identity and applied ethics : a historical and
    philosophical introduction / by Andrea Sauchelli.
Description: 1 [edition]. | New York : Routledge, 2017. | Includes
    bibliographical references and index.
Identifiers: LCCN 2017032020 | ISBN 9781138185685 (hardback : alk.
    paper) | ISBN 9781138185692 (pbk. : alk. paper) |
    ISBN 9781315644288 (e-book)
Subjects: LCSH: Self (Philosophy) | Self-knowledge, Theory of. | Self. |
    Identity (Philosophical concept) | Identity (Psychology) | Applied
    ethics.
Classification: LCC BD438.5 .S28 2017 | DDC 126—dc23
LC record available at https://lccn.loc.gov/2017032020

ISBN: 978-1-138-18568-5 (hbk)
ISBN: 978-1-138-18569-2 (pbk)
ISBN: 978-1-315-64428-8 (ebk)

Typeset in Times New Roman
by Apex CoVantage, LLC

Contents

Acknowledgements   vi

**Introduction: personal identity, personal ontology,
and ethics**   1

1   **The simple-soul approach and dualisms**   30

2   **Buddhist no-self approach and nihilism**   52

3   **Relational approach and Confucian role-person**   76

4   **Locke and the psychological approach**   97

5   **The physical approach and animalism**   123

6   **Practical and narrative approaches**   145

7   **What matters in survival and life-extending
    technologies**   166

8   **The beginning and the end**   197

Glossary   231
Index   238

Acknowledgements

Much of the intellectual pleasure that philosophy gives me derives from thinking about philosophical problems by myself. Perhaps as a consequence of this preference, and a resulting 'isolationist' attitude, I have not received much help from other 'professional philosophers' in developing and writing this book. However, some people did read the entire manuscript (among them, the anonymous referee for Routledge and Paisley Livingston, whose help has been immensely important), while others read one or more chapters (Rafael De Clercq and P. J. Ivanhoe). Their comments have been helpful and I would like to thank them for their time. Also, I want to thank those people who have been giving me that 'non-philosophical' support that was perhaps even more essential to complete this project: my mom (Emanuela), my dad (Vincenzo), my grandmother (Maria), my two aunties and uncle (Cristina, Luisella, Virgilio), and Hyelin.

This project was supported by a Grant from the Research Grants Council of the Hong Kong Special Administrative Region, China (Project No. LU23400314).

Introduction

Personal identity, personal ontology, and ethics

Sunday morning, you are waking up. You forgot to put your phone on silent and a promotional message did the rest. Now, you can't even focus on the display to read the time. Finally, the mental machinery starts to put together all the various pieces of the puzzle: memories, desires, and impulses that remind you to satisfy various bodily urges. Suddenly you form – or perhaps simply retrieve – the usual compelling map of priorities. Is there a sense in which you, right now, are the same individual who went to bed the night before? If so, what makes this sense of continuity through time not just an illusion, an impression, something that certain wise men of the past (and the present) claim you should get rid of to obtain 'enlightenment'? You remember that you have a lunch appointment with your family. You promised your friend you would meet him or her at the gym later on. There is a pseudo-important meeting the day after, on a dreadfully anticipated Monday morning. Is this network of relations with people and of responsibilities part of what makes you what and who you are? The phone rings again; evidently last night you said something terrible that hurt someone's feelings: there is someone who now resents you, or so you are told. Apparently, you are also a moral agent who has to take responsibility for your actions. Does this – taking responsibility for actions – constitute part of what being a *person* is, in addition to just being a human animal, a digestive tube that strives to survive? Never mind, it is time to prepare your gym bag, fill up your shaker with some protein powder (and maybe something else). 'Is it safe to drink these things? Am I slowly damaging myself and my body?' you think. But should this really worry *you*? After all, it is very unlikely that you will have kidney failure in the near future. 'It will be a problem, if at all, that some future *me* will have to deal with.' But now you think again. 'Should I be concerned with the future of an old(er) self that will have my same body but that will likely have a significantly different mind or way of thinking? Does it matter whether this person will be really me?' Then you look at the watch, shrug off these worries and your life continues; some play backgammon, some lift weights, merry with their friends.

This book introduces the reader to various replies to the questions asked by this awakening consciousness, in the hope that you have sometimes felt like that self or at least once have fallen into a similar philosophical melancholy. One of the general guiding ideas behind what follows is that what we think we are and how (and whether) we persist through time is conceptually and metaphysically – and not just psychologically – connected to a variety of practical issues, some of them of considerable moral relevance. In fact, far from being of a purely theoretical interest, debates in personal identity are of great importance for matters of life and death – even if only for defining what life and death are. For example, a belief in the existence of an enduring soul, although not popular among professional philosophers nowadays, seems to play a significant role in the lives of those people who still believe in, e.g., rebirth or resurrection. But what theories of the soul are compatible with the view according to which it is really *you* who is resurrected when the time comes – or with the view according to which you may come back to life as, say, a cow or a cat? As it turns out, there are theories saying that we are essentially psychological entities that continue to exist through time only if certain psychological connections are maintained. So, on these views, the belief that you may become a cat – without any of those memories, desires, capacities, and character traits that distinguish you now – would be false.

What are the key concepts and terms we use to think about ourselves? Some of the most important include the concepts of a self and of a person, personal pronouns such as 'I', 'you', etc., the notion of a subject of experience, of our nature, and so on. Among these, the book focuses on the concept of a person and on the conditions a person should meet to persist through time – what we may call the metaphysics of personal identity. Another centre of focus is the current debate on what we are, on our nature. Such a debate is nowadays understood as an enquiry into the ontological category to which we belong – that is, an investigation of the general category or categories of entities to which we belong. It is important to notice that the ontological study of our nature – an investigation aimed at clarifying the question 'what are we?' – is conceptually different from a discussion of what makes us persons and of the conditions of identity that an individual must satisfy to persist through time *as* the same person. Much of the past debate on personal identity is framed under the assumption that when we think about our own nature, about the kind of entities we are, we are thereby thinking about the nature of entities that are essentially persons and/or of entities that essentially have psychological states. The two questions – one concerning the identity over time of persons and one about our own nature – are certainly related. For instance, many contemporary thinkers believe that we are, indeed, essentially persons. However, others have argued that, although we are now also human persons, we are not *essentially* persons. In particular, the supporters of a theory called **animalism** say that you and I are animals, and that there was a time in which we were human **organisms** but not persons, e.g., when we were foetuses at an early stage of development.

In introducing and assessing various accounts of personal identity and of our nature, I will sometimes take a stand with regard to their plausibility and highlight how some of the considerations that count against one approach have been developed in other theories. Now, a good starting point for clarifying these issues is to distinguish the questions that the theories discussed in this book are supposed to answer.

1 The questions

These are some of the key questions that are addressed in the current debate on personal identity and our nature:

- What are the necessary and sufficient conditions that an entity should satisfy to be a person?
- What are the necessary and sufficient conditions that a person should satisfy to persist through time as the same person?
- What are we? What is our nature? What is the most general ontological category to which we belong?
- When did we begin? When will we end? What is (our) death?
- How do philosophers from different backgrounds and times discuss these issues?
- Under the supposition that our identity through time is akin to an illusion, is it desirable or rational to refrain from thinking of ourselves in terms of persisting entities?
- What is the contribution of other people and of our social background to the determination of our own identity, both as metaphysically individuated entities and as persons?
- What is the contribution of those stories or narratives we tell about ourselves to personal identity? Do these narratives only contribute to our biographical or social identity, or should they be included in the specification of the metaphysical **conditions of personal identity** through time?
- Is there a sense in which we can personally survive death? What do different theories of personal identity imply with regard to the rationality of certain self-directed attitudes towards our own future (e.g., self-concern for survival)?
- What are the theoretical consequences of metaphysical theories of identity for debates on the morality of **abortion** and the rationality of different types of life-extending technologies – both hypothetical and actual?

Now that the main questions and problems have been more clearly specified, what are the main approaches or families of theories that attempt to answer them?

2 Main approaches

Not all of the theories and approaches discussed in the subsequent chapters provide explicit answers to all of the previous questions. For instance, the Buddhist approach (Chapter 2) was not originally devised to discuss certain contemporary life-extending technologies (e.g., mental [or mind] uploading). However, whenever it is reasonable to do so, I try elaborate the consequences of these approaches for issues not directly discussed by their proponents, especially in the last two chapters. The organising principle of the book is to first introduce the main approaches in the current metaphysical debate (Chapters 1 to 6) and then investigate some of their conceptual consequences for a selected number of issues in applied ethics (Chapters 7 and 8).

In general, an *approach* to an area X is here understood as a family of theories or theses having some key conceptual features in common. I use both the expressions 'the family of X-theories' (for example, the family of psychological theories of personal identity) and 'the X-approach' (for example, the psychological approach), to group together various theories that are significantly similar with respect to some fundamental conceptual dimensions of variation.

The main approaches to personal identity and our nature discussed in this book are:

1   **The simple-soul approach** (e.g., simple-soul theories, dualism about our nature). The main idea behind these theories, which belong to the broader family of soul-based theories, is that personal identity over time depends on the continuity of a simple soul. The versions of this approach explored in Chapter 1, which are elaborations on Plato's and some theistic thinkers' ideas, hold that the soul is a mereologically simple entity, that is, an entity that has no proper parts. In addition, such a simple entity is generally taken to be immaterial. In other words, on these views, a soul is an entity that cannot be further (metaphysically) divided into more basic components and that has no (non-derivative) physical properties. Theories of our nature belonging to this approach further state that we are simple souls or that we are compounds of soul and body, although perhaps only the soul is responsible for our continuity over time. One of the problems of this approach is that the existence of (immaterial) souls is, to say the least, controversial. In addition to recent criticisms by contemporary philosophers of mind, also Buddhist philosophers have argued that the belief in *enduring* or *persisting* souls is mistaken (Chapter 2).

2   The **Buddhist no-self** approach and nihilism (e.g., Buddhist nihilism). This approach generally (but not always) includes the claim that we should deny the existence of persons and other similar complex (i.e., non-simple) entities along with the existence of permanent souls. For instance, some early Buddhist schools seem to firmly deny the existence of an enduring soul of the kind discussed by Plato and some Christian thinkers. In addition, several Buddhist schools claim that the alleged holding of the relation of personal identity is an artificial projection onto reality that it would be best to discard or do without. Some of the characteristic claims of the Buddhist approach also imply that, strictly speaking, *we* (or you or I) do not exist – at least under certain understandings of the purported reference of personal pronouns or proper names. On these views, what really or literally exists is just a series of interrelated fleeting mental and physical occurrences. Even the staunchest advocates of these theories, however, recognise that 'person' stands for a concept that we can hardly dispense with in our everyday lives. One of the challenges to the Buddhist approach is thus that of making sense of the idea that this and related concepts seem to be fundamental and strictly connected to our social nature. This social and relational aspect is emphasised in what I call the Confucian

role-person theory, one version of the relational approach discussed in Chapter 3. (The relational nature of personal identity is also associated with John Locke's theory.)

3   The relational approach (e.g., early Confucian role-person, relational narrative theories). Theories that belong to this approach emphasise our relational nature and that of persons. For instance, the early **Confucian role-person theory** holds that a necessary condition for the existence of a person is that such a person be appropriately related to a social background. On this view, the concept of a person is essentially relational in the sense that an entity can become and/or continue to be a person only if such an entity undergoes a certain process of development within a community and/or if the relevant community continues to exist. Although this view has been presented as an alternative to, e.g., Locke's version of the psychological approach, the relational approach can be specified in ways that are compatible with various other psychological theories. The main idea as to why these approaches can be compatible – or even require each other – is that certain relational aspects of persons (e.g., some of the psychological states required to interact in a community and cultivate ourselves) presuppose the development of psychological features in the individual in question, which in turn seems to presuppose that persons persist through time also in virtue of their psychological properties.

4   The psychological approach (e.g., psychological and **person essentialism**, non-structured or **generic psychological theories**). This approach is broad and includes a great variety of theories. The characterising feature of generic psychological theories is the claim that the relation of personal identity depends on (the continuity or connection between) certain psychological properties/faculties throughout time. In turn, these theories differ in the specification of these psychological facts and in how these facts are related. For instance, generic psychological theories include in their lists of relevant mental faculties some forms of memory, character, agency, and so on – what I call 'identity-sustaining psychological connections'. For expository reasons, I first discuss non-structured or generic psychological theories (Chapter 4), a series of objections raised against these theories (Chapter 5), and then other versions of the psychological approach (Chapter 6) based on the idea that the psychological connections that sustain the relation of personal identity should have a specific structure (e.g., the identity-sustaining psychological connections should also ensure the continuity of the same moral/rational agent that depend on such psychological connections). Some of the problems of this approach are related to what Bernard Williams calls the attempt to prise apart considerations regarding the continuity of our body and the psychological features that are supposed to ground the relation of personal identity. In particular, some philosophers claim that the continuity of certain physical facts (e.g., our brains) is a necessary condition for the identity through time of persons.

5   The **physical approach** (e.g., theories including the idea that bodily continuity is a necessary condition for personal identity, animalism). Not many

contemporary accounts claim that individuals *qua* (i.e., as) persons are merely bodies, in the sense that the identity conditions of a person exclusively coincide with the identity conditions of a human organism. In fact, bodily theories of personal identity, from early Biblical references to claims made by recent analytic philosophers, seem to be better understood as simply stating one or more necessary conditions for the holding of the relation of personal identity. However, there are theories of our nature – *not* of personal identity – claiming that we are essentially living human organisms (one version of animalism). These theories offer interesting philosophical alternatives to the previously dominant psychological approach to our nature. However, theories such as animalism sometimes fall short of providing a convincing account of the apparent plausibility of some of our beliefs regarding the importance of at least some psychological connections for our own identity and nature – these beliefs have been discussed especially in relation to various thought experiments such as brain-transplant or fission scenarios (more on this in what follows). Theories that fare better in this respect are classified as belonging to the **practical approach** and/or to the narrative approach – the next item in our list.

6   The practical and narrative approaches (e.g., the **volitional theory**, self-constituting narrative view). These theories are understood as specifications of some of the psychological theories discussed in Chapter 4 and criticised in Chapter 5. One of the motivations behind these views is that, despite the best efforts of defenders of animalism, some of our deeply rooted intuitions about our nature seem to crucially involve beliefs regarding the holding of certain psychological connections in assessing claims about our identity and persistence over time. Practical approaches clarify some of these beliefs by providing an account of the relationship between being a moral agent and the process of constitution of personal identity, as for example in Epictetus's view. The narrative approach holds that our identity and/or our nature essentially involve our capacity to connect some of the events of our lives into a (coherent) narrative. However, whether having a narrative is a necessary and sufficient condition for being a (human) person and/or persisting through time is itself controversial.

So much for an initial list of approaches or families of theories. How, one may now wonder, are they connected? Are these theories all mutually exclusive? Now, it seems to me that many of these theories (or, at least, some of the main claims that are parts of these theories) are not mutually exclusive. On the contrary, some versions of these approaches seem to be more fundamental than or presuppose the others. For instance, certain versions of the self-constituting narrative approach presuppose certain basic claims made by generic psychological theories. More specifically, certain versions of the narrative approach presuppose that a self-constituting person has persisting psychological features – or, at least, that the self-constituting narrator does (see Chapters 4 and 6 for details). Similarly, some relational and role-based theories implicitly assume or presuppose that the identity through time of persons also involves psychological continuity. In addition, certain criteria proposed by some physical theories can be integrated with criteria of the psychological approach. For instance, some psychological theories include, as a necessary condition for the holding of the identity-sustaining psychological connections, that certain forms of causal and physical continuity (e.g., the continuity of the same brain) hold as well. For these reasons, drawing clear-cut distinctions among these approaches is sometimes artificial and not entirely accurate. To better understand some of the connections and differences between the approaches introduced previously, we need further preliminary clarifications of the key terms and concepts used to formulate them.

3 Basic concepts: identification, persons, selves, persistence, identity through time, survival, practical concerns

In the contemporary debate, a great variety of concepts and terms are usually discussed under the general heading 'personal identity', although the topic of personal identity, in a strict sense, is just one among them.[1]

- Identification and individuality

The notion of **identification (and individuation)** can be understood in at least two senses: metaphysical and epistemological/cognitive. An epistemological/cognitive act of identification or individuation consists in the mental recognition or isolation of one or more entities as individual objects of attention or thought.[2] For example, when we individuate a computer and a chair in front of us, we mentally individuate, isolate, or distinguish two distinct entities. Some philosophers argue that such a mental act – if it is an act – generally requires, on the side of the identifier, the possession of some kind of description or concept taken to apply to the identified entity. The idea is that for me to identify – to isolate in cognition – an object, say, a chair, I must have, even implicitly, the capacity to single out chairs from the other elements presented to me by the senses, and such a capacity is mediated by certain basic and/or broad classifiers. The details of such a process or even how this capacity is acquired do not concern us now. The main point to remember is that 'identification' can refer to an epistemological or cognitive process the result of which is the recognition or creation (in thought) of one or more objects of attention of thought. On the other hand, the metaphysical, as opposed to the epistemological/cognitive, identification or individuation of an object is not a mental act but is a fact about the world. Such a fact is sometimes taken to be determined by a series of other facts that specify the identity of an object as an entity, at least under a certain respect, as distinguished from others. For example, the conditions of metaphysical identification described by a kind K (e.g., 'cat') are those conditions the satisfaction of which is necessary and sufficient for an entity ('Kitty') of kind K ('cat') to be of that kind and/or to exist. The number of times that such conditions are satisfied at a time is the number of objects of kind K that exist at that time. The conditions of metaphysical identification of an object are supposed to be those general conditions that an object has to satisfy to exist at all.

This book focuses on general issues about the metaphysical identification of persons and of ourselves. Theories addressing these issues are understood as being about the conditions of *numerical* identity of persons and ourselves, not simply about the conditions of *qualitative* identity of persons and ourselves. The difference is that conditions of numerical identity are those conditions that metaphysically identify the numerically same object, while conditions of qualitative identity involve only the qualities possessed by an object. To illustrate the difference, imagine that a perfect replica or copy of an object is metaphysically or nomologically possible. For example, imagine a perfect qualitative replica of, say, a watch right next to the other. The two watches are *qualitatively* identical (i.e., they may have the same intrinsic properties) whilst *numerically* different (there are two watches, rather than one). Or, imagine a situation in which you tell a salesperson 'I want that watch' while pointing at a watch on display. After having paid, the person in question will give you an almost qualitatively identical watch, and you will probably not object to that. You did not want the numerically identical watch on display, rather you were expressing the desire to buy an object of that type – an object qualitatively identical (or relevantly so) to the one you were pointing at. Another example: imagine a futuristic 3D printer capable of scanning each single molecule composing your body – ignore for the moment the nomological constraints that may make this machine technologically impossible. Imagine also that this machine is capable of making an exact replica of your body without thereby destroying you. After the copying procedure has been performed, a natural description of the outcome is that now there are two qualitatively identical entities (two bodies), each numerically different from the other, albeit qualitatively almost identical (at least for a brief amount of time). Unless otherwise specified, the concept of personal identity (and of our nature) discussed in the book is that of *numerical* personal identity (and of ourselves).[3]

What are the metaphysical facts that determine the numerical and metaphysical identification of things (including ourselves)? Some Medieval philosophers, for example Aquinas (1225–1274) and some Averroists (followers of certain doctrines proposed by Averroes [1126–1198]), claimed that matter is the principle of individuation: the spatio-temporal material existence of an entity properly informed by (moulded after) a form or principle is a sufficient condition for an entity to be metaphysically individuated, that is, to count as one sample of its kind. In turn, Aquinas and some Averroists seem to identify our individuating form with the soul, although their accounts differ regarding the way in which a soul can be individuated. More specifically, the former (seems to have) held that the soul can still be individuated independently of the matter it informs; for instance, even after the relevant material body dies. On the other hand, Averroists are generally understood as holding that the soul is not independently individuated, and this is sometimes understood as implying that after death there is no individual or personal survival, possibly just a form of non-personal survival. The scholastic philosopher

Francisco Suarez (1548–1617), whose work was known and appreciated by Descartes and Leibniz, claimed that (actual) existence is not a necessary condition for individuation and that also possible entities may have individuality. The essence of a man is what individuates such an entity and, in discussing resurrection and immortality, Suarez also claims that an entity is rightly re-identified through time for as long as the same soul persists. Questions of human and personal identification and re-identification in a metaphysical sense, especially due to the debate to which John Locke (1632–1704) made crucially influential contributions, were later finally framed in terms of *personal* identity. However, general criteria of individuation (i.e., criteria that apply to all kinds of objects) are still debated in contemporary metaphysical disputes.[4]

• Personhood and persons

Theories of personal identity are involved in at least these two projects:

1 The project of specifying the **synchronic** (i.e., at one time) conditions of personhood – what features does an entity have to possess in order to count as a person?
2 The project of specifying the **diachronic** (i.e., through time) conditions of identity for persons – what features must two entities existing at different times have to be identified as the (numerically) same person?

As already specified in the previous section, this book deals mostly with theories about the metaphysical and numerical identification of persons at a time and through time, but what do we mean by 'person'? The concept of a person and the conditions of personhood discussed by philosophers are various and even substantially different. In certain cases, as when I discuss the early Confucian role-person view, my use of 'person' can be usefully understood as standing for a concept that is functionally equivalent, in a way to be specified, to other concepts expressed by foreign language terms. When the concept of a person is employed in such a way, it can be useful to adopt very broad application standards; for instance, as a concept that groups together individual beings that (1) have certain cognitive/psychological capacities, (2) can persist through time, and (3) are morally or practically relevant to a considerable degree, e.g., they are said to have (a high degree of) **moral status**. In turn, the cognitive and psychological capacities included in this broad definition can be specified in different ways: as memory, reason, character traits, and so on. The moral or practical part of the definition may involve the notion of moral responsibility, concern for future personal survival, and even considerations regarding the role of other people in the formation of our identity. It seems to me that, sceptics notwithstanding, cultures sophisticated enough to produce what we may call philosophical thinking, whether early Chinese Confucians or ancient Greek philosophers, all had terms in their languages standing for rational/psychological individuals with a significant moral and practical dimension. The details of their relevant concepts and terms may certainly differ. However, a broad understanding of what a person is – even if the aim is just to claim that persons are illusions (Chapter 2) – seems to be hardly avoidable in the conceptual frameworks of any sophisticated literary and philosophical culture.

Many scholars have pointed out that the term 'person' comes from the Latin *persona*, which in turn was used to translate the Greek term πρόσωπον (*prosopon*). The Greek term seems to have been connected to the theatrical world; in particular, it was used to refer to the mask used to inform the audience about which roles were being played by the actors in the performance. Christopher Gill claims that another term used in ancient philosophy related to our use of 'person' is ἄνθρωπος (*anthrō-pos*), sometimes translated as 'man', in the generic sense of member of the human species, or 'human'. These terms were frequently taken to have a moral dimension or bearing – for instance, in Aristotle's *Nicomachean Ethics*, where the proper function of a human being (an activity of the mind in accordance with reason and virtue) was taken to determine the well-being of the members of our species. The concepts of a human being and of a person have often been taken to be equivalent; however, an increasing number of philosophers claim that a person does not necessarily have to be human. For instance, some have argued that 'person' is a more general term that can apply to, say, gods, intelligent aliens (if there are any), or even some animals (e.g., certain greater apes or even dolphins). In the rest of the book, I focus on human persons, unless otherwise stated, but I do not assume that the concept of a human being and that of a person are equivalent. The use of the Latin term 'persona' was extended from its early association with the theatre to refer to the more general role or function played by an individual in society. An example of this use is in Cicero's (106–43 BCE) theory of the four persons. Gill describes the aim of this theory as that of providing a series of normative reference points that should be taken into account in developing personal *decorum* or appropriateness.[5] The idea seems to be that an individual, to develop appropriately, should keep in mind that she is: (1) a human being, thus endowed with special physical and rational capacities common to other human beings, (2) an entity with specific talents and skills, (3) an entity with a social status, embedded in a social context that specifies certain obligations based on her role, and (4) an entity that can choose, up to a certain point, the way in which she can be seen – as an orator, a philosopher, or a gladiator. The association of the notion of a person with a social role is present also in later diverse thinkers such as Lorenzo Valla (1407–1457) and Miguel Serveto (1511?–1553).

Other important uses of the concept of a person emerge in the legal system. In the Roman legal system, for instance, a *persona* was conceived as being not merely a *res* (thing); rather, a *persona*, whether an individual human being or a corporate entity, was considered as an entity that has legal rights. This legal or forensic aspect of the concept of a person is not further explored in the rest of the book, with a brief exception in Chapter 4.[6] The use of 'persona' and 'prosopon' spread to the theological context, in particular to describe some of the features of the Christian God. For instance, Tertullian (160–220) is reported to have used the expression *una substantia, tres personae* ("one substance, three persons") to describe and refer to the trinity. Udo Thiel claims that the use of 'persona' for referring to the various persons that (allegedly) characterise God has been adopted in the Christian tradition since at least the Council of Alexandria (362). Around the year 500, the Roman philosopher Boethius (475/477–526?) used 'persona' to refer to an essentially rational individual substance – "the individual substance of a rational nature". Subsequently, Aquinas claimed in his *Summa Theologiae* (1a.29.1) that persons are substances that, due to their rational nature, have control over their actions. The concepts of a human person and of an individual human being were taken to be (almost) the same, but, as is amply discussed in Chapter 4, Locke made an influential and widely recognised contribution to the debate by more clearly distinguishing these concepts. In particular, his understanding of what a person is refers to (1) a person's rational and psychological nature, (2) certain features of the type of consciousness that persons are supposed to have, (3) the moral, relational, and social aspects of persons, and (4) the religious and eschatological consequences of such an understanding. In recent times, contributors to the metaphysical debate on personal identity have not all emphasised the moral, relational, and social aspects of the concept of a person. These aspects, however, have been discussed in the context of debates on moral agency and on the role of the individual in society. As a result of this divergence of interests, many philosophers in the last two centuries seemed to be discussing (and took themselves to be discussing) two different concepts, that is, the 'metaphysical person' and the 'moral person' – and some have even claimed that a conception of the latter is independent from a conception of the former (and vice versa).

One contemporary influential philosopher, David Wiggins, writes: "[o]n occasion, almost everyone feels difficulty in holding in a single focus three very different ideas: (a) the idea of the person as object of biological, anatomical, and neurophysiological inquiry; (b) the idea of the person as subject of consciousness; (c) the idea of the person as locus of all sorts of moral attributes and the source or conceptual origin of all value."[7] Sense (c) has been described by Amelie Oksenberg Rorty as containing the promise of a dream; more specifically, the idea that a whole series of moral rights and obligations – even moral principles – can be derived from a clear definition of what a person is.[8] As a consequence of the disparate variety of understandings of the concept of a person, A. Rorty claims that there is no unique and/or correct understanding of it, but rather different aspects that may even be in conflict with each other.[9]

This plurality of definitions of 'person' can be taken to reveal a divergence of methodological approaches to the study of the concept(s) at issue. For instance, certain authors whose interests are closer to issues in practical ethics (e.g., Peter Singer) generally tend to use 'person' as a term with a *thin* metaphysical or merely functional content but rich in practical consequences. More specifically, some authors have claimed that, to the degree that an entity is capable of feeling pain – where this may also be intended as involving the capacity to have a basic form of self-awareness or perspective on the world – such an entity ought to be classified as a person. Throughout the book, I will adopt the simple but good practice of specifying, when relevant, which use of 'person' (and which understanding of the related concepts) is intended in each case. A further complication is that many authors also use 'self' and 'person' interchangeably or as denoting the same kind of entities. In the next section, I discuss some of the concepts associated with the term 'self' and suggest that, given this variety, it is theoretically useful to distinguish them.

- Selves, subjects of experience, and ourselves

In a recent paper, Sydney Shoemaker writes: "I think that insofar as 'selves' are a kind of entities, they are no different from persons. The term 'self' is used to refer to a person as that person conceives and knows itself. Locke's definition asserts a close connection between the nature of selves, or persons, and the access they have to themselves and their identities."[10] Other philosophers, psychologists, and neuroscientists have used the term 'self' differently. For instance, some have associated the notion of a self with the concept of a minimal subject, that is, the concept of a basic, minimal metaphysical and/or phenomenological and/or epistemological unit that (allegedly) accompanies all our experiences. Along these lines, some describe the minimal subject as an entity the existence of which is required for having experiences at all and sometimes as being pre-reflective. On this understanding, the perception or deduction of the existence of a minimal subject may come from the phenomenological aspects of our conscious experiences – i.e., we always perceive from a perspective, the perspective of our own self, and this testifies to its existence. Following this line of reasoning, a **minimal self** is taken to provide (or be) the subjective point of view through/from which we know the external world or our inner mental lives. A minimal or basic self is also sometimes described as being almost featureless, in particular, as having essentially only the property of being conscious (akin to a Cartesian ego). In addition, a minimal subject is sometimes characterised as being capable of existing independently of all our experiences; as such, it is an entity the existence of which may be testified solely by the perspectival nature of our subjective experiences. A possible worry related to this way of characterising the idea of a subject of experience – as an almost featureless point of view – is that the deduction of the existence of an entity purely from the phenomenological quality of our experiences may be dubious. For example, some recent cognitive scientists (e.g., Thomas Metzinger) have criticised this methodology and claimed that the (sense of) self is a kind of illusion generated by the cognitive architecture of our brains. In addition, the self, intended as the entity essentially related to our experiences or mental states, does not have to be minimal or basic to be regarded as that which has such experiences or mental states.

In a recent survey on the literature on the self, Shaun Gallagher claims that the concept of a minimal self is generally understood as standing for a self that is accessible to immediate self-consciousness – where self-consciousness is supposed to be a form of awareness internally directed. Gallagher distinguishes the minimal self from the narrative self, that is, a self extended in time that also has a more complex structure. However, the term 'narrative self' has been used also to refer to the author or narrator of what is called instead a person-narrative, where it is only the latter, but not the former, that is supposed to essentially have a more complex (non-minimal) structure and/or temporal dimension. On this understanding, the narrative (or better *narrating*) self is the actual agential unit that composes or creates complex entities or ways of looking at entities that we generally call persons (or person-narratives). It is persons that have narrative structure, whilst it is an open question whether the narrator is itself structured or whether it coincides with the created person-narrative.

The current academic literature includes uses of 'self' in which the term is understood as standing for the way an individual presents herself to the world – a use of 'self' that is very similar to that of 'person', intended as a placeholder for a nexus of social roles. Other philosophers claim that the self is our true inner core, that is, what remains after all the societal accretions have been removed or left aside. Another source of confusion (or simply a different way in which the term is used) is that the self is sometimes taken as the referent of the personal pronoun 'I'. Many (e.g., Ludwig Wittgenstein) have also distinguished at least two referential uses of 'I': we can use first personal pronouns, when we self-refer, to indicate a subject or a physical object. Some associate the first use with sentences that express thoughts containing at least one element with regard to which we cannot fail to properly identify the referent of part of what is said. For example, the thought 'I think that Hong Kong is very humid in summer' contains an element – 'I think that' – about which the speaker cannot be wrong about who is having the thought that Hong Kong is very humid in summer.[11] An objective use of personal pronouns is characterised by the use of such pronouns to describe oneself from an external perspective and/or to describe some of our bodily features and states.

To complicate things even more, the term 'self' is frequently used to signal a specific way in which we may come to know some of our inner states; for instance, when we talk about *self*-knowledge. In turn, this form of knowledge can be understood as an internally directed way in which we come to know also some features of the subject of our experiences – although some have criticised this understanding of self-knowledge as involving a form of internal perception or inference. The term 'self-' in this and similar contexts is generally understood as introducing a level of *self*-referentiality to the term to which it is attached.

One of the most important distinctions to the understanding of this book is that between debates about *our selves* and debates about *ourselves*. The two debates may coincide if, for instance, we hold that we are selves; however, generally debates concerning ourselves are nowadays intended as debates regarding our nature, that is, debates aimed at clarifying the ontological kind to which we (essentially) belong (a sub-field of ontology called **personal ontology**). On an understanding of selves as essentially psychological entities (i.e., as entities that essentially have mental properties), many recent philosophers argue that we are not essentially selves/psychological entities. For example, Eric Olson claims that we are human animals, where the concept of a human animal is understood as equivalent to that of a (living) human organism. The details of this theory, called 'animalism', are explored in Chapter 4, but to a first approximation, some of its main versions imply that it is not essential to have mental states (i.e., to be psychological entities) for us to exist (or be the same through time).[12] In the rest of this book, I frequently use the expressions 'ourselves' and 'our own nature' in reference to debates regarding the ontological category/ies to which we belong, without thereby implying that we are selves/psychological entities.[13]

- Persistence and time

Contemporary philosophers describe the existence of an entity at different times by saying that x *persists* over times. This way of describing the relationship between an entity and time is supposed to be neutral with respect to various metaphysical theories of time and change. For reasons of space and given the introductory nature of this book, I do not investigate also how different theories of time influence theories of persistence and consequently of personal identity. However, some brief remarks are in order. One of the fundamental questions in the debate on the nature of time and persistence is whether time should be thought of as another dimension in which entities can extend. One popular way of understanding how objects persist over periods of time, in fact, is that of thinking of persistent entities as entities extended in time, not just in space. On this view, a familiar three-dimensional object such as a table or a chair has one additional dimension, the dimension of time, in which it extends and thereby persists. This approach, sometimes called four-dimensionalism, is generally associated with the view called eternalism, that is, the theory according to which temporal events – i.e., events that happen in time – exist *simpliciter*: past, present, and future events are all equally real and existent. A past object, say, the Colossus of Rhodes, is an object that exists in the past, say, in 250 BCE. The Great Pyramid of Giza is an object that exists in the past and in the present, that is, it is a present object that extends in the past. This past extension is no less real than its present extension – it simply exists at some other time. On this version of four-dimensionalism, we say that objects persist through time by having temporal extensions or stages at different times. A different approach to time and the persistence of objects may assign a special role to the present moment. For example, according to presentism, only the present moment exists and/or is real. This view is generally combined with the idea that past and future objects have a different ontological status compared to present objects: only the latter exist. Generally associated with this view is also the belief that an object persists through time by enduring, that is, by being fully present at the present time.

   Why would anyone believe a theory as counter-intuitive as eternalism? One of the arguments in favour of eternalism is based on Einstein's Special Relativity. In a nutshell, the main point of the reasoning is that, according to Special Relativity, whether an event is simultaneous with another depends on one's perspective.[14] Since which events are past, present, or future depends on whether these events are simultaneous with the present moment, and the determination of simultaneity is subjective, it seems to follow that whether certain events are past, present, or future is subjective. However, what exists and/or what is real does not seem to be entirely up to someone's perspective. So, given that presentism implies that the reality of certain objects depends on whether they are present, past, or future, it follows that presentism is false. Since eternalism is the best alternative theory of time, we have reasons to believe it. Presentists have proposed various replies to the previous argument, but I will not discuss them here (or in what follows). Rather, in the rest of the book, I try to state the main theories of personal identity and of our nature in a way that is as neutral as possible with regard to specific theories on the nature of time – although it can be argued that to make further progress in the debate on diachronic identity, discussions on the ontology of time should play a more prominent role.

- Survival, practical issues, and applied ethics

One of the main points of this book is to show how various metaphysical theories bear on (some) debates in applied ethics. One example of such a connection is the debate that started with the publication of Derek Parfit's works on personal identity in the '70s and '80s. Since then, much academic effort has focused on the connection between personal identity and (1) our rational concern for **personal survival** and (2) various theories in normative ethics (e.g., utilitarianism). For reasons of space, I will focus only on the first of these two lines of inquiry. In particular, through a series of thought experiments and appeals to intuitions, Parfit has come to the conclusion that persisting in a way that is not equivalent to personal survival – a situation in which we do not survive as the same and unique entity through time – is not to be rationally considered as bad as death, that is, as bad as when we do not personally survive. Other philosophers in the past reached similar if not equivalent conclusions (see Chapter 7). Now, our concern for personal survival is only one of those self-directed attitudes towards some future events that we may have special reasons to care about. This claim needs to be further specified, but the main gist of what is involved is intuitively simple. Suppose you are told that someone is going to be tortured tomorrow. Perhaps you may feel pity or even be indifferent. However, a whole series of different attitudes are likely to be activated in case you are also told that the person who will be tortured is, well, *you*. The point is that in knowing that you are the same person who will be tortured or possibly killed, you will have a different kind of mental attitude towards the expected events. For instance, you may *anticipate* some of the future states from a particular perspective or point of view. Or, you may be particularly *concerned* (in the sense of preoccupied) for these future events.[15] The intensity of such attitudes may just be contingent on your character: for instance, you may feel even more distressed if told that the person who is going to be tortured is your partner. In this last case, you may be concerned to the highest degree you are capable of although you may not anticipate experiencing certain events from an internal point of view.

There are several other debates in applied/practical ethics in which theories of personal identity and of our nature play a crucial role – if only as presuppositions or hidden premises in the main arguments debated by ethicists. In particular, I have chosen to discuss, in Chapter 7 and 8, several different life-extending technologies (**cryonics** and **mental uploading**) and some ethical problems related to our beginning (the morality of abortion) and our end (the debate concerning the definition of death and its consequences for that on the morality of **organ transplantation**). The philosophical consequences of the metaphysical theories explored in the rest of the book are not limited to issues in applied ethics, but extend to general issues in moral theory. For instance, various approaches to personal identity may involve different attitudes towards our attributions of moral responsibility over time. If we adopt a theory of personal identity according to which the temporal extension of person P is determined solely by the extension of P's memories, this may have important consequences for ascriptions of responsibility. Take the case of a person who has lost her memories and the capacity to recall a significant part of the events that led her to do A. Suppose that a necessary condition for a person to be responsible over time for certain actions is that she should be at least identical to whoever performed the action for which she is supposed to be responsible. Now, certain theories of personal identity imply that the person who has forgotten doing A is not the same person who did A – and thus that this forgetful person is not responsible for A. Other moral issues associated with the debate on personal identity include the question whether we are (morally and/or rationally) justified in distributing certain goods intrapersonally (for example, to ourselves at different times) rather than (or as much as) interpersonally (that is, to different individuals).

Several mundane practices presuppose or assume views about the continuity of persons, e.g., marriage, friendship, even the practices of depositing money in a bank (and expecting to get it back later on) or paying insurance to cover some possible future expenditures. According to certain philosophers, theories of personal identity implying that these social practices are systematically irrational (for instance, because they would be based on gross misunderstandings of reality) and/ or groundless are, for this same reason, not plausible. Others, such as certain Buddhist philosophers, claim that if we come to truly believe the idea that personal identity and/or the self is a kind of illusion, we may well have to revise some of our attitudes towards many everyday practices, but we would also gain a higher level of well-being. For example, Buddhist thinkers claim that we could get rid of our existential pain or anxiety caused by our awareness of mortality. However, even Buddhist theories have to provide an account of the reasonableness of at least some of our basic everyday practices.

In this book, I assume that, among the criteria for assessing theories of personal identity, we should include the plausibility of their account/explanation of the alleged rationality of those beliefs that guide our lives. However, this does not imply that a theory should provide a justification of *all* of the social practices involving people – some may well turn out to be metaphysically/rationally unsound.

4 Dimensions of variation

Families of theories may differ with respect to whether certain dimensions of variation are relevant at all (say, whether psychological continuity is to be taken into account in a theory of our nature), the degree to which one of these dimensions counts, and how the conditions specified by these dimensions are framed in the theory at issue. Now, approaches to personal identity and to our nature may differ with respect to:

- *Theoretical aims*. That is, the analyses/conditions of personal identity proposed by various philosophers can be:

  1   Semantical: the necessary and sufficient conditions that an approach employs to discuss specific statements involving personal identity may be taken to specify the truth conditions of statements involving personal identity and/or to specify how the relevant terms are or should be used;
  2   Metaphysical: the necessary and sufficient conditions specified by an approach are supposed to state the metaphysical foundations of claims of personal identity. According to this understanding, accounts of personal identity clarify which entities, relations, properties, etc. are supposed to exist or hold in order for the relation of personal identity to hold as well;
  3   Epistemological: on this understanding of the aim of an account of personal identity, the point is to specify what constitutes evidence for claims of personal identity. Many philosophers have clearly distinguished metaphysical from epistemological approaches because, for example, what constitutes our evidence for believing that a friend of yours is the same person through time (e.g., mere physical appearance), may not constitute what is metaphysically necessary and sufficient for this entity to metaphysically persist through time;
  4   Conceptual: on this understanding, the necessary and sufficient conditions specified by theories of personal identity are devised to provide or outline a series of other more fundamental/clearer concepts in terms of which the notion of personal identity can be understood.

  The aims of the approaches to personal identity discussed in the next chapters generally oscillate between (2) and (4). I use expressions such as 'personal identity is constituted by X' or 'personal identity is metaphysically grounded in X' to discuss the metaphysical project. The idea is that many theories of personal identity are devised to provide necessary and sufficient conditions that a relation should have for such a relation to be the metaphysical foundation of the identity of persons (as persons) at different times.

- The recognition that our identity over time as persons and/or as ourselves is:

  (1) a brute fact and/or whether there are informative criteria for such an identity;

(2) an illusory/fictional/conventional fact (these three characterisations are not equivalent) and/or whether there are no criteria for personal identity (or no mind-independently and intentionally established criteria); or

(3) dependent on something else (e.g., psychological connections, physical connections, narrative chains of continuity, and so on).

(1)-approaches may claim that the holding of the relation of personal identity does not depend on anything metaphysically more fundamental and/or that the *concept* of personal identity is simple/fundamental and thus not further analysable in terms of other concepts. So-called anti-criterialists claim that personal identity does hold, but that there are no (informative) criteria for personal persistence. In this context, a criterion of personal identity is informative only if it does not include the relation of personal identity itself. So, for instance, a theory that is viciously circular would be non-informative.[16] Certain anti-criterialist accounts are sometimes associated with soul-based approaches to personal identity and with the so-called simple view. However, a soul-based approach, in itself, is not also thereby committed to anti-criterialism and/or to a brute fact view. In particular, in Chapter 1, I discuss soul-based theories that offer non-trivial criteria of personal identity. The discussion of (3)-approaches is the main focus of the book. In fact, most of the theories in the next chapters seek to provide informative criteria of personal identity and of our nature (whether they succeed is a different issue). (The three types of approaches illustrated in this section are not mutually exclusive.)

- The assumption of psychological and/or person essentialism. Accounts of our own nature and of personal identity, especially before the '80s and '90s, generally assumed that we are essentially persons and that, given that persons are essentially psychological entities, we are essentially psychological entities – that is, entities that essentially have mental states, or, at least the actual capacity to have certain mental states. However, the idea that we are essentially persons is controversial and, according to certain views of our own nature (e.g., animalism), false. In the rest of the book, I will not assume that it is true.
- The specificity of the definition of the sustaining conditions of the personal identity relation (or **identity-sustaining relations**). Certain theories (e.g., narrative theories) are more specific than others (e.g., generic psychological theories) in spelling out the details of their defining necessary and sufficient conditions. Being more specific does not imply that a theory is thereby better: the narrative approach may turn out to be implausible precisely because the conditions imposed on the relevant identity-sustaining psychological connections are too strict or complex.
- The emphasis put on the extrinsic or relational aspects of personal identity and of our nature. For instance, many accounts of personal identity and of our nature generally assume that the identity between you at t_1 and you at t_2 is determined exclusively by the singular entity referred to by 'you' at t_1 and the singular entity referred to by 'you' at t_2. In the current debate, this idea

is sometimes called the only-x-and-y principle. Some philosophers maintain that this principle is obvious and/or that it is a formal requirement of any theory of personal identity (Chapter 5). Others, especially those thinkers particularly interested in the political, social, or moral aspects of the debate, have claimed that relations to other people are metaphysically relevant, not just for our **biographical identity**. The underlying idea is that certain notions such as that of personhood are essentially relational: we are persons also because we have a language to communicate, we belong to various human communities, we interact with other intelligent beings, and so on. In addition, we became persons also because we grew up in a certain environment that gave us a series of conceptual resources such that our cognitive capacities have developed to their actual level.

5 Methodological remarks

5.1 Thought experiments, descriptions of outcomes, and future technologies

The methodology employed by contemporary philosophers to study personal identity is a mixed bag. Some philosophers have used the traditional method of thought experiments (Locke, Parfit, Shoemaker, and countless others) to discuss, elicit, and evaluate our intuitions or basic beliefs about cases involving personal identity. Parfit quotes this passage from Quine's work: "The method of science fiction has its uses in philosophy, but . . . I wonder whether the limits of their method are properly heeded. To seek what is 'logically required' for sameness of person under unprecedented circumstances is to suggest that words have some logical force beyond what our past needs have invested them with."[17] In reply to this worry, Parfit says that when we are confronted with certain imaginary cases we have strong reactions (nowadays, I suspect these reactions would be called 'intuitions'). The way in which we describe certain imaginary scenarios, Parfit claims, reveals some of our beliefs not just about words, but about ourselves. Also, imaginary cases may help us isolate some relevant aspects of the concept of personal identity that may be blurred in real life. In addition, the plausibility of the way in which theories imply that the outcome of a specific thought experiment should be described is sometimes taken as providing reasons in favour or against such a theory – thought experiments are thus also used as test cases for *evaluating* the plausibility of theories. However, this evaluative process should not be taken as unidirectional: thought experiments or real cases can also provide reasons to modify or formulate theories in a specific way – on this understanding, thought experiments are test cases for *modifying* the theories to which they are applied.

Thought experiments do not have to be understood as necessarily involving fictional stories. In a broad sense of the concept, a philosophical thought experiment can be just any case study selectively presented to us in order to discuss philosophical issues or theories. So, some case studies can be extrapolations or slight alterations of real events. Or, they can be fictional stories inspired by real events: as in the case of narrative works, the separation between fictional stories – intended as not involving facts that really happened – and events that took place may not be always so clear cut. In any case, theories of personal identity are evaluated not only in relation to how they imply that certain fictional stories should be described, but also in relation to how such theories describe real case scenarios (for instance, cases at the beginning or at the end of life). What are the most popular thought experiments discussed in the current literature?

5.1.1 Reduplication and fission scenarios

A **reduplication thought experiment** usually includes a scenario involving at least three individuals, two of which begin to exist at a time later than when the third did. These two later individuals are both relevantly connected – relevantly connected for the discussion of a theory of personal identity – to the earlier individual. In particular, the connection between the earlier individual and the other two would generally be regarded as sufficient to ground (or be) the relation of personal identity over time in case such a connection held between the early individual and only one of the other two individuals separately. For instance, A may be relevantly psychologically connected with both B and C at t_1 in a way that if only B had existed at t_1, we would have claimed that, on a specific psychological theory, B is the same person as A. The nature of the relevant connection varies among thought experiments of this kind – one of the most popular being a functionally defined notion of psychological connection. A **fission thought experiment** has a similar structure, with the exception of an emphasis on the apparent division or split of an original entity into two – as in the case of a surgeon who divides a brain in two parts to cure a severe case of epilepsy.

5.1.2 Brain-transplant scenarios

Brain-transplant scenarios vary greatly in their details, but the basic case is what follows. Imagine that, in the future, scientists (surgeons) are able to successfully transplant a human brain from one body into another human body. Now, it is likely that most of our mental features depend on the brain. If your brain is transplanted into another body and the brain in that other body is transplanted into yours, will your body still be the body of the same person, namely, yours? Brain-transplant cases, the way they are described, and their evaluation vary greatly in relation to: (1) the similarity of the bodies from and into which brains are transplanted (e.g., the body of your twin, the body of a human being of a different sex, the body of an infant); (2) whether the brain is split into two hemispheres and whether these different parts are in turn transplanted into two different bodies; (3) whether more than one person is involved in the operations and whether the brains and bodies of these persons are exchanged.

In general, psychological theories of our nature/personal identity tend to support the intuition that, in cases involving hypothetical brain transplants from body A to body B – on the supposition that our brains are responsible for at least many of our psychological states – the person previously associated with body A goes where her brain goes (i.e., body B). So, psychological theories generally describe the outcome of the (simple) brain transplant case as involving a person's change of body. Versions of the approach according to which organism continuity grounds our identity through time would generally claim that (exceptions and clarifications should apply here), after a brain transplant operation (better, a transplant of that part of the brain responsible for some of our higher mental functions), the outcome can be described as that of a radical organ transplant. On these views, it is appropriate to say that, in principle, we can get a new brain – and possibly become new persons. Early versions of this kind of scenario, not framed in terms of brain-transplant but in terms of soul-exchange and/or consciousness transfer, played a crucial role in Locke's discussion of personal identity (Chapter 4).

5.1.3 Tele-transportation and mental uploading scenarios

Tele-transportation scenarios generally involve a fictional scanning device capable of recording our present physical state, down to the last detail, and of translating it into some kind of informational state. Imagine that this device scans your body and that the resulting information is then sent to some other planet where a receiving machine uses it to produce a copy of yourself, down to the last physical detail (and, presumably, psychological detail).[18] A popular version of this scenario also asks us to imagine that the original person, after the information has been beamed to the faraway planet, is subsequently destroyed. Parfit also discusses a situation in which the tele-transporting machine malfunctions and the original is not destroyed but rendered terminally ill. Some of the tele-transportation cases may be considered as specific (or more detailed) instances of the reduplication- or fission-scenario templates.

One variation on this kind of scenario is nowadays discussed as if it were a possible and foreseeable life-extending technology: mind or mental uploading. Although the idea of surviving through uploading our consciousness (or, at least, some of our relevant psychological features) to a computer seems plausible only in the context of science fiction (e.g., Greg Egan's *Permutation City*, 1994, a novel that explores the complicated life of 'copies' and their difficult interactions with people not yet uploaded), it is interesting that certain AI enthusiasts and/or influential philosophers of mind (e.g., David Chalmers) have seriously debated this hypothesis, especially in relation to the astonishing technological progress in fields such as computer science. Scenarios involving the uploading of our consciousness to a computer (and/or perhaps to the Internet) are thus ambivalent thought experiments: some take them as interesting but *merely* fictional scenarios, others as a possible future means of surviving (biological) death. One of the key questions related to the plausibility of mental uploading scenarios as a form of life-extending technology is whether a program running in a computer can be conscious at all. And even if it were, can such a program be properly metaphysically identified with the same person as the person whose consciousness has been uploaded? More on this in Chapter 7.

Despite the general positive influence that such thought experiments have had for the advancement of the debate, some philosophers claim that fictional scenarios may not be a necessary tool for investigating our beliefs about personal identity and our nature. In particular, some (e.g., Kathleen Wilkes) have claimed that there is already, especially in the literature on mental disorder, a great variety of interesting and challenging real life cases to investigate. For instance, the stories masterfully narrated by the neurologist Oliver Sacks can inspire some deep reflections on the relationship between our mental capacities and our identity through time without recurring to sometimes off-putting phantasies and far-fetched scenarios having little or no obvious bearing on our actual experiences and choices.

5.2 A note on the inclusion of Buddhist and early Confucian theories

I refrain from using the expression 'Western approach(es)' to refer to some of the theories discussed here because the differences among theories usually grouped together under such a heading are so wide that the term 'Western' does not seem to stand for anything theoretically distinctive. Similarly, I do not use expressions such as 'Chinese approach(es)' or 'Indian approach(es)': again, there are so many different theories that are usually grouped under these headings that these labels seem to suggest a misleading theoretical unity. Using such labels is misleading also for other reasons; in particular, it wrongly amplifies differences between different geographically individuated approaches. It seems to me that certain metaphysical beliefs held by, say, Heraclitus in Ancient Greece (or by certain ancient Greek sceptics) are more similar to the beliefs held by some early Buddhists than to the beliefs held by certain Medieval Scholastics. Similarly, claims to the effect that the 'Western conception' of the individual is different from the 'Chinese conception' of the individual are gross generalisations that do not take into account large portions of each geographically individuated tradition – whatever 'tradition' may actually refer to in this context. For example, the idea that the identity of persons is (also) relational is a recurring theme also in much 'Western' philosophy and is not something that is peculiar, exclusive, or characteristic of all of the early 'Chinese' schools of thought.

The point of discussing Buddhist (rather than *Indian*) and early Confucian (rather than *Chinese*) approaches is not that of providing an inclusive (or politically correct) introduction to personal identity that pleases the alleged troubled consciences of certain contemporary critics, but rather that of showing how concerns about our own nature and about our persistence through time (and their moral and practical consequences) are part of our common human predicament. In addition, Buddhist and Confucian approaches have been chosen also because they are interesting and have been significantly influential in the cultures in which they developed, to the degree that a well-informed contemporary philosopher of personal identity cannot completely ignore some of their main theses.

Suggested readings

General introductions

Carruthers, Peter, *Introducing Persons* (London and New York: Routledge, 1986).
Dennett, Daniel and Douglas Hofstadter, *The Mind's I* (New York: Basic Books, 1981/2000).
Gallois, Andre, *The Metaphysics of Identity* (London and New York: Routledge, 2017).
Ganeri, Jonardon, *The Self: Naturalism, Consciousness, and the First-Person Stance* (Oxford: Oxford University Press, 2015).
Hall, David and Roger Ames, *Thinking From the Han* (Albany: State University of New York Press, 1997).
Kind, Amy, *Persons and Personal Identity* (Cambridge: Polity Press, 2015).
Martin, Raymond and John Barresi, *The Rise and Fall of Soul and Self* (New York: Columbia University Press, 2006).
Metzinger, Thomas, *Being No One* (Cambridge, MA: MIT Press, 2003).
Ney, Alyssa, *Metaphysics: An Introduction* (New York: Routledge, 2014).
Noonan, Harold, *Personal Identity, 2nd Edition* (London and New York: Routledge, 1989/2003).
Olson, Eric, *What Are We?* (Oxford: Oxford University Press, 2007).
Olson, Eric, 'Personal Identity', in *Stanford Encyclopedia of Philosophy* (2015). https://plato.stanford.edu/entries/identity-personal/
Perry, John, *A Dialogue on Personal Identity and Immortality* (Indianapolis, IN: Hackett Publishing Company, 1978).
Shoemaker, David, *Personal Identity and Ethics* (Ontario, CA: Broadview Press, 2009).
Shoemaker, David, 'Personal Identity and Ethics', in *Stanford Encyclopedia of Philosophy* (2015). https://plato.stanford.edu/entries/identity-ethics/
Sorabji, Richard, *Self* (Chicago: University of Chicago Press, 2006).

Definitions of key terms

Carrithers, Michael, Steven Collins, and Steven Lukes (eds.), *The Category of the Person* (Cambridge: Cambridge University Press, 1985).
Gallagher, Shaun, 'Philosophical Conceptions of the Self', *Trends in Cognitive Sciences*, 4, 1 (2000), pp. 14–21.
Gill, Christopher, 'Personhood and Personality: The Four-Personae Theory in Cicero, *De Officis I*', *Oxford Studies in Ancient Philosophy*, 6 (1988), pp. 169–199.
Gill, Christopher, 'The Human Being as an Ethical Norm', in Christopher Gill (ed.) *The Person and the Human Mind* (Oxford: Clarendon Press, 1990), pp. 137–164.
Morrison, Kirstie, 'The Self', in Samuel Guttenplan (ed.) *A Companion to the Philosophy of Mind* (Oxford: Blackwell, 1994), pp. 550–558.
Naffine, Ngaire, *Law's Meaning of Life* (Portland, OR: Hart Publishing, 2009).
Olson, Eric, 'There Is No Problem of the Self', *Journal of Consciousness Studies*, 5, 5–6 (1998), pp. 645–657.
Parfit, Derek, *Reasons and Persons* (Oxford: Clarendon Press, 1984/6/7).

Rorty, Amelie Oksenberg, 'Persons and Personae', in Christopher Gill (ed.) *The Person and the Human Mind* (Oxford: Clarendon Press, 1990), pp. 21–38.

Shoemaker, David, 'Personal Identity and Practical Concerns', *Mind*, 116, 462 (2007), pp. 317–357.

Shoemaker, Sydney, 'Personhood and Consciousness', in JeeLo Liu and John Perry (eds.) *Consciousness and the Self* (Cambridge: Cambridge University Press, 2011), pp. 198–213.

Thiel, Udo, *The Early Modern Subject* (Oxford: Oxford University Press, 2011).

Tur, Richard, 'The "Person" in Law', in Arthur Peacocke and Grant Gillet (eds.) *Persons & Personality* (Oxford: Blackwell Publishing, 1987).

Wiggins, David, 'The Person as Object of Science, as Subject of Experience, and as Locus of Value', in Arthur Peacocke and Grant Gillet (eds.) *Persons & Personality* (Oxford: Blackwell Publishing, 1987), pp. 56–74.

Dimensions of variation

Gasser, Georg and Matthias Stefan (eds.), *Personal Identity: Complex or Simple?* (Cambridge: Cambridge University Press, 2012).

Merricks, Trenton, 'There Are No Criteria of Identity Over Time', *Nous*, 32, 1 (1998), pp. 106–124.

Lowe, E. J., 'The Probable Simplicity of Personal Identity', in Georg Gasser and Matthias Stefan (eds.) *Personal Identity: Complex or Simple?* (Cambridge: Cambridge University Press, 2012), pp. 44–62.

Olson, Eric, 'In Search of the Simple View', in Georg Gasser and Matthias Stefan (eds.) *Personal Identity: Complex or Simple?* (Cambridge: Cambridge University Press, 2012), pp. 44–62.

Parfit, Derek, 'Experiences, Subjects and Conceptual Schemes', *Philosophical Topics*, 26, 1 and 2 (1999), pp. 217–270.

Williamson, Timothy, *Vagueness* (London and New York: Routledge, 1994).

Methodology

Daly, Chris (ed.), *The Palgrave Handbook of Philosophical Method* (London: Palgrave Macmillan, 2015).

Egan, Greg, *Permutation City* (San Francisco: Night Shade Books, 2014). (Original work published in 1994)

Flanagan, Owen, *The Problem of the Soul* (New York: Basic Books, 2003).

Gendler, Tamar Szabó, 'Personal Identity and Thought Experiments', *Philosophical Quarterly*, 52, 206 (2002), pp. 34–54.

Sacks, Oliver, *The Man Who Mistook His Wife for a Hat* (New York: Simon & Schuster, 1985).

Shoemaker, Sydney, 'Brown-Brownson Revisited', *The Monist*, 87, 4 (2004), pp. 573–593.

Wilkes, Kathleen, *Real People* (Oxford: Oxford University Press, 1988).

Appendix I

Basic logical properties of identity

Some recurring terms and concepts in the contemporary debate (e.g., the transitivity of the relation of personal identity) have originated in technical discussions on identity in formal logic. The relation of identity is generally symbolised in logic with the equality sign '=', which stands for a relation that is supposed to hold between an entity and itself. The logical relation of identity is:

- Reflexive: $(\forall x)\,(x=x)$ [For every entity x, x is identical to itself];
- Symmetric: $(\forall x)\,(\forall y)((x=y)\rightarrow(y=x))$ [For every x and y, if x is identical with y then y is identical with x];
- Transitive: $(\forall x)\,(\forall y)(\forall z)((x=y\ \&\ y=z)\rightarrow x=z)$ [For every x, y, and z, if (x and y are identical and y and z are identical) then x and z are identical].

In addition, identity is also taken to follow the principle of indiscernibility of the identicals (sometimes called Leibniz's law):

$(\forall x)(\forall y)((x=y)\rightarrow(\forall F)(Fx\leftrightarrow Fy))$ [For every x and y, if x and y are identical, then, if F is a property of x then it is also a property of y, and if F is a property of y then it is also a property of x.]

Some philosophers claim that personal identity, being one kind of numerical identity, should have the stated properties, in addition to the other necessary and sufficient conditions that distinguish *personal* identity from mere identity. For instance, some have claimed that the logical structure of the relation of personal identity should be that of a one-to-one relation, that is, a relation that cannot hold between more than two entities each existing at different times.

Appendix 2

Other classifications: simple/complex, reductionism/ non-reductionism

Many contemporary philosophers have followed Parfit in distinguishing between simple and complex views of personal identity. However, as Eric Olson has recently and persuasively pointed out, this distinction is anything but clear, in addition to not being particularly helpful in carving significant theoretical joints – especially considering what theories some philosophers nowadays tend to classify as simple.[19] However, since many current philosophers have employed the simple-complex distinction, I here briefly summarise some of the ways in which it has been drawn.

In their introduction to a recent volume on the simple/complex distinction, Georg Gasser and Matthias Stefan claim that: "the complex view analyses personal identity over time in terms of simpler relations. The fact that a person persists over time is nothing more than some other facts which are generally spelled out in either biological or psychological terms, or both. [. . .] It [the complex view] aims to provide necessary and sufficient conditions for personal identity, thereby reducing it to the holding of basic biological or psychological relations." Gasser and Stefan then characterise the simple view as the view that "denies that a person's identity through time consists in anything but itself. Biological and psychological continuity may be regarded as epistemic criteria for diachronic identity, but they are neither necessary nor sufficient conditions for personal identity. There are no non-circular, informative, necessary and sufficient conditions for personal identity: personal identity consists in nothing other than itself."[20] This characterisation of the difference between simple and complex views is standard in the literature. However, the same authors, in providing more details about the general features of the simple view, also write: "[t]he claim that personal identity is simple implies that it cannot be analysed because it is not possible to appeal to other entities of a suitable kind for formulating in a non-circular way what personal identity consists in. This does not imply that the simple view is entirely uninformative. The discovery – if it is a discovery – that personal identity is not analysable is a kind of progress in understanding it."[21] These remarks highlight the conceptual ambiguities that the simple/complex distinction may engender. For instance, one paradigmatic example of a simple view is the simple-soul approach. In the versions defended by Descartes or Richard Swinburne, the main idea is that we are substances that are essentially thinking (or that essentially have the capacity to think).[22] Moreover, on their views, these thinking substances are mereologically simple. Clearly, these theories do not meet the previously stated requirements for being classified as simple: after all, the relation of personal identity is reduced to something else, namely, to the identity of a (mereologically, not conceptually) simple soul – soul-based theories claim that personal identity over time between P and Q holds iff P's soul is identical with Q's soul at different times. Moreover, the entity that metaphysically grounds such a relation is conceptually and metaphysically further specified using concepts, e.g., those of a simple and thinking substance, that may not involve the relation of personal identity. So, certain versions of the simple-soul approach may not count as simple, although simple-soul theories are generally taken to be paradigmatic examples of the simple view. One of the reasons of the protracted confusion between soul and anti-criterialist/brute fact approaches is that philosophers do not always clearly distinguish the kinds of projects they are engaged in. More specifically, it is not always clear whether they are proposing a conceptual analysis of the concept of personal identity or whether they are discussing, say, the simplicity of the meta-physical entities or relations responsible for the holding of the relation of personal identity. For example, someone may defend a view according to which personal identity holds in virtue of a metaphysically simple entity (e.g., a soul), without thereby being committed to the view that her metaphysical criteria of identity are not informative.

Another way of understanding the simple view is by characterising it as that family of theories according to which there is always a definite answer to questions regarding the existence of persons (or ourselves), although there can be cases in which we may never know the correct answer. This approach is in contrast with the view according to which, given the inherent vagueness of some of our concepts (among them that of a person), there can be cases – even imaginary ones – in which it is indeterminate whether personal identity holds. **Epistemicism** is a general (and not very popular) theoretical stance discussed in the philosophical debate on vagueness.[23] According to supporters of epistemicism, our alleged difficulty in assessing the vagueness of certain concepts is a form of ignorance. In particular, it may involve our ignorance regarding the threshold of the application of the concepts at issue. In the case of personal identity, epistemicists may hold that the concept of a person has precise boundaries, but we may never be able to come to know them. Belief in this claim applied to the case of personal identity is generally accompanied by a belief in the existence of an irreducible further (mental or physical) substance that accounts for our identity over time. Generally, such an entity is taken to be an immaterial soul.

Parfit rejects this epistemicist stance towards personal identity and claims that his approach is *reductionist* in the sense that facts about personal identity can be reduced to other kinds of facts, in particular, facts about physical configurations of matter and psychological events – the latter not necessarily metaphysically individuated by using the relation of personal identity. Simple theories are sometimes identified with non-reductionism (or further-fact views), that is, theories holding that, in addition to configurations of matter and psychological events, not characterised by using the relation of personal identity, there is a further fact that is responsible for our identity. However, as already discussed previously, it is not clear whether this further fact (generally identified with the soul), is not, in itself, reducible to other kinds of facts and/or whether this further fact has to be essentially characterised in terms of the relation of personal identity. Also, non-reductionism, in the sense just explained, should not be confused with a theory about the irreducibly perspectival or subjective phenomenal quality of our experience. For instance, we may claim that a *description* of our subjective experience may essentially involve reference to a self, but not hold that the metaphysical grounding of such experiences must include the relation of personal identity. Additional arguments are needed to draw such a connection.[24]

Some philosophers (e.g., Mark Siderits) have also emphasised the distinction between reductionist and eliminativist theories of personal identity. According to the former, facts about personal identity are reducible to facts about something else, for instance, specific configurations of matter and psychological events. Eliminativists would add to this stance that talk about personal identity can or should be in principle dispensed with. This view may be taken to imply that alleged statements regarding the identity through time of persons are systematically false. Reductionism, in itself, is not characterised as having this consequence: although a reductionist theory of personal identity may hold that personal identity is nothing over and above certain further facts, it does not also thereby imply that statements to the effect that A and B are the same person through time are systematically false and/or to be dispensed with.

Notes

1 In the second and third chapter, I also introduce some relevant terms and concepts used in different languages (e.g., Sanskrit and classical Chinese). The differences between these terms and those introduced above are clarified in the respective chapters.

2 We may further distinguish between identification and individuation, both at a metaphysical and epistemological/cognitive level, but in what follows I will assume that they coincide.

3 As is the case with all philosophical concepts, the above way of presenting the notions of identification and individuation is disputed and controversial, e.g., according to certain philosophers, there are no objective – already out there in the world – metaphysical conditions of identification.

4 Admittedly, using the expression 'metaphysical facts' can be taken to imply that there are other kinds of facts (biological facts, sociological facts, and so on). To a first approximation, metaphysical facts are facts relevant to metaphysical considerations. No attempt to reduce or further specify what is metaphysical is made here.

5 Gill (1988).

6 See Tur (1987) and Naffine (2009) for references.

7 Wiggins (1987).

8 Rorty (1990).

9 In particular, she claims that the notion of a person works as a kind of insurance policy: once an entity qualifies as a person, it will not lose some benefits related to the recognition of its dignity, even in old age.

10 Shoemaker (2011).

11 Gallagher, drawing on the work of various neuroscientists and psychiatrists, reports that there can be exceptions to the immediacy and transparency of this form of self-reference. For instance, he reports that some schizophrenic patients claimed that some of their occurring thoughts were not really their own thoughts, despite it being clear that they were thinking them – this is called "the phenomenon of thought-insertion". How to understand these cases is still controversial.

12 I use 'mental' and 'psychological' interchangeably in this book.

13 Another use of 'self' is to refer to temporal stages. Suppose that ordinary persons are temporally extended objects composed of different temporal stages. On this view, the name 'Charles Baudelaire' refers to a temporally extended entity that stretches through time from the 9th of April,

1821, to the 31st of August, 1867. This temporal entity is extended in time — a time that is no more actual — as it was extended in space and is composed of different temporal stages or *selves* each existing at specific moments (say, the temporal stage or self Charles Baudelaire-on the 3rd of August, 1841).

14 See Ney (2014), pp. 143–144 for a clear formulation of the argument.

15 The two different attitudes of *anticipation* and *concern* are frequently discussed as if they were one single attitude; however, they are conceptually different. See Shoemaker (2007).

16 Merricks (1998).

17 Parfit (1984/6/7), p. 200.

18 Certain theories of mental content (e.g., externalism) may disagree with some characterisations of this thought experiment. Although I do not explicitly discuss externalist theories of mental content, they are crucially important in evaluating the plausibility of certain theories of personal identity, as it will emerge in my discussion of Williams's reduplication argument in Chapter 5.

19 Olson (2012).

20 Gasser and Stefan (2012).

21 Gasser and Stefan (2012), p. 15.

22 Swinburne seems to claim that we are compounds of body and souls, but we can leave this complication aside for the moment. See Chapter 1 for details.

23 Williamson (1994).

24 See Parfit (1999).

1   The simple-soul approach and dualisms

1	Wandering souls and ψυχή (Psuchê)	32
2	The soul in Plato's Phaedo	33
3	Soul_Platonic-Phaedo and personal identity	35
4	Early Christian views on the nature of the soul: Saint Augustine	37
5	Early Christian views on the origin of the soul	38
6	Descartes and the soul_mind	40
7	Contemporary soul-based theories: Richard Swinburne and compound dualism	42
8	Personal identity and dualism: clarifications and criticisms	45
9	Summary	47

[Crito:] '. . . but in what fashion are we to bury you?'

'However you wish', [Socrates] said; 'provided you catch me, that is, and I don't get away from you.' And with this he laughed quietly.

—Plato, *Phaedo*, 115c 4–5

Why is Socrates laughing, though quietly, at Crito's request? The situation is momentous for the history of philosophy: Socrates has been condemned to death and is about to end his life by drinking hemlock, or so the story goes. Despite this context, however, Socrates and his friends start a discussion on nothing less than the nature of the soul and whether we are rationally justified in believing that death is not the end of our existence. This alleged debate is recorded in Plato's (429?– 347 BCE) *Phaedo*, a seminal work, along with the *Republic* and the *Timaeus*, for subsequent philosophical reflections on the nature of the soul. In particular, Plato (or Socrates) argues in the *Phaedo* that the soul is a simple, impartite entity – an entity not composed of different parts – that does not decompose along with the body. Whether Plato continued to hold that the soul is a simple entity also in later dialogues is still a matter of dispute. What is beyond dispute is that Aristotelian, Late Antiquity, and Medieval Christian theologians, along with Muslim and Jewish thinkers, elaborated Plato's ideas on the soul in various ways in their attempts to extrapolate a coherent doctrine from their respective religious scriptures.

The other philosophers discussed in this chapter, Augustine (354–430 CE), René Descartes (1596–1650), and Richard Swinburne (b. 1934), have been chosen among a great variety of equally influential and original figures whose doctrines show a certain continuity with Plato's. Both Augustine and Descartes discuss the mental faculties of which a soul is capable – among them, the capacity to immediately perceive its own existence and thoughts. Among the *dissimilarities* between these two thinkers is the idea that the soul, according to Descartes, is not the principle of life of the body – an idea that Augustine inherited from the Greek tradition – that is, a necessary requirement for a body to be alive. In particular, in Descartes's mechanistic philosophy, the soul is an immortal mental substance responsible for our thinking, i.e., responsible for – if not identical with – the mind. The idea that the soul is responsible both for our thinking and for the animation of the body is still present – although understood in slightly different terms – in certain views of our own nature defended by some contemporary Catholic thinkers (e.g., Norman Ford).[1] Some arguments for the distinction between mind and body in the context of the discussion on personal identity have been recently revamped by Swinburne, a contemporary theistic thinker. In some of his works, Swinburne claims that human beings *on Earth* are a compound of a Cartesian soul and a body where only the soul is essential to our continuity through time. Several philosophers have noticed that the thesis according to which we are essentially a compound of soul and body – a view of human nature called **compound dualism** – is frequently also accompanied by claims to the effect that what we essentially are is just a soul. Clearly the two theories are conceptually different, and two versions of compound dualism should be distinguished: according to an *essentialist* version of compound dualism, we are essentially compound entities, namely, a compound of body and soul. In order for a person – supposing that we are essentially persons – to exist, a soul and a body must be relevantly conjoined and thus both existing. A non-essentialist version of compound dualism simply claims that we are a compound of body and soul only contingently – and this seems to be Swinburne's latest (2013) position. Versions of what is called **simple dualism**, the view according to which we are essentially souls (I am aware of no philosophers who claim that we are contingently simple souls), deny that it is necessary for a person to exist and/or to continue to exist as the same person to have the same body – or even a body at all.[2]

The theories discussed in this chapter have in common the belief that the soul is simple and immortal, and that it is responsible for a great number of our psychological states. This family of views is sometimes called *the simple view*, although probably this label is misleading and does not truly capture a homogeneous **approach to personal identity**.[3] Nonetheless, the simple view is sometimes characterised as the approach according to which there is always a yes or no answer as to whether the same person still exists even in cases of complicated versions of thought experiments such as the brain-split or brain-transplant scenarios – a stance that resembles epistemicism, a contemporary theory of vagueness. In particular, an epistemicist about the concept of personal identity would claim that a determined yes or no answer can always be given, even though we, entities with limited cognitive

capacities, may never know the correct answer. Now, Swinburne holds this epistemicist belief along with the idea that personal identity holds because of a further
fact, *further* in the sense of being over and above physical and psychological facts –
that is, the existence of soul(s).

The plausibility of the soul-based approach is nowadays closely connected to the
plausibility of substance dualism in the study of the nature of the mind, a theory that
few still think as worthy of serious scrutiny. The declining popularity of substance
dualism, at least among non-religious philosophers, has been variously ascribed to
the development of a series of scientific discoveries on the nature of the brain and
of human beings in general. At the end of this chapter, I discuss some of the problems that hinder substance dualism. However, contemporary philosophers of mind
are not the sole critics of this view: the main theories discussed in the subsequent
chapters, in fact, can be seen as developments of criticisms to this approach. For
instance, some of the earliest philosophical investigations of the Buddhist tradition
stem from a critical stance against the existence of enduring substances, which is
what souls have been supposed to be.

I Wandering souls and ψυχή (*Psuchê*)

The term 'soul' is generally used to translate the Ancient Greek term 'ψυχή'
(*psuchê*), the meaning of which has assumed different nuances since its first
attested literary appearances in Homer to the times of Plato and Aristotle. In turn,
'*psuchê*' was translated into Latin as '*anima*', a term still used in certain modern languages. The English term 'soul' has a different, Proto-Germanic origin
('sáwol'). Here I distinguish only those aspects of '*psuchê*' in the pre-Socratics
(roughly, from 850 to 400 BCE) that have some bearing on the subsequent Platonic
dialogues. First, an entity having *psuchê* is an entity that is alive. However, from
the Homeric usage, it is not always clear whether the *psuchê* also perishes and is
destroyed at the moment of death. Part of this lack of clarity comes from the fact
that sometimes the term was used to indicate a shadow – what remains of an individual after death – possibly in the underworld. *Psuchê* was also associated (and
sometimes identified) with breath, intended as the principle of life. In the 6th and
5th centuries BCE, the *psuchê* was considered as an entity responsible for various
kinds of activities, only some of which we would classify as strictly psychological
or mental. Some scholars claim that '*psuchê*' could also stand for an entity capable
of extra-corporeal travels, as it was used in stories of wandering spirits that leave
the body in a trance. At some point in the 5th century BCE, the *psuchê* was taken
to be responsible for our moral character, as it was identified with the bearer of virtues such as courage, temperance, and justice. Various pre-Socratics (Empedocles
and perhaps Pythagoras) did not think that having a soul, in itself, distinguishes
humans or persons from plants or other animate beings – in fact, they believed that
also non-human entities have souls. There are passages and fragments suggesting
that Pythagoras identified the *psuchê* with the bearer of significant personal traits,
especially in cases of transmigration. (The story goes that Pythagoras allegedly

recognised the soul of a friend in a non-human animal.) However, *psuchê* was not always regarded by ancient thinkers as being incorporeal, immaterial, or immortal (more on materialist conceptions of the soul in 5.1).

2 The soul in Plato's *Phaedo*

Plato does not argue in favour of the existence of the soul (henceforth I will use 'soul' instead of '*psuchê*') for the simple reason that he could take its existence for granted among his peers. If a proof of the existence of individual souls were demanded, an educated Greek man of the period would have politely had us acknowledge that he was alive. It was the immortality of the soul that was contentious, not its existence: Simmias, one of the interlocutors of Socrates in the *Phaedo* (at 77b), says that the "view of the majority" was that the soul is mortal. So, Plato (or Socrates) simply had to argue for the immortality of the soul. The arguments offered in favour of this belief, four in total, are better seen as forming a cumulative case because each of them, taken separately, does not seem to be sufficient to make a case that the soul cannot perish. Among these arguments, the *affinity argument* (78b-84b) is the one that provides most details about the properties that a soul is supposed to have. The main passages of the argument can be summarised as follows. Souls are more similar to the Forms than to visible (sensible and/or material) entities such as those we perceive through our senses. The Forms have a set of properties. More specifically, they are, among other things, invariant (in contrast to material and changeable objects), partless (or incomposite as whatever is invariant was taken to be incomposite), and indissoluble because everything that is incomposite is indissoluble (or so it was suggested by Socrates). So, since souls are relevantly similar to the Forms, souls are, among other things, indissoluble and thus immortal. This argument will not satisfy those who do not already believe in the theoretical or philosophical utility of (and thus in the necessity of postulating) the Forms. To sum up, souls in the *Phaedo*, henceforth souls$_{\text{Platonic-Phaedo}}$, are: (1) partless or incomposite, (2) immaterial, (3) invariant, (4), indissoluble, and (5) immortal.

Theory of Forms: A metaphysical and epistemological doctrine that has consequences also for value theory. This theory is developed and criticised in many Platonic dialogues (e.g., *Phaedo, Republic, Sophist, Statesman, Parmenides*), although sometimes it is rather presupposed than explicitly argued for (and even harshly criticised, as in the *Parmenides*). One of the main reasons to believe in the Theory of Forms is that by assuming the existence of certain kinds of immaterial entities (see the main text for their essential features), we would solve many difficult philosophical problems. For instance, such eternal and unchangeable immaterial objects would provide (and secure) the correct answer to questions concerning the objective features of important concepts such as justice, beauty, and the good – thus also providing a remedy against certain forms of relativism or scepticism. In addition, the Forms are taken to be the proper objects of knowledge through what is characterised as a non-representational, non-propositional form of acquaintance (a kind of direct knowledge). Forms are what is real and can be known by recollection, contrary to the physical universe, which is in flux and thus not an appropriate source of knowledge – this last claim is still debated among Plato scholars. Also, Forms provide the objective truths of morality.

There are passages suggesting that souls$_{\text{Platonic-Phaedo}}$ exist before their own embodiment – as allegedly demonstrated in the recollection argument – and are capable of cognising the Forms, also by recollecting them. Cognising the Forms is an ennobling feature that testifies to the superior nature of the **soul$_{\text{Platonic-Phaedo}}$**, which is thus apt to rule the body. In particular, an interpretation of what Plato means by claiming that the soul$_{\text{Platonic-Phaedo}}$ is divine – one way of being superior to the body – is that it has all that is required to lead and tame bodily desires; for instance, it is capable of choosing certain things instead of others despite the urges of the body. A perhaps anachronistic but evocative suggestion is that the soul$_{\text{Platonic-Phaedo}}$ is the source of free human action. Noble souls$_{\text{Platonic-Phaedo}}$ (it is not clear whether all of us have or are noble souls) can generate some noble desires, e.g., the desire for learning, and are the subject of reward and punishment. However, souls$_{\text{Platonic-Phaedo}}$ are not inert and/or not affected by the body; in fact, they can be corrupted as a consequence of their embodiment and are even seen as the principle of life – that is, they animate the body.

Are *we* souls$_{\text{Platonic-Phaedo}}$? Do we continue to exist after our bodies die? Some passages of the *Phaedo* suggest that only pure intellect survives after death – not all of our mental capacities can thus survive. In other places, Plato describes the souls$_{\text{Platonic-Phaedo}}$ of ordinary men (and, more generally, of non-philosophers) as being afraid, retaining memory, trying to persuade each other, and showing various character traits. In the disembodied state, we are immaterial knowers, whilst in the embodied state, we are images in need of philosophical purification. Still, textual evidence is sometimes difficult to assess: in the *Phaedo*, there are passages in which Socrates claims that we are part body and part soul$_{\text{Platonic-Phaedo}}$ (79b 1) and others where Socrates says that when he dies, he cannot be buried – meaning that he is his soul$_{\text{Platonic-Phaedo}}$ and hence immaterial. Socrates also claims that *he* will be dissociated from the body and go to the philosophers' paradise. However, in this context, Socrates may be interpreted as making an ironic remark about his fate. It is even compatible with textual evidence to maintain that, according to Plato in the *Phaedo*, being a person and being a soul$_{\text{Platonic-Phaedo}}$ are different properties – for instance, in case souls were pure knowers and did not retain any psychological states that characterised their previous earthly existence as persons. More specifically, suppose that retaining some of our previous mental states (e.g., memories) is essential for our persistence as persons. If we are essentially souls$_{\text{Platonic-Phaedo}}$ and such souls did not retain our memories, then it can be argued that we are not essentially persons. According to this view (souls$_{\text{Platonic-Phaedo}}$ essentialism) we are essentially neither human beings nor persons, but rather souls$_{\text{Platonic-Phaedo}}$: we happen to be persons for a certain amount of time, but this is not essential for our persistence.

The *Phaedo* is not the only dialogue in which Plato examines the nature of the soul. For example, he famously discusses it also in the *Republic*. For reasons of space, I do not discuss this other conception in detail but only summarise some of its key points. In particular, there are two apparently striking modifications to the account of the soul found in the *Phaedo*. First, in the *Republic*, Plato seems to claim that the soul is composed of three parts: the reasonable/reason, the spirited, and the appetitive. Second, some of these parts seem to be responsible for some of the functions that were ascribed to the body in the *Phaedo*, e.g., certain appetites or desires. In fact, in the *Phaedo*, Plato had argued that the origin of certain appetites is not the soul itself, although it is the embodied soul that feels certain physical sensations. Thus, Plato's conception of the soul in the *Republic* (and in other subsequent dialogues, such as the *Timaeus*) seems to be at odds with the conception of the simple soul that is under consideration in this chapter. One of the additional worries emerging from these subsequent dialogues regard the alleged incompatibility between a conception of the soul as a mereological simple entity and its alleged functional complexity. For example, we may wonder whether a soul must be mereologically complex, that is, composed of different parts, if we can properly ascribe to it different motivational forces (appetites and spirited desires) – as Plato did in the *Republic*. Some scholars have claimed that concluding that the soul must be composed of different parts from the apparent multiplicity of its different psychological functions is not justified or obvious. In particular, they claim that it is possible for a soul to have multiple psychological functions and yet be ontologically simple. According to this understanding, the conception of soul in the *Republic* can still be compatible with the view that the soul is mereologically simple. For our purposes of extrapolating a criterion of personal identity in terms of a simple soul, however, it is not immediately important to assess which interpretation is the most accurate. If Plato's theory of the soul in the *Republic* implies that the soul is composed of different parts, then a metaphysical theory of personal identity and of our nature based on it would count as (mereologically) complex rather than simple. This difference may have some consequences in terms of the plausibility of claims to the effect that the soul is immortal because, according to Plato, a complex entity will eventually dissolve and thus cannot be immortal. In the next section, I formulate various theories of personal identity based solely on the relatively less controversial, from an interpretative perspective, account of the soul in the *Phaedo*.

3 Soul$_{\text{Platonic-Phaedo}}$ and personal identity

Plato did not explicitly argue for a criterion of personal identity based on the soul$_{\text{Platonic-Phaedo}}$ and what follows is one way in which such a criterion can be made more precise.

(Soul$_{\text{Platonic-Phaedo}}$ Theory of the Metaphysical Foundation of Personal Identity)#1

For all t, P at t$_1$ is one and the same person as Q at t$_2$ iff P's soul$_{\text{Platonic-Phaedo}}$ at t$_1$ = Q's soul$_{\text{Platonic-Phaedo}}$ at t$_2$.

According to this theory, the metaphysical foundation of the relation of personal identity over time is provided by the identity of soul$_{\text{Platonic-Phaedo}}$. In other words, the metaphysical fact grounding the identity of two persons over time is the possession or existence of the same persisting soul$_{\text{Platonic-Phaedo}}$. This view should not be confused with the view of our nature according to which we are (essentially) a composite of body and soul (compound dualism) and/or with the related theory of personal identity according to which we persist through time iff the same compound of body and soul persists. If we are essentially a composite or compound of body and soul, *and* the previously stated criterion for personal identity is correct, then it may be argued that for us to exist at different times, we also always need our soul to be embodied. On this view, a whole person and/or ourselves cannot exist without a body, although it would be possible for a person and/or ourselves to come back to life if our soul were embodied again after our earthly demise – provided that a soul can exist disembodied. If we take the view that we are essentially persons and that we are souls, then the previous theory can be reformulated as follows:

(Soul$_{\text{Platonic-Phaedo}}$ Theory of the Metaphysical Foundation of Personal Identity)#2

P at t$_1$ is one and the same person as Q at t$_2$ iff P-soul$_{\text{Platonic-Phaedo}}$ at t$_1$ = Q-soul$_{\text{Platonic-Phaedo}}$ at t$_2$. (Where t$_1 \neq$ t$_2$.)

On the view that we are essentially compounds of body and soul, (earthly) death can be defined as the separation of body and soul. Some may also believe that the soul itself can perish, perhaps after having been separated from the body. On this view, it is the death of a soul that is to be identified with our complete annihilation – assuming that a soul cannot come back into existence once destroyed. Plato holds that philosophy itself can be seen as an activity that resembles dying, intended as a form of separation. In fact, for him, the activities of the body are something that distracts the nobler (and rational) activities of the soul and, by doing philosophy, we can gradually detach ourselves from what is inessential to our identity and from the attachments created in/by the embodied life/soul. The idea that philosophy is a kind of preparation for dying will be further developed in different ways by later thinkers (e.g., Cicero in his *Tusculanae Disputationes* and Michel de Montaigne in his *Essays*, in particular in the essay XVII).

Is this approach to personal identity plausible? Is the previous conception of soul$_{\text{Platonic-Phaedo}}$ adequate to play the theoretical role of sustaining the relation of personal identity? Probably the answers to these questions are both negative (see the final section of this chapter). Despite this, a slightly different but very similar conception of the nature of the soul has played a crucial role in the subsequent history of the debate on personal identity and of our nature. For example, Plato's theory has influenced different theories developed by various theistic thinkers, such as those belonging to the Christian tradition.[4]

4 Early Christian views on the nature of the soul: Saint Augustine

The Christian scriptures are open to a multiplicity of interpretations regarding the nature of the soul, e.g., whether the soul is akin to a Platonic Idea/Form or a material and perhaps very rarefied entity. In addition, although the doctrine of the resurrection of the dead is crucial to Christianity, writers such as Paul the Apostle were anything but philosophically precise in specifying the role played by the soul in this process or event. Instead, metaphors abound – for example, the mortal body is a seed which will sprout into a new spiritual body at the moment of resurrection (see Chapter 5, section 1). In the early Christian tradition, a certain level of philosophical sophistication was achieved by the Greek Fathers (Irenaeus of Lyons, Clement of Alexandria, Origen of Alexandria, etc.) and the Latin Fathers (Tertullian, Augustine, etc.). One of the most influential of the Latin Fathers was Aurelius Augustine (354–430 CE), a converted Christian who helped shape the debate on a variety of issues in the philosophy of his nascent religion. Augustine discussed the nature of the soul in different works, remaining uncertain about some important details of his doctrine. However, some main points on the nature of the soul seem to be constant throughout his vast intellectual production, such as the ideas that, similar to what was believed by several Greek philosophers, the soul – Augustine used the term 'anima' – is the principle of life and that the soul functions as a unifying force in the organism (*De Immortalitate Animae*, 'On the Immortality of the Soul', 3.3). Similar to what Plato (*Timaeus*) and Aristotle (*De Anima*) had maintained before him, Augustine also holds that all living beings have a soul, including animals and plants. In some works, he also seems to believe that the world itself has a soul. Now, even though all living beings may have a soul, reason distinguishes the human soul from that of other living beings. In *On the Greatness of the Soul* (*De Quantitate Animae*, 13.22), he maintains that the soul is a substance that guides the body. In *On the Trinity* (and in other works), Augustine also claims that human beings are substances consisting of soul and body (a form of compound dualism, although it is not clear the modal status of the theory endorsed, i.e., whether according to him we are *essentially* a compound of soul and body or just contingently so). On his view, the soul is directly aware of its own existence and cannot fail to know that it exists. In a famous anticipation of Descartes's *cogito* argument, Augustine argues that doubting the existence of the soul is in itself a proof that something exists, namely, that which is doubting, a mental substance. The capacities of the soul to turn away from thoughts of material entities and to entertain concepts such as 'God' support the idea that the soul itself is not material. In addition to not being material, the soul is also simple.

How can we reconcile the possibility of spiritual conversions, so well represented in Augustine's own *Confessions*, with the idea that the soul is a simple entity? Moreover, our own experience seems to tell us that in many cases, we feel as though our internal mental life, for which the soul is responsible, is phenomenologically complex and, in a sense, non-unitary. For instance, we experience many internal conflicts, with the pull of two or more desires tearing our internal tranquillity apart. One solution to these worries, which we have already seen in our discussion of Plato's conceptions of the soul in the *Republic*, is to claim that the soul can be phenomenologically complex and mereologically simple at the same time (*De Trinitate*, XII.4). Thus, if we accept the idea that a simple substance can have multiple functions and retain its metaphysical simplicity (or unicity), then we can maintain, without contradiction, that the soul is a simple substance that supports a complex array of psychological states. Now, the idea that phenomenal/ psychological complexity is compatible with ontological simplicity is crucial for the plausibility of those theories of personal identity based on this conception of soul. For instance, by accepting this thesis, we can maintain that a soul can be the same through time, despite various changes in the personality or character of the human being of which it is a component, without thereby losing its mereological simplicity. A more general point that can be inferred from this reasoning is that the phenomenological or experiential aspects of our mental life may not have a direct bearing on the underlying metaphysical structure responsible for our thinking. However, whether ontological simplicity and psychological complexity are compatible is a matter of dispute. Now, supposing that souls really exist, what is their origin?

5 Early Christian views on the origin of the soul

Augustine discusses various theories of the origin of the soul in his *On the Free Choice of the Will* (*De Libero Arbitrio*, 3.20–23.21). Some of these theories had already been discussed by other philosophers and theologians, such as Plato, Plotinus, and Tertullian. The dimensions of variations in the debate include whether souls (1) pre-exist their embodiment or whether God creates them *ex nihilo* (out of nothing), (2) can be regarded as voluntarily becoming attached to a specific body at the moment of creation of the latter, (3) are being transmitted by, and thus derive from, the parents to the newborn at the moment of conception. A possible consequence of this last hypothesis, called 'traducianist', would be that, at least in the Christian tradition, all souls are connected to Adam's soul, thus providing a link that would (partially) explain or account for the doctrine of original sin. This traducianist hypothesis may support a specific view of human beings as irremediably bearing guilt and thereby being in need of (among other things) atonement or salvation through divine Grace. Sin would also be involved in the voluntaristic hypothesis, the view according to which pre-existing souls decided to be embodied: why would a soul, if not sinful, desire to descend into a human being? However, the voluntaristic hypothesis, along with those views that imply the pre-existence of the soul, seem to have troubled Augustine who, in a letter to Jerome (Letter 166), expressed doubts about the compatibility of the Platonic idea of a cycle of various incarnations and certain moral aspects of salvation. In particular, the problem would be that, if souls are bearers of moral responsibility and blame (in this context, sin) and if souls can re-incarnate, it may turn out that dying in a state of grace is not always sufficient for salvation; after all, post-mortem sin and pre-incarnate sin are possible. An evaluation of these theories is difficult, if only because debates on these issues are frequently influenced by what is taken to be ultimately authoritative – for example, a specific passage of the Bible – or by other theoretical *desiderata* – for instance, providing a better explanation of other relatively better understood philosophical or religious doctrines.

If we believe that we are essentially souls and/or composites of body and soul, then the coming into existence of a soul – on the assumption that our souls have not always existed – determines the coming into existence of one of us and/or the coming into existence of part of us. This point is of relevance for the debate on, among other things, the morality of abortion, as we will see in Chapter 8.

Substance: In the Scholastic tradition, which provided the theoretical background of Descartes's philosophy, philosophers endorsed different conceptions of substance. One of these conceptions is the *subject view*, the main idea of which is that a substance is the subject in which properties (called also accidents) inhere and that does not inhere itself in any other subject. On this view, a substance is a thing in virtue of which properties can be said to exist, though not independently of it. According to a second understanding of substance, the *independence conception*, a substance is a thing that exists independently, as it does not inhere in anything. In his *An Essay Concerning Human Understanding* (1690), John Locke provides the following definition of (the idea of) a "pure substance in general": "[t]he idea [. . .], to which we give the general name substance, being nothing, but the supposed, but unknown support of those qualities, we find existing, which we imagine cannot subsist, *sine re substante*, without something to support them, we call that support *substantia*, which, according to the true import of the word, is in plain English, standing under or upholding."

Contemporary philosophers use the concept of substance in a variety of different ways, so it is important to pay attention to the specific context in which this concept is used. For instance, in an Aristotelian fashion, some employ the notion of substance as that of a simple or composite entity (composite in the sense of having parts) that is knowable and that bears or sustains certain properties (e.g., organisms like cats and dogs). Substances are also sometimes taken to be entities that *instantiate* or *exemplify* properties and that may last through time. Certain substances may exist without all of their actual properties, although not all properties can be peeled off from a substance without thereby changing the kind of substance at issue (or, in alternative accounts, without destroying the substance). There are significant similarities between the previous understandings of substance and the analogous concept criticised by certain Indian philosophers discussed in the second chapter. For instance, both philosophical traditions include the concept of an independent entity (a substance) that ultimately exists, persists through time, and has properties.

6 Descartes and the soul$_{mind}$

One of the first paragraphs of Descartes's *The Passions of the Soul* (*Les passions de l'âme*, 1649) already makes clear one important point of disagreement between him and other earlier philosophers regarding the nature of the soul (the term he used is '*âme*'). In particular, according to Descartes, it is an error to think that it is the absence of the soul that causes the cessation of movement and heat in the body. On the contrary, Descartes argues, it is because of the cessation of the possibility of bodily movement and heat that the soul takes its leave. In turn, movement in the body and its heat are determined by our internal organs and animal spirits, that is, the "most lively and rarefied parts of the blood." The soul is solely responsible for our thoughts ('*nos pensées*'), which include actions and passions. The former (actions) are our volitions, which originate in the soul itself and can be directed at non-material objects, as when we direct our thinking at the nature of the soul itself, or at actions that terminate in the body, as when we desire to raise an arm. The passions, in a broad sense, are those states that affect the soul. Descartes also provides a narrower definition of the passions as "those perceptions, sensations or emotions of the soul which we refer particularly to it, and which are caused, maintained and strengthened by some movement of the spirits."[5]

Descartes argues for a mind-body substance dualism – a view according to which mind and body are two different kinds of substances – by reflecting on the content of the "clear and distinct perceptions" we have of the mind, or soul, as a thinking and non-extended entity, contrary to that of an extended and non-thinking body. Additionally, the mind, which he claims is nothing less than the soul, is a pure substance, indivisible, and thus incorruptible. Let us call this conception '**soul**$_{mind}$'. According to Descartes, the soul$_{mind}$ is simple, and the term 'I' generally refers to this thinking thing that is indivisible and united to the body. The faculties of each single mind are not metaphysical parts of the soul; rather one mind's sense, perception, intellect, and will can be all different functions of a single indivisible soul$_{mind}$. In other words, one and the same soul$_{mind}$ can sense, perceive, cognise, and desire. Although the human soul is said to be whole in the whole body, Descartes claims that there is a privileged part in which soul$_{mind}$ and body interact, namely, the infamous pineal gland, or *conarium*, located in the centre of the brain. According to many scholars, the account of this interaction is mysterious and a weak point of the whole Cartesian approach to the nature of the mind. His dualism, Descartes says in the *Meditations*, gives hope in an afterlife because if dualism is true, then it does not follow that we are annihilated at the moment of bodily death – provided that the soul can exist without interacting with a body. Regarding the origin of the $soul_{mind}$, Descartes claims in various places that souls are created by God.

Descartes also draws a connection between morality, particularly the virtues, and the $soul_{mind}$: the virtues are habits of the $soul_{mind}$, and their effect is also that of disposing the $soul_{mind}$ to have certain specific thoughts. Although thoughts can be produced solely by the $soul_{mind}$, movements of the animal spirits frequently influence them. Another interesting remark is that $souls_{mind}$, Descartes claims, are not all equally noble and capable of the same kind of generosity, although they all have free will. A good upbringing and frequent reflections on the nature of free will may correct certain "defects of birth".

Dualism: In general, a dualistic view of a specific domain of discourse claims that the domain in question requires for its existence and/or explanation two fundamental principles or kinds of entities. The kind of principles generally taken to be relevant to a dualistic position are ontological. In philosophical accounts of the mind, substance dualism is generally understood as involving the idea that mind and body are of two distinct ontological categories. The thesis can be further specified as stating that the explanation of mental phenomena, such as consciousness, requires the existence of a nonphysical reality, sometimes classified as purely mental. Another interpretation of substance dualism claims that any substance with mental properties lacks material properties and any substance with material properties lacks mental properties (Rodriguez-Pereyra 2008). Contemporary dualistic views frequently do not refer directly to the existence of an immaterial *soul*, but only to a non-material, non-physical mind – a connection between the concept of an immaterial soul and that of an immaterial mind, such as Descartes's, is neither obvious nor logically necessary. Some contemporary philosophers of mind, especially those influenced by the work of David Chalmers, hold that, although there is only one kind of substance (e.g., physical substances), mental *properties* are not reducible to physical properties (the meaning of 'reducible' is itself a matter of controversy). This position is known as property dualism.

Descartes also holds that the human body is numerically identical through time so long as it is informed by the same $soul_{mind}$. Thus, the $soul_{mind}$ seems to have the function of preserving our identity as well as the identity of our bodies. Some scholars have interpreted Descartes as holding the view that $soul_{mind}$ and body, when united, form a *further* substantial unity, that is, another substance over and above the two independent substances of body and $soul_{mind}$, taken separately. Sometimes this interpretation of Descartes is combined with the view that a human being *is* this third substance and, as a consequence, that *we* are this third substance (and thus we are not solely a soul$_{mind}$). A contemporary account of the connection between soul$_{mind}$ and personal identity is offered by Swinburne, which I discuss in the next section.

7 Contemporary soul-based theories: Richard Swinburne and compound dualism

Swinburne, an influential theistic thinker, has been defending an increasingly elaborated theory of personal identity since the 1970s. According to one of its early formulations, which he classifies as a version of the so-called simple view (see appendix 2 in the introduction), answers to questions regarding problematic scenarios involving personal identity – for instance, brain-split scenarios – are not a matter of degree but always involve a yes-or-no answer (what I called an epistemicist version of the simple view).[6] More specifically, Swinburne thinks that it is in principle possible to give a yes-or-no answer – at least for an ideal observer, say, God – to existential questions regarding persons (e.g., is person A still existing at t_2?) raised by certain thought experiments involving brain split, tele-transportation, and so on even for borderline cases. In fact, according to him, there is always a further fact, over and above physical and specific mental facts (e.g., personal memories), that would justify an ascription of personal identity between individuals at different times. Imagine the following scenario. A future scientist divides A's brain in half and transplants each part into two bodies relevantly similar to the body in which A's brain resided before the operation. Suppose that each half of the brain retains significant psychological connections with A's previous mental states – for instance, suppose that A's memories and/or character traits are equally distributed in the two halves. Now, Swinburne claims that, even in such convoluted cases, there will always be a further fact, over and above the configuration of mental properties and brain structure such that A can, in principle, always be said to either exist or not 'in' either of the two resulting post-operation bodies (or, perhaps, in none of them). The structure of Swinburne's reasoning is: given that there is always such a yes-or-no answer to questions of existence for persons, it follows that personal identity cannot be analysed solely in terms of similarity of memory (or other mental properties) and brain continuity, because (1) brain split scenarios (or similar thought experiments) would otherwise imply that the holding of personal identity may be a matter of degree and/or vague, and (2) given that the holding of the relation of personal identity cannot be a matter of degree and/or vague. In addition, he also maintains that this epistemicist stance amounts to a theory of personal identity when it includes, as a criterion of identity, a soul$_{mind}$ (or, at least, one version of substance dualism, whether Cartesian or not). Thus, we have in Swinburne a thinker in whom three conceptions or specifications of the simple view – epistemicist, further-fact view, and mind-body substance dualism – are held together.

According to Swinburne, the functioning of the soul$_{mind}$ (I do not further terminologically distinguish Descartes's understanding of soul$_{mind}$ from Swinburne's in this paragraph; simply assume that I am discussing Swinburne's version here) consists in its having a mental life. In turn, the mental is defined – at least in one of his early works – as that to which substances have privileged access.[7] A substance is understood, as by Descartes, as "a thing that can exist independently of all other things of that kind" (other than its parts). Swinburne claims that a mental property is a property the instantiation of which is necessarily accessible, in a privileged way, to the substance that instantiates this property. Having a privileged access means "having access to whether a property is instantiated by a substance that is further in respect to the access to it that other substances may have". In other words, one mental substance has a manner of accessing her mental states that is distinctive – and privileged – from any other (mental) substances' manner of accessing those same states. The thesis according to which the mark of the mental – that is, what makes a property mental – is that such states provide a specific and privileged access to them is controversial in contemporary philosophy of mind and psychology. Developing Descartes's idea that souls are minds, Swinburne maintains that souls$_{mind}$ are structures formed by, among other things, beliefs and desires. The character of a person is composed of some of the core beliefs and desires of the person, which in turn should be seen as forming a web. This metaphor suggests that beliefs and desires do not exist in isolation but rather form patterns of responses crystallised in time. The character of an individual is thus localised in the soul, intended as an immaterial mental structure.

The main strategy adopted by Swinburne to argue that personal identity is independent from psychological and bodily continuity involves the use of imaginative thought experiments. In particular, he claims that we can imagine that we could become disembodied and that we could survive a complete change of personality and loss of memory. This would prove that, since what is imaginable/conceivable is *prima facie* (metaphysically) possible and that such scenarios are imaginable, it is possible to have cases in which the relation of personal identity holds between entities at different times independently of the holding of psychological and/or bodily continuity. Hence, psychological and/or bodily continuity are not essential to our identity over time. Swinburne also discusses certain relevant phenomenological and qualitative aspects of our conscious experience. In particular, he maintains that there are not only experiences of the successive experiences of a common subject but also simultaneous experiences of a common subject. More specifically, he claims that a subject has forms of non-inferential knowledge related to her own self when she is experiencing, that is, a subject S experiences her experiences as overlapping in a continuous singular stream. In other words, a subject not only experiences certain continuous events but also experiences that certain events are happening to the same subject. Thus, a subject has experience of her own self as a unitary subject of experience. The subject does not need any further evidence to believe that she is having a certain experience because its unity is something that she is already aware of (and that does not depend on anything more fundamental).

This unity of the self and of its experiences is supposed to provide further evidence for the existence of a simple soul$_{mind}$.

Swinburne claims that it is possible that the soul$_{mind}$ may not be able to function on its own, that is, when it does not inform a body. Rather, the soul$_{mind}$ may function as a principle of our identity that becomes conscious when linked to a body. According to this conception, which Swinburne only alludes to without apparently endorsing, a soul$_{mind}$ would thus essentially have the capacity to have mental properties, although it may exist without exercising such a capacity. Swinburne also claims that human beings ("men on Earth") are bodies plus souls, although he also repeatedly uses the expression "I am a pure substance", which is a non-essentialist formulation of the view according to which we are souls$_{mind}$. Some of these claims are rather confusing, but I think that the best way of understanding his most recent (i.e., 2013) version of dualism is the following. We are a compound of soul$_{mind}$ and body, but not essentially so; rather, what we are *essentially* is just souls$_{mind}$.[8] On this interpretation, Swinburne is not an essentialist compound dualist, but rather an essentialist simple or pure dualist who also claims that we are contingently (that is, when we are on Earth) compounds of two substances. Another way of specifying his theory is that of saying that we are essentially pure mental substances that have physical properties only derivatively. On this view, we are essentially souls somehow connected to a body, which is not one of our parts. Ascriptions of physical properties to us (e.g., I have two arms) should be understood along the following lines. A person A has a physical property P in the sense that the body to which A is connected has P. Literally speaking – or directly – we do not have physical properties (surprisingly enough, literally speaking, I thus do not have two arms).

In line with certain Christian beliefs concerning the resurrection of the dead, Swinburne suggests that the soul may even cease to exist and come back into existence once it exercises again its essential capacities. For instance, a soul may go out of existence when what is necessary for its functioning (say, a brain) disappears, but come back to life when another (material) support for thinking is once again linked to the soul. Additionally, Swinburne maintains that it does not immediately follow from the fact (if it is a fact) that souls are indivisible that they are also indestructible. A soul may lose its capacity to experience without losing its indivisibility (a point already made by Kant in his first *Critique*).

Swinburne explicitly links soul$_{mind}$, personal identity, and his (anomalous) dualistic view of our nature in a way that can be thus summarised:

(Swinburne's Dualistic Soul$_{mind}$ Theory of the Metaphysical Foundation of Personal Identity)#1

For all t, where P and Q are each contingently a composite of body and soul$_{mind}$, P at t_1 is one and the same person as Q at t_2 iff P's soul$_{mind}$ at t_1 = Q's soul$_{mind}$ at t_2, provided that if $t_1 \neq t_2$ and P existed at t_1, then the conditions that allowed the soul$_{mind}$ to function properly at t_1 are realised at t_2. For instance, if the soul$_{mind}$ requires a body to function, then the soul$_{mind}$ must inform a body with mind-related equivalent functions.

Alternatively, his account can be formulated as follows.

> (Swinburne's Dualistic Soul$_{mind}$ Theory of the Metaphysical Foundation of Personal Identity)#2
>
> For all t, where P and Q are each essentially a soul$_{mind}$, P at t$_1$ is one and the same person as Q at t$_2$ iff P-soul$_{mind}$ at t$_1$ = Q-soul$_{mind}$ at t$_2$, provided that if t$_1 \neq$ t$_2$ then the conditions that allowed the soul$_{mind}$ to function properly at t$_1$ are realised at t$_2$. For instance, if the soul$_{mind}$ requires a body to function, then the soul$_{mind}$ must inform a body with mind-related equivalent functions.

The plausibility of this approach to personal identity is inextricably linked to the plausibility of substance dualism.

8 Personal identity and dualism: clarifications and criticisms

As Eric Olson has recently claimed, the exact details of many dualistic accounts of personal identity and of our nature are frequently spelled out in terms that are not equivalent or not even entirely internally consistent, given other presuppositions.[9] For instance, the ambiguity that Swinburne inherits from the Platonic tradition is that it is not always clear whether the manner in which he classifies the referent of 'I' and what he says about the nature of persons and human beings are compatible. More specifically, suppose that I am essentially a person. Then, if a person is essentially composed of two parts, a body and a soul, and 'I am only a pure soul', is true, then it follows that I am a proper part of a person. So, contrary to our supposition, I am not a person. It would be a mistake to infer, from essentialist compound dualism about persons and from the claim that I am only a pure soul, that I would be a person because I am a proper part of a person: it would be similar to saying that a window is a skyscraper because the window is a proper part of the skyscraper. Unless a further argument or explanation is provided, we cannot say that we are persons merely by starting from the previous premises. This is not just word-play but one of the possible conceptual confusions that may hint at serious problems related to how certain versions of the soul-based approach can account for certain basic beliefs about our own nature and personal identity through time.

Recent thinkers (e.g., Olson) have claimed that pure dualism is more plausible than compound dualism. However, the former also seems to have problems in explaining some of the ascriptions of properties we generally make to ourselves. For instance, if you are a pure immaterial soul, then *you* do not (literally or directly) grow old and do not have weight. Supporters of pure dualism need an account of how, by merely being pure souls$_{mind}$, we can consistently claim to have certain physical properties or even be spatio-temporally located. In fact, if a soul is an immaterial entity, it is not clear how it can have a spatio-temporal location because it is not literally true that *you* are in a particular location right now as you read this sentence. As hinted previously, we may argue that if we are immaterial souls_{mind}, we may occupy space *derivatively*, that is, by having or being connected to a body. Whether this is an appropriate solution is controversial.

Descartes's defence of his version of dualism has been crucially influential in shaping the debate on the nature of the mind. Gonzalo Rodriguez-Pereyra reconstructs one of his most famous arguments, which can be found in the *Sixth Medita-tion*, as follows: "(1) If I clearly, distinctly, and completely conceive or understand A apart from B, then A is a substance and it is possible that A exists without B. (2) If it is possible that A exists without B, then A and B are numerically distinct. (3) I clearly, distinctly, and completely understand the mind apart from the body (any mind and any body), and I clearly, distinctly, and completely understand the body apart from the mind (any body and any mind). (4) The mind (any mind) is a substance, and it is possible that it exists without the body (any body), and the body is a substance, and it is possible that it exists without the mind (any mind). (5) Therefore, the mind and the body (any mind, any body) are numerically distinct substances."[10] This argument, however, does not entail that any substance with mental properties lacks material properties and any substance with material properties lacks mental properties – which corresponds to Rodriguez-Pereyra's understanding of substance dualism (see the explanatory box on dualism). If anything, this argument entails the real ontological distinction between mind and body. Descartes provides other arguments from which substance dualism follows. In particular, he claims that the notions of a thinking thing and that of an extended thing are different – they can at least be conceived as separable. He also maintains that attribute and substance coincide; more specifically, that the principal attribute (e.g., thinking or extension) of a substance and the substance are not distinct entities. One (the substance) cannot exist without the other (the principal attribute) *and* the two principal attributes of thinking and extension are separable. Now, a thinking thing is a substance that has thinking as its principal attribute, as an inseparable feature of the substance itself. From these premises, substance dualism follows.

Specific objections against substance dualism have been explored at least since Descartes had Mersenne circulate the manuscript of his *Meditations*. Among them is the interaction problem, that is, the problem of finding an adequate explanation of how a physical body may enter into a causal relation with an immaterial body and vice versa. Another way of expressing similar worries is the so-called pairing problem. Suppose that soul A and soul B are immaterial and non-spatial. Imagine that A and B engage in an act of will W the result of which is a material body grabbing an apple. If A and B are immaterial and non-spatial, the puzzle a dualist faces is that of explaining what relation holds between one of these souls and one body such that it is just one of them that grabs the apple: what makes it the case that my soul is paired with only my body instead of somebody else's body given that if we exclude hypotheses similar to Descartes's pineal gland as the seat of their interaction, souls and bodies do not share any parts?

Another strategy to rebut substance dualism is that of making a case against the theoretical appeal of some of the intuitions that support this view. For instance, dualism can be appealing because it explains or accounts for the strong intuition that a description, no matter how accurate, of a series of physical facts related to mental phenomena, say, neurones and/or dispositions of relevant matter, will always be incomplete in an important sense. In particular, no matter how many details, e.g., a neuroscientist can accumulate about the internal structure of the brain, she will never be able to know, just by looking at the long description of these facts, what it feels like to be in the mental states described by the states of the brain unless she has experienced them *subjectively*. From this, dualists infer the existence of a further domain of existence that does not coincide with the physical, a domain that can be understood in terms of mental properties and/or mental substances alone. In turn, some materialists or physicalists have replied that the previous observations do not have to be taken as indicating that there are two radically different types of substances and/or properties, but rather that there are (at least) two radically different ways of understanding or describing brain states (or other physical states that may be responsible for our mental properties). The idea is that we use, on one hand, *phenomenal concepts* to describe our access to certain brain states by, e.g., introspection and, on the other hand, *descriptions of physical states* to access mental states from an external point of view. However, the radical difference between these two ways of accessing mental states – and the intuitions of separateness that they engender – does not reveal the existence of different kinds of substances or properties, rather only two different ways of accessing physical substances or properties that happen to be instantiated in our brains (that is, material entities).[11]

Other criticisms to the soul-based approach – and some of its applications to debates in applied ethics – are discussed in the next chapters. In particular, some Buddhist thinkers have argued that the belief in the existence of enduring substances such as souls is misguided and even conducive to morally wrong behaviours (Chapter 2). In fact, one of the main principles of many Buddhist schools is that reality is constantly changing (everything exists just momentarily), which implies that the appearance of the existence of immutable substances is a kind of illusion. In turn, relational accounts of personal identity and of our nature may argue against the simple-soul approach that, since we are essentially relational/social entities and souls do not seem to be essentially relational/social entities, we are not essentially souls or compounds of soul and body (Chapter 3). Another influential account that critically discusses the simple-soul approach is Locke's. In particular, he argues that, even granting the existence of souls and since what grounds personal identity is a special kind of psychological relation the continuity of which seems to be independent from the continuity of the same soul, identity of soul is not what grounds the relation of personal identity (Chapter 4).

9 Summary

In this chapter, we explored the simple-soul approach to our nature and personal identity. Such an approach relies on an account of the soul according to which the soul is a simple and immaterial entity connected in various ways to our capacity to think and reason. In particular, we saw that certain accounts of the nature of the soul hold that it is a *mereologically* simple entity (e.g., Plato's in the *Phaedo*, Descartes's, Swinburne's). Many pre-modern philosophers (e.g., Plato, Augustine) also believed that the soul was not solely responsible for our mind, consciousness, or some other mental faculties, but that it was the principle of life of the body itself. Some philosophers (Plato, some Christian thinkers, Descartes, etc.) claimed that souls are immortal, immaterial, and/or irreducible to combinations of matter. The origin of the soul is a debated topic and theories about it differ significantly; for instance, some argue that the soul is created by God, others that the soul is transmitted by the parents to the newborn.

We distinguished various theories of our nature based on the notion of a soul. In particular, an essentialist version of simple dualism states that we are essentially souls, whilst a non-essentialist version claims only that we are souls. Similarly, there is an essentialist and a non-essentialist version of compound dualism, the theory according to which we are (essentially) a compound of soul and body. Theories of personal identity based on the notion of a simple soul all have in common the idea that the relation of personal identity holds in virtue of the continuity or identity of the same soul over time. The plausibility of some of the main arguments in favour of the existence of certain forms of dualism depend on the claim that an explanation of the mental requires positing the existence of non-physical mental substances. However, an increasing number of scholars in various disciplines have questioned the very existence of souls and/or the plausibility of the idea that an explanation of the mental should involve immaterial entities. For instance, contemporary non-religiously inclined philosophers of mind are generally dismissive of the explanatory value of positing the existence of souls. Other approaches to personal identity and our nature raise different objections to the simple-soul approach – e.g., Buddhist theories generally hold that the belief in persisting substances, including souls, relies on a misunderstanding of the nature of reality, as we will see in the next chapter.

Essentialist compound dualism, intended as a theory of our nature, may hold that, although we persist in virtue of the continuity of the same soul, our existence requires embodiment. On this version of dualism, the soul is responsible only for retaining our capacity to continue to exist through time as the same entity. Simple dualism does not directly imply this and is compatible with the view that a sufficient condition for our persistence through time is that the same soul continues to exist. Supporters of compound dualism and of simple dualism tend to hold the view according to which we are essentially persons and frequently do not distinguish between theories of personal identity and of *our* persistence through time.

Notes

1 These other views on the nature of the soul are discussed in Chapter 8, 3.1.
2 I use the expressions '*qua* person' and 'as a person' interchangeably.
3 See Appendix 2 in the introduction.

4 I do not claim that the Biblical scriptures are directly inspired by Greek philosophy. My point is only that (some) important later Christian philosophers were. See Cooper (1989/2000) for discussion.
5 *The Passions of the Soul*, Chapter 27.
6 Swinburne (1984).
7 Swinburne (1984).
8 This reading seems to be confirmed by his most recent discussion of these issues in Swinburne (2013): Chapter 6.
9 Olson (2007): Chapter 7.
10 Rodriguez-Pereyra (2008), p. 73.
11 Other strategies to rebut Descartes's (and Swinburne's) arguments include that of questioning the connection between conceivability/imaginability and metaphysical/logical possibility. The phenomenal concept strategy against substance dualism is clearly explained in Papineau (2002).

Suggested readings

Plato and Greek conceptions of the soul

Primary sources

Phaedo, translated by David Gallop (Oxford: Clarendon Press, 1975).
The Republic, translated by Reginald E. Allen (New Haven: Yale University Press, 2006).

Secondary literature

Apolloni, David, 'Plato's Affinity Argument for the Immortality of the Soul', *Journal of the History of Philosophy*, 34, 1 (1996), pp. 5–32.
Barney, Richard, Tad Brennan, and Charles Bittain (eds.), *Plato and the Divided Self* (Cambridge: Cambridge University Press, 2012).
Bostock, David, *Plato's Phaedo* (Oxford: Clarendon Press, 1986).
Bremmer, Jan, *The Early Greek Concept of Soul* (Princeton: Princeton University Press, 1983).
Ferrari, Giovanni R.F., 'The Three-Part Soul', in G.R.F. Ferrari (ed.) *The Cambridge Companion to Plato's Republic* (Cambridge: Cambridge University Press, 2007), pp. 165–201.
Gerson, Lloyd P., *Knowing Persons* (Oxford: Oxford University Press, 2003).
Lorenz, Hendrik, 'Plato on the Soul', in Gail Fine (ed.) *The Oxford Handbook of Plato* (Oxford: Oxford University Press, 2008).
Shields, Christopher, 'Plato's Divided Soul', in Mark McPherran (ed.) *Plato's Republic: A Critical Guide* (Cambridge: Cambridge University Press, 2010), pp. 147–170.

Early Christian views on the soul and Augustine

Primary sources

Augustine, *The Works of Saint Augustine: A Translation for the 21st Century* (Hyde Park, NY: New City Press, 1990).

Secondary literature

Bynum, Caroline Walker, *The Resurrection of the Body in Western Christianity, 200–1336* (New York: Columbia University Press, 1995).

Cooper, John W., *Body, Soul and Life Everlasting* (Grand Rapids, MI: William B. Eerdmans Publishing Company, 1989/2000).

King, Peter, 'Body and Soul', in John Marenbon (ed.) *The Oxford Handbook of Medieval* Philosophy (Oxford: Oxford University Press, 2012).

Matthews, Gareth B., *Thought's Ego in Augustine and Descartes* (Ithaca and London: Cornell University Press, 1992).

Descartes and the soul-mind

Primary sources

Descartes, René, *Meditations on First Philosophy: With Selections From the Objections and Replies*, translated by Michael Moriarty (Oxford: Oxford University Press, 2008).

Descartes, René, *Passions of the Soul*, translated by Stephen H. Voss (Indianapolis: Hackett, 1989).

Secondary literature

Broadie, Sarah, 'Soul and Body in Plato and Descartes', *Proceedings of the Aristotelian Society* 101, 3 (2001), pp. 295–308.

Broughton, Janet and John Carriero (eds.) *A Companion to Descartes* (Oxford: Blackwell Publishing, 2008), in particular essays 15 and 23.

Cottingham, John, *Cartesian Reflections: Essays on Descartes's Philosophy* (Oxford: Oxford University Press, 2008).

Hawthorne, John, 'Cartesian Dualism', in Peter van Inwagen and Dean Zimmerman (eds.) *Persons: Human and Divine* (Oxford: Clarendon Press, 2007), pp. 87–98.

Pasnau, Robert, *Metaphysical Themes: 1274–1671* (Oxford: Oxford University Press).

Rodriguez-Pereyra, Gonzalo, 'Descartes's Substance Dualism and His Independence Conception of Substance', *Journal of the History of Philosophy*, 46, 1 (2008), pp. 69–90.

Schechtman, Anat, 'Substance and Independence in Descartes', *Philosophical Review*, 125, 2 (2016), pp. 155–204.

Shapiro, Lisa, 'Descartes's Passions of the Soul', *Philosophy Compass* 1, 3 (2006), pp. 268–278.

Williams, Bernard, *Descartes: The Project of Pure Enquiry* (London: Penguin Books, 1978).

Richard Swinburne and other contemporary soul-based views

Chisholm, Roderick, *Person and Object* (LaSalle, IL: Open Court, 1976).

Spackman, John, 'Consciousness and the Prospects for Substance Dualism', *Philosophy Compass*, 8, 11 (2013), pp. 1054–1065.

Swinburne, Richard, 'Personal Identity: The Dualist Theory', in Sydney Shoemaker and Richard Swinburne (eds.) *Personal Identity* (Oxford: Blackwell, 1984), pp. 3–66.

Swinburne, Richard, *The Evolution of the Soul* (Oxford: Oxford University Press, 1986/97).

Swinburne, Richard, *Mind, Brain, and Free Will* (Oxford: Oxford University Press, 2013).

Philosophy of mind, dualism, and criticisms

Chalmers, David J., *The Conscious Mind: In Search of a Fundamental Theory* (Oxford: Oxford University Press, 1996).

Churchland, Paul M., *Matter and Consciousness* (Cambridge, MA: MIT Press, 1984/88).

Ford, Norman, *The Prenatal Person* (Oxford: Blackwell Publishing, 2002).

Goetz, Stewart and Charles Taliaferro, *A Brief History of the Soul* (Oxford: Wiley-Blackwell, 2011).

John Heil, *Philosophy of Mind, Third Edition* (London and New York: Routledge, 2013)

Kim, Jaegwon, *Mind in a Physical World: An Essay on the Mind-Body Problem and Mental Causation* (Cambridge, MA: MIT Press, 1998).

Olson, Eric, 'A Compound of Two Substances', in Kevin Corcoran (ed.) *Soul, Body, and Survival* (Ithaca and London: Cornell University Press, 2001), pp. 73–82.

Olson, Eric, *What Are We?* (Oxford: Oxford University Press, 2007), chapter 7.

Papineau, David, *Thinking About Consciousness* (Oxford: Clarendon Press, 2002).

Robinson, Howard, 'Dualism', in *Stanford Encyclopedia of Philosophy* (2011). http://plato.stanford.edu/entries/dualism/

Sturgeon, Scott, *Matters of Mind* (London and New York: Routledge, 2000).

2 Buddhist no-self approach and nihilism

1	The Buddha, *Anātman*, and suffering	53
2	*Abhidharma*, *skandhas*, and Vasubandhu	56
3	The emptiness of the self and Nāgārjuna	63
4	Buddhist no-self views and ethics	66
	4.1 Intra-personal ethics and no-self	66
	4.2 Relational ethics and no-self	68
5	Nihilism and our nature	70
6	Summary	72

> Bhikkus, all is burning. And what, bhikkus, is the all that is burning? The eye is burning, forms are burning, eye-consciousness is burning, eye-contact is burning, and whatever feeling arises with eye-contact as condition – whether pleasant or painful or neither-painful-nor-pleasant – that too is burning. Burning with what? Burning with the fire of lust, with the fire of hatred, with the fire of delusion; burning with birth, aging, and death; with sorrow, lamentation, pain, displeasure, and despair, I say.
>
> —*The Connected Discourses of the Buddha*, SN 35.28

The Buddhist tradition has produced a variety of intricate and apparently counter-intuitive ideas regarding the nature of the self and personal identity. Drawing from the rich Indian intellectual and religious traditions, the Buddha – whose real name is said to have been Gautama – laid the foundations of what he took to be a path towards the removal of suffering. A crucial step of this path is a correct understanding of the nature of reality and of ourselves. Although the details of Gautama's life are interspersed with myth, some sources claim that he lived from 566 BCE to 486 BCE (alternatives to these dates place his death at 404 BCE). Contemporary Buddhism includes a variety of different schools, practices, and rituals that differ greatly in relation to the cultural traditions of the regions with which they interacted (India, Sri Lanka, Thailand, China, Korea, Japan, etc.). Despite this variety, Buddhist intellectuals have all emphasised a series of doctrines and ideas that connect metaphysics and ethics in particular ways. One of these ways is the claim, already made by the Buddha in some early sutras, that believing in an enduring self or soul (in a sense to be specified) is a harmful illusion that leads to suffering. Although the conceptions of a persisting self criticised by the Buddhists are not exactly those discussed in the previous chapter, the similarities are sufficient to support the claim that many of the Buddhist arguments can be applied to the Platonic and Christian notions of soul.

This chapter is organised as follows. First, I discuss some general Buddhist doctrines, with particular emphasis on the nature of the self and on how, according to the Buddha, some metaphysical views on the self are connected to suffering. To clarify the Buddhist no-self approach, I provide the required background in classical Indian philosophy. In this regard, I outline two accounts of *ātman,* the concept in the Indian tradition closest to the notions of soul explored in the previous chapter, and then formulate two theories of personal identity based on *ātman.* In the second section, I outline some arguments proposed by the Buddha against the previous conceptions of *ātman* and against theories of personal identity based on them. I then clarify some crucial points of the debate on no-self views by taking into account the elaboration of the Buddha's early sutras advanced by *Abhidharma* thinkers – early philosophers devoted to the clarification and expansion of some central Buddhist doctrines. In this regard, I briefly discuss some exegetical points advanced by Vasubandhu, an important Indian philosopher-monk of the 4th century CE, and outline a first no-self theory of personal identity, the 'Buddhist no-self View#1'. In the third section, I illustrate some doctrines proposed by a different, though related, school of Buddhism called *Madhyamaka.* One of the main theoretical theses of this school is that everything is empty, a claim that can be understood as meaning that there are no entities having an intrinsic or independent nature. I summarise a series of ideas derived mostly from Nāgārjuna's works and elaborate what I call the 'Buddhist no-self View#2'. In the fourth section, which is divided into two sub-sections, I first investigate some connections of the no-self views with issues in personal ethics and then the relation between no-self views and some other-regarding moral attitudes (e.g., compassion). In the final sections, I discuss one view of our own nature, nihilism, which has been variously associated with some interpretations of *Madhyamaka.* One of the challenges that revisionist approaches such as the Buddhist faces is that of providing an account of the rationality of at least some of our everyday and social practices that appear to be fundamentally connected to (a belief in) the existence of persons.

I The Buddha, *Anātman,* and suffering

One of the main teachings transmitted by the Buddha to his disciples is that suffering is intimately connected to the structure of existence itself.[1] In fact, suffering lurks almost inevitably in human (and non-human) affairs in different forms – poverty (for some), sickness (for most), old age (for those who survive poverty and sickness), etc. A particular form of suffering, which is sometimes called 'existential suffering', is connected to the awareness of our own mortality. Gautama allegedly realised that ignorance of certain truths about existence, such as the impermanence of everything and the doctrine of no-self, is partially responsible for such unnecessary existential suffering. As a result of this realisation, the Buddha decided to teach certain doctrines, the understanding of which can expunge such suffering and eventually pave the way to ***nirvana***, which for now can be understood as a state of liberation and bliss. One of the main effects of reaching *nirvana* is the interruption of the (eventually) painful series of rebirths regulated by the Karmic rules in which we are immersed. In fact, Buddhists see the continuous cycle of rebirths as a condition from which it is desirable to escape. Realising that an enduring self is an illusion – this realisation being one of the conditions the fulfilment of which would liberate us from the cycle of rebirths – is thus of central importance for the Buddhist project of salvation. In the Buddhist tradition, self, personal identity, and ethics are thus tightly connected in at least this sense: ignorance of our metaphysical nature obstructs our path to the removal of suffering. In turn, removing suffering is seen by some Buddhists as a reason motivating compassionate beings to remain in the painful cycle of rebirths and help those who have not yet achieved enlightenment. The desire to alleviate suffering is thus also seen as a source of moral motivation.

The Buddha argued that suffering is also due to a process of appropriation – the linguistic aspects of which are the use of terms such as 'I' and 'mine' – which is essentially bound to disappoint us, given a sufficiently long span of time. More specifically, the formation of various forms of attachments, based on the illusion of an enduring self that strives to own, among other things, material possessions, is bound to generate further desires and aversions in a seemingly endless cycle. Before exploring in more detail the ethical consequences of the no-self doctrines (section 4.1 and 4.2), we should specify the concept of a self that is criticised by the Buddha and other later Buddhist philosophers – that is, we have to discuss some of the philosophical background of the early Buddhist tradition derived from the *Upanishads*.

In the tradition of the *Upanishads*, a series of texts compiled at different times that allegedly contain descriptions of rituals and truths concerning the nature of reality, the self (*ātman* in Sanskrit) is sometimes described as concealed or hard to spot. This self may be hidden because of its size (in a passage of the *Chāndogya*, one of the oldest *Upanishads*, the self is said to be "smaller than a grain of rice") or because it does not enter into the field of sensory perception. In the *Chāndogya Upanishad*, our true *ātman* is associated with our true desires, which in turn, according to some interpretations, can be seen as desires for what is stable or immortal. Jonardon Ganeri suggests that this hidden self in the early *Upanishads* is not itself an object of perception.[2] On this interpretation, the *Upanishadic* self is not an object of perception but rather is the subject of consciousness, an agentive self that controls the body: "Know the self as a rider in a chariot,/and the body, as simply the chariot. Know the intellect as the charioteer, and the mind, as simply the reins." (*Katha Upanishads* 3.3) In this respect – that is, as an agent in control of the body – the conception of the self in the *Upanishads* is similar to the conception of soul discussed in the *Phaedo*. However, an important difference between the Platonic soul and the *Upanishadic* self is that the hidden *ātman* is sometimes described as being impersonal. In fact, the principle behind a specific person's *ātman*, called *brahman*, is the same for all of us. Some later Indian philosophers, such as Śankara (788–820 CE), even claim that *ātman* is identical with *brahman*, where the latter can be understood as the ultimate reality or being of the cosmos. There are several ways of interpreting such claims, some of which may lead to radically different metaphysical conceptions of reality. In fact, the understanding of *brahman* throughout the *Upanishads* significantly varies: sometimes it is taken to be a formulation of truth, other times the essence of reality. Thus, equating *ātman* to *brahman* may mean different things in different *Upanishads*. Keeping in mind that such complications exist, I will now focus only on two ways of understanding the previous claims about the nature of *ātman* and relate them to criteria of personal identity.

*Ātman*₁ thesis: Each of us has an imperceptible agential individual essence that is the owner or subject of our experiences. This subject is a substance of a divine nature (hence its similarity with *brahman*), though it is ontologically distinct from such an underlying higher reality.

It is not clear whether this also implies that we are essentially such an *ātman*. If this is the case, we can articulate a theory of our nature claiming that we are (essentially) *ātman*s. A related theory of personal identity goes as follows.

($\bar{A}tman_1$ Theory of the Metaphysical Foundation of Personal Identity)#1

For all t, P at t_1 is one and the same person as Q at t_2 iff P's *ātman*₁ at t_1 = Q's *ātman*₁ at t_2.

*Ātman*₂ thesis: Each of us has an imperceptible, agential individual essence that is the owner or subject of our experiences. Reality, contrary to the merely apparent perceivable world, is monistic: there is only one underlying substance. That is why *ātman* is *brahman*. If this is taken to be a claim about our own nature, then we are (essentially) *brahman*. A related theory of personal identity goes as follows.

($\bar{A}tman_2$ Theory of the Metaphysical Foundation of Personal Identity)#2

For all t, P at t_1 is one and the same person as Q at t_2 iff P's *ātman*₂ at t_1 = Q's *ātman*₂ at t_2.

According to the *Upanishads*, what is perceived through our senses is deceitful and imperfect; what exists "beyond the veil of ignorance" is a reality that is divine. The difference between *ātman*₁ and *ātman*₂ concerns the metaphysical nature of this hidden reality, which may generate different problems for the theories of personal identity built on them. For example, if we hold ($\bar{A}tman_2$ Theory) and/or ($\bar{A}tman_2$ Theory of the Metaphysical Foundation of Personal Identity)#2, we may have the following problem. Suppose that P and Q are perceived in the world of appearances as two distinct persons. Because P's *ātman*₂ and Q's *ātman*₂ are the same (or because P is an *ātman*₂ and Q is an *ātman*₂), given that they are both equivalent with *brahman* and that identity is a transitive relation, P and Q are the same. Unless we specify a way in which *brahman* individuates persons, this view implies that, in reality (beyond the veil of ignorance), we are all identical to the same underlying divine reality and thus also identical to each other (supposing that we are persons). The alleged distinction between individual persons would thus be only a sort of illusion. As Śankara puts it, "[j]ust as the contents of illusions have no real existence apart from consciousness, so everyday experience of differentiation has no real existence apart from consciousness."[3] The main idea seems to be that the experiences of individuality we have in everyday experience is similar, in regard to its existence, to an illusion. Individual differences are the product of our consciousness (or imagination), devoid of independent real existence. Another consequence of this view is that, in reality, I am identical to you (and to the rest of being).

Now, the Buddha is generally taken to have denied the existence of *ātman*, in both of the senses specified previously. In particular, the Buddha has claimed in many sutras that everything is impermanent. As a consequence, Buddhists uphold the Heraclitean principle that there is no such thing as an enduring substance that persists unchanged through time. From this, it seems to follow that the Buddhists deny the existence of not only $ātman_1$ and $ātman_2$ but also of $soul_{Platonic\text{-}Phaedo}$. Although various interpretations of the Buddhist no-self have been proposed, we shall take the main point of the no-self approach (that is, what makes it a no-self theory) to be the claim that, since everything in reality is impermanent – akin to an Heraclitean flux – there are no enduring $ātman_1$ or $ātman_2$ (or relevantly similar entities such as souls). In the rest of (only) this chapter, I will use 'self' as equivalent to these conceptions of *ātman*, unless otherwise specified.

2 *Abhidharma, skandhas,* and Vasubandhu

In the centuries after Buddha's death, a corpus of studies containing various interpretations and elaborations of his teachings expanded into what is called *Abhidharma*. Various translations of this Sanskrit term are used, 'higher teachings' or 'concerning the teachings' among the most frequent. These texts, the exact list of which varies in relation to different Buddhist schools (e.g., *Sarvāstivāda* or *Theravāda*), are generally distinguished from various collections of Buddha's and his disciples' discourses, as well as from texts containing monastic and meditational rules for Buddhist practitioners and monks. The content of *Abhidharma*, intended as a prolonged attempt to systematise certain teachings of the Buddha, has been crucially influential in the sense that subsequent Buddhist schools and traditions defined themselves also in relation to their agreement or disagreement about specific arguments and disciplines elaborated in these philosophical treatises. In particular, *Abhidharma* texts elaborate some of the early sutras with the purpose of offering an ontological catalogue and hierarchy of the ultimate kinds of components – called **dharmas** – that constitute reality. In other words, *Abhidharma* texts provide an account of the various categories of objects – including persons – and of the more fundamental ontological components of reality.

To illustrate what is at issue here, imagine a car. A car belongs to the category of physical objects. However, this category (and its tokens) can be further divided into more fundamental kinds of elements: for instance, engine, bumper, window, etc. These categories can be further analysed into more fundamental ones and so on until we eventually find what is ultimately indivisible. *Abhidharma* philosophers were interested in providing an analysis of the various physical and mental categories (or kinds) that ultimately compose reality, that is, those elements that cannot be further analysed. *Abhidharma* texts differ in the proposed taxonomy and organisation of the *dharmas*, or ultimate components. For instance, the tradition associated with the *Theravāda* school proposed a system of eighty-two *dharma* categories, whereas the *Sarvāstivāda* introduced a system of seventy-five basic types. It may be improper to call these ultimate components of reality 'categories'; in fact, some recent scholars have proposed that *Abhidharma* philosophers, or at least some of them, did not understand these basic *dharmas* as being universals – that which can have multiple instantiations or exemplifications – but rather as momentary and particular individuals or events. More specifically, some contemporary Buddhist scholars have compared *dharmas* – whether intended as tokens or types – to *tropes* that have their own intrinsic and/or essential properties.

Tropes: Among those who revived a tradition going back at least to Aristotle, Donald C. Williams (1899–1983) argued that the basic components of reality are abstract particulars, also known as *tropes*. According to D. Williams's understanding, tropes are the particular cases of (alleged) general features – the particular token-properties that we encounter in our experience; for instance, this specific shade of colour, or x-colour-at t_1, that you perceive in this specific situation at this particular time. Keith Campbell (b. 1938), another influential contemporary trope theorist, claims that ascribing the property of being abstract to tropes should be understood as simply claiming that the specific features a trope has can be "brought before the mind only by a process of selection, of systematic setting aside" the other qualities we may perceive in a specific object – e.g., this specific roundness as distinct from this vividness, which both coexist in a specific object. In contrast, a concrete object would be "the totality of the being" from which we mentally abstract the specific colours, shape, and so on. Some claim that the particular features that we called tropes exist as individuals independently of our minds, and they are not instantiated in many different situations simultaneously – this last feature distinguishes them from repeatable universals. The characterising feature of D. Williams's approach is that he also claims that tropes are the fundamental ontological category, thus excluding the necessity of postulating the existence of universals. The individuality, fundamentality, and non-repeatability of tropes are features ascribed to *dharmas* as well. Possible differences include the momentariness or impermanence of *dharmas* (e.g., tropes in contemporary metaphysics are not necessarily taken to be momentary) and the lurking idea in the Buddhist tradition that entities are only apparently composed of all of the *dharmas* that we may abstract in/from them. In fact, according to the Buddhists, there is no entity called, say, 'the Nagasena's chariot': the basic components of reality, in the Buddhist tradition, do not add up to and compose objects.

To summarise, a *dharma* in the *Abhidharma* tradition can be interpreted as an entity contained in our ultimate ontology such that it (1) bears its own essential or intrinsic properties, (2) is impermanent (not persisting in time), (3) is partless (or simple), and (4) unique.[4]

The previous discussion is important for our purposes because *Abhidharma* texts also include a discussion of the components or aggregates – called *skandhas* in Sanskrit – into which persons can be divided. The five categories generally used to classify the *skandhas* are: (1) *Rūpa*-form/material object/body, (2) Feeling or sensation (of hedonic states such as pleasure, pain, and indifference), (3) Perception, (4) Volition, and (5) Consciousness. Form-matter or *rūpa* is itself divisible into momentary material entities of different kinds. In his *Pañcaskandhaka-prakana* ('A Discussion of the Five Aggregates'), Vasubandhu, in line with traditional classifications, claims that the first *skandha* (*rūpa*) is what has dimensionality and is constituted by the four great elements – that is, earth-element, water-element, fire-element, and wind-element. For example, the various sense-organs (eye, ear, nose, tongue, etc.) are derived from these great elements. The second *skandha*, feeling, corresponds to the mental episodes of pain, pleasure, or neutral sensations that accompany our experiences. The category of perceptions includes, according to Mark Siderits, those mental events that allow us to grasp the phenomenal aspects of perceptible objects. Charles Goodman claims that this category includes the categories of thought used to organise and cognise what we perceive or think about. Vasubandhu holds that these perception-cognitions (or cognitions in perception and sensing) are of three kinds: indefinite, definite, and immeasurable. The *skandha* of volition includes mental dispositions or attitudes responsible for various bodily and mental activities. Vasubandhu uses episodes of hunger, maliciousness, desire to harm, mental attention, vigour, tranquillity, lack of shame, and many others as examples to illustrate this category. The last broad category, consciousness, stands for our awareness of mental and bodily events. Various subdivisions of these five broad categories are possible, but one of their main common features is that the momentary existence of an aggregate never involves a persisting self. The point seems to be that, in our mental experiences, we are never directly aware of the owner of such mental states; nor are we conscious that our thoughts contain such a self. Some *Abhidharma* traditions (e.g., the *Sarvāstivāda* and the post-canonical *Theravāda*) understood the notion of impermanence in terms of momentariness: all successive singular mental and physical *dharmas* form series of discrete, momen-tary events that go out of existence as soon as they have originated. The account of our mental life presented here is that of a succession of momentary and imperma-nent mental states, the nature and content of which do not include any reference to an owner-self in addition to their specific content. In other words, although we may obviously have a perception of what may appear as ourselves, the content of such a thought does not include, as one of its essential constituents, an enduring self that is also the owner of such a state. For example, if you are perceiving what appears to be yourself in the mirror, the content of your resulting thought would have the struc-ture <the-appearance-of-[the-aggregates-allegedly-constituting-me]-in-the-mirror> but *not* <an inner subject (an *I*); the-appearance-of-[the-aggregates-allegedly-constituting-me]-in-the-mirror >.

Keeping in mind the notions of *ātman* and *skandha*, I will now present two arguments against the existence of a persisting self allegedly proposed by the Bud-dha himself. I then offer an interpretation of these arguments according to certain *Abhidharma* texts. Siderits summarises one version of the argument from imper-manence contained in different forms in various passages of the *Saṃyutta Nikāya*, a canonical collection of discourses and texts in *Theravāda* Buddhism, along the following lines.

1   If there were a self, intended as either *ātman*$_1$ or *ātman*$_2$, it would be permanent.
2   None of the five types of psychophysical elements (*skandhas*) into which a person can be analysed or reduced is permanent.
3   Thus, there is no self. (S III.66–68)

A related argument, called 'the control argument', which can be found in various sutras, holds that:

1   All of the five kinds of psychophysical elements are suffering – they all lead to affliction.
2   The self is an agential entity or controller of its own states.
3   None of these psychophysical elements is the self, since if they were, they would be under our control and thus they would not lead to suffering.
4   Thus, there is no self.

These arguments, extracted from the *Anatta-lakkhana Sutta* (Pali, translated as 'The Discourse on the Characteristic of Not-self'), have a hidden premise, called the 'Exhaustiveness Claim' (EC) by Siderits: there is no constituent of a person (or ourselves) that is not listed in one or more of the five categories of *skandhas*. In other words, the EC says that, if we analyse and divide a person into her ultimate components, all of these components would figure in the list of *skandhas*. The main underlying reasoning behind the two previous arguments would thus be that, given the nature of *skandhas*, since a self (*ātman*) is not one of these aggregates (or their sub-varieties), and because the aggregates are all there is that (supposedly) compose a person, it follows that there are no selves. This thought is then taken to be justified by the fact that, because everything that allegedly composes a person is impermanent, there is no such thing as an impermanent self. The crucial hidden premise of EC may imply several things, e.g., that also persons are completely analysable into more basic *skandhas*, depending on the exact meaning of '*pugdala*', the corresponding term for 'person' in Sanskrit. In fact, the term '*pugdala*' is generally translated with 'person', but we should keep in mind that it does not have exactly the same semantic extension as its English counterpart. (For instance, the Sanskrit term seems to be also associated simply with the notion of an individual and it is sometimes used to refer also to what extends over various lives after rebirths.) More specifically, an analysis of the concept of a person in terms of its *dharmas* – which is the process that justifies the EC – can be intended in two ways: (1) as an ontological reduction of an entity to one or more other entities, or (2) as a conceptual analysis of the notion of a person into other notions.[5] The difference between the two can be stated as follows. A full or complete (or non-circular) conceptual analysis or reduction of a concept C in terms of something else, T, usually involves a series of specifications of C in terms of T, where T does not include C. In other words, the concept C is fully specified or reduced to other concepts Ts if these Ts do not include C. As a result of this analysis, if we substitute all of the occurrences of C with Ts, the understanding of what was involved in C would not be compromised if we are able to grasp the concepts Ts. An ontological reduction does not imply, in itself, a conceptual reduction (and vice versa). For instance, from the fact that a concept C can be reduced to concepts Ts, it does not follow, without further arguments, that the entities referred to in Ts are also metaphysically or ontologically more fundamental than or reducible to the entities referred to in the concept C. (From the fact that the concept of the number 2 can be defined by using the concepts of the number 1 and of addition, it does not immediately follow that 1 is ontologically more fundamental than 2.) Applied to our main discussion, the idea would be that there are at least two possible ways of understanding the EC. According to an ontological understanding of EC, a full analysis of the *skandhas* that seem to compose a person is an analysis of all there is in reality with regard to a reduction of a person. *Abhidharma* philosophers have frequently combined this point with the idea that once we have specified the basic *dharmas* that are taken to be proper parts of a person we do not have to posit an additional entity over and above them. For example, the claim 'there are persons' can be taken as fictional or, at least, as involving a convention that does not map onto how reality is independently of our conceptual schemes. I take this claim to be applicable also to ourselves, as the previous discussion does seem to presuppose that we are persons. On this view, ultimately, there are only *dharmas*; wholes, such as persons or us, are, if at all, fictional, conventional, or illusory aggregates of *skandhas*.

According to a conceptual understanding of the EC, its main point would be that every constituent of a person or of ourselves, whether volitions, perceptions, consciousness, or other mental phenomena, can be properly understood without positing a concept that includes a persisting self. Some have objected to this conceptual reduction on the basis that some of the mental phenomena to be analysed cannot be properly understood from a third person perspective, a perspective that does not essentially involve a subjective aspect. The dispute just described is still alive, in different forms, in the current debate.[6]

Even if Buddhist philosophers are correct in holding that a person can be onto-logically analysed into simpler (or more fundamental) parts, we may still claim that, although there are no persisting selves, there are persons; in particular, we may claim that the relation of composition holds between a person and its proper parts (or between us and our proper parts): as the existence of all of the proper parts that compose a car, when properly arranged, can imply that there is a car, simi-larly, the existence of a certain number of *skandhas*, when properly arranged, may imply that there is a person and/or that we exist. Among the others, Vasubandhu in his *Abhidharmakośabhāṣya* ('Commentary to the Treasury of the *Abhidharma*', or 'Commentary' for short) seems to hold that, in a sense to be specified, parts do not compose wholes. Vasubandhu's Commentary is usually attached as a critical compendium to a summary in verse written by the same Vasubandhu of the *Sarvās-tivādin* system. (Vasubandhu's own position throughout his prolific career does not seem to be easily labelled as belonging to only one Buddhist school. Some scholars even posited the existence of two Vasubandhus, one more related to *Sautrāntika* and other earlier Buddhist schools, and another to a *Yogācāra* system.) Now, there are different ways of understanding Vasubandhu's claim that aggregates or proper parts do not compose, in reality, a further entity. One is in terms of a theory in con-temporary metaphysics called '**mereological nihilism**'. According to mereological nihilism, the relation of composition never holds/cannot hold: an answer to the question 'when do parts compose a whole?' does not have an answer and/or cannot be answered because the relation of composition does not/cannot hold. If we also believe that at least partless or impartite or simple entities exist, then these entities are all there is/can be. On this view, once a certain number of *skandhas* (or sim-ple aggregates) have been described, we do not need to include also an entity – a person or one of us – composed of these *skandhas* to provide a complete descrip-tion of reality. Rather, when we use expressions such as 'this person is 36 years old', we may be imposing a fictitious unity onto a reality of constantly changing parts/*skandhas*. In other words, we are projecting into reality, which involves just chains of causally related momentary *dharmas*, a fabrication, the result of which may ultimately lead to suffering.

To summarise our discussion so far, Vasubandhu can be interpreted as making the following claims:

- There is no persisting self;
- *Skandhas* can account for all the phenomena that seem to require persons and ourselves for their explanation or analysis;
- Claims to the effect that there are persons, as well as claims ascribing proper-ties to persons or to us, are to be understood as being at best conventionally or fictionally true as ultimately there are no selves and there are no persons;

- The relation of composition never holds and/or cannot hold, so, on the supposition that at least impartite entities exist, the latter are all there is and the apparent existence of wholes is just the result of mental projections or conventions.

According to this interpretation of Vasubandhu, there are neither persons nor selves, and claims to the effect that persons exist are to be understood as being true only conventionally. Let us call this view the 'Buddhist No-self View#1'. A possible implication of this view is that, properly speaking, we do not exist. Only our transient parts do – and not for long. The claim that we exist may be understood as being conventionally true and/or as to be made in the context of a fictional operator. For instance, we may claim that, although we do not exist, according to a specific fiction (e.g., the socially regulated person-fiction), we exist. The reference of personal pronouns such as 'I' and 'we' are conventionally determined selections of *skandhas*.[7] A supporter of the Buddhist no-self view#1 may also claim that such a theory does not amount to a full-blown version of eliminativist nihilism about ourselves because, on this view, claims about ourselves can still be considered as *conventionally* true, or true according to some fictional or conventional practice. In other words, statements referring to persons may still have their use, although their truth-conditions have to be understood as essentially involving a fiction or a convention.

One contemporary Buddhist scholar, James Duerlinger, has interpreted Vasubandhu as making a slightly different ontological claim about the existence of persons and ourselves. In particular, Duerlinger maintains that Vasubandhu simply asserts that persons – understood as the references of personal pronouns – are "the same in existence as a collection of aggregates."[8] This point is further understood as implying that what Vasubandhu was suggesting is that the existence of a person (or ourselves) is nothing over and above the existence of its parts. A similar but more general claim is understood in contemporary metaphysics as the thesis of composition as identity (CAI). One formulation of CAI says that a whole is identical to its parts. For example, on this view, a person just *is* her components: insofar as some parts arranged person-wise exist, we can also say that a person exists.[9] It is not clear whether Vasubandhu really held this view, but, if this interpretation is correct, we may even claim that persons and ourselves (ultimately) exist: if parts (*skandhas*) causally related in the relevant way are identical to relevant wholes, then the corresponding person (or persons, if appropriate) exists and this person is nothing over and above the *skandhas* at issue. A possible problem for this interpretation is that, if Vasubandhu also held CAI, then it seems that he would be committed to the claim that, after all, persons are ultimately real since their parts are. However, other commentators have suggested that Vasubandhu often classifies persons as mere conceptual constructs, mere conventions (**prajñapti**), and/or that which is not to be included in the catalogue of really existing things. In addition, for Vasubandhu, being classified as a conceptual construct means not being causally efficacious. Given that the *skandhas* are in the flow of causality, if a person is his/her *skandhas*, then the person cannot also be conventional – otherwise the *skandhas* would not be causally efficient.

3 The emptiness of the self and Nāgārjuna

Nāgārjuna's (150–250 CE) contribution to Buddhism has been so influential that he is often regarded as one of the founders of *Madhyamaka*, an important school of the *Mahāyāna* tradition. One of the central points of his philosophical investigations, often pursued in the form of dense and slightly obscure verses, is that everything, including the self and the aggregates, is empty, in a sense to be specified. To understand the concept of emptiness (*śūnyatā* in Sanskrit) at issue, we have to understand the notion of **svabhāva**, because the claim that everything is empty is generally taken to be equivalent to the claim that everything does not have *svabhāva*. Thus, to understand the claim 'the self is empty', we have to understand what, according to Nāgārjuna, the self or its parts are deprived of – *svabhāva*.

Jan Westerhoff, following a commentary tradition on Nāgārjuna's main works, distinguishes various senses of *svabhāva*: ontological, cognitive, and semantical.[10] (I discuss only some of these senses in what follows.) In turn, the ontological understanding of *svabhāva* can be spelled out in different ways. For instance, the *svabhāva* of an object can be understood as its characterising feature and/or its essence. According to this understanding, which is called 'essence-*svabhāva*', the *svabhāva* of X is the property that X cannot lose without ceasing to be what it is. An example used in the Buddhist literature is that of fire and heat, where the latter is the *svabhāva* of the former. Sometimes this sense of *svabhāva* is taken to include also the idea that these essential properties are intrinsic, intended as properties the possession of which does not depend on anything else apart from its possessor – that is, a property that an entity has solely in virtue of itself, e.g., the property of having a specific mass. According to this school of Buddhism, an intrinsic property is also simple, in the sense that it is not a combination of various other properties. In contrast, an extrinsic property is a property that an entity has in virtue of something else, for example, in virtue of its relation to some other entity.[11] Westerhoff claims that this understanding of *svabhāva* in terms of essence is not the main sense employed by Nāgārjuna, although it has played an important role in the subsequent commentarial tradition. Rather, according to Westerhoff, the prevailing sense in Nāgārjuna's works is substance-*svabhāva*. According to this understanding, an entity having substance-*svabhāva* is ontologically fundamental and has real existence. More specifically, an entity having, displaying, or being a substance-*svabhāva* is something the existence of which does not depend on anything else, that is, an object that exists in an ultimate and fundamental sense. For instance, drawing from our prior discussion of *Abhidharma*, the primary and ultimately existent entities, the *dharmas*, would have substance-*svabhāva*.[12] In turn, the concept of substance-*svabhāva* is sometimes associated with the idea that an entity having substance-*svabhāva* is not further analysable or divisible. In addition, entities having substance-*svabhāva* have intrinsic properties if they have any properties at all – ultimately existing entities have their own nature intrinsically, a nature not borrowed from anything else, not even from what we may call, erroneously, their parts.

The cognitive understanding of *svabhāva* relies on the idea that our minds – or at least the momentary figments that allegedly or fictionally compose them – in perception naturally tend to project or superimpose on reality conceptualisations involving ultimately existing entities, without recognising the conventional nature of such projections. The point is that we tend to perceive certain objects as having *svabhāva*, as, for example, when we tend to perceive that the self is a unitary entity without understanding that there is nothing in reality to which such a conceptualisation corresponds. In a sense, we tend to read into the world what we project into it and think that our conceptualisations – for example, the self – are not solely a product of our own projections.

Another understanding of the claim that everything is empty is semantic. On this interpretation, 'everything is empty' means that there are no ultimate truths. An argument in favour of this view that combines elements from the previous understanding goes as follows. Given that everything is devoid of an intrinsic nature and thus does not have independent existence – an existence that is independent of other things – there is no mind-independent reality to which we may ascribe emptiness as its essence-*svabhāva*. According to this semantic interpretation of emptiness, the concept of an ultimate truth itself should be abandoned, possibly along with a realist conception of the connection between reality and truth (for instance, one based on one version of the correspondence theory of truth). A deeper understanding of the Buddhist doctrines may thus involve the realisation that the view of a mind-independent reality to which true propositions may correspond is incoherent or simply wrong. This semantic understanding of emptiness is sometimes contrasted with an ontological understanding according to which nothing exists. This nihilistic interpretation is based on the following reasoning. Given that, according to this Buddhist school, a requisite for non-conventional or non-derivative existence is having intrinsic features, entities the nature of which is determined extrinsically lack *svabhāva* (both in the essential and the substantial sense) and thus do not really exist, and since all of the entities that would allegedly compose reality are empty, there is nothing at all from an ultimate point of view. Everything, including the alleged fundamental components proposed by *Abhidharma*, is conventional, where this is understood as a type of illusion. Which interpretation – the semantic or the nihilist one – is better (or their compatibility) is still debated.

Nāgārjuna does not propose a single general argument for the conclusion that all different types of entities are empty; rather, he offers several related but specific remarks on various concepts and notions, such as those of causation and of motion. For example, Nāgārjuna argues that all of the possible ways in which we can understand the relation between a cause and its effects are incompatible with their having the various types of *svabhāva* discussed previously. Relevant to our discussion of the self, Nāgārjuna argues that the aggregates into which a self can be analysed are themselves empty. Matter, volition, consciousness, and the other aggregates derived from them are not fundamental entities. He seems to reach the conclusion that there are no possible ultimate components of the self starting from certain rather restrictive metaphysical and epistemological premises. An interesting point in this regard is that, according to Nāgārjuna, we cannot identify the self as an entity over and above the aggregates because this identification would make the self unknown to us. More specifically, the self would be unknown to us because, in introspection, we cannot identify it as an entity that exists independently of a specific mental aggregate – a particular feeling, a specific bout of anger, and so on. In other words, the existence of an independent self can be neither directly experienced nor inferentially deduced from the particular momentary mental events that we experience. This interpretation of Nāgārjuna's sometimes obscure verses on the possibility of knowing a self is similar, though not equivalent, to David Hume's famous remarks on the same topic:

> For my part, when I enter most intimately into what I call myself, I always stumble on some particular perception or other, of heat or cold, light or shade, love or hatred, pain or pleasure. I never can catch myself at any time without a perception, and never can observe anything but the perception.
>
> (*Treatise on Human Nature*, 1.4.6.3)

In addition to the claim that all the alleged components of a person are empty, and thus devoid of intrinsic properties, Nāgārjuna also adds the point that personal identity is an illusion. For instance, in certain passages of 'The Fundamental Wisdom of the Middle Way', he claims that "3. To say 'I was in the past/Is not tenable./What existed in the past/Is not identical to this one. 4. According to you, this self is that,/ But the appropriator is different./If it is not the appropriator,/What is your self?'". The point at issue here is an alleged refutation of the idea that the self continues through time and that such a self is the identical appropriator of several different mental states. Using expressions such as 'I' may lead to the illusion of the existence of an entity that persists unchanged through time and that appropriates or owns different successive mental states. According to Nāgārjuna, an act of appropriation of a mental state is itself momentary and differs from other acts in relation to the appropriated mental state. Given these assumptions, the act of appropriation cannot thus be the immutable self or done by an immutable self. The crucial idea here is that mental acts or events, and in particular the acts of mental appropriation – for instance, the act (or event) of recognising a specific mental state as being one's own self – are distinguished from other acts also in virtue of their components, at least one of which is momentary. Thus, one mental act will never be identical to a subsequent one. It follows that such an act or its components cannot be a persisting self.

I summarise and group some of Nāgārjuna's points, which we can call the 'Buddhist no-self View#2', as follows.

- *Ātman* (in both senses described in the first section) is empty; that is, it is devoid of substance-*svabhāva*;

- The aggregates, and all the rest of what was the ultimate reality for *Abhidharma* philosophers, are themselves empty;
- Given the emptiness of everything that exists, the distinction between ultimate and conventional truth, along with a realist picture of truth as a form of correspondence between language and reality, should be rejected;
- Personal identity is a sort of illusion;
- The appearance that there is an appropriator of our mental states through time does not imply that there is such an appropriator. Rather, it is just another illusory mental projection.

4 Buddhist no-self views and ethics

Buddhist ethical systems include a variety of rules, precepts, and virtues the complexity of which cannot be properly discussed here. In what follows, I explore only some of the ways in which the previous metaphysical doctrines, whether related to *Abhidharma* or proposed or inspired by Nāgārjuna, were intended to affect people's behaviour and morality. A first distinction in the domain of the ethical consequences of the various no-self doctrines is between (1) Intra-personal/self-regarding consequences and (2) Relational/other-regarding consequences. (This distinction would be considered as a conceptual mistake by some Buddhists. It is here used only for expository reasons.)

4.1 Intra-personal ethics and no-self

The subjective or personal effects of no-self theories include the alleged connection between these doctrines and the well-being of the individual who believes them – for instance, an individual who understands herself (or her alleged persistence through time) as being a convention out of a chain of causally related *skandhas*. One way of spelling out such a beneficial connection is this: realising that an enduring *ātman* (in both senses) is an illusion is itself conducive to what is called *nirvana*. The concept of *nirvana* is understood in a variety of different ways by different schools, sometimes as a state of eternal bliss and other times as the ineffable end of meditational practices about which nothing meaningful can be said. Despite this variety, a characteristic aspect of Buddhism is that nirvana is always referred to as desirable. The enterprise of achieving nirvana is presented with a moral tone, i.e., it is morally good to achieve nirvana and, whether to become a saint or out of compassion, to help others achieve it. The early Buddhist sutras convey a sense that ignorance of the doctrine of no-self is not only instrumentally and extrinsically morally wrong – *instrumental* to the achievement of higher moral ends – but it is also intrinsically disgraceful and bad for its own sake, as it is a particular form of ignorance. In turn, ignorance of the nature of the self (and, more in general, of reality) is one of the causes of suffering. More specifically, suffering is described in early sutras as having three heads: greed, aversion or hatred, and delusion. Greed and aversion are classified as types of cravings, which are frequently described as rooted in ignorance, intended as a distorted way of perceiving things – for instance, the perception of a projected or conventional self. From an intra-personal/self-regarding ethical perspective, realising that the self does not exist would also be liberating – nirvana is sometimes characterised as a sort of liberation from the cycle of rebirths – because as soon as we form a conception of an isolated *I*, we immediately also use expressions such as 'This is mine, this I am, this is my self'. The use of these expressions is conducive to a belief in a detached and independently existing self, and thus to the generation of some of those cravings that will lead us to suffering. Realising that the self does not exist is important for persons to achieve nirvana or, at least, personal well-being, where the latter can be understood as a pain-free state.

The previous line of reasoning can be made more precise in different ways, for instance, as making a psychological and/or a metaphysical point. Assuming the Buddhist no-self view#1, the psychological thesis can be articulated as follows.

- Psychological premise 1: certain cravings that lead to suffering are determined (or caused) by certain self-centred and self-directed desires – for instance, greed.
- Metaphysical premise 1: one of the Buddhist no-self view#1's principles holds that claims to the effect that there are persons, as well as claims ascribing properties to persons, are at best only conventionally true as ultimately there are no selves and there are no persons – if what we can be is just persons, then we do not exist.
- Psychological premise 2: if an alleged person P realises that the Metaphysical premise 1 is true, then P will be less *motivated* to have (at least some) self-centred and self-directed desires, as P will realise that the alleged subject of these states does not really exist.
- Thus, P's holding the Buddhist no-self view#1 would lead, for psychological reasons, to a certain desirable state of well-being for P.

One way of adapting the previous argument for Buddhist no-self view#2 can start from the substitution of Metaphysical premise 1 with the claim (Metaphysical premise 1*) that personal identity is an illusion (a principle of Buddhist no-self view#2). In addition, Psychological premise 2 can be modified to include a temporal element. For instance, it can be restated as Psychological premise 2*: if an alleged person P realises that the Metaphysical premise 1* is true, then P will be less motivated to have (at least some) self-centred and self-directed desires that, over time, lead to suffering. The rest of the argument would be similar (given intuitive minor adjustments).

A metaphysical reading of the connection between no-self theories and suffering would emphasise that greed and other undesirable mental attitudes and states are metaphysically linked to the illusion of a persisting self:

- Metaphysical premise 1: greed (and those desires that lead to suffering) essentially involves a belief in the existence of a persisting self and/or in the holding

of the relation of personal identity – at least for those cases of greed related to the accumulation of, e.g., wealth over time.
- Metaphysical premise 2: according to both Buddhist no-self view#1 and Buddhist no-self view#2, a persisting self does not exist and the relation of personal identity does not hold.
- Thus, a sincere endorsement and realisation of Metaphysical premise 2 would prevent the possibility of occurrences of greed and other disruptive mental attitudes and thus of (a certain kind of) suffering.

There are other aspects of various Buddhist ethical systems worth remembering in relation to our discussion of intra-personal aspects of ethics. For instance, some Buddhist schools emphasise that the sole rational recognition of the validity or soundness of arguments such as those stated previously may not suffice to support any change. In fact, many Buddhist thinkers emphasise that in addition to rational or conceptual understanding, certain truths must also go through a process of internalisation or personal realisation, a crucial component of which is meditation. The idea is that a simple rational assent to the idea that, say, personal identity is a sort of fiction or illusion may not be sufficient to bring about the cessation of suffering. Certain truths, in fact, need to be interiorised to become part of our set of reasons for action, and various Buddhist schools provide different means to achieve this.

Other fundamental notions of moral significance within Buddhism are those of Karma and rebirth. However, these concepts may appear to be in contrast with the two Buddhist no-self views discussed previously. In particular, most Buddhist ethical systems recognise the possibility of accumulating and spending good or bad Karma throughout various rebirths. If we also believe that a fair distribution of good or bad Karma depends on a distribution that is based also, though not exclusively, on the individual merits and demerits of those who performed good or bad actions, then providing an account of the basis of such a distribution is crucial. However, if personal identity through time and across different lives does not hold, then on what basis would good and bad Karma be distributed fairly across different lives? Why would some good Karma be distributed to A instead of B if neither of them were in the relation of personal identity with C, the entity who has done some good Karmic deed? One way around this difficulty, available for instance to Buddhist no-self view#1, is that although the relation of personal identity does not hold through different lives, it is still conventionally true that C will ripen the Karmic fruits of her actions in the future: so long as there is a causal connection between the *skandhas* apparently constituting C and those conventionally constituting A, we can say that it is conventionally true that C's good Karmic consequences are fairly passed on to A. It is certainly questionable whether this is a satisfying solution.

4.2 Relational ethics and no-self

The Buddhist *Madhyamaka* monk and philosopher Shantideva (8th century CE) famously illustrates the connection between Buddhist metaphysics and ethics in his

Bodhicaryāvatāra by arguing that, since an individual who experiences suffering does not exist, all episodes of suffering are not owned by anybody and they are not different from each other in terms of importance. Some of the relevant passages in Shantideva's work are:

> 101. The continuum of consciousness, like a series, and the aggregation of constituents, like an army and such, are unreal. Since one who experiences suffering does not exist, to whom will that suffering belong?
>
> 102. All sufferings are without owner, because they are not different. They should be warded off simply because they are suffering. Why is any restriction made in this case?
>
> 103. Why should suffering be prevented? Because everyone agrees. If it must be warded off, then all of it must be warded off, and if not, then this goes for oneself as it does for everyone else.
>
> (Shantideva, *Bodhicaryāvatāra*)

Although these passages have been interpreted in a variety of different ways, one of the main points is that altruism, compassion, and, in general, other-caring attitudes are influenced by seeing reality as it is, namely, impermanent and thus without persisting selves. Now, reasons for actions should not be justified or grounded on illusory views of reality. Thus, given that there is no distinction in terms of ownership between, for instance, 'my' suffering and 'your' suffering – although we may claim that, in a sense, they impersonally exist – both sufferings should be (equally) warded off (provided that they have the same intensity). The conclusion can then be extended to all instances of suffering – no-self views would thus imply that since suffering is ownerless and suffering is morally bad, all episodes of suffering are to be warded off. Granted that all episodes of suffering are bad, we do not have special selfish reasons – e.g., reasons related to the existence of a persisting self – to relieve only what appears to be our personal pain. It can still be argued that the priority to extinguish certain episodes of suffering rather than others may vary in relation to their intensity.

An important other-regarding moral attitude in the Buddhist tradition is compassion (Skt. *karunā*) – Goodman says that in several Indian Buddhist texts there is a classification of types of compassion connected to the moment or level of enlightenment. For instance, a Bodhisattva, that is, an enlightened being who wishes all humanity to achieve Buddhahood, would first be compassionate towards living beings without any specific conception of their metaphysical nature and then, after realising that wholes do not ultimately exist, direct her compassion to the impersonal events that appear to constitute persons. *Mahayana* schools include a third and final stage in which the bodhisattva would act towards others with awareness of the emptiness of everything. The Buddhist no-self view#2 would have the further ethical consequence of producing moral agents that act spontaneously. A morally spontaneous action is a moral action that (1) does not require any additional rational debate, and (2) is nonetheless right. Such an action is similar to the action of the skilled artist who seems to execute complex movements naturally and effortlessly.

Buddhist no-self views can also be used in arguments against forms of ethical and/or rational egoism. For example, according to one version of the former, it is a necessary and sufficient condition for an action to be morally good that it maximises one's own self-interest over time. One version of rational egoism maintains that it is a necessary and sufficient condition for an action to be rational that it maximises the agent's own self-interest over time.[13] Suppose that these versions of egoism are taken to be ultimately true theories – as expressing non-conventional truths. If this is the case, then it seems that they both require that something akin to the relation of personal identity hold between different selves at different times – as usually episodes of egoistic behaviour are actions directed at the accumulation of resources over time. However, according to both Buddhist no-self views, personal identity is not a relation that holds at the ultimate level. Thus, if we accept either Buddhist no-self view#1 or #2, we would have to abandon an unqualified belief in these forms of egoism since one of the fundamental presuppositions of egoism would be false, namely, that ultimately there is a continuous self-interested agent over time. In conclusion, Buddhist no-self views can be seen as implying a rejection of simplistic forms of egoism. It may still be rational to behave as if personal identity sometimes held – if only at a conventional level – even though our behaviour should be filtered by an awareness that, at the ultimate level, personal identity is a sort of illusion.

5 Nihilism and our nature

Some (or most) Buddhist theories seem to imply that, literally speaking, we do not exist. However, the understanding of the proper meaning and implications of this counter-intuitive consequence is still a matter of controversy. Scholars also debate whether the Buddhist theories discussed previously imply ontological nihilism, the view according to which nothing exists. Among the others, Westerhoff provides textual evidence from different sources to argue that certain *Madhyamaka* philosophers (e.g., Nāgārjuna and Candrakīrti) did not believe that the doctrine of emptiness entails the claim that nothing, in a broad sense, exists – otherwise, the doctrine of emptiness would negate also the existence of appearances, which it does not do. After all, Nāgārjuna asserts that even empty phenomena or appearances such as chariots or pots can fulfil certain functions. In addition, Westerhoff suggests that Buddhist nihilism does not have to be taken as self-refuting or incoherent: although there are no entities with *svabhāva*, we do not have to adhere to a foundationalist view in ontology to the effect that if there are no basic entities – understood as substances that exist by themselves – then nothing exists. On the contrary, certain phenomena can be seen as having a relational or, like nodes in a web, a coherentist/conventional existence. One articulation of this idea, in relation to persons and ourselves, is explored in the next chapter. Is this the best way of understanding the Buddhist theories described previously? Westerhoff maintains that finding the right or sole interpretation of certain Buddhist doctrines may prove difficult also because *Madhyamaka* arguments are best seen as opponent-relative. So, when their opponents are naïve realists, *Madhyamaka* would claim that the world is not how appearances seem to describe; when their opponents are radical error theorists who claim that reality irremediably lies behind an impenetrable veil of shadow, they would deny that the source of knowledge lies exclusively outside of this illusory appearance.

If it is necessary for X to exist that X exists independently or substantially, then it seems fair to say that, according to many Buddhist schools, we do not exist. On this understanding of existence, Buddhist scholars would better find a way of providing an account of our deeply rooted intuitions about ourselves – e.g., the way we describe ourselves as entities that persist over time – and how we interact with the world. In fact, leaving aside whether a form of personal nihilism is the best interpretation of the stance on our nature and on persons of the Buddhist schools described previously, we should evaluate whether these theories are persuasive or plausible. Now, one of the proposed criteria to evaluate theories of personal identity is their capacity to make sense of our social and practical lives. So, is a form of personal nihilism, e.g., a theory holding that we do not exist or that persons do not exist, plausible in this regard? Probably the best strategy to support this revisionist approach is that of considering it as a part of a broader project. More specifically, it seems more plausible to argue that we do not exist in the context of other more general theories or conclusions that involve broader aspects of the so-called reality. For instance, some may claim that it is more plausible to be nihilists about ourselves if we do not deny solely our existence but also the existence of a variety of other entities as well, say, trees, tables, or mountains. The principle supporting this negation may be an unrestricted (or universal) version of mereological nihilism, or other revisionist theories of the ontological structure of reality. Supporters of nihilist theories may also want to question the requirement that theories of personal identity should explain our everyday practices rather than explaining them away. However, if we hold that part of the plausibility of a theory of personal identity is its capacity to explain or be compatible with our everyday practices, then one of the nihilist's main problems is that of providing its own account of the way we perceive the world and our practical lives – not to mention our intuitions regarding our own existence, cf., Augustine's and Descartes's *cogito* arguments. One option open to a supporter of the Buddhist no-self view#1 is that of claiming that we do exist, but in the sense that personal pronouns – 'I', 'we', etc. – refer only to momentary and fleeting mental and/or physical events. So, although it is not the case that we exist as temporally extended entities, there is still a sense in which we exist, namely, when personal pronouns are intended to refer to one of the momentary existing *skandhas*. This view may not be available to those Buddhist theories holding that not even *skandhas* exist. Another attempt to provide an account of our everyday talk about persons and ourselves within the nihilist metaphysical worldview is this: when we seem to refer to persons or ourselves, what we should really be saying (or what our sentences express) is that, for instance, certain X-particles arranged person-wise are being individuated through certain linguistic or conceptual devices (proper names, personal pronouns, etc.) and mental acts. So, occurrences of, e.g., 'Andrea' should be replaced with or understood as referring to the Andrea-particles or the particles arranged Andrea-wise at a specific time. Our understanding of predicates applying to names would also have to be modified accordingly. Another possibility is that of understanding claims about persons as claims about fictional entities or as expressions within the context of a story. For example, although the claim that 'Sherlock Holmes is a detective' is false, the statement '*according to the fiction F*, Sherlock Holmes is a detective' can be true – depending on how we specify F, for example, if we substitute 'F' with 'Conan Doyle's *A Study in Scarlet*'. Similarly, our talk about persons can be understood as having an implicit reference to the conventional and social fictions we live by. The general idea behind these solutions is that, even though our talk and reasoning about persons is literally false, this does not imply that we have to eliminate all alleged references to persons and/or that there are no norms to account for the fact that only certain claims involving people seem to be correct. Alternatively, supporters of Buddhist no-self view#2 may claim that there is a sense of existence, call it relational-existence, according to which persons exist. In particular, on this view, persons are entities that, although they do not have independent existence, may exist as/because they are nodes in an interconnected web of (social) relationships and/or roles. This view, along with the importance of other social aspects of personal identity, is discussed more in detail in the next chapter.

6 Summary

Some of the main principles of Buddhism imply a view of reality that is at odds with the existence of persisting souls of the kind described in the previous chapter. The disagreement between these two approaches is not limited to ontological issues, but is extended to beliefs regarding the *desirability* of the existence of such a continuous entity through time: one of the main tenets of Buddhism is, in fact, the idea that a belief in a persisting soul or self is not just wrong, but also conducive to suffering. Whilst, e.g., Christian thinkers attempt to ensure the rationality of divine retribution and judgment following our earthly death by claiming that *we* will be rewarded in an afterlife – where this is possible also if not exclusively in virtue of having a persisting soul – Buddhists maintain that by abandoning the illusion of our own persistence over time we will thereby be liberated from certain (immoral) cravings.

The Buddhist theories discussed in this chapter are elaborations on some of the main philosophical discussions offered by a series of different thinkers, for instance, Vasubandhu and Nāgārjuna (and their interpreters, e.g., Siderits and Westerhoff). According to the no-self Buddhist view#1, which is an elaboration on some of Vasubandhu's early doctrines, there are independently existing elements of reality, or *dharmas*. *Dharmas* are sometimes characterised as particular (i.e., non-repeatable) and transient psycho-/physical simple entities. Some of these elements *seem* to compose us and/or persons, but, in reality, the relation of composition does not hold. As a consequence, literally speaking, we do not exist – and the same reasoning is applied to other everyday objects such as tables and chairs, that is, literally speaking, everyday objects do not exist either. There are various interpretations of how to understand the approach to reality prescribed by the Buddha, as it is to be expected in a long and rich tradition such as the Buddhist. In fact, it would be foolish to claim that all Buddhist schools hold the same views on the nature of reality. For instance, another interpretation of the Buddha's teachings, attributed to Nāgārjuna, holds that there are no *independently* existing fundamental elements of reality – an idea sometimes expressed with the claim that everything is empty. Westerhoff has recently suggested that this claim does not have to be understood only paradoxically (e.g., as implying or meaning that nothing exists). Perhaps, he argues, we may fruitfully interpret some of Nāgārjuna's insights as a form of criticism against a foundationalist view in ontology that also points to a relational or holistic ontology: entities and/or appearances do not have independent existence but may (in some sense) exist as dependent entities, that is, as entities that exist only in relation to each other and not in isolation. This relational approach to the existence of persons/ourselves is the major topic of the next chapter.

Buddhist views seem to provide a revolutionary ontology – at least with respect to some of our beliefs about the existence of ourselves and of everyday objects – that do not seem to be easily reconcilable with some of our everyday practices and/or ways of reasoning. However, Buddhists argue that, despite their counter-intuitiveness, their metaphysical beliefs lead to a better morality: for instance, some have claimed that a belief in the non-existence of the self is conducive to altruism, intended as the moral behaviour characterised by an equal regard for all of the instances of suffering. In addition, a revolutionary ontology that denies the existence of many everyday objects may still have the conceptual resources to account for our talk of alleged non-existent entities, e.g., by regarding them as fictional entities.

Notes

1 My understanding of Buddhism is largely based on Mark Siderits's work. See Siderits (2003) and (2007).
2 Ganeri (2007).
3 *Upadasa Sahasrī*, p. 68.
4 There are also other interpretations of the notion of *dharma*. See the suggested readings for details.
5 See Introduction, section 4 ("Theoretical aims").
6 See the debate on quasi-memory in Chapter 4, section 4.
7 See Sauchelli (2016) for more details.
8 Duerlinger (2003), p. 280.
9 Some metaphysicians have argued that mereological nihilism (at least in its non-modal formulation) and CAI, spelled out in a particular way, are equivalent. In this case, Vasubandhu can be taken to hold both.
10 My understanding of Nāgārjuna is largely based on Westerhoff (2009).

11 In the contemporary debate, the notion of an intrinsic property is taken to be distinct from that of an essential property as it is not necessary for the essential properties of an entity to be also intrinsic to the entity in question.

12 Things are not so simple because in the *Abhidharma* tradition, as Westerhoff notices, an object having *svabhāva* may not be entirely independent of anything, as such an object may depend on its own causes and conditions.

13 Not all versions of this theory include a temporal element.

Suggested further readings

The Buddha, Anātman, and suffering

Primary sources

Edelglass, William and Jay L. Garfield (eds.) *Buddhist Philosophy: Essential Readings* (Oxford: Oxford University Press, 2009).
Samyutta Nikāya ('The Connected Discourses of the Buddha'), translated by Bhikkhu Bodhi (Somerville, MA: Wisdom Publications, 2000).

Secondary literature

Bartley, Christopher, *An Introduction to Indian Philosophy* (London: Continuum, 2011).
Black, Brian, *The Character of Self in Ancient India* (Albany, NY: State University of New York Press, 2007).
Carpenter, Amber, *Indian Buddhist Philosophy* (London: Routledge, 2014).
Ganeri, Jonardon, *The Concealed Art of the Soul* (Oxford: Oxford University Press, 2007).
Keown, Damien, *Buddhism: A Short Introduction* (Oxford: Oxford University Press, 2005).
Siderits, Mark, *Buddhism as Philosophy* (Indianapolis, IN: Hackett Publishing Company, Inc., 2007).

Abhidharma, skandhas, and Vasubandhu

Primary sources

Duerlinger, James, *Indian Buddhist Theories of Persons* (London and New York: Routledge-Curzon, 2003).
Seven Works of Vasubandhu, translated and edited by Stefan Anacker (New Delhi: Motilal Banarsidass Publishers, 2005).

Secondary literature

Albahari, Miri, *Analytical Buddhism* (London: Palgrave Macmillan, 2006).
Collins, Steven, *Selfless Persons* (Cambridge: Cambridge University Press, 1982).
Cox, Collett, 'From Category to Ontology: The Changing Role of Dharma in Sarvāstivāda Adbhidharma', *Journal of Indian Philosophy*, 32 (2004), pp. 543–597.
Gethin, Rupert, 'He Who Sees Dhamma Sees Dhammas: Dhamma in Early Buddhism', *Journal of Indian Philosophy*, 32 (2004), pp. 513–542.
Gold, Jonathan, *Paving the Great Way* (New York: Columbia University Press, 2015).

Goodman, Charles, 'The Treasury of Metaphysics and the Physical World', *The Philosophical Quarterly*, 54, 216 (2004), pp. 389–401.

Ronkin, Noa, 'Abhidharma', in *Stanford Encyclopedia of Philosophy* (2014). https://plato.stanford.edu/entries/abhidharma/

Siderits, Mark, *Personal Identity and Buddhist Philosophy* (Aldershot, UK: Ashgate, 2003).

The emptiness of the self and Nāgārjuna

Primary sources

Nāgārjuna, *The Fundamental Wisdom of the Middle Way*, translation and commentary by Jay L. Garfield (Oxford: Oxford University Press, 1995).

Secondary literature

The Cowherds, *Moonshadows: Conventional Truth in Buddhist Philosophy* (New York: Oxford University Press, 2011).

Garfield, Jay L., *Empty Words* (Oxford: Oxford University Press, 2002).

Siderits, Mark, 'Causation and Emptiness in Early Madhyamaka', *Journal of Indian Philosophy*, 32 (2004), pp. 393–419.

Westerhoff, Jan, *Nāgārjuna's Madhyamaka* (Oxford: Oxford University Press, 2009).

Westerhoff, Jan, 'On the Nihilistic Interpretation of Madhyamaka', *Journal of Indian Philosophy*, 44, 2 (2016), pp. 337–376.

Buddhist no-self views and ethics

Flanagan, Owen, *The Bodhisattva's Brain* (Cambridge, MA: MIT Press, 2011).

Goodman, Charles, *Consequences of Compassion* (Oxford: Oxford University Press, 2009).

Harvey, Peter, *An Introduction to Buddhist Ethics* (Cambridge: Cambridge University Press, 2000).

Liu, Jeeloo and Douglas Berger (eds.), *Nothingness in Asian Philosophy* (New York: Routledge, 2014).

Thompson, Evan, *Waking, Dreaming, Being* (New York: Columbia University Press, 2015).

Williams, Paul, *Altruism and Reality* (Richmond: Curzon Press, 1998).

Nihilism and our nature

Baxter, Donald and Aaron Cotnoir (eds.), *Composition as Identity* (Oxford: Oxford University Press, 2014).

Olson, Eric, *What Are We?* (Oxford: Oxford University Press, 2007).

Rosen, Gideon and Cian Dorr, 'Composition as a Fiction', in R. Gale (ed.) *The Blackwell Guide to Metaphysics* (Oxford: Blackwell), pp. 151–174.

Sauchelli, Andrea, 'Buddhist Reductionism, Fictionalism About the Self, and Buddhist Fictionalism', *Philosophy East and West*, 66, 4 (2016), pp. 1273–1291.

Sider, Theodore, 'Against Parthood', *Oxford Studies in Metaphysics*, 8 (2013), pp. 237–293.

Unger, Peter, 'I Do Not Exist', in Graham F. MacDonald (ed.) *Perception and Identity* (London: Palgrave Macmillan, 1979).

Varzi, Achille, 'Mereology', in *Stanford Encyclopedia of Philosophy* (2016). https://plato.stanford.edu/entries/mereology/

3 Relational approach and Confucian role-person

1	Individuation, heart-mind (心, *xin*), and the Confucian self	78
2	The Confucian relational person and its origin	80
3	The Confucian role-person and *li* (禮)	83
4	Role-personhood and personal identity	87
5	Our nature: Mencius's four roots	88
6	Self-cultivation in the ECT	89
	6.1 Self-cultivation and personal identity	91
7	Further directions	92
8	Summary	93

> The Master said, "At age fifteen I set my heart upon learning; at thirty I took my stand; at forty I became free of doubts; at fifty I understood the Heavenly Mandate; at sixty my ear was attuned; and at seventy I could follow my heart's desire without overstepping the bounds of propriety."
>
> —Confucius, *The Analects*, 2.4

One of the main aims of this chapter is that of providing one way of articulating the idea according to which we do not have to think of ourselves or of the conditions of personal identity through time as being determined solely by our intrinsic features and/or by an individual soul. An entity the conditions of identity of which are not solely determined by these intrinsic features is relational. Now, the identity conditions of a relational entity may be determined by a variety of different elements that are external to what we consider our intrinsic features. The Confucian role-person view is one way of specifying the relational approach.

Harmony between the individual and the social order, self-cultivation, and appropriateness are some of the central values of the Confucian tradition. The historical originator of this tradition, Confucius (孔子 or *Kǒngzǐ*, 551?–479? BCE), lived in a period of fragmentation in Chinese history, that is, the time of conflict between local aristocratic families that followed the fall of the western Zhou dynasty. Confucius seems to have promoted his teachings as a way of retrieving the good that had been lost and did not present himself as an innovator or as the initiator of a new tradition. Although Confucius used terms and concepts that are not easily or fully translatable into English, he and some of his early followers nevertheless had – if only implicitly – a conception of human beings and of their roles from which interesting views on our nature and personhood can be extracted. In particular, this chapter presents a series of ideas on our own nature and on personal identity that can be extrapolated from thinkers such as Mengzi (孟子, also known as Mencius, 372–289 BCE) and Xunzi (荀子, 310–235 BCE), both belonging to the early Confucian tradition (ECT). Their views have been variously interpreted by contemporary scholars of Chinese philosophy, and this chapter relies on these valuable recent contributions. I do not claim to have always followed the most accurate reconstruction of the Confucian theories; rather, I focused on those interpretations that are more fecund for the current debate.

In the first section of this chapter, I introduce some key general notions used in the early philosophical discourse in China to express the idea that certain objects and events can be epistemically and metaphysically identified, along with other terms used to describe individuated entities relevant to our discussion (e.g., 'heart-mind'). In this context, I distinguish between a Confucian *self* and a Confucian *person*. The former is the subject of experience that seems to be assumed to exist given certain doctrines in the Confucian tradition, while the notion of a Confucian person embodies the idea that a person is one kind of relational entity. In turn, this distinction is used to specify the notion of a Confucian *role*-person. In particular, a Confucian role-person is a relational entity individuated by its roles in a particular society. The concept of a Confucian role-person is here understood as specifying not solely our biographical identity but also as determining the metaphysical conditions of synchronic and diachronic identity of persons. The second section presents various general (non-Confucian) ways of understanding the relation between an individual and society. Now, the idea that the social context identifies individual persons is hardly a feature of only the ECT. In fact, despite many exaggerated statements regarding the alleged irreconcilable differences between what is called 'Western' and Confucian approaches to the self and personhood, a variety of non-Chinese thinkers have explored these topics in similar or related manners (e.g., Friedrich Hegel, various Marxist philosophers, contemporary communitarians, feminists, philosophers of social sciences, etc.). The concept of a Confucian role-person is thus one of the many ways in which the relational approach can be articulated.

In the third section, I specify in more details what features a Confucian role-person may have. In particular, on this view, a person is ontologically relational, that is, an entity the existence of which depends on specific social patterns and ceremonies – those prescribed by Confucius and his more or less direct followers. In the fourth section, I formulate a rigorous account of personal identity and of our nature based on the ideas outlined before. The fifth section discusses Mengzi's account of our nature in terms of natural or innate perfectible moral beginnings or sprouts. The related idea of self-cultivation is discussed in the sixth section, along with different models of thinking about self-cultivation in the ECT, with particular reference to the work of P. J. Ivanhoe. I then summarise a view on personal identity to which Mengzi's model of self-cultivation seems to be committed, and an account of personal identity that takes into account both Mengzi's model of self-cultivation and the concept of a Confucian role-person. One of the critical remarks emerging from this chapter is that, although relationality can plausibly be taken as determining a necessary condition for being a person, it can hardly provide a full analysis of personhood. One of the reasons is that certain forms of sociality, such as those described in the Confucian approach, seem to presuppose the development and cultivation of certain psychological features (e.g., character traits, memory). The role that psychological considerations have assumed in the current debate is discussed in Chapter 4.

1 Individuation, heart-mind (心, *xin*), and the Confucian self

Pre-Qin Confucian philosophers elaborated their views on human nature and on virtue starting from various metaphysical presuppositions about the nature of reality. More specifically, Franklin Perkins argues that pre-Qin thinkers assumed that what underlies everyday phenomena is explained by notions such as *qi* (氣, frequently translated with 'vital energy') and the interaction of certain positive and negative principles. Although this underlying reality was conceived sometimes as undifferentiated or always mutable, our everyday cognitive life – including our inescapable interactions with the world – requires us to individuate things, at least epistemically and/or conceptually, in the environment around us. Perkins claims that various words and annexed concepts were used to satisfy such a necessity. In particular, *wù* (物) played the role of indicating an individual(ised) entity. For example, if I claim that a cup is a *wù*, this implies that I am talking about an individuated object. The concept of a *wù* did not become more widely used in a philosophical context until the 4th century – especially in various Daoist cosmogonies. Calling something a *wù* was similar to calling a thing a particular, distinguishable individual – a usage that was extended to events (e.g., a somersault) – with a beginning and an end. In the Confucian text *Xunzi* (荀子, third century BCE), a *wù* is distinguished from other particulars either in virtue of its having a different form/shape or by having a different spatial location. A *wù* can alter its form without being distinct or ceasing to exist, that is, it can transform or change without thereby losing its identity – probably on the condition of displaying spatial continuity. Being a *wù* also appears to imply that, at least in certain passages of the *Mengzi*, a particular can be individuated also in virtue of a model or pattern of development. For instance, in the *Mengzi* our human nature can be distinguished and classified as such also in virtue of some of our dispositions. Perkins emphasises that *wù* cannot be properly understood in terms of a kind of metaphysical substance that composes the deeper structure of reality. Instead, he claims that the articulation of the individuating discourse in these early Chinese texts does not seem to be informed by an interest in mapping the objective structure of reality. Rather, the main focus of these investigations was on the nature and structure of the ways in which phenomena are given to us.

Despite a widely emphasised (and exaggerated) alleged distinction between certain pre-Qin metaphysical views and substance-based or realist metaphysical theories of Greek origin, Chinese thinkers thus had to think in terms of differentiated individuals in the world, not just in terms of undifferentiated and endlessly transforming underlying forces. In addition, the previously stated characterisation of the scope of the metaphysical distinctions in the aforementioned early Chinese texts can be understood as a form of what is called nowadays 'descriptive metaphysics', one way of doing metaphysics in contemporary 'Western' philosophy.[1] It should also not be forgotten that, in the Chinese context, other terms were devised to talk about certain more fundamental aspects of reality (e.g., *dao* 道, the way).

Our next questions are: what kind of *wù* are we? If we are Confucian persons, what are (some of) the individuating features of a Confucian person? The answers to these questions require a preliminary description of one of the things that make it possible for us to be persons, that is, the Heart-Mind (**xin**, 心) and its reflective functions. Again, although some scholars have emphasised an alleged absence of any descriptions or emphasis on interior mental aspects in the early Confucian tradition – "Do not psychologise the Confucian self!" they say – such an alleged sharp difference with 'Western' and/or early Greek conceptions of our internal mental activities seems to be in conflict with the available textual evidence.[2] In fact, as other scholars have pointed out, there are several passages even in the *Analects* showing an understanding of how certain mental faculties are supposed to be important for the development of our virtues.[3] In particular:

> The Master said, "When you see someone who is worthy, concentrate upon becoming their equal; when you see someone who is unworthy, use this as an opportunity to look within yourself."
>
> (4.17)

> The Master said, "I should just give up! I have yet to meet someone who is able to perceive his own faults and then take himself to task inwardly."
>
> (5.27)

> Sima Nu asked about the gentleman.
>
> The Master replied, "The gentleman is free of anxiety and fear."
>
> "Free of anxiety and fear" – is that all there is to being a gentleman?
>
> "If you can look inside yourself and find no faults, what cause is there for anxiety or fear?"
>
> (12.4)

So, even in one of the most fundamental documents of the Confucian tradition, it is clear that agents are characterised as having self-reflexive mental capacities. In the ECT, these self-reflexive mental capacities are ascribed to *xīn* (心), usually translated with 'heart-mind'. The reason behind this translation is that the heart was thought of as being responsible for our cognitive, affective, and conative capacities. In the ECT, the heart-mind is not what gives life to an organism – a kind of *qì* (氣) was taken to be responsible for that. Kwong-Loo Shun also claims that *xīn* can have desires (欲, *yù*), emotions (情, *qíng*), and can deliberate about a situation as well as focus upon certain aspects of what we perceive.[4] In addition, the heart-mind is capable of directing a person towards certain virtuous acts – such directions are called *zhì* (志), a term translated also with 'will'. Shun claims that the difference between *zhì* and *yù* is that the first is exercised exclusively by the heart-mind, whilst the second can be ascribed also to the body or to its parts – in the latter case, we can think of *yù* as forms of attractions, propensities, or tendencies rather than desires. On this understanding, *yù* can be propensities or urges felt in the body that we may choose to resist, a function executed by the heart-mind. Of course, this brief list does not exhaust the rich vocabulary used to discuss our mental faculties and the various ways in which sentences involving self-reflection can be articulated in (classical) Chinese. The main point is that the heart-mind is an organ the functions of which can be compared to those played by a functionally complex soul – for instance, the kind of soul described in Plato's *Republic* – minus the capacity to give life to the organism. Another difference with certain immaterialist conceptions of *psuchê* is that the heart-mind seems to be a material entity. It has to be remembered that there are also certain conceptions of soul in various Greek schools that shared with the ECT the idea that the soul is material (e.g., Stoicism). Several scholars of comparative philosophy also emphasise that the ECT was a secular tradition, where speculations about spirits, supernatural objects, and immortal souls were generally avoided. However, Jiyuang Yu also correctly points out that in ancient China, the worship of ancestral spirits was a highly regarded practice regulated by codified rituals. The metaphysical status of these spirits is not easily reconcilable with a purely materialistic ontology.

The Confucian self, intended as the subject of experience presupposed by the philosophical discourse of the ECT, is a self the main faculties of which are not significantly different from the faculties ascribed to the mind or soul$_{mind}$. In the rest of the chapter, we will take the Confucian self as residing in or as being constituted of/by – or even *be* – the heart-mind. Such a heart-mind is a material object that is not solely responsible for various self-reflective capacities, but also for various conative, affective, and decisional (volitional) faculties. Additional aspects of how the Confucian self has to interact with certain environmental aspects to develop or generate a Confucian person will be explored in the next sections.

2 The Confucian relational person and its origin

Advocates of the Confucian role-person theory support their ideas by referring to certain metaphysical principles. In particular, Roger Ames claims that, in the cosmological and metaphysical views presupposed by the Confucian, the principle of individuation is not to be understood as specifying those aspects that distinguish substances independently of their existence in a context. Rather, the main point seems to be that entities are individuated (or "achieve their distinctiveness", using Ames's terminology) only within a network of relations. However, David Wong claims that frequently philosophers fail to make crucial distinctions between (1) the context in which a self or a person may emerge, (2) the relevance of such a context for the persistence of the persons thus generated, and (3) the realisation of a certain ideal state for a person – the state of the exemplary person or *jūnzî* (君子). Wong calls the view according to which people need the help of others to develop as agents the *developmental sense of relationality*. Another sense of relationality distinguished by Wong is the *social conception of the person*, the main point of which is that "we begin life as biological organisms and become persons by entering into relationship with others of our kind."[5] However, despite this useful distinction, it is not clear whether Wong has in mind also a claim about the ontology of persons. What follows is my reconstruction of some of the key distinctions figuring in the current debate that, in turn, can determine various specifications of the relational approach.

- Relational-origin approach

According to the **relational-origin approach**, an individual can become a person only by interacting with certain (other) individuals. Another way of formulating this idea is that the origin of a person is essentially relational. This approach emphasises the alleged inherently social nature of persons. A Confucian (and more disputable) version of this approach (Confucian relation-origin theory) also includes a specification of the identity-generating context within which a person may emerge, for instance, a family of a specific kind – more specifically, a family that follows certain codified patterns of ritual behaviour called *lî* (禮). The relational-origin theory of a person should not be confused with a relational origin theory of selves. According to the latter, a self *qua* self, that is, as a subject of experience, can come into existence only relationally. This theory holds that our becoming subjects of experience requires the development of certain cognitive capacities that essentially involves certain interactions with other individuals – a claim not to be confused with the idea that all subjects of experience have been causally created by other entities. The relational origin theory of selves can be further clarified as making an empirical and/or an evaluative claim. More specifically, it can be understood as an empirical claim regarding the necessary conditions for developing certain forms of consciousness – say, our interactions with other humans – that coalesce, with time, into the constitution of a subject of experience. Developmental and evolutionary psychology may contribute or cast doubt to the plausibility of these theses. A different claim is that a *proper* subject of experience may emerge only relationally.

The Confucian versions of the previously stated theories specify the relational aspects of the process of self/person formation as primarily a social context of a specific kind – a family regulated by certain patterns of ritual behaviour. In addition, Confucian theories reject the view that selves or persons are individual entities independent from interactions with other entities. However, despite several attempts by various scholars to draw sharp distinctions between philosophical traditions, other contemporary philosophers agree with the point that part of what constitutes the identity of a person *qua* person is essentially related to the context in which such a person lives – in other words, there are non-Confucian versions of the relational approach and thus relationality is not an exclusive feature of Confucian theories. The ideal targets of those who emphasise the distinction between the Confucian approach to personhood and other traditions seem to be those views according to which we are pure souls – e.g., Descartes's ontological claim according to which we are essentially disembodied subjects of experience – or souls$_{mind}$. The point of disagreement seems to be that Confucian theories deny that selves and/or persons can become or be the entities they are if they were disembodied or, at least, in a form that precludes certain kinds of significant social interactions. Few (if any) contemporary developmental psychologists would nowadays defend the hypothesis that the various faculties responsible for our mental lives, and thus for our becoming selves or persons, could emerge in isolation from a social context – language acquisition and the various capacities that it entails is an obvious case in point.

Another theory to be distinguished here regards *our* relational origin. According to a relation-origin view of our own nature, we are essentially entities the origin of which is relational. Again, this claim should not be understood as merely implying that we are the result of a causal process involving entities similar to us. Rather, on this view, it is necessary for us to undergo a process of development, the main features of which are relational (social). A Confucian version of this view implies that such a relational process is the one prescribed by the Confucian rites. The plausibility of this last claim is rather dubious.

- Relational-necessity approach

A **relational-necessity theory** holds that it is a necessary and sufficient condition for a self or person to exist that they be relational entities, given a specific understanding of the relevant relations an entity has to have. Weaker versions of this theory can appear more plausible as, for example, those distinguished by the claim that a necessary (but not sufficient) condition on being a person is that of being a relational entity. Theories of our own nature can be specified in similar ways: we are essentially relational entities. On this view, we cannot exist but as entities having a certain kind of relation R, where R is a series of social relations. These theories are conceptually different from those according to which a self, person, and/or ourselves must have a relational *origin*. Given an understanding of R as involving various forms of social relations, the previous views can be all specified as stating that selves, persons, and/or us are (essentially) socially related entities – e.g., we are essentially members of a family or other social networks. The early understanding in the Roman context of the concept of a person as a mask or as a social actor resonates with this view. If we understand existence as entailing identification, we can also understand the previous theories as claiming that entities are properly classified as selves, persons, and/or ourselves only if such entities are related to other social entities. The relational-necessity approach, depending on what it is supposed to include, e.g., necessary and sufficient conditions or simply a necessary condition, can be specified in different ways, for example,

(Relational-necessity theory of personal identity)#1

For all t, P at t_1 is the same person as Q at t_2 only if Q at t_2 partakes of the same social-relational structure of which P at t_1 partakes.

One version of this relational-necessity theory that is specifically Confucian can contribute to the stated formulation with a clarification of the kind of relationality that provides the conditions of identification of selves, persons, and/or ourselves. A consequence of these relational theories is that, among the conditions of identity of the entities involved, we must include facts that *prima facie* may appear to be external to the individual at issue – for instance, facts about the social composition of the relevant community in or through which a self or a person is metaphysically identified. As a result, society may play a metaphysically transformative role on certain individuals: as a piece of paper becomes money only in a social context, so an individual can be a person only in a social context. Early Confucians did not frame their theses using the terms I used to characterise the role-person approach; however, the previously stated theories are elaborations of some of their key points. In particular, the Confucian role-person view is one way in which the social relation-necessity theory can be elaborated.

3 The Confucian role-person and *lǐ* (禮)

The Confucian role-person view is one instance of the social relation-necessity view. Henry Rosemont, one of the proponents of a role-view of personhood inspired by Confucian principles, states some basic principles behind the Confucian understanding of persons as follows:

> For the early Confucians there can be no me in isolation, to be considered abstractly: I am the totality of roles I live in relation to specific others. [. . .] They [the Confucians] emphasise the interrelatedness of what I am calling 'roles', that is to say, they are cognisant of the fact that the relations in which I stand to some people affect directly the relations in which I stand with others, to the extent that it would be misleading to say that I play or perform these roles; on the contrary, for Confucius I *am* my roles. Taken collectively, they weave, for each of us, a unique pattern of personal identity, such that if some of my roles change, others will of necessity change also, literally making me a different person.[6]

It is clear from this passage that the author is not solely trying to specify a social theory about the structure of early Chinese society or a theory about the biographical identity of the entities that play a role in the social context at issue. Rather, the passage also seems to contain a series of metaphysical theses; at least this is how I interpret the expression "literally making me a different person". Among these metaphysical theses, there is the idea that the conditions of synchronic identity for a person and for us are given by the totality of interrelations that coalesce into individualities. This thesis seems to imply that the societal structure is ontologically prior to or more fundamental than the existence of individuals and/or persons. Also, it is only in a structured social pattern – for instance, a structure in which certain roles are defined – that we can identify who or what we are. In addition, Rosemont seems to be assuming one version of person essentialism, the claim according to which we are essentially persons. (See Chapter 4 for details.) There are at least two ways of further clarifying the theory at issue: (1) I am a role-person, that is, the totality of the social and relational roles in a society specified by Confucian social relations (strict Confucian role-person view of our nature); (2) A necessary and sufficient condition for X to be a person is that of being a point of focus of various roles, in particular, those roles specified by the Confucian social relations.

As discussed in the first section, there are interpretations of the Confucian stance on personhood that do not properly take into account Confucius's, Mencius's, and other Confucians' insights about our reflective mental capacities – and thus, relative to the discussion of role-persons, the importance of these self-reflective capacities in the determination of a proper role-person. In fact, as we will see in the next sections, early Confucians conceived of the notion of an exemplary person as an entity that is certainly the point of focus of various roles, but that also has a variety of internal mental states that develop through time. So, it is reasonable to assume that a Confucian relational role-person approach would not be complete without a discussion of the mental faculties that role-persons are supposed to have. This point seems to imply that this relational approach should at least specify (1) which mental or psychological capacities are required for certain types of social interactions, and (2) the way in which such capacities can develop and still be considered as belonging to the same person.

As we will see in Chapter 8, there are certain approaches to narrative identity that question the idea that it is a necessary condition for having social roles to display complex psychological features that seem necessary for establishing social relations. For instance, the feminist philosopher Hilde Lindemann claims that having complex psychological features may not be a necessary condition for being part of a social narrative – a narrative that is essentially socially mediated – that, in turn, may constitute the identity of entities like us.

General versions of the role-person theory are not solely an intellectual product of the ECT. On the contrary, many such views have been variously proposed, not least by contemporary communitarians in their polemical discussions of liberalism. In addition, other features that are sometimes taken as characterising the specific kind of context that determines the various roles that define role-persons – for instance, an emphasis on the role of the family – are not found solely in the ECT. Still, in what follows, I flesh out one version of the social relational-necessity approach by taking into account the kind of social relations discussed in the ECT, in particular, those social relations partially identified with or regulated by the rites or rituals (*lǐ*, 禮) – the entire body of codified behavioural patterns, customs, institutions, and life-styles, the best exemplification of which was in the early Zhou Dynasty.[7] These rites represent the appropriate context in which an exemplar role-person (a *jūnzǐ*) can develop. The roles frequently discussed in the ECT are family-based and ritualised. Ames summarises the approach by referring to *human becomings*, entities that co-develop with these socially determined roles:

> [there] is a fundamental, default distinction between individuated, self-sufficient, and thus discrete human beings, and situated, relational human becomings who grow and realise themselves as distinctive persons through a sustained commitment to their always-collaborative, transactional roles within the nexus of family and community.

In the ECT, the roles that define a person (or a human becoming) are determined by certain specific conventions, and such conventions prescribe certain familiar practices that, in turn, are meant to inculcate the right expression of certain virtues – for instance, the virtue of filial piety (孝, *xiào*). The connection between personhood and morality is thus an essential feature of what it takes to be a person and/or one like us. Since being one like us necessarily involves a relational and moral aspect (encoded in the rites), being a person has, also in this tradition, an inherent moral dimension. The Confucian model of transmission of learning is related to the idea that the elderly and, in particular, the paternal figure deserves particular or special reverence. Among the various rituals and behavioural patterns meant to convey or foster the virtue of filial piety, we can find in the ECT (as well as nowadays) the idea that our physical body derives, as a kind of gift, from our parents. Therefore, the reasoning goes, we should not injure our bodies and we should keep them intact. The rituals discussed in the various classical texts of the ECT are also described as including a peculiar aesthetics of existence, e.g., the rites prescribe which colours should be used in certain ceremonies as well as suggest the appropriate kind of music for different occasions. These societal- and person-grounding practices are not supposed to be solely enacted, but also felt by the proper person through a process of self-cultivation (more on this in the last section of this chapter). Unfortunately, in some of the contemporary scholarship in comparative philosophy, the difference between alleged 'Western' views of the person and Confucian is greatly exaggerated and does not take into account the role that society, family, and social class have been taken to play in various parts of the so-called 'Western' tradition. Portraying a so-called 'Western view of personhood' as exemplified by an autonomous, egoist, self-absorbed, over-indulgent Wall Street lone wolf or politician ("I pray to myself for myself") is a gross mischaracterisation.

When Confucius was asked about governing, he allegedly replied "Let the ruler be a true ruler, the ministers true ministers, the fathers true fathers, and the sons true sons" (Analects, 12.11). In addition, Confucians also believed that the good order of society – and thus the proper social roles to be prescribed – is the one that grounded the good political order of the early Zhou, which is based on the five fundamental relationships. In turn, these relationships are specified in the *Book of Rites* (禮記, *liji*: one of the books in the Confucian canon that contains a variety of rules for proper *li*) as: "Ruler and subject, father and son, husband and wife, elder brother and younger brother, and friend and friend." The social structure that prescribes the roles that define persons in the ECT is hierarchical, a social structure in which people are supposed to find their place and respect – with feeling – their superiors and their roles.

To sum up, a Confucian role-person account of the conditions for personhood claims that:

- A necessary and sufficient condition for X to be a person is that of being a point of focus, an individuated node in a network composed of/constituted by various social roles, where such roles are those prescribed in the rites of the ECT.

This theory is anachronistic and hardly acceptable. In particular, if the defining roles are taken to be necessarily and exactly those of the Zhou dynasty (or of any other time-specific period or dynasty), then this implies that persons, in a proper sense of the term, are entities that can develop only in a very specific tradition. As a consequence, no members of, say, the Roman senate or any individual far removed from the ECT, say, Abraham Lincoln, were ever persons. This is a *reductio* of the Confucian role-person account stated previously.

A more charitable understanding of a non-culture/non-tradition specific Confucian role-person account of the conditions for personhood can be formulated as follows:

- A necessary and sufficient condition for X to be a person is that of being a point of focus, an individuated node in a network composed of/constituted by various social roles, where such roles have a general form that resembles the form of the social roles prescribed in the ECT.

However, it is not clear what is so special, from a metaphysical point of view, about the social roles prescribed by the rituals of the ECT. A reply would be that those patterns of behaviour were those that best represented or follow the way, or *Dao*. Given the broad diversity of ways of life in both the historical past and in the contemporary world that seem to involve persons, even this weaker view does not seem plausible. Perhaps a general, non-culture specific (and thus, in a sense, not distinctively Confucian) formulation of this approach may or should simply dismiss any reference to a specific tradition or social structure and rather specify some more general conditions for the appropriateness of the social roles at issue. For instance,

A necessary and sufficient condition for X to be a person is that of being a point of focus, an individuated node in a network composed of/constituted by various social roles, where such roles have a general form such that certain social roles in the network are specified and, overall, in harmony with each other.

4 Role-personhood and personal identity

Given the different criteria of personhood specified previously, we can formulate several related theories of personal identity:

(Role-Person Theory of the Metaphysical Foundation of Personal Identity)#1

For all t, P at t_1 is one and the same person as Q at t_2 iff P at t_1 is determined by the same social roles R that constitute Q at t_2.

If the conditions for being a person are taken to be dependent upon a very specific set of rites and behavioural patterns embodied in a living community, then the existence and persistence of the persons appropriately embedded in them are contingent upon the continuous existence of this community. So, on this view, a necessary condition for the existence and persistence of individuals as the same persons is the persistence of the same community of which they are members. A possible problem is that the stated theory does not seem to be specific enough to justify or ground claims of personal identity. In particular, it is not clear how those roles relevant to the specification of an entity are to be distinguished from those that are not conducive to a person's individuation. For instance, a social role can be 'husband' or 'chief executive', but it can also be 'Regina Tong's husband' or 'the chief executive of Hong Kong SAR in 2016': it is not clear whether the relevant social roles at issue should be indexed to specific times, places, or other nodes in the social network and/or whether they are all relevant (and to what extent) to the identification of an individual. It seems plausible that, in order for the previous theory to provide conditions of identity that properly individuate persons in a society, such roles must be indexed to specific times, places, or other nodes: after all, there are many people in the same society who have the same generic roles. For example, if we take it that a proper specification of a sufficient relevant R is simply that of being a taxi driver, this generic social role does not seem to provide conditions of synchronic identity sufficient to individuate or distinguish in the same society one taxi driver from another as different persons – unless additional conditions for the identification of individuals are provided. This result is clearly unacceptable.

A Confucian version of the role-person theory is:

(Confucian Role-Person Theory of the Metaphysical Foundation of Personal Identity)#1

For all t, P at t_1 is one and the same person as Q at t_2 iff P at t_1 is constituted by the same social roles R that constitute Q at t_2 and such roles are those prescribed in the rites of the ECT.

Again, a general problem of this formulation – a problem shared with a Confucian role-person account of the conditions for personhood – is that, given that the types of relevant social roles are strictly connected to a more or less precise and limited tradition, it follows that individuals in different traditions cannot persist through time as persons – not to mention the idea that this account does not adequately take into account the mutable and continuously changing structure of the social world. In brief, this theory, as it stands, does not provide a plausible account of personal identity.

A more general version of the role-person view may still retain the idea that persons are constituted by their social roles, but also claim that the relevant social roles are themselves the result of a society, the identity conditions of which are to be understood in terms of an evolving structure. More precisely,

(Role-Person Theory of the Metaphysical Foundation of Personal Identity)#2

For all t, P at t_1 is one and the same person as Q at t_2 iff P at t_1 is composed of/constituted by a series of related social roles that belong to an evolving social structure S that constitutes Q at t_2.

The identity conditions of S are to be understood in terms of relations of historical or causal continuity: a role-determining social structure S is the same through time provided that a sufficient degree of causal and historical connections exist between the roles determined by such a society over time. A related view on our nature can be spelled out as follows: we are essentially a series of social roles in an evolving social structure S (General social-role theory of our own nature).

Although there may be cases of unclear or vague boundaries between societies at different times and different places, especially considering extended time-lines, there are also cases in which such boundaries seem better discernible. Specifying the identity conditions of a society would be the next task for those interested in defending such an approach to personal identity. There are several studies on the topic of social ontology which may provide interesting ideas about how to further articulate the theory in question.[8] Unfortunately, contemporary scholars in Chinese and comparative philosophy have not yet (2017) availed themselves extensively of these theoretical resources. If individual psychology and its philosophical underpinnings are to be reduced or connected to social groups, 'getting more serious' about the ontology of social entities seems advisable.

5 Our nature: Mencius's four roots

Despite the great emphasis put in the previous sections on the social nature of human persons, the ECT integrates such a relational approach with a variety of views on our own nature as perfectible entities. In particular, the main idea is that, we can perfect ourselves through the cultivation of our moral and psychological features. For instance, consider this passage from the *Analects* (2.7):

Ziyou asked about filial piety. The Master said, "Nowadays 'filial' means simply being able to provide one's parents with nourishment. But even dogs and horses are provided with nourishment. If you are not respectful, wherein lies the difference?"

In this context, respect (敬, *jìng*) involves both a behavioural pattern and an emotional response, clearly a (series of) psychological state(s). The development of an internal emotional attitude towards certain virtues – or, at least, towards certain rituals – is possible because we are, according to Mengzi, naturally inclined to the good. In particular, according to Mengzi, our nature as humans (人性, *rén xìng*) is such that a proper development of some of our inner dispositions can eventually result in a virtuous person. More specifically, Mengzi characterises these four inner moral dispositions as sprouts or beginnings (端, ***duān***). These sprouts or beginnings of virtue are not hidden or inert, but visible and active. It is not always clear whether the metaphor of the four sprouts should be intended as suggesting that there are four independent faculties responsible for each of them or whether they are all aspects or functions of the same heart-mind. For simplicity, let us assume that the sprouts are dispositions of the Confucian self, which in turn depends on (or is identical with) the heart-mind. In *Mengzi* 2A6, Mengzi claims that no person is devoid of a sensitive heart, i.e., everybody is prone to moral sentiments. This point is made by claiming that everybody would feel compassion at the sight of a young child about to fall into a well. In particular, a man seeing a child falling into a well would feel compassion independently of any advantage he may achieve by acting on the impulse to save the child – the man would be moved to act not (just) following the desire to prevent the water in the well of his village from being contaminated. On this account, compassion is the emotional beginning of the virtue called *rén* (仁, variously translated with 'benevolence', 'virtue' [in a general sense], 'humaneness', etc.). Mengzi also claims that our heart-mind is naturally ashamed in certain situations: even a beggar would refuse to eat the rice that has been trampled upon disrespectfully. If properly tended to, the emotion of shame will develop into the virtue of *yì* (義, righteousness, right conduct). The heart-mind also feels courtesy – as when a young person almost instinctively feels the need to show respect for an elderly figure – and has a sense of right and wrong. Under the right conditions, these two sentiments develop respectively into *li*, the virtue of properly respecting rites, and wisdom, the virtue that involves the capacity to grasp the spirit of certain moral rules such that these rules can be applied appropriately. In short, normally there are no sociopaths.

A. C. Graham claims that Mengzi's account of our nature should not be understood in terms of a set of stable and essential features, but rather in terms of a qualification of the various ways in which a human entity develops and declines when not injured or inadequately nourished. This development and decline is connected to an internal moral energy common to all men. Mengzi sometimes characterises such an energy as a special kind of *qi*. Our special vital energy is accumulated in our bodies and can function in a magnetic way, as a charismatic power that attracts other people to the good. Even bodily development is allegedly influenced by such a growth of inner moral energy.

6 Self-cultivation in the ECT

The main thinkers generally associated with the Confucian tradition have all discussed and emphasised the importance of self-cultivation for developing our virtues – 'virtue' is the translation of '德' (*dé*). In the early pre-Confucian period, this term was used to refer to an alleged power that people develop when they act favourably toward some entities, such as ancestors or spirits. *Dé* subsequently acquired also a moral dimension, for instance when an individual performs some of her social functions appropriately. The criteria of appropriateness are given by the nature of these social functions and by the *li* (rituals). For instance, a *proper* king would be virtuous when he enacts the kingly functions and duties appropriately – which are the ways a just king treats his subjects according to the rites. A basic idea in the Confucian tradition is that a virtuous king can inspire and command even without being active or taking the initiative: his virtue would radiate and facilitate the correct functioning of the empire almost automatically. Similarly, the morally perfect man has a virtuous power that influences those around him.

Ivanhoe has isolated various different models, developed by various Chinese thinkers since Confucius, or ways of thinking about how virtues develop through self-cultivation. Among those developed in the ECT, Ivanhoe distinguishes between: (1) Confucius's acquisition model; (2) Mengzi's developmental model; and (3) Xunzi's reformation model. More specifically, Confucius proposed an educational programme focused on a continuous practice aimed at mastering certain key texts and rituals. A constant attention to the details of the objects of this practice would contribute to the formation of habits and skills, as for instance the capacities to focus on and care for others. In fact, Confucius believed that the study of, say, edifying odes was not supposed to be a mere repetitive exercise, but a way of acquiring certain character traits and skills. The aim of self-cultivation through the practice of rituals was that of nurturing people who will then be able to act willingly upon their knowledge of what a virtue is and dictates. For example, in the case of filial piety, people were supposed to act out of filial piety through an *acquired* capacity to pay attention to certain ritual ceremonies that regulate the proper way of interacting with family members.

Although self-cultivation is a process that crucially involves the development of an individual, it is seen here as a process that is also aimed at the formation of character traits that are in harmony with social life. Confucius's ideas were sufficiently general and generic that other thinkers could then develop them in different directions. For instance, Mengzi suggests that the task of self-cultivation is that of *developing* one's own Heavenly conferred nature. Ivanhoe claims that, according to Mengzi, the process of self-cultivation of the moral sprouts of our own nature should take place in an adequate environment. Only a few moral heroes are capable of developing in the harshest environments, while most of us normal people need a series of minimal conditions in order to develop our naturally good tendencies. Another important figure in the ECT, Xunzi (310–219 BCE), held a different view about the kind of resources we are equipped with at the beginning of our journey of self-cultivation. In particular, Ivanhoe ascribes to him the idea that self-cultivation is a process of *reformation* of our nature. According to this interpretation, Xunzi maintains that our moral development is an artificial process carried out through 'deliberate action'. Tradition provides us with models of behaviour, which are to be emulated in order to achieve social order. Learning such models seems to add something new to the learning individual; for example, the individual seems to acquire a new kind of sensibility.

The metaphors used by Xunzi to explain his understanding of self-cultivation are not akin to those based on natural growth used by Mengzi. Rather, Xunzi uses metaphors meant to underline that self-cultivation is a deliberative, artificial, and fundamentally transformative process. Ivanhoe claims that despite Xunzi's pessimistic view regarding the status of human beings in a pre-social context, he was optimistic about our capacity to perfect ourselves. Still, self-cultivation is seen by Xunzi as a demanding task that requires constant effort because our nature is, if untamed, rather capricious. Despite their differences, according to both Mengzi and Xunzi, the process of self-cultivation can bring about a deep psychological change (e.g., of our character traits). The relevance of self-cultivation to theories of personal identity is discussed in the next section.

6.1 Self-cultivation and personal identity

There are more models of self-cultivation in the long Confucian tradition than those outlined in the previous section, but their underlying presuppositions about the identity conditions of persons are all similar. More specifically, models of self-cultivation seem to presuppose that an individual or a person can undergo even drastic psychological changes without thereby ceasing to exist or be the same. The following account is meant to capture more precisely the idea that persons persist through time in virtue of their taking part in the same process of self-cultivation, which in turn involves the notion of *duān*.

(Mencius *Duān* and Self-cultivation Metaphysical Theory of Personal Identity)#1

For all t, P at t_1 is one and the same person as Q at t_2 iff and P at t_1 and Q at t_2 belong to only one and the same development of a series of 端, *duān* (sprouts).

To conclude our discussion of the often-implicit theories of personal identity to which certain theories in the ECT are committed, we can also formulate a more complex theory that combines both the idea that persons are identified by their roles and a reference to self-cultivation. More specifically, we can combine Mengzi's self-cultivation model with (Confucian Role-Person Theory of the Metaphysical Foundation of Personal Identity)#1 in the following way:

(Confucian Role-Person/Mengzi Cultivation Model Theory of Personal Identity)#1

For all t, P at t_1 is one and the same person as Q at t_2 iff (1) P at t_1 is composed of/ constituted by the same social roles R that compose/constitute Q at t_2, where such roles are those prescribed in the rites of the ECT; and (2) P at t_1 and Q at t_2 belong to only one and the same development of a series of 端, *duān* (sprouts).

7 Further directions

The idea that the relational origin of certain mental features is essential for person-hood seems to be supported by a number of studies in developmental psychology. The general claim is that an infant's interactions with her caregivers provide her with some crucial material of what will become her perceived self-image; for instance, the language in which she will formulate her basic conception of reality. This point does not seem to be significantly controversial, although some of its philosophical consequences are. In particular, certain post-modern and structuralist thinkers have inferred from the social and contextual origin of language a more controversial con-clusion to the effect that rationality is itself, in a strict sense, plural. In turn, this claim is understood as implying that there are no universal norms of rationality, and that the self or persons (intended as persisting entities through time) are pre-modern (or pre post-modern) delusions. Other lines of enquiry on the social origin of per-sons have been explored by thinkers such as Michel Foucault (1926–1984) and his epigones. One of these prolific lines of research has emphasised that, by recognising the relational and social origin of much of what constitutes our own identities, indi-viduality, and/or personhood, we may also uncover how certain structures of power operate and contribute to the formation of our identities. This process of discovery would, in turn, contribute to the recognition and eventually subversion of certain intrusive or exploitative practices. If persons are constituted by social structures determined by power dynamics characteristic of certain social institutions, the study of these power dynamics offers important insights into certain aspects of our own identities that may not be immediately accessible to us. In fact, some of these power structures may be so deeply rooted in certain identity-constituting social structures that persons may not be able to realise that such forces actively contribute to the formation of their identities, both biographical and metaphysical.

Among the most plausible points discussed in the previous sections, there is the idea that personhood is also a relational concept. Unfortunately, this aspect is frequently forgotten and/or omitted in contemporary metaphysical discussions. Although the various theories discussed previously may not be appealing if under-stood as providing an exhaustive account of the identity conditions of persons and of ourselves, it is important to remember that a plausible account of our nature and of personal identity may have to recognise in one way or another our relational nature and/or the relational nature of the concept 'person'. This point is recognised, even implicitly, and implemented in some of the views discussed in the following chap-ters. For instance, Locke himself claims that the concept of a person is, among other things, also forensic – that is, 'of the forum' and thus related to society (Chapter 4). Practical and narrative theories of personal identity also acknowledge the relational role of some of the features that characterise us as persons and/or of what we are.

Relational theories can provide the ground for several lines of criticism against the simple-soul and the Buddhist no-self approaches. In particular, against the for-mer, and to the degree that souls can exist independently of other souls and/or in a disembodied, non-social form, some versions of the relational approach imply that we cannot identify ourselves with souls. The main reason is that we are essentially social entities, while souls are not, hence we are not souls.[9] In turn, social/relational theories may argue against some Buddhist no-self views that a plausible theory of personal identity and of our nature should explain and not explain away some of our intuitions about our social and/or moral lives. The supporter of the relational approach may further hold that a condition for performing our social functions is that we exist. Hence, the extreme revisionism that seems to be implied by some Buddhist theories – especially in their nihilistic forms – may count as a reason to reject them.[10] To sum up, the legacy of the relational approach may be that of reminding us that an adequate account of personal identity and/or ourselves should recognise, perhaps only as a necessary condition, that human individuals and/or persons are relational beings that develop in social structures.

8 Summary

The relational approach holds that persons and/or ourselves are entities the origin or continuous existence of which do not depend exclusively on the intrinsic properties that such entities have. For example, whether you are a person does not depend only on your body, psychological faculties, or soul (if souls exist), but also on your belonging to a network of relations with other individuals. This chapter has described some of the ways in which this basic intuition can be made more precise. Although I have chosen to discuss more in detail a series of theories related to the Confucian tradition, this does not mean that only in such a tradition persons and/or ourselves have been understood as relational entities (e.g., contemporary communitarians and some feminist philosophers have similar views on our nature).

In general, the relational approach may include a claim about our relational origin (or that of persons) and/or one about the necessity of a relational structure for our persistence through time (or that of persons). According to the former, a person/ourselves can come into existence only relationally, that is, as the result of certain social interactions. A Confucian version of this view, which seems to be clearly implausible, is that persons (in a general understanding of the concept) can come into existence only when nurtured in a specific context (e.g., a context determined by the Zhou dynasty rites). Weaker forms of the relational-origin theory are more plausible – that is, versions that simply state that a self and/or a person require a certain relation context to develop some of their basic functions (e.g., the capacity to comprehend a language). A relational-necessity theory holds instead that persons/ourselves are entities the continuous existence of which essentially depends on a social structure. In turn, this point can be articulated as implying that a person's continuous existence is possible only if the social structure in which she developed continues to exist. Another understanding of the relational-necessity theory simply makes a generic claim about the necessity for a person's continuous existence to be embedded in at least one social structure. Again, the latter idea seems more plausible. I classified the Confucian role-person theory as one version of the relational-necessity theory, in particular, as a theory claiming that the social structure required for a specific person's existence is the one determined by the Confucian rites. Again, this theory does not seem plausible. Still, it is important to emphasise that it is not clear whether the original doctrines in the ECT were also intended as making any explicit claims about the ontology of persons.

A common feature of the ECT is its emphasis on self-cultivation. The process of self-cultivation is variously described by Confucius, Mengzi, Xunzi, and other thinkers in the same tradition. However, despite some important differences among their accounts – differences testified by the variety of contrasting metaphors used to describe the process at issue – self-cultivation is understood as essentially involving the development of certain psychological features. For instance, Mengzi's discussion of our nature in terms of four beginnings seems to rely on (1) the idea that persons can develop and thus change, and (2) that such a change is brought about also by a process of psychological development. In short, self-cultivation seems to presuppose the idea that psychological features are part of what makes an individual a social agent and that the identity of individuals in a social context over time is compatible with their developing psychological features. The role that psychological properties/faculties (e.g., memory) play in the debate on personal identity is further analysed in the next chapter.

Supporters of theories that emphasise our relational or social nature are likely to find some of the nihilistic formulations of certain Buddhist doctrines as particularly unpalatable – given the alleged difficulties that these theories have in accommodating some of our everyday and social practices.

Notes

1 The term 'descriptive metaphysic' is generally associated with the approach to metaphysics discussed in the introduction to Strawson (1959).
2 See Raphals (2009).
3 See Wong (2004), Shun (2004), and Yu (2005).
4 See Shun (2004).
5 Wong (2004), p. 421.
6 Rosemont (1991), p. 90.
7 There are other conceptions of what *li* or rites are. See the interesting discussion in Van Norden (2007), pp. 101–112.
8 For instance, Searle (1995).
9 Perhaps a theistic supporter of the soul-based approach may reply that, in a sense, we are always in a form of social relation with at least another person, namely, God.
10 As we have seen in Chapter 2, there are ways of understanding some Buddhist schools as implying that we are relational entities – or, at least, that although we do not exist as independent substances, we exist only relationally. However, on many Buddhist accounts, also this form of existence (if at all) is generally considered illusory and/or misleading.

Suggested readings

Chinese philosophy and Confucianism

Primary sources

All the relevant texts in the early Confucian tradition can be found at the Chinese Text Project http://ctext.org.

Confucius, *Analects*, translated by E. Slingerland (Indianapolis: Hackett, 2003).

Ivanhoe, Philip J. and Bryan W. Van Norden (eds.), *Readings in Classical Chinese Philosophy, 2nd Edition* (Indianapolis: Hackett Publishing, 2005).

Mengzi: With Selections From Traditional Commentaries, translated by B. Van Norden (Indianapolis, IN: Hackett Publishing, 2008).

General introductions

Gardner, Daniel, *Confucianism: A Very Short Introduction* (Oxford: Oxford University Press, 2014).

Ivanhoe, Philip J., *Confucian Reflections* (New York and London: Routledge, 2013).

Lai, Karyn, *An Introduction to Chinese Philosophy* (Cambridge: Cambridge University Press, 2008).

Liu, JeeLoo, *An Introduction to Chinese Philosophy* (Oxford: Blackwell Publishing, 2006).

Van Norden, Bryan, *Virtue Ethics and Consequentialism in Early Chinese Philosophy* (Cambridge: Cambridge University Press, 2007).

Van Norden, Bryan, *Introduction to Classical Chinese Philosophy* (Indianapolis: Hackett Publishing, 2011).

Individuation and the heart-mind

Perkins, Franklin, 'What Is a Thing (wù 物)?', in Chenyang Li and Franklin Perkins (eds.) *Chinese Metaphysics and its Problems* (Cambridge: Cambridge University Press, 2015), pp. 54–68.

Perkins, Franklin, 'Metaphysics in Chinese Philosophy', in *Stanford Encyclopedia of Philosophy* (2015). http://plato.stanford.edu/entries/chinese-metaphysics/

Raphals, Lisa, 'Thirteen Ways of Looking at the Self in Early China', *History of Philosophy Quarterly*, 26, 4 (2009), pp. 315–336.

Shun, Kwong-loi, 'Conception of the Person in Early Confucian Thought', in Kwong-loi Shun and David B. Wong (eds.) *Confucian Ethics* (Cambridge: Cambridge University Press, 2004), pp. 183–202.

Strawson, Peter, *Individuals* (London: Methuen, 1959).

Yu, Jiyuan, 'Soul and Self: Comparing Chinese Philosophy and Greek Philosophy', *Philosophy Compass*, 3, 4 (2008), pp. 604–618.

Van Norden, Bryan (ed.) *Confucius and the Analects: New Essays* (Oxford: Oxford University Press, 2002).

Confucian relational self

Ames, Roger, 'The Chinese Conception of Selfhood', in Eliot Deutsch and Ron Bontekoe (eds.), *A Companion to World Philosophies* (Oxford: Blackwell, 1997), pp. 148–154.

Ames, Roger, *Confucian Role Ethics* (Honolulu: University of Hawai'i Press, 2011).

Fingarette, Herbert, *Confucius: The Secular as Sacred* (New York: Harper, 1972).

Kim, Sungmoon, 'The Anatomy of Confucian Communitarianism: The Confucian Social Self and its Discontent', *Philosophical Forum*, 42, 2 (2011), pp. 111–130.

Rosemont, Henry Jr., 'Rights-Bearing Individuals and Role-Bearing Persons', in Mary Beckoner (ed.) *Rules, Rituals, and Responsibility* (La Salle, IL: Open Court, 1991).

Searle, John, *The Construction of Social Reality* (New York: Simon and Schuster Inc., 1995).

Wong, David B., 'Relational and Autonomous Selves', *Journal of Chinese Philosophy*, 31, 4 (2004), pp. 419–432.

Yu, Jiyuan, 'Confucius' Relational Self and Aristotle's Political Animal', *History of Philosophy Quarterly*, 22, 4 (2005), pp. 281–300.

Yu, Jiyuan, *The Ethics of Confucius and Aristotle: Mirrors of Virtue* (London and New York: Routledge, 2007).

Mengzi and self-cultivation

Graham, A. C., 'The Background of the Mencian Theory of Human Nature', in Xiusheng Liu and P. J. Ivanhoe (eds.) *Essays on the Moral Philosophy of Mengzi* (Indianapolis, IN: Hackett Publishing Company, 2002), pp. 1–64.

Ivanhoe, Philip J., *Confucian Moral Self Cultivation, 2nd Edition* (Indianapolis, IN: Hackett Publishing Company, 2000).

Ivanhoe, Philip J., *Ethics in the Confucian Tradition, 2nd Edition* (Indianapolis, IN: Hackett Publishing Company, 1990/ 2002).

Schwitzgebel, Eric, 'Human Nature and Moral Education in Mencius, Xunzi, Hobbes, and Rousseau', *History of Philosophy Quarterly*, 24, 2 (2007), pp. 147–168.

Van Norden, Bryan, 'Mencius', in *Stanford Encyclopedia of Philosophy* (2014). http://plato.stanford.edu/entries/mencius/

Relational self and contemporary developments

Christman, John, *The Politics of Persons* (Oxford: Oxford University Press, 2009).

Crittenden, Jack, *Beyond Individualism* (Oxford: Oxford University Press, 1992).

Feldman, Robert, *Child Development, 7th Edition* (Glenview, IL: Pearson, 2015).

Foucault, Michel, *The Hermeneutics of the Subject: Lectures at the Collège De France, 1981–1982* (London: Palgrave Macmillan, 2005).

Kymlyka, Will, *Liberalism, Community, and Culture* (Oxford: Clarendon Press, 1989).

Reddy, Vasudevi, *How Infants Know Minds* (Cambridge, MA: Harvard University Press, 2008).

Taylor, Charles, *Sources of the Self* (Cambridge, MA: Harvard University Press, 1989).

4 Locke and the psychological approach

1	Locke, identity, and person	98
2	Lost souls and lost bodies	102
	2.1 The prince, the cobbler, and the night-man	104
3	Consciousness and personal identity	106
4	The circularity objection and quasi-memory	110
5	Contemporary psychological theories	112
	5.1 Adequacy conditions for contemporary psychological	
	theories of personal identity	113
	5.2 Parfit's psychological theory of personal identity	114
6	Summary	118

So you want to have gone to Mars. Very good.
—Philip K. Dick, *We Can Remember It for You Wholesale*, 1966

The twenty-seventh chapter of the second book of John Locke's *An Essay Concerning Human Understanding*, included in the second edition published in 1694, contains one of the most influential theories of personal identity in the history of philosophy. In that chapter, called 'Of Identity and Diversity', Locke (1632–1704) proposes a theory that many scholars consider the starting point for the contemporary debate on personal identity. According to Locke, sameness of soul is neither necessary nor sufficient for personal identity. Rather, one of the main ideas of his theory is that personal identity through time is a relation that should be analysed in terms of sameness of consciousness. Part of the influence of Locke's account comes from the criticisms it has received. For instance, many contemporary psychological theories of personal identity have been influenced by a series of arguments against one interpretation of Locke's account – that is, the interpretation according to which Locke's notion of sameness of consciousness should be understood solely in terms of sameness (or continuity) of memory. Contemporary psychological theories hold that personal identity is a relation that should be analysed in terms of the continuity of a *variety* of different mental faculties and/or mental contents, not only memories but also character, desires, and sometimes agency.

In this chapter, I devote a great deal of attention to the details of Locke's theory, given its great importance for the current debate. In particular, in the first three sections (4.1, 4.2, 4.3) I introduce Locke's understanding of the *ideas* of identity and person – Locke famously claims that "idea" ". . . stands for whatsoever is the Object of the Understanding, when a man thinks" (*Essay* I, i, 8); more on this in what follows. Locke's criticism of the soul-based approach to personal identity is discussed in 4.2, along with one of his other important contributions to the debate, that is, the use of thought experiments (e.g., the famous **prince and the cobbler scenario**). Section 3 is devoted to a discussion of how Locke's theory of personal identity has been recently interpreted. The last two sections (4.4 and 4.5) contain a discussion of the circularity objection, the notion of quasi-memory – a theoretical device introduced to reply to some objections against certain versions of the psychological approach – and Derek Parfit's (1942–2017) psychological theory. In section 5, I list a series of requirements that psychological theories and, in general, all theories of personal identity are supposed to satisfy. I then introduce in some detail Parfit's influential psychological approach, the main idea of which is that personal identity involves the holding of different types of psychological relations in a non-branching form. Parfit and other contemporary philosophers have variously explored how adopting one version of the psychological approach may also modify the assessment of various issues regarding our ethical and rational choices. This connection between morality and personhood was also emphasised by Locke, who argues that our ideas about legal and moral responsibility through time essentially inform our concept of a person. Two lines of criticism against the psychological approach – at least in the generic form discussed in this chapter – are discussed in the next two chapters. In particular, supporters of the physical approach have emphasised a series of problems related to discussing psychological states without taking into due consideration their physical or causal pre-conditions (this line of criticism is pursued by Bernard Williams). Another problem, explored in Chapter 6, is that the holding of the relation of personal identity should be specified in terms of more structured psychological connections than those employed in generic psychological theories. The point is that our identity over time is not just the result of any series of sufficiently numerous psychological connections, but it rather depends on sufficiently numerous psychological connections structured in a certain way.

1 Locke, identity, and person

In Locke's time, theories of personal identity circulated in intellectual and religious circles both in England and on the continent, and the dominant position in the debate was that persistence of a soul-substance was at least a necessary condition of personal identity.[1] A continuous and identical soul-substance would also provide part of the rational foundation for believing in our personal resurrection. Although some argued that persons (or we) are compounds of body and soul, the identity through time (and death) of the resurrected person was thought to be sustained solely by sameness of soul. A new body, eternal and/or reassembled by God, would be informed by the same pre-mortem soul at the time of the final judgment. One of Locke's aims was that of providing an account of personal identity not dependent on sameness of soul but still compatible with the possibility of our personal resurrection and final judgment.

In keeping with his empiricist view of the mind and its working, Locke claims that the *idea* of identity comes from experience; in particular, from the comparison between two distinct ideas of the same thing. Without entering into the depths of Locke scholarship, the notion of a simple idea can be here understood as a unit of mental content that we do not create but receive (passively) from experience, that is, the material upon which our minds apply our various mental faculties. To a first approximation, simple ideas can be taken as basic mental representations, such as percepts and thoughts derived from experience. In addition to simple ideas, there are also complex ideas, which are combinations of simple ideas. The idea of identity is a complex one. More precisely, the complex idea of identity comes from the comparison between two idea-representations taken to refer to the same object. Locke maintains that the idea of identity is crucial to our discussion because knowing what individuates an entity tells us how to distinguish one entity from the others and its conditions of identity through time.[2] In fact, Locke claims that the principle of individuation of particular entities specifies what makes it possible for an entity to exclude other entities of the same kind from its spatio-temporal location. (In general, a principle of individuation tells us, for each entity, how to identify and distinguish such an entity from all others.) Locke specifies a general principle of individuation or identity for substances in the following way. A substance P at t_1 is identical to all and only those substances of the same kind that occupy the same spatio-temporal location. Given an understanding of existence as the occupation of a location in space and time, existence itself – having a location – is what individuates substances of the same kind. The exact interpretation of this principle, sometimes called the '**Place-time-kind principle**' is controversial in contemporary scholarship.[3] On one understanding of the principle, the relevant kinds to which the principle applies are not *any* kinds of entities, for there are passages in which Locke claims that the principle applies only to infinite immaterial substances (e.g., God), finite immaterial substances (e.g., spirits or souls), and material substances (e.g., bodies). Other interpretations (e.g., Gideon Yaffe's) hold that the principle applies to any kinds of things and substances. I suspect that non-specialists in Locke's scholarship have understood Locke's principle in the latter way, that is, as applying to all kinds of entities and substances.[4] In what follows, I will assume this reading as well – two existing things of the same kind cannot occupy the same place at the same time.

According to Locke, the idea of a man – which I take here to be equivalent to what we understand as the idea of a human being, intended as a biological organism – is the idea of an entity the individuation of which depends on the existence of a living organised body. A particular life – the life of a living organised body – is the principle of unity of such an entity, and thus what determines the conditions under which it persists through time. For example, the identity over time of a cat is sustained by the existence of various particles or atoms of matter that 'partake of' the same cat-life. The existence of the same specific particular atoms composing a cat at a specific time is not a necessary condition for the continuous existence of the same cat at other times. In fact, according to Locke, the continuous existence of a cat as a living organism depends on the taking part of some atoms in the same continuous life. The identity conditions through time of a living organism differ from that of a mass of matter or of a single particle. In fact, Locke maintains that the identity over time of masses of matter depends solely on the atoms that compose the mass. Keeping in mind that here 'mass of matter' stands for a sum of atoms that is not taken to compose a *functional* whole, removing a specific atom alters the identity of that specific mass. For example, consider a collection of three atoms, C, randomly assembled and Homer, a cat. C remains the same through time as long as the three atoms remain the numerically same atoms. If one atom ceases to exist, so does the specific mass of matter. On the other hand, Homer may lose some of its atoms – say, some of those that compose its fur – and gain some new atoms – for instance, when Homer eats some of auntie's shrimps. However, Homer at t_1 will still exist at a different time t_2 in case a sufficient number of atoms or particles that compose Homer at t_1 still partake of Homer's life at t_2, even though not all of Homer's particles at t_2 are exactly the same particles that composed Homer at t_1. Homer, and other living organisms such as oak trees, wolves, and monkeys are the same through time so long as atoms partake of the same life or organised functional whole.

Locke does not only distinguish the idea of a human being from that of a mass of matter, but also the idea of a person from the idea of a human being. In fact, Locke claims that while the identity conditions of human beings are similar to those of other animals and plants, the identity conditions of persons follow different criteria. Among others, Thomas Hobbes (1588–1679) had already distinguished the concept of a person from that of a human being and also discussed the possibility of attributing personhood to non-human agents. More specifically, in the *Leviathan* (1651), Hobbes associates the concept of a person with that of an entity that *owns* actions, i.e., an entity to whom actions can be properly ascribed. However, Hobbes contends, such ascriptions of responsibility do not have as a necessary condition that the responsible entity be of any specific biological kind. For instance, even fictitious entities – or artificial persons – can be considered as responsible for their actions.

Locke's definition of 'person', a term that he uses interchangeably with 'self', is presented in at least four different passages:[5]

(1) we must consider what *Person* stands for; which, I think, is a thinking intelligent Being, that has reason and reflection, and can consider it self as it self, the same thinking thing in different times and places; which it does only by that consciousness, which is inseparable from thinking, and as it seems to me

essential to it: It being impossible for any one to perceive, without perceiving, that he does perceive.

(II, xxvii, 9)

(2) For it is by the Consciousness it has of its present Thoughts and Actions, that it is *self* to it *self* now, and so will be the same self as far as the same consciousness can extend to actions past or to come.

(II, xxvii, 10)

(3) Self is that conscious thinking thing, (whatever Substance made up of whether Spiritual, or Material, Simple, or Compounded, it matters no) which is sensible, or conscious of Pleasure and Pain, capable of Happiness or Misery, and so is concern'd for it *self*, as far as that consciousness extends.

(II, xxvii, 17)

(4) Person, as I take it, is the name for this self. Where-ever a Man finds, what he calls himself, there I think another may say is the same Person. It is a Forensick Term appropriating Actions and Merit; and so belongs only to intelligent Agents capable of a Law, and Happiness and Misery. This personality extends it *self* beyond present Existence to what is past, only by consciousness, whereby it becomes concerned and accountable; owns and imputes to it *self* past Actions, just upon the same ground, and for the same reason, that it does the present.

(II, xxvii, 26)

On this view, a person is an entity that is capable of recognising itself as the subject of perception at a specific time and through time. A subject's perceptions are accompanied by an awareness of herself perceiving, a thesis already proposed by Descartes. Also, a person is an entity that has emotions and is capable of feeling happiness and misery. Some of these emotions have the form of concerns for things to come, to the degree and extent that a person's consciousness can take these things to come as belonging to her own future existence – Locke uses the term 'appropriation' to describe the process through which we recognise future (and past) states as our own. This future-oriented aspect of Locke's theory is suggested also in II, xxvii, 25 where Locke claims that the self may have an uncertain duration in the future – "that this self has existed in a continued Duration more than one instant, and therefore 'tis possible may exist, as it has done, Months and Years to come, without any certain bounds to be set to its duration". Locke also holds that 'person' is a forensic term, that is, a term that denotes an entity that, in virtue of its capacity to think of herself as extended in time, is accountable for her actions, both subjectively and legally.

Bringing these various threads together, Locke's definition of (the idea of) person can be summarised as follows:

A person is (1) an intelligent and rational being that is (2) conscious – where this involves self-awareness – of her perceptions, (3) capable of thinking of herself as an entity extended in time, (4) capable of sensations and emotions such as pleasure and pain, (5) concerned for herself, (6) capable of appropriating her past, present, and future actions, and (7) responsible for her actions before the law.

On this view, being a person has an internal or subjective aspect – for instance, a person is supposed to be conscious and capable of appropriating mental states *from the inside* – and an external or relational one – the fact that a person is also an entity that is accountable for her actions by other persons.

In addition, two related views of our own nature are generally ascribed to Locke:

- Person essentialism: we are essentially persons.
- **Psychological essentialism**: we are essentially psychological entities.

In what follows, I assume that Locke holds these two views, at least implicitly. Psychological essentialism can be understood in at least two ways: (1) we are essentially entities that have the actual capacity to have mental states, and (2) we are essentially entities that actually have mental states. The first version is preferable because on certain understandings of the second it seems to follow that when we are not conscious (e.g., when we sleep and do not dream) we thereby cease (perhaps momentarily) to exist – a consequence that many find rather odd.

2 Lost souls and lost bodies

Locke puts his conception of what a person is to work in his criticism of theories based on the concept of a soul. These theories of personal identity were usually accompanied by the belief that consciousness depends on an immaterial substance (e.g., a soul$_{mind}$), as it was generally taken for granted that matter cannot think. It has to be noticed that Locke does not claim that souls or immaterial thinking substances do not exist or that they are not responsible for our consciousness; rather, he maintains that there are good reasons to believe that the idea of a soul and that of a person are distinct. Thus, Locke's critical focus was on the theory that sameness of soul is a necessary and sufficient condition for personal identity, not on the existence of souls. Some of his arguments to this effect can be summarised as follows.

1   We can imagine a case in which the soul of a person who lived in the past transmigrates or informs a body in the present. Given our limited knowledge of what a soul is, there is no metaphysical or conceptual contradiction in supposing that a soul can inform different bodies. This point is supported by the many different stories about the transmigration of souls, which, however implausible, do not seem metaphysically or conceptually contradictory. Again, for all we know about the nature of thinking substances, we are not in the position to rule out the possibility of transmigrations.

2   (From 1.) It is metaphysically and conceptually possible for a soul to inform different bodies.

3   It is metaphysically possible for a soul to lack any memories of its past life. The reason is similar to the one one given previously: stories of transmigrations or even entire religious traditions based on *memoryless* transmigrations are implausible, but do not seem metaphysically or conceptually impossible – although some probably are. Again, the point is that, for all we know, the nature of the soul does not rule out the possibility for it to survive (e.g., by transmigrating) without memories.

4   However, given Locke's definition of what a person is, it is not metaphysically and conceptually possible to be the same person over time and to be completely and/or irremediably oblivious of our past actions and/or not having the same consciousness.

5   The case of, e.g., the transmigration of a soul into different bodies associated with completely different mental states at different times is best described as a case in which there is one soul and unrelated persons at different times.

6   So, it is metaphysically and conceptually possible to have a case in which the same soul-substance informs bodies associated with different persons. (Locke's original discussion is at II, xxvii, 14.)

7   So, the idea (and concept) of a person and that of a soul are, in principle, extensionally different – they cover different cases – and, in addition, sameness of soul is not a sufficient condition of personal identity.

Locke advances other considerations in support of (6). More specifically, he asks whether a person existing now, in coming to know that her soul transmigrated from a dead individual, say, Nestor or Thersites (if they existed), should be egoistically or personally concerned with their past actions. Locke answers negatively, and adds that if we came to know that we share the same soul with Nestor or Thersites, we would *not* be justified in attributing their actions to ourselves. This intuition seems to constitute one basic feature of the process of appropriation: *prima facie*, we tend to consider ourselves as less responsible for or attached to actions we cannot bring back to our present consciousness.

Locke does not believe that having the same soul is a necessary condition of personal identity either. This conclusion seems to follow from the concept of a person: what is necessary for personal identity is sameness of consciousness and, for all we know, sameness of consciousness is not identical to sameness of thinking substance. His reasoning can be summarised in the following argument.

1   For all we know about the nature of immaterial thinking substances, it is metaphysically and conceptually possible for one consciousness to be transferred from one thinking substance to another. Again, there is nothing in the concept of a soul that rules out this possibility. For all we know, if God wanted, He could transfer our memories and other relevant mental states from one thinking substance to another.

2   It is metaphysically and conceptually possible for different substances to be responsible for sameness of consciousness.

3   So, there is no necessary one-to-one correspondence between one thinking substance and one consciousness.
4   So, sameness of consciousness may depend on more than one thinking substance.
5   Given Locke's definition of 'person', sameness of thinking substance is not a necessary condition of personal identity over time.

Personal identity may not depend on an immaterial substance, but are persons substances at all? Contemporary scholars disagree on this point. Now, Locke claims that ideas of various kinds of substances represent particular things that exist by themselves, i.e., that do not depend on something else for their existence. Ideas of modes stand for things that depend on substances. Examples of modes include beauty, theft, joy, sorrow, hope, and fear, as well as events like duelling, wrestling, etching, or imagining, reasoning, and remembering. Antonia Lolordo claims that Locke uses the term 'mode' in a way we would understand as standing for both a property and as a thing resulting from the exemplification of a property – this would show that the distinction between substances and modes is not that between things and their properties.[6] Lolordo further claims that ideas of modes are mind-dependent, in the sense that they are determined by us rather than by the real features of the world.[7] The distinction between ideas of substances and of modes has relevant consequences for understanding Locke's distinction between (the idea of) a human being and (the idea of) a person. In particular, on one interpretation, Locke would be addressing the metaphysical individuation of two *substances* (not of two modes or one substance and one mode), that is, two substances that happen to occupy the same space – a human being and a person. Hence, according to this view, a person is not a mode of a substance, but a substance itself, that is, something that exists independently. The point is that the idea of a person and the idea of a human being would not refer to or represent the same individual in different ways; rather, they specify different identity conditions for at least two distinct substances. If this interpretation is correct, then Locke may be committed to the view that there are two entities/substances – a human being and a person – that co-exist at the same location – what Vere Chappell calls the "doctrine of double existence".[8] In itself, this would not contradict anything Locke said since, according to him, two substances of different kinds can co-exist in the same location. However, there is no consensus among Locke scholars as to which interpretation of the alleged metaphysical status of persons is to be preferred and harmonised with his place-time-kind principle.[9]

2.1 The prince, the cobbler, and the night-man

What reasons does Locke offer to distinguish between the ideas of person and of human being? The way Locke argues in favour of this distinction, which includes the use of the thought-experiment methodology, is one of the most enduring legacies of his work. In particular, his methodology involves the discussion of imaginary cases or thought experiments designed to question or articulate the reader's relevant (conceptual or metaphysical) intuitions. One of Locke's most famous thought experiments is that of the prince and the cobbler. In the context of a discussion concerning the distinction between the persistence conditions of human beings and souls, Locke writes:

> For should the Soul of a Prince, carrying with it the consciousness of the Prince's past Life, enter and inform the Body of a Cobler [sic] as soon as deserted by his own Soul, every one sees, he would be the same Person with the Prince, accountable only for the Prince's Actions: But who would say it is the same Man? The Body too goes to the making of the Man, and would, I guess, to every Body determine the Man in this case, wherein the Soul, with all its Princely Thoughts about it, would not make another Man: but he would be the same Cobler to every one besides himself.
>
> (II, xxvii, 15)

In this passage, Locke imagines that the soul of a prince carries with it his consciousness – we have already seen that Locke thinks this is not necessarily true. If the prince's consciousness and/or whatever is responsible for it comes to inform the body of a consciousness-emptied cobbler, then Locke claims that we would say that there is a body that was not the original body of the prince, and that such a body is now associated with the prince. The prince's life as a person continues also in virtue of the new body that before was informed by the cobbler's conscious soul. By claiming that this is the best description of the thought experiment, Locke is thereby claiming that the use of the concept of a person is distinct from that of a human being or human body.

Another thought experiment proposed by Locke is the strange case of the night- and day-man.

> Could we suppose two distinct incommunicable consciousnesses acting the same Body, the one constantly by Day, the other by Night; and, on the other side the same consciousness, acting by Intervals two distinct Bodies: I ask in the first case, Whether the *Day* and the *Night*-man would not be two as distinct Persons, as Socrates and Plato; and whether in the second case, there would not be one Person in two distinct Bodies, as much as one Man is the same in two distinct clothing?
>
> (II, xxvii, 23)

Again, Locke is here suggesting that consciousness alone is what is responsible for personal identity. Novels and movies provide us with a plethora of even more elaborate examples, from Robert Louis Stevenson's *Dr. Jekyll and Mr. Hyde* (1886) to Chuck Palahniuk's *Fight Club* (1996) and David Fincher's (1999) cinematic adaptation of the latter. One of the points that Locke's thought experiment is meant to make is that our intuitions about how the concept of a person is to be applied and how it is applied to the case of the day- and night-man lead to the conclusion that identity of consciousness, and not identity of body, is what matters for personal identity. In particular, the best description of a case in which we have two incommunicable consciousnesses and one body is, according to Locke, one that includes reference to at least two persons and one body.

The consequences of Locke's distinction between persons and human beings are significant. An obvious one is that such a distinction informs Locke's account of personal identity, which will be discussed in the next section.

3 Consciousness and personal identity

An initial working formulation of Locke's metaphysical theory of personal identity can be stated as follows.

> (Lockean Theory of the Metaphysical Foundation of Personal Identity)#1
>
> For all t, P at t_1 is one and the same person as Q at t_2 iff P's consciousness at t_1 is Q's consciousness at t_2.

Any adequate interpretation of Locke's theory of personal identity must take into account the fact that he constantly refers to the notion of consciousness. One of the earliest interpretations of Locke's understanding of consciousness (in the context of his account of personal identity) basically reduces it to *memory*. Inspired by passages such as "as far as this consciousness can be extended backwards to any past Action or Thought, so far reaches the Identity of that Person; it is the same self now it was then; and 'tis by the same self with this present one that now reflects on it, that that Action was done" (II, xxvii, 9), many understand Locke as offering a view equivalent to the following:

> (Lockean Theory of the Metaphysical Foundation of Personal Identity)#2.1
>
> For all t, P at t_1 is one and the same person as Q at t_2 iff P's memory at t_1 is contained in Q's memory at t_2.

On this view, a person at a specific time is identical to a person at a different and later time if and only if the person that exists at a later time remembers or can remember what the earlier person did or remembered. The main point seems to be that sameness of consciousness is sustained by or depends on the content of someone's memory. More refined versions of this interpretation may include further requirements constraining what counts as an appropriate identity-sustaining memory.[10] In particular, it may be argued that remembering oneself as the same person may involve a particular kind of remembering – e.g., a mental act of remembering that includes feelings and emotions, in addition to some propositional content (autobiographical remembering). However, many contemporary Locke scholars do not think that consciousness simply amounts to memory alone.

A different interpretation of Locke's notion of consciousness is in terms of *reflection*. There is textual evidence (II, i, 4 and II, i, 19) to the effect that reflection is, for Locke, an operation of our own mind; more specifically, an act of perception of the operations of our own mind. According to Locke, reflection is an inwardly directed mental-perceptual operation that generates experiences:

> By Reflection then, [. . .] I would be understood to mean, that notice which the Mind takes of its own operations, and the manner of them, by reason whereof, there come to be Ideas of these Operations in the Understanding.
>
> (II, i, 4)

Such reflective experiences whereby the mind takes notice of its own operations furnish the understanding with new ideas of our own mental operations; for instance, the ideas of perception, thinking, doubting, believing, reasoning, knowing, and so on. Some recent scholars claim that Locke understands the idea of consciousness as the perception of what passes in our own minds (see II, i, 19 for example). So, they conclude, Locke believes that consciousness *is* reflection and thus reflection is the fundamental notion of his theory of personal identity. However, it is not easy to formulate a precise theory of personal identity in terms of consciousness understood as reflection. One formulation can be made in terms of the content of the reflective experience:

(Lockean Theory of the Metaphysical Foundation of Personal Identity)#2.2

For all t, P at t_1 is one and the same person as Q at t_2 iff P's content of reflection at t_1 is the same as or is contained in the content of Q's reflection at t_2.

The main insight of this formulation is that diachronic identity is sustained by/ consists in/depends on sameness or inclusion of the content of our mental faculties or its operations. In particular, personal identity through time is sustained by the content of reflection, where by 'reflection' we refer to an internal perception of the operations of the mind. Perhaps a more plausible specification of this view should not be in terms of mere numerical identity of the content of reflection, but in terms of continuity of those parts – in this case, instances of the faculty of reflection – that take part in the same mental life of the faculty of reflection. Similar to accounts of identity over time for living organisms, we may argue that what is necessary and sufficient for personal identity is that all of the various reflective experiences take part in the same life of a continuous reflective faculty. More precisely,

(Lockean Theory of the Metaphysical Foundation of Personal Identity)#2.3

For all t, P at t_1 is one and the same person as Q at t_2 iff P's content and operations of reflection at t_1 partakes in the same mental life of Q's faculty of reflection at t_2.

The understanding of consciousness in terms of reflection has been criticised by recent scholars. For instance, Udo Thiel claims that there is textual evidence showing that Locke did not entirely identify consciousness with reflection. In particular,

Thiel argues not only that consciousness is not identified by Locke with reflection, but also that consciousness is not one kind of higher-order perception. One argument in favour of this interpretation is that Locke repeatedly claims that consciousness is inseparable from thinking, consciousness is one of the essential features of thought, and being conscious involves an immediate awareness that always accompanies all our experiences. Since reflection is not responsible for all of our experiences and does not accompany all of our experiences in the way consciousness is supposed to do, Thiel concludes, consciousness is not reflection. One passage used to support the equivalence between consciousness and reflection – "Consciousness is the perception of what passes in a Man's own mind" (II, i, 19) – can be understood differently, for example, by noticing that what passes in Man's own mind can also be ideas of sensations, thus ideas not deriving from reflection. Thiel characterises Locke's view of consciousness as a "presence of the mind to itself that is more fundamental than the objectifying reflection." According to this interpretation, consciousness accompanies both sensation and reflection, which in turn are not always accompanied by reflection. If the previous points are correct, consciousness cannot be identified with reflection. Thiel also maintains that when Locke uses the expression "sameness of consciousness", we should understand him as claiming that what matters for personal identity are not individual acts or episodes of consciousness, but rather the continued life or connectedness between acts of consciousness in the same conscious mental life.

Locke claims that it is absurd to say that we perceive or think without thereby being conscious of perceiving or thinking, as consciousness is an essential feature of all of the objects of our mental lives (our Ideas), not an external or accessory object of perception itself. The inseparability of thinking and consciousness is a point that Descartes also made, the main difference from Locke being that, according to the latter, although perception is accompanied by self-awareness, we do not thereby also have knowledge of the nature of the subject of such self-awareness. More specifically, Locke's account of consciousness involves a form of self-awareness that informs us of the existence of an experiencing subject but that does not inform us also of the nature of such a subject. In other words, conscious experiences do not include, as such, experiences that reveal our nature to us (as, for instance, that we are immaterial substances). In addition, we should also remember that, according to Locke, the concept of a person has a relevant moral dimension. In fact, he claims that it is the person that is the proper object of moral and legal judgments as when he explicitly says that "punishment is annexed to personality". The person is the proper object of judgment not only in the courts of law, but before God on the Day of Wrath. On that revelatory day, all the "secrets of the hearts shall be laid open" and God will declare which persons merit his divine grace. Some scholars have suggested that a crucial aspect of Locke's account of personal identity is the notion of appropriation, which would seem to constitute the link between consciousness and morality: conscious self-awareness seems to be involved in establishing connections or appropriations of past and future states, which in turn determine what we can properly be considered as responsible for.[11]

To sum up, a Lockean account of personal identity and of our nature based on the previous observations should include the following points:

1 We are essentially persons and persons are capable of self-concern, which includes a variety of emotional states.
2 Consciousness is a form of self-awareness, which is manifested not only in reflection, but in all perceptions. Consciousness is an essential feature of thinking and of the way in which we perceive.
3 Consciousness, intended as a form of self-awareness, does not directly reveal the metaphysical nature of the conscious subject. All we are entitled to infer from the activity of thinking is that a subject of experience is aware of certain perceptions and reflections.
4 Consciousness constitutes personal identity in the sense that it plays an active role in the constitution of the identity of a person through time, possibly through a process called 'appropriation'.
5 Memory plays a crucial but not exclusive role in sustaining personal identity through time.
6 What is responsible for personal identity through time is not identity through time of particular acts of consciousness, but the contribution of such acts to a single conscious activity. (Thiel does not think that this point justifies ascribing to Locke an understanding of the life of one consciousness as having the identity conditions of a functional whole.)
7 Personal identity through time gives a temporal dimension to responsibility, concern, and other reactive attitudes.[12] The reason is that, according to Locke, responsibility is grounded also on our consciousness of past actions. In addition, becoming or being conscious – self-aware – of certain past actions determines or grounds certain attitudes such as concern for our future, responsibility, and so on. Personal identity is not exclusively backward looking, but also forward-looking, as this latter dimension is essential to planning and agency.
8 A person's true extension through time will be revealed by God on the Final Day (and judged accordingly).

One way of formulating this view concisely is the following:

(Lockean Theory of the Metaphysical Foundation of Personal Identity)#2.4:

For all t, P at t_1 is one and the same person as Q at t_2 iff P's consciousness/self-awareness at t_1 takes part in the same mental life of Q's consciousness/self-awareness at t_2. This consciousness/self-awareness is responsible, at least partially, for (1) the emotional life of P, (2) the inclusion of P's past-experiences into an organic whole, (3) the moral/legal standing or status of P.

4 The circularity objection and quasi-memory

One of the most well-known objections against Locke's account of personal identity, the circularity objection, has been proposed in various forms. Among the early proponents of this line of reasoning, we can count John Sergeant (1623–1707 or 1710), Joseph Butler (1692–1752), Thomas Reid (1710–1796), and others. One way of putting what their arguments have in common is the idea that Locke confuses what constitutes personal identity with what provides evidence for it. For instance, some scholars understand Butler as making a criticism of the alleged confusion between epistemological and ontological issues – how we know that something is the case should not be confused with what grounds the truth of what we come to know. So, according to this way of understanding the objection, consciousness and memory may provide us with *evidence* for personal identity because, through them, we come to know when such a relation holds. However, since consciousness and memory are forms of knowledge and knowledge presupposes the truth of what is known, consciousness cannot produce the truths it knows. Circularity would occur if we try to define or analyse something (personal identity) in terms of what already includes or presupposes it (e.g., consciousness, or memory, or knowledge).[13]

Other versions of the circularity objection have been discussed intensely from the 1950s to our days because many philosophers developed their own views – views which have become popular, mainstream, or considered as worthy of attention – also in response to arguments similar to the one sketched previously. Unfortunately, the starting point of many of these discussions is the belief that, in brief, Butler showed that Locke's account of personal identity, interpreted as a memory-based account, is circular. Keeping in mind the probable historical inaccuracy of this interpretation of Locke, I outline one version of the circularity objection in terms of memory – with the proviso that, in order for this objection to be entirely cogent against better readings of Locke's theory, some key terms have to be changed.[14]

1 Assume that one person (P) is in the state (S) of remembering having a specific experience (E).

2 The content of the state S is qualitatively identical or very similar to the past experience E.

3 One person (Q) really experienced E at a time earlier than P's state of remembering S and is remembering it. So, for instance, a subsequent episode of Q remembering E is a genuine state of remembering the past experience E.

4 P's identity with Q depends on a sufficient number of states related to Q's experiences in a way similar to how S and E are related.

5 Identity between P and Q is *presupposed* in the previously stated explanation because the identity between P and Q is what guarantees that S is a genuine state of remembering E.

6 So, memory cannot appear in a non-circular analysis of the concept of personal identity since a genuine occurrence of remembering presupposes personal identity.

This reasoning is grounded on the idea that memory (or a sufficient number of mental states of remembering) must be veridical and/or appropriate to constitute or analyse the relation of personal identity. The point here is that not just any memory properly sustains the relation of personal identity: delusions do not (or should not) constitute personal identity – or, at least, many contemporary philosophers argue so. The appropriateness condition in the previous reasoning can be spelled out as follows: P=Q is a requirement for Q's memory to be one of P's real memories. So, the relation of personal identity sustains proper memory connections and cannot, on pain of circularity, be sustained itself by proper memory connections.

A group of philosophers – Sydney Shoemaker, Derek Parfit, John Perry, and others – have replied to this objection. Now, these philosophers do not believe that (personal) memory is the sole relevant condition of personal identity. In fact, almost all of the psychological accounts of personal identity proposed in the 1960s and '70s included, to various degrees, other psychological features such as character, emotions, desires, and so on, as constitutive components of personal identity. However, many attempts to respond to the circularity objection took personal memory as a starting point, moving on to generalise their results to other psychological states. The most influential among these replies is generally taken to be Shoemaker's formulation of a memory-like mental state, called quasi-memory, a notion that generated a series of important works in various fields, including philosophy of mind and philosophy of language. 'Quasi-memory' is a technical term coined to refer to a theoretical or possible mental state that, as the name itself suggests, is relevantly similar to a state of normal remembering. Shoemaker maintains that, as in normal cases of remembering, quasi-memories are generated by causal connections between the experience of an event and the subsequent memory of such an experience. However, a claim to the effect that P quasi-remembers Q's experience E does not entail that P=Q. In other words, having an appropriate or real quasi-memory does not thereby imply that the remembered past experience was an experience of the same person who subsequently remembers the event. Remembering an experience, even an experience *from the inside* – from a subjective point of view – does not imply that remembering such an experience excludes the possibility that the remembered experience happened to someone else (e.g., the fictional memory agency Rekall in the film *Total Recall*, 1990, sells quasi-memories). A case of remembering that is connected in the appropriate causal way to the episode that would normally generate the memory trace but that does not imply identity between the perceiver and the person who remembers is a case of quasi-memory. If quasi-memories are a real metaphysical or conceptual possibility – at our world and time, all memories and quasi-memories coincide – then a non-circular definition of personal identity in terms of quasi-memory is possible. The definition is non-circular because the appropriateness condition for quasi-memory to constitute personal identity would not be met by saying that this kind of memory involves or presupposes the identity of the person at issue (see point 5 of the previous argument), but would be spelled out in terms of an appropriate causal connection. A quasi-memory can be an appropriate identity-sustaining mental state provided it is in the right causal connection between persons at different times. So, a psychological account of personal identity can be defined in terms of sameness or continuity of quasi-memory without thereby being circular. If the relation of quasi-memory holds for the right reasons – say, because of the right causal connection – between P and Q, then P and Q may be the same person, or, at least, such a quasi-memory connection can be a necessary condition of personal identity. The main point of this reasoning is that the identification of an appropriate member of the set of mental states that constitute personal identity through time does not have to presuppose that such a mental state has been previously had by the same person – which would make the account circular. In fact, we can specify the conditions that a causal connection should satisfy to sustain personal identity non-circularly, e.g., by referring to the causal connections responsible for our brain continuity.

However, things are not so simple. If Q's remembering from the inside P's doing X (or a number of memories or mental states regarded as sufficient to sustain personal identity) does not have as an adequacy condition that P and Q are identical, then a whole series of apparently puzzling scenarios may seem to be conceptually and metaphysically possible. For instance, it may be possible (conceptually and metaphysically) that two individuals existing at the same time, S and Q, may both quasi-remember doing X from the inside, given the appropriate causal connections. Would then P be identical to both Q and S? We can imagine different scenarios involving such a possibility. For example, P may divide or split – for instance, by a surgical intervention to her brain – into two distinct individuals, Q and S, each having an appropriate causal connection with P. Suppose that Q's and S's mental states of quasi-remembering are causally connected with P's past experiences. It seems that, on a simple memory-based psychological theory of personal identity, the relation of personal identity should hold between P and Q, but also between P and S. However, given the transitivity of identity, we should also say that Q and S are the same person, which seems wrong – after all, they are two distinct individuals in different locations each having different streams of consciousness. In the next section, I discuss how some contemporary philosophers have attempted to reply to these and related worries.

5 Contemporary psychological theories

One of the relevant points emerging from the previous discussion is that more criteria should be added to the analysis of personal identity in terms of psychological connections. These further conditions should exclude wrong attributions of personal identity in branching, fission, and reduplication cases. A wrong attribution is generally taken to be an application of a theory of personal identity to a real or imaginary scenario that is in contrast to what we take to be some of the crucial features of the concept of personal identity. In what follows, I first describe these conditions and then introduce a contemporary psychological theory that includes some of them.

5.1 Adequacy conditions for contemporary psychological theories of personal identity

1   **The intrinsic condition or the only-x-and-y principle**: Personal identity between P and Q is an intrinsic relation between P and Q – that is, in determining whether P and Q are the same person, we should take into account only the nature (intended as the sum of the intrinsic properties) of the related entities. In other words, in determining the identity between P and Q, other entities or individuals are not relevant. In the previous chapter, this condition was openly violated by the various relational theories under discussion.

2   **The one-to-one condition**: Personal identity must be a one-to-one relation. This condition seems to follow from the logical properties of the relation of identity, namely, that the formal structure of the relation of identity is that of a one-to-one relation, and is sometimes also called the *uniqueness* condition. Some relate this condition to another condition, called the *non-branching* condition. According to the latter, personal identity cannot take a branching form, i.e., personal identity cannot hold between P and more than one entity at a single later time. It is not clear whether implementing the non-branching condition amounts to a rejection of the only-x-and-y condition (e.g., Shoemaker has recently argued that it doesn't).

3   **The transitivity condition**: Given that personal identity is a transitive relation, a relation in terms of which personal identity can be properly analysed should be transitive as well. An early argument against a memory-based account of personal identity was famously defended by Thomas Reid. In particular, he claimed that Locke's account, understood to be solely in terms of memory connections, which are not transitive – cannot be right because personal identity is transitive.[15] The example Reid used to argue for this is known as the Brave (or Gallant) Officer case:

> Suppose a brave officer to have been flogged when a boy at school, for robbing an orchard, to have taken a standard from the enemy in his first campaign, and to have been made a general in advanced life: Suppose also, which must be admitted to be possible, that when he took the standard, he was conscious of his having been flogged at school, and that when made a general he was conscious of his taking the standard, but had absolutely lost the consciousness of his flogging.
> These things being supposed, it follows, from Mr LOCKE's doctrine, that he who was flogged at school is the same person who took the standard, and that he who took the standard is the same person who was made a general. When it follows, if there be any truth in logic, that the general is the same person with him who was flogged at school. But the general's consciousness does not reach so far back as his flogging, therefore, according to Mr LOCKE's doctrine, he is not the person who was flogged. Therefore the general is, and at the same time is not the same person as him who was flogged at school.[16]

4   The psychological complexity condition: Memory (and its continuity) is not the only relevant mental faculty necessary for being a person or for persisting through time. Other conditions for being a person and for personal identity through time may include the identity or continuity of various psychological aspects of our minds such as character, the connection over time between desires, plans, and action, emotions, and so on.

5   The moral accountability condition: An account of personal identity should: (1) explain, (2) be compatible with, and/or (3) at least provide reasons to revise some of the relevant ascriptions of moral and legal responsibility to agents through time. This requirement was strongly emphasised in Locke's original formulation, but it did not always play a central role in the debate in the '60s and '70s. However, recent practical and narrative approaches seem to emphasise this condition again (see Chapter 6).

6   The reactive attitudes condition: An account of personal identity should (1) explain, (2) be compatible with, or (3) at least provide good reasons to revise our attitudes towards some of our concerns for practical issues that involve our identity through time – for example, our concern for personal survival – and other attitudes such as shame, guilt, and so on. More recently, especially in versions of the psychological theory related to the practical and narrative approaches, such an aspect has been emphasised again. Some Buddhist views seem to prescribe a radical re-description and re-evaluation of such practices.

Not all of these additional conditions have been taken to be desirable or required in a theory of personal identity; in fact, some philosophers have explicitly rejected some of them.

5.2 Parfit's psychological theory of personal identity

Parfit has proposed an influential psychological theory, which nicely summarises part of our previous discussion, in terms of **psychological connectedness** and continuity. First, he defines psychological connectedness as the "holding of particular direct psychological connections" and psychological continuity as the "holding of overlapping chains of strong connectedness." The holding of the relation of connectedness is a matter of degree, and specifying what counts as a sufficient and/or specific degree of connectedness may prove (conceptually) impossible or ill-conceived in certain cases – there can be cases in which it is indeterminate whether personal identity holds. Parfit attempts to make more precise the relevant degree of connectedness by saying that a high degree of connectedness between P and Q occurs in case the psychological connections between P and Q are at least as numerous as half of the psychological connections that hold in the lives of continuous persons in normal cases over every day. Parfit claims that when there are enough – a high degree of – direct connections between two persons at different times, we have a case of strong psychological connectedness. The relation 'strong psychological connection' is not transitive: it may be that, at different times in the life of the same human organism, an infant has a strong psychological connection with an adolescent and that the same adolescent has a strong connection with an adult. However, this adult may not have a strong psychological connection with the infant – or any psychological connection at all. When there are strong over-lapping chains of psychological connections between P and Q, we say that P and Q are psychologically continuous. The relation 'X is psychologically continu-ous with Y' is transitive. In certain passages, Parfit claims that a non-branching relation of psychological continuity is what should analyse the relation of per-sonal identity, although he also claims that psychological connectedness is more important "both in theory and in practice".[17] It is not always clear whether Parfit believes that the causal connection between psychological states is a relation that entirely determines psychological continuity. If this is the case, then psycholog-ical connectedness plays an ancestral or grounding role.[18] Another possibility is that psychological connectedness *and/or* psychological continuity sustain personal identity. For simplicity, let us regard the holding of the relations of psychological connection and/or psychological continuity as the holding of relation R. Now, the account at issue says that personal identity is constituted by relation R, provided that R has a non-branching form.

Some differences among versions of the psychological approach are determined by how we specify the nature of the causal connections sustaining psychological connectedness and/or continuity. For instance, human psychological connectedness may hold because of a *normal* causal chain (i.e., brain-continuity), any *reliable* cause (e.g., a series of integrated and well-functioning neural implants), or *any* cause (e.g., divine interventions or unreliable tele-transportation devices, to the degree that these events can properly involve causation). In his *Reasons and Persons*, Parfit suggests that we do not have to choose among these different versions of the psycho-logical theory and that some cases may even be indeterminate as to whether personal identity holds.[19] Rather, he claims that we better focus on discussing whether the relevant relations that do hold are at least as good as personal identity.[20]

To sum up, two different versions of Parfit's psychological theory – on an under-standing that relation R involves psychological connectedness and/or continuity – can be summarised as follows.

(Normal-cause Parfit's Theory of the Metaphysical Foundation of Personal Identity)

For all t, P at t_1 is the same person as Q at t_2, provided a definition of psychological continuity in terms of overlapping chains of strong psychological connectedness, iff (1) P is psychologically continuous with Q (relation R holds), (2) psychological connectedness and/or psychological continuity have the *normal kind* of causes, and (3) they have not taken a branching form (uniqueness condition).

The wide or any-cause psychological approach can be specified as follows:

(Any-cause Parfit's Theory of the Metaphysical Foundation of Personal Identity)

For all t, P at t_1 is the same person as Q at t_2, provided a definition of psychological continuity in terms of overlapping chains of strong psychological connectedness, iff (1) P is psychologically continuous with Q, (2) psychological connectedness and/or psychological continuity are sustained by *any* cause, and (3) they have not taken a branching form.

An application of the normal-cause theory is the following. Vincenzo goes to bed on the 5th of October 2015 and plans to sell a welding machine the day after. An entity wakes up on the 6th of October and remembers having fixed an appointment to sell a welding machine in a few hours, has a desire to sell a welding machine, and has a series of psychological states relevantly connected – through the normal means of brain continuity – to those experienced by Vincenzo the night of the 5th. The entity (still) named Vincenzo on the 6th has strong and overlapping psychological connections with Vincenzo on the 5th. So, Vincenzo on the 5th is psychologically connected and continuous with Vincenzo on the 6th. Vincenzo on the 6th does not remember what he ate on the 3rd of August 1980. However, there is psychological continuity between, say, Vincenzo on the 3rd of August 1981 and Vincenzo in 1980 – psychological continuity holds because there are strong chains of psychological connections between Vincenzo in 1980 and Vincenzo in 1981. So, Vincenzo in 1981 and Vincenzo in 1980 are the same person. The relation of psychological continuity is similarly sustained over the years by normal means: Vincenzo in 1982 and Vincenzo in 1983 have the same brain. So, although there may not be strong psychological connections between Vincenzo in 1980 and Vincenzo in 2015, they are psychologically continuous in virtue of the various intermediary strong psychological connections over the days and years. So, Vincenzo in 1980 is the same person as Vincenzo in 2015. On Parfit's theory, this situation is a case of normal, non-branching psychological continuity, a case in which personal identity through time holds.

   The previous theories can meet Berkeley's and Reid's transitivity objection: although the general of the story does not remember the boy, the officer remembers the boy, so it is likely that the boy and the officer are psychologically connected and/ or continuous. The general is sufficiently psychologically connected to the officer; hence, they are continuous. So, the general and the boy are psychologically continuous, although not connected. In addition, for this reply to work, personal identity should consist in/be constituted by (or be) a non-branching causally appropriate psychological continuity relation. Other versions of Parfit's theory can be formulated by modifying the relevant form of causal relations that sustain relation R – which in turn can be understood in different ways depending on how psychological continuity and connectedness are supposed to be structured. Psychological theories of personal identity that do not specify or impose particular structural constraints on the psychological connections that sustain personal identity (e.g., whether certain psychological connections should be organised amongst themselves to form a narrative structure) are classified as *generic*.

   Parfit characterises his theory (at least in one edition of his *Reasons and Persons*) as a form of reductionism, where a theory is reductionist in case it satisfies these requirements: (1) the primitive facts upon which the relation of personal identity holds can be described in an impersonal way (this condition is discarded in a later paper); and (2) a person's identity over time does not consist in the holding of facts more primitive than those specified in (1); (3) a person's existence consists solely in the existence of relevant bodily parts (a brain or even the whole body) and in the occurrence of various physical and mental states.[21] Parfit seems to take (3) as the core of his theory *qua* reductionist. According to Parfit, a description of R does not require also reference to an independently existing owner of such mental states that is identical at different times for such a description to be a useful or complete analysis of personal identity.

Many of the other contemporary generic psychological theories seem to be terminological or minor variations of the views we have just explored, for instance, the best-candidate or closer-continuer view defended by Robert Nozick. (Some of their differences do not seem to be differences in their metaphysical principles.) The characterising idea of this theory is that the relation of personal identity is such that it holds between a person at t_1 and the best candidate to its succession as a person at t_2. So, in cases of branching, fission, or other problematic scenarios, being the best candidate may amount to having the strongest and most numerous memory or psychological connections with the original person – specific versions of the theory may apply different criteria to determine what counts as the best candidate. If the specifications of what constitutes the best candidate are equally met by two (or more) different individuals, then there is a tie and neither is identical to the earlier person. So, according to this theory, questions of personal identity may admit of indeterminate answers. Nozick holds that personal identity is a one-to-one relation and that it may not be always determined whether such a relation holds in so-called borderline cases. In addition, this theory seems to reject the idea that personal identity is an intrinsic relation between only two individuals – the rejection of such a principle is explicit in Nozick's view. On Parfit's view, the condition that the relation of personal identity holds only in case it does not have a branching form may be taken to rely on the idea that if there is more than one entity to which the original person is psychologically connected and/or continuous in the right way then it may be indeterminate whether personal identity holds or not. In other words, the holding of the relation of personal identity between P and Q at t_1 is also determined by the relation between P and R at t_1, where Q and R are distinct individuals at t_1.[22] So, whether personal identity holds between P and Q depends also on the relation between P and R at the same time, hence personal identity between P and Q, two persons existing at different times, may hold also in virtue of features extrinsic to P and Q. While some may claim that this dependence on extrinsic features is a problem (Bernard Williams), others may even welcome it.

The psychological approach is connected with the relational approach, e.g., Locke explicitly claims that 'person' is a forensic term, and being forensic, I assume, involves relationality. Being responsible for actions – also in courts of law – and, by extension, being the proper object of certain reactive attitudes implies, for at least some of these attitudes, being a relational entity. Criticisms against some aspects of the psychological approach are explored in detail in the next chapter – in particular, the reduplication argument and the arguments that animalists have proposed against the view that we are essentially persons. The practical and narrative approaches discussed in Chapter 6 are presented as attempts to improve on generic versions of the psychological approach – that is, as improvements on psychological theories that do not specify or include conditions on the internal structure of the relevant psychological connections. Whether these practical and narrative theories are really improvements is a matter of dispute.

6 Summary

Locke's psychological theory of personal identity has played a pivotal role in the debate on personal identity – and this explains the long discussion of his views in this chapter. He offered an account of the concepts (or ideas) of identity and of personal identity based on a general theory of the identity conditions of individuals (or, at least, of the ideas we use to think about them). According to Locke, the conditions of identity of individuals are determined by the kind to which they belong. In particular, he claims that, since the idea of a human being, understood as a biological kind, and that of a person are different, the identity conditions of human beings are different from the identity conditions of persons. Since we are essentially persons (person essentialism), we are not merely human beings but persons. The exact interpretation of Locke's general principle of identity is disputed in the current literature. However, beyond dispute is that Locke makes one important distinction between the idea of a soul and that of a person; in particular, he claims that, for all we know about souls – that is, given the way we employ this idea – there are conceivable situations or thought experiments in which souls and persons are not things of the same kind (if they are things at all). The consequence of Locke's distinction between the two ideas – 'person' and 'soul' – is that his account of personal identity does not rely on sameness of soul. In fact, since persons are essentially conscious agents, personal identity is sustained by sameness of consciousness, which is independent from sameness of soul. Unfortunately, it is not clear how we should understand Locke's notion of consciousness. For example, some have taken Locke as claiming that sameness of consciousness amounts to sameness of memory – and various interpretations have been offered of this last claim as well. This understanding, however, has been disputed by some contemporary Locke scholars who have proposed alternative interpretations, for instance, in terms of reflection and of self-awareness. As a consequence, there are different and contrasting more precise formulations of Locke's theory of personal identity depending on how we understand the key notion of consciousness. Regarding our nature, many ascribe to Locke the view that we are essentially persons and that persons are capable of self-concern and moral agency.

Contemporary psychological accounts of personal identity derive in part from an attempt to answer certain objections against an interpretation of Locke's theory in terms of memory (that is, the interpretation according to which, on Locke's view, consciousness is memory). In particular, Shoemaker and Parfit (among many others) have proposed psychological theories of personal identity that are capable of replying to various versions of the circularity and of the transitivity objections by employing the notion of quasi-memory. In the rest of the chapter, I analysed a series of principles and criteria that an adequate psychological theory of personal identity is supposed to satisfy (5.1) and an introduction to Parfit's psychological theory of personal identity (5.2). According to one version of Parfit's account – in his *Reasons and Persons*, he outlines different versions of the psychological approach – personal identity holds over time iff strong psychological connectedness and/or psychological continuity hold, provided that they do not take a branching form, at least over the span of time under consideration. Different formulations of his psychological account depend on the way in which we think that psychological connections should hold. For instance, we may believe that, in order to sustain personal identity, psychological connections should hold in virtue of their normal causes (i.e., because we have the same brain over time).

Some of the main contemporary objections to the psychological approach are discussed in the next chapters. In particular, the previous (generic) psychological theories of personal identity do not further specify whether the relevant identity-sustaining psychological connections should also assume a particular structure. In fact, these theories are frequently spelled out solely in terms of the required approximate number of connections over time. Practical and narrative theories discussed in Chapter 6 can be understood as criticising such generic psychological theories and as attempts to specify these non-qualitative versions of the psychological approach – that is, as attempts to clarify in more detail the form that the psychological connections should have to sustain personal identity over time.

Notes

1 This rich intellectual landscape is masterfully charted in Thiel (2011).
2 It has to be remembered that Locke rejects substantial forms and also the possibility of human knowledge of the real essences of substances.
3 See Gordon-Roth (2015a) for a recent survey and a list of references.
4 Gallois (2017), pp. 31–37.
5 See Galen Strawson, *Locke on Personal Identity* (Princeton: Princeton University Press, 2011), Appendix 1 for a translation of Locke's text into modern English.
6 Lolordo (2010) and (2012: 74–82).
7 This does not mean that, e.g., mixed modes are arbitrary. In fact, not every composition of simple ideas is equally useful for our practical concerns.
8 See Chappell (1989).
9 See Weinberg (2011), Lolordo (2010), and Gordon-Roth (2015a), (2015b).
10 See Stuart (2013), Chapter 8 for a defense of the attribution to Locke of one version of the memory view.
11 Richard Sorabji claims that there is a connection between Locke's and the Stoics' notions of appropriation. See Thiel (2011), pp. 99–100 for discussion. Lolordo emphasises the constitutive aspect of appropriation in her interpretation of Locke's theory of personal identity.
12 The term 'reactive attitudes' comes from Strawson (1962). The term was originally intended to refer to those attitudes we express when we hold persons morally responsible. However, I use it more broadly to refer to all those attitudes we express in practical dealings with other people (e.g., resentment, love, gratitude, forgiveness, anger, etc.).

13 If the *analysans*, the concept or notion that is supposed to do the analysing, presupposes or contains the *analysandum*, the concept or notion that is supposed to be analysed or defined, then we have not found an analysis that reduces (conceptually or metaphysically) the *analysandum* to something that does not contain reference to it.

14 This version of the objection is discussed in Slors (2001).

15 George Berkeley in his *Alciphron*, which was published before Reid's discussion, advanced a relevantly similar objection. See Thiel (2011), p. 211 for discussion.

16 See Reid's *Essays on the Intellectual Powers of Man*, Essay 3, Chapter 6.

17 Parfit (1984/6/7), p. 206.

18 Paul Grice had already proposed a similar weakened memory condition in the '40s.

19 In a note added to the 1986-edition of *Reasons and Persons*, Parfit claims that he has withdrawn his support for the Wide Psychological Criteria of personal identity (one version of the theory according to which psychological connections and/or continuity may be determined by any cause). There are three editions of *Reasons and Persons* (1984, 1986, and 1987), each containing slight variations on the formulations of the psychological criteria.

20 See Chapter 7 for further discussion on the consequences of this point for the evaluation of claims regarding what matters in survival.

21 See Parfit (1999).

22 See Shoemaker (2004) for discussion.

Suggested further readings

General introductions to Locke

Ayers, Michael, *Locke. Epistemology and Ontology* (London and New York: Routledge, 1991).

Barresi, John and Raymond Martin, *Naturalization of the Soul* (London and New York: Routledge, 2000).

Chappell, Vere, *The Cambridge Companion to Locke* (Cambridge: Cambridge University Press, 1994).

Mackie, John L., *Problems From Locke* (Oxford: Clarendon, 1976).

Thiel, Udo, *The Early Modern Subject* (Oxford: Oxford University Press, 2011).

Uzgalis, William, 'John Locke', in *Stanford Encyclopedia of Philosophy* (2012). http://plato.stanford.edu/entries/locke/

Locke on identity and ontology

Primary sources

Locke, John, *An Essay Concerning Human Understanding,* edited by Peter H. Nidditch (Oxford: Clarendon Press, 1975/1694).

Perry, John (ed.) *Personal Identity* (Berkeley, CA: University of California Press, 1976) for Reid's and Butler's criticisms.

Strawson, Galen, *Locke on Personal Identity* (Princeton: Princeton University Press, 2011), Appendix 1 ('Of Identity and Diversity' by John Locke) and Appendix 2 ('A Defence of Mr. Locke's Opinion Concerning Personal Identity' by Edmund Law).

Secondary literature

Atherton, Margaret, 'Locke's Theory of Personal Identity', *Midwest Studies in Philosophy*, 8, 1 (1983), pp. 273–293.

Bolton, Martha, 'Substances, Substrata, and Names of Substances in Locke's Essay', *Philosophical Review*, 85 (1976), pp. 488–513.

Chappell, Vere, 'Locke and Relative Identity', *History of Philosophy Quarterly*, 6, 1 (1989), pp. 69–83.

Flew, Antony, 'Locke and the Problem of Personal Identity', *Philosophy* 26, 96 (1951), pp. 53–68.

Gallois, André, *The Metaphysics of Identity* (London and New York: Routledge, 2017).

Gordon-Roth, Jessica, 'Locke's Place-Time-Kind Principle', *Philosophy Compass*, 10, 4 (2015a), pp. 264–274.

Gordon-Roth, Jessica, 'Locke on the Ontology of Persons', *The Southern Journal of Philosophy*, 53, 1 (2015b), pp. 97–123.

Lolordo, Antonia, 'Person, Substance, Mode and "the moral Man" in Locke's Philosophy', *Canadian Journal of Philosophy*, 40, 4 (2010), pp. 643–668.

Lolordo, Antonia, *Locke's Moral Man* (Oxford: Oxford University Press, 2012).

Noonan, Harold, *Personal Identity, 2nd Edition* (London and New York: Routledge, 2003), Chapter 2.

Stuart, Matthew, *Locke's Metaphysics* (Oxford: Oxford University Press, 2013).

Uzgalis, William, 'Relative Identity and Locke's Principle of Individuation', *History of Philosophy Quarterly*, 7, 3 (1990), pp. 283–297.

Yaffe, Gideon, 'Locke on Ideas of Identity and Diversity', in Lee Newman (ed.) *The Cambridge Companion to Locke's "Essay Concerning Human Understanding"* (Cambridge: Cambridge University Press, 2007), pp. 192–230.

Locke and consciousness

Kriegel, Uriah and Angela Coventry, 'Locke on Consciousness', *History of Philosophy Quarterly*, 25 (2008), pp. 221–242.

Scharp, Kevin, 'Locke's Theory of Reflection', *British Journal for the History of Philosophy*, 16 (2008), pp. 25–63.

Weinberg, Shelley, 'Locke on Personal Identity', *Philosophy Compass*, 6, 6 (2011), pp. 398–407.

Weinberg, Shelley, *Consciousness in Locke* (Oxford: Oxford University Press, 2016).

Winkler, Kenneth, 'Locke on Personal Identity', *Journal of the History of Philosophy*, 29 (1991), pp. 201–226.

Circularity objection and quasi-memory

Butler, Joseph, 'Of Personal Identity', in Joseph Butler (ed.) *Analogy of Religion, Natural and Revealed, to the Constitution and Nature* (London: Knapton, 1736).

McDowell, John, 'Reductionism and the First-Person', in Jonathan Dancy (ed.) *Reading Parfit* (Oxford: Blackwell, 1997).

Northoff, Georg, 'Are 'Q-Memories' Empirically Realistic? A Neurophilosophical Approach', *Philosophical Psychology*, 13, 2 (2000), pp. 191–211.

Shoemaker, Sydney, 'Persons and Their Past', *American Philosophical Quarterly*, 7 (1970), pp. 269–285.

Slors, Marc, 'Personal Identity, Memory, and Circularity', *The Journal of Philosophy*, 98, 4 (2001), pp. 186–214.

Strawson, Peter, 'Freedom and Resentment', *Proceedings of the British Academy*, 48 (1962), pp. 1–25.

Parfit's and other psychological theories

Grice, Paul, 'Personal Identity', *Mind*, 50 (1941), pp. 330–350.

Nozick, Robert, *Philosophical Explanations* (Oxford: Clarendon Press, 1981).

Parfit, Derek, *Reasons and Persons* (Oxford: Clarendon Press, 1984/86/87).

Parfit, Derek, 'Experiences, Subjects, and Conceptual Schemes', *Philosophical Topics*, 26, 1 (1999), pp. 217–270.

Shoemaker, Sydney, *Identity, Cause, and Mind: Philosophical Essays, Expanded Edition* (Cambridge: Cambridge University Press, 2003).

Shoemaker, Sydney, 'Brown-Brownson Revisited', *The Monist*, 87, 4 (2004), pp. 573–593.

Shoemaker, Sydney and Richard Swinburne, *Personal Identity* (Oxford: Blackwell, 1984).

Sidelle, Alan, 'Parfit on "the Normal/a Reliable/Any Cause" of Relation R', *Mind*, 120, 479 (2011), pp. 735–760.

5 The physical approach and animalism

1	Stoic body, Christian sin, and resurrection	124
2	The varieties of physical continuity	128
3	Thought experiments and Bernard Williams's reduplication argument	131
4	Our physical nature: animalism	135
5	The thinking animal argument, the embodied mind view, and constitutionalism	137
	5.1 The embodied mind view and constitutionalism	139
6	Summary	140

If the dead are not raised, "Let us eat and drink, for tomorrow we die."

—1 Corinthians, 15:32

Various thought experiments involving brain transplants, reduplications of persons, and other bizarre scenarios have played a crucial role in shaping the debate on personal identity and our nature. Although several philosophers have vigorously challenged a perhaps excessive emphasis put on the theoretical value of the intuitions deriving from some of the most abstruse scenarios, it is undeniable that imaginary cases have inspired interesting theories and objections. In general, theories of personal identity and of our own nature that involve reference to material, bodily, or organic continuity will be here understood as including different forms of *physical* criteria. Bernard Williams (1929–2003) argued that, although some thought experiments can be used to support certain versions of the psychological approach to personal identity, other thought experiments (or even the same, just carefully re-phrased) can be devised to support the view that bodily, causal, or other forms of spatio-temporal connections provide a necessary condition for personal identity through time. These ideas have a long history. In fact, debates about the importance of a form of physical continuity for personal identity go back at least as far as early discussions by Christian thinkers on how to make sense of their belief in the resurrection of the dead. More specifically, these philosophers discussed questions regarding, e.g., how one individual who dies can return to life and still be the same person.

In the first section of this chapter, I describe the Stoic conception of what a body is and how some early Christian philosophers implemented such a view into their discussions of personal resurrection. The main reason for exploring these debates is to extrapolate the implied beliefs regarding the connection between physical continuity and personal identity over time. In the second section, I discuss several ways to make more precise the intuition that physical continuity is a necessary condition for personal identity and ways to extend this condition to theories that refer to physical criteria as also sufficient conditions for personal identity. In the third section, I focus on a series of arguments based on a thought experiment – the reduplication scenario – devised to support the view that physical continuity is at least a necessary condition for personal identity. Theories about personal identity claiming that only physical continuity, where such a continuity does not involve any reference to psychological criteria, is both a necessary *and* sufficient condition for an entity to be the same *person* through time do not seem to be popular nowadays, so I do not discuss them extensively.[1]

A more promising theory that involves physical continuity – in particular, the continuity of a human organism – has recently been developed as an account of our own nature, that is, about what we are. According to this theory, called 'animalism', physical criteria do not provide necessary and sufficient conditions of synchronic and/or diachronic identity for *persons*, but only for *us*, i.e., for the entities we are. According to animalism, we are human animals, hence, given an understanding of the kind 'human animal' in terms of 'human organism', our identity conditions are those of human organisms – some also add the identity conditions of *living* human organisms. A stronger version of animalism holds that we are *essentially* animals, that is, we are animals and we cannot but be animals, that is (living) human organisms. An animalist would generally hold that being a person is not essential to us: the conditions of identity of a human animal and the identity conditions of a person, depending on how they are specified, may not coincide – and, at least according to Locke, they do not coincide. In this context, I discuss the brain-transplant thought experiment, along with a prominent argument in favour of animalism – i.e., **the thinking animal argument**. In the final sub-section of this chapter, I introduce two different theories of our own nature, the **embodied mind** or part view, as defended by Jeff McMahan and Derek Parfit, and one version of the constitutional view (Sydney Shoemaker's).

1 Stoic body, Christian sin, and resurrection

According to the early Stoic Chrysippus, the human soul is corporeal and its functioning is divided into eight faculties.[2] These faculties include the five senses, the power of reproduction, the power of speech, and the *hēgemonikon* – the part that rules. Chrysippus claims that the substance of the soul is corporeal or material, albeit of a particularly thin and rarefied kind. In addition, he argues that the human soul is spread throughout the body, and the seat of the ruling part is in the chest or heart, the place where we feel emotions. Anthony Long maintains that the early

Stoics understood the nature of human beings as that of entities composed of body and (material) soul – a materialist compound theory of our nature.

The Stoics distinguish various types of bodies: bodies composed of separated parts (a team), bodies composed of contiguous parts (a house), unified bodies (stones or logs) and bodies that grow together (organisms). The unity of this last type of bodies is given by the soul. Christopher Gill uses the label 'psychophysical holism' to characterise the Stoic view, partly because of the Stoic belief in the strict cohesion and interdependence between soul and body. In fact, there is a sense in which the soul was taken to have a structuring role in the unity of the body: certain bodies would not be unified and (metaphysically) identifiable objects without a soul. According to the Stoics, proper names such as 'Socrates' stand for a composite of *sōma* (body) and *psuchê* – on this view, Socrates, the person, is an ensouled, rational, mortal body. The flesh-and-bone body becomes self-moving and sentient when it is conjoined to the corporeal soul. The material soul is literally contained in the flesh-and-bone body, where the latter provides the former with those organs essential to sentience and movement. On this view, we are a compound of two corporeal substances, blended together. A soul is not just an organ of the flesh-and-bone body because all bodily organs exist before the soul comes into being. The Stoics also have a semi-scientific explanation of how the soul is transmitted through the semen and, although the details of such an explanation do not directly concern us here, it is important to notice that they attempted to provide an empirical explanation in support of their claims. In addition, the material soul is frequently characterised as divine and as pervading other parts of the universe – this could be a feature that made the Stoic view appealing to certain Christian thinkers. God, which is sometimes described as *pneuma* ('intelligent breath') or the divine that pervades the universe, is characterised also as being crucial for the (metaphysical) individuation of even a stone: the divine soul, in pervading the material world, provides its various parts with the possibility of being individuated (metaphysically) or distinguished as independent entities.

The idea of a corporeal or material soul has been employed also by some Christian thinkers to argue in favour of specific conceptions of personal resurrection. Even though their discussions may appear relevant only to those who believe in their religious world-views, specific conceptions of what is essential for personal resurrection, along with the reasons given to believe such conceptions, may reveal more general ideas concerning what is necessary for a person to persist through time and for what matters in our survival (more on this in Chapter 7). 'Personal resurrection' stands here for an event in which a person is resurrected after her death and in which such a person is the same person that died at an earlier pre-resurrection time. Now, by specifying what is taken to be necessary for personal resurrection to happen, we can evaluate the reasons given to believe specific views on what matters for personal continuity and survival more generally, even in contexts in which divine interventions or resurrections are not at issue. After all, personal resurrection is one way of surviving, i.e., of persisting over time. A further point is that this discussion does not have to be framed in terms of 'persons'. So, although I assume one form of person essentialism – the view that we are essentially persons – in presenting most of the debates on the possibility of resurrection, the whole discussion can be re-phrased as an enquiry about how *we* can be resurrected – that is, as a discussion involving us, and thus not necessarily *persons*.

One of the oldest Christian metaphors used to illustrate personal resurrection is that of the seed, as in St. Paul's 1 *Corinthians* 15 (53–54 CE):

> But someone will ask, "How are the dead raised? With what kind of body will they come?" 36 How foolish! What you sow does not come to life unless it dies. 37 When you sow, you do not plant the body that will be, but just a seed, perhaps of wheat or of something else.

> [. . .]

> So will it be with the resurrection of the dead. The body that is sown is perishable, it is raised imperishable; 43 it is sown in dishonour, it is raised in glory; it is sown in weakness, it is raised in power; 44 it is sown a natural body, it is raised a spiritual body.

Some philosophical presuppositions required to make sense of the previous passages include the idea that the identity of a person (or of something like us) through resurrection is secured also by a physical or corporeal causal chain. In particular, the passage suggests that when we die our bodies 'leave a seed' or trace that will grow into a new imperishable body. Although it is not explicitly stated, we may argue that personal resurrection consists also in – or is explained also in terms of – the existence of a new spiritual body growing from the seed or trace left behind by a mortal body. If the metaphor is understood literally, the idea is that it is not necessary that a complete and functioning body, intended as a functioning organism, be required to persist through time for personal resurrection; a chain of relevant causal continuity, a kind of continuity provided by the seed (or physical trace), suffices. It is not here specified whether psychological continuity is also a requirement for persisting through time.

The Medieval scholar Caroline Walker Bynum has persuasively argued that in many writings in the early Christian tradition the resurrection of the body was seen as a necessary condition for personal resurrection. Such a belief was also sometimes coupled with various descriptions of an earthly paradise, a kind of Heaven the full enjoyment of which requires physicality. Bynum maintains that even during the high Middle Ages – when greater emphasis was put on the psychological or rational aspects of our souls – bodily or causal continuity was still taken by many Christian thinkers to be essential to personal resurrection. Again, the main presupposition here seems to be that some form of physical continuity is necessary for our identity through time, whether as persons or simply as individuals. One of the first early Christian apologists who discussed the importance of material continuity in resurrection was Justin Martyr (100–165 CE). According to him, God collects our dispersed bits at the moment of death and subsequently reassembles them. A possible problem for this view is that some of the parts that compose us at the moment of our death may subsequently end up composing other animals. For instance, sometimes human corpses are eaten by scavengers, which in turn are eaten by other organisms. So, certain bits of matter, which previously formed a human body, may become parts of other animals. It is not clear what would happen to us or to these animals at the moment of resurrection. Apologists such as Athenagoras (133–190 CE) claim that God is so powerful that He can still trace back the original bits of matter that composed the original human body and reassemble them at the moment of resurrection. However, human beings may (and do) eat other human beings (or, for what matters, animals that ate human beings). Some episodes of cannibalism would thus make it difficult, even for God, to reassemble everybody at the moment of resurrection, at least in those cases in which the parts that composed a human being at a specific time later become parts of another dying human being. For example, a cannibal may die after having and/or after having assimilated a human meal (or part of it). As a consequence, it seems that, when the time comes, one of the two resurrected individuals will not have at least some of the parts that composed her at the moment of their respective deaths. Athenagoras's (implausible) reply is that human flesh cannot be properly absorbed and thus cannot become part of other human beings.

Another early Christian apologist, Tertullian (c. 160–230), combined Stoic ideas with Christian scripture to provide an account of personal resurrection. In particular, in his *A Treatise on the Soul*, Tertullian claims that the soul is material, although apparently of a substance different from that of the body. More precisely, Tertullian claims that, if there were immaterial substances, they would not be capable of interacting with corporeal substances since these two kinds of substance belong to two radically different categories of being. However, the soul interacts with the body; for example, it shares the body's pain and other sensations. So, since the body is material and given that several interactions between body and soul occur, the soul must be corporeal too. (This argument had already been proposed by the Stoics.) Tertullian uses other Stoic arguments to support the same conclusion. In particular, he argues that, given that the soul is what originates motion in the body, and since this 'spring of action' is received by the body, the soul must be of a nature such that an interaction with the body must be possible. Thus, Tertullian (and the Stoics) concludes, the soul is corporeal. According to him, the soul is a simple substance spread throughout the body the natural function of which is (the generation of) the mind. Since the soul is simple, Tertullian claims that it is immortal as well.

Tertullian believed that, although some philosophical arguments can be given to believe certain views about the nature of the soul, all we need to discover the truth about these matters is already contained in the Christian scriptures. In fact, Tertullian maintains that the Gospels provide ample evidence for believing in the corporeal nature of the soul. He makes his point by discussing an unpleasant example: the torments of hell. In particular, Tertullian reminds us of the physical nature of some of the torments inflicted upon an unrepentant sinner's soul – burning or suffering from excruciating thirst for eternity. Such torments have a peculiar physical nature, so the substance to which they are inflicted has to be of a corporeal or physical nature. In conclusion, Tertullian seems to believe that (1) punishment requires personal identity through time; (2) the kind of punishment described in the Bible involves suffering; more specifically, physical pain inflicted to the body that sinned. One of the main general philosophical points of this discussion is that Tertullian, perhaps implicitly, seems to hold that moral responsibility is based on or is essentially related to the identity through time of the sinner. In turn, such an identification presupposes at least a causal connection between the body that sinned, which provides the seed, and the resurrected one.

2 The varieties of physical continuity

Taking the notions of personal resurrection and responsibility as necessarily involving bodily continuity seems to presuppose that (1) the correct application of the two concepts – personal resurrection and responsibility – to two individuals at different times requires that the relation of personal identity hold between these two persons; and (2) bodily or causal continuity is at least a necessary condition for personal identity. An objection to this line of reasoning is that it excludes *a priori* the possibility that persons without physical properties may persist through time, since they cannot meet the requirement of having the same body at different times. While this may not be taken as problematic – for instance, by those who claim that everything is physical or corporeal – it may become less appealing depending on how the nature of this physical continuity is specified. In particular, if we understand the relevant notion of physical continuity solely in terms of the continuity of a biological organism, then we are excluding the conceptual and metaphysical possibility of non-organic persons persisting through time as persons. Again, this may not be a particularly troubling objection, but if the possibility of non-organic persons, e.g., intelligent robots or cyborgs, is to be acknowledged, then the following discussion should be understood as restricted only to certain kinds of entities, that is, *human* persons, not to persons in general. In other words, we may claim that, when the conditions of personhood are satisfied by an entity that is also a human being, then certain forms of physical continuity are necessary for the persistence through time of this entity *as a human person*.

The nature of the relationship between physical continuity and personal identity can be made more precise in different ways. First of all, criteria involving physical continuity may either prescribe necessary or necessary *and* sufficient conditions for our identity through time (as persons). Some of these conditions are formulated here only as prescribing a necessary condition on personal identity, but they can be easily modified so as to provide also sufficient conditions.

- Material continuity condition: for all t, a necessary condition for P at t_1 to be the same person as Q at t_2 is that Q at t_2 be composed of the same material/matter P is/was composed of at t_1.
- Bodily continuity condition: for all t, a necessary condition for P at t_1 to be the same person as Q at t_2 is that Q's body at t_2 be the same body as P's body at t_1.

- Living **organic (or biological) continuity condition#1**: for all t, a necessary condition for P at t_1 to be the same person/individual as Q at t_2 is that Q's organism at t_2 be part of the same life in which P's organism is/was partaking at t_1.

Instead of using the expression 'P's organism', the previous condition may also be spelled out as:

- Living organic (or biological) continuity condition#2: for all t, a necessary condition for organism P at t_1 to be the same person/individual as organism Q at t_2 is that the activities of organism Q at t_2 be part of the same life in which the activities of organism P was partaking at t_1.

Both versions of the living organic continuity condition can be further articulated depending on how the notions of an organism and of a life are understood. The problem (if it is a problem) is that these notions have been debated in recent philosophy of biology and how they should be defined is controversial.[3] Nonetheless, organisms are generally taken to have at least these features:[4]

- A dynamic stability, i.e., organisms tend to maintain the same form and structure through continuous exchange of material.
- The proper parts of an organism are organised in an internal teleological manner.
- The internal structure of an organism is regulated by a complex set of basic operating instructions.

A life is the life of an organism in case its proper parts take part in the same dynamic, teleological, and self-directing biological system. Following Peter van Inwagen, these last conditions can be further elaborated as follows. If the activities of Xs (the parts of an organism) at t_1 constitute/compose/result from a life, and the activities of Ys (the parts of an organism) at t_2 constitute/compose/result from a life, then the organism composed of Xs at t_1 and the organism composed of Ys at t_2 are the same organism if and only if the activities of the Xs at t_1 and the activities of the Ys at t_2 constitute/compose/result from the same life.[5] In other words, an organism remains the same through time if and only if its parts constitute/compose/result from the same life. Based on these considerations, we can formulate the following criterion of diachronic identity for organisms:

- Criterion of diachronic identity for organisms: for all t, an organism P at t_1 is the same organism Q at t_2 iff the parts/activities of organism Q at t_2 and the parts/activities of organism P at t_1 constitute/compose/result from the same life.

The stated criterion encapsulates the idea that an organism persists through time if and only if its parts or activities belong to the same life. Some philosophers disagree with criteria that involve the notion of a life because these criteria imply that when an organism dies – i.e., when its parts or activities are no more partaking in the same life – a person/individual ceases to exist. According to these philosophers, the problem is that an organism can persist through time even after its parts are no more alive, e.g., as a corpse. We will discuss this idea in relation to animalism.

In addition to the previous criticism, certain philosophers have also noticed that not all of the proper parts of an organism are necessary for the continuity of organisms and/or persons through time. In particular, some have claimed that what is necessary (and sufficient) for the persistence through time of (living) human organisms and/or persons is just one organ: a functioning brain (or some of its relevant parts). This idea, in turn, can be clarified in different ways:

- **Whole-brain condition**: for all t, a necessary condition for P at t_1 to be the same person/organism as Q at t_2 is that Q's whole-brain body at t_2 be part of the same brain-life in which P's whole-brain is/was partaking at t_1.
- **Brain-part condition**: for all t, a necessary condition for P at t_1 to be the same person/organism as Q at t_2 is that the relevant parts of Q's brain responsible for some relevant higher forms of cognition (awareness, character, planning, etc.) at t_2 be part of the same brain-life in which the relevant part of P's brain is/was partaking at t_1.

The brain-part condition is generally considered a more appropriate addition to the identity conditions of persons than the whole-brain condition. The main reason is that the considerations that may justify a preference for the persistence of only certain parts of a human organism – in this case, its higher or upper brain – seem to justify the brain-part condition rather than the other. More precisely, since what may motivate choosing the brain as the relevant organ for the continuity of a person/individual is generally related to its capacity to sustain consciousness (or other higher cognitive faculties), and since only the higher brain (or cortex) seems to be directly (although not exclusively) responsible for our consciousness (or other higher cognitive faculties), many philosophers think that only certain parts of the brain are necessary for personal identity.[6] So, the brain-part condition is to be preferred to the whole-brain condition.

The criterion of diachronic identity for organisms outlined previously does not as yet specify in detail what it takes for a life to persist through time. In some discussions on the continuity of human organisms, it is presupposed that the continuity of the brainstem (not the higher brain or cortex) is a necessary condition for the continuous unitary activity of the relevant human organism and thus a necessary condition for sameness of human life. The main reason behind this view is that the brainstem was taken to be essential to the functioning of those systems that keep the human organism alive (e.g., those systems responsible for our thermal regulation, etc.). However, the importance of the brainstem for the continuous functioning of human organisms has been recently disputed. For example, Alan Shewmon has documented various cases in which the teleological unity of several human organisms – and thus their persistence through time as human lives – was not decisively hindered by the destruction of their brains.[7] Further details are discussed in Chapter 8, but for the moment I assume that the previously stated criterion for the continuity of living human organisms in terms of continuity of life is sufficiently clear for the purposes of this chapter.[8]

An important point to keep in mind is that, although the previous conditions can certainly be modified so as to specify necessary *and* sufficient conditions for the continuity of persons as persons, the view that criteria of diachronic personhood rely solely on physical criteria is not popular in the current debate. In other words, not many contemporary philosophers believe that an entity that is a person at t_1 would still be the same person at a later time t_2 iff solely physical and non-mental criteria were met – even if these requirements were intended to apply only to human persons. On the other hand, views according to which some form of physical continuity is a necessary condition for personal identity are more popular. Theories to the effect that our identity conditions as individuals, as the entities we are, may involve only physical criteria have found a surge of supporters in the recent 20 to 30 years. In particular, many have claimed that, although we are now human persons, we are entities the persistence conditions of which may differ from the persistence conditions of persons. More specifically, recent views on our nature have questioned some of the implicit assumptions made by some psychological theories of personal identity in regard to our own nature. As discussed in the previous chapter, psychological theories of personal identity tend to assume person essentialism, the thesis according to which we are essentially persons, and psychological essentialism, the thesis according to which we are essentially psychological/mental entities. These claims are questioned by certain forms of animalism, the view according to which we are animals (sections 4 and 5). Before discussing animalism, I present one argument that is supposed to show that physical continuity is at least a necessary condition for personal identity: Williams's reduplication argument.

3 Thought experiments and Bernard Williams's reduplication argument

As explained in the introduction to this book (in section 5.1), a basic reduplication scenario includes three individuals – one existing at t_1 and two at a later time t_2 – connected by a relation R such that, if only one among the two later individuals existed, one theory of personal identity – in our case, a generic psychological theory – would entail that at t_2 such an individual is metaphysically identical with the earlier individual.[9] In the history of the debate, different versions of the reduplication thought experiment have been proposed, some of which explicitly devised to argue against generic psychological theories that do not include any form of physical continuity as a necessary condition for personal identity through time.[10] In this section, I focus on a seminal paper on the topic (published in 1956), in which Williams defends the idea that bodily identity (or continuity) is a necessary condition of personal identity by using another version of the reduplication argument.[11] The precise nature of this physical condition is not specified, although Williams holds that it should involve some form of spatio-temporal continuity. The critical targets of the argument are those psychological theories that include only continuity of psychological states and their contents (memories, beliefs, intentions, etc.) as a necessary and sufficient condition for personal identity, where such mental states are metaphysically individuated independently of physical matter and/or spatio-temporal location.

Williams's strategy is to present a series of scenarios and then ask which concepts should be used to describe each situation. The first scenario involves a case of radical change of personality. Imagine that one person, call him Charles, wakes up and claims to have witnessed a series of events that were not known to him the night before. How should we describe this case and verify Charles's claims? Williams maintains that, in order to assess the normal functioning of the mental operations of remembering, we should include considerations related to physical or causal continuity. To make a case in favour of this point, Williams proposes a second scenario. Imagine that this time Charles claims to remember a series of events that coincide with someone else's life, say, Guy Fawkes. Williams holds that, if we apply to this case (one interpretation of) Locke's theory of personal identity then we would have to say that Charles is the same person as Guy Fawkes. However, Williams maintains that we should choose a different description: we should say that Charles has become a person *like* – that is, *similar* to – the late Guy Fawkes. In other words, Charles is not numerically identical to Guy Fawkes; rather, Charles is simply a person that is similar to Guy Fawkes. What follows is a slightly modified version of my reconstruction of Williams's reduplication argument in favour of choosing the latter description (the one in terms of similarity).[12]

1   Suppose that Charles (C) and his brother Robert (R) both live and have lived at times that do not coincide with the time when Guy Fawkes (GF) lived. Now, if it is logically possible that C accurately remembers GF's life-story [e.g., to a degree we may regard as sufficient to sustain personal identity through time] then it is logically possible that also R can accurately remember GF's life-story.

2   "But C and R cannot both be GF because:

   2.1 If they were, GF would be in two places at the same time, which is absurd.
   2.2 If they were both identical with GF, they would be identical with each other, which is also absurd.

3   In addition, it is not the case that either C or R could be said to be identical with GF because:

   3.1 There is no ground for (metaphysically) identifying GF with at most one between C and R, since the relation between C and GF and the relation between R and GF is the same, or, at least, the two relations hold in virtue of the same facts (i.e., alleged memory connections)."[13]

4   So, the best description is that both C and R had mysteriously become *similar to* GF, not identical with GF.

5   Call the alleged identity-sustaining psychological relation between C and GF, 'R_1'; and the relationship between R and GF, 'R_2'. So far, we have assumed that $R_1 = R_2$.

6   The holding of the relation of personal identity between A and B depends only on the two *relata* (i.e., A and B) and what relates them (e.g., R_1) – one formulation of the only-x-and-y principle.

7   Given (6), and since there is a situation in which the holding of R_1 and the holding of R_2 are not sufficient for personal identity (premise 4), it follows that R_1 and R_2 are each independently insufficient for personal identity.

8   Hence, it follows that the best description of the case in which only C is R_1-related to GF should be in terms of similarity. In other words, what R_1 (and R_2) can provide is at most similarity, not personal identity.

According to Williams, there is a conceptual distinction between claims of similarity (qualitative identity) and identity (numerical identity), and such a distinction can be drawn, in the case of personal identity, only if we introduce a physical condition into our account. My reconstruction of Williams's argument in support of this point goes as follows.[14]

1   Consider again the case of C and GF. Both individuals are metaphysically individuated *also* by their different bodies, B-C and B-GF respectively. Suppose that these two bodies do not spatio-temporally overlap.

2   Where A is a singular action, that is, an action performed by only one person, A is metaphysically individuated also by one spatio-temporal body (e.g., the single action of raising the cup of coffee in front of you is individuated also by your body's motion). 'M_A' refers to the memory of doing A.

3   The individuation of memory M_A metaphysically and/or causally depends on A. One way of specifying this principle is: where t_1 is a time prior to t_2, a veridical memory M_A at t_1 = a veridical memory M_A at t_2 only if M_A at t_2 has the same content as M_A at t_1 and only if such a content is individuated/caused by the same action A.

4   Let us define the notion of an ersatz memory of M_A (ME_A) as follows. ME_A is a memory relevantly similar to M_A (e.g., a memory that is phenomenologically identical or almost identical with a veridical memory) but that is individuated as a memory neither in virtue of the agent who performed A nor in virtue of A itself.

5   Given that C does not have the same body as GF, it follows from the previous premises that C can only have ME_A at t_2. In other words, C can only have memories that may be qualitatively identical with GF's memories, but C cannot have GF's same memories.

Williams claims that "when we prise apart 'bodily' and 'mental' criteria; . . . we find that the normal operation of one 'mental' criterion involves the 'bodily' one."[15] The difference between 'M_A at t_1 = M_A at t_2' and 'M_A at t_1 is similar to ME_A at t_2' is the difference between an episode of proper remembering and an experience of a similar memory at different times. Charles is not literally remembering what happened to GF, he is just experiencing a qualitatively similar mental state. A corollary of the previous argument is that scenarios in which bodily/spatio-temporal continuity is not a necessary condition for personal identity are not cases involving personal identity:[16]

6   Assume a memory-based theory of personal identity and suppose that bodily/ spatio-temporal continuity is not a necessary condition for personal identity and/or for the identity of memories.
7   It follows from (6) that this scenario is possible: C 'remembers' doing a number of singular actions that we would take to be sufficient to ground personal identity in normal cases.
8   However, given (5), C cannot have any M_A. So, the scenario described in (7) is not possible.[17] The case generalises to similar cases – that is, to all cases that assume (6).

Williams's reduplication scenario and the other arguments discussed previously can be seen as making a case for a specific view on the identity of mental content, in particular, of episodic memories.[18] It may be argued that, on my reconstructions, the arguments do not have to be understood as going against all possible versions of a memory or psychological theory of personal identity. Rather, they can be taken as making a case for a theory of personal identity that includes the further condition that identity-sustaining psychological states must be individuated also by physical criteria. Other complications can be added to the previously stated reasoning by including a more sophisticated metaphysics of memory and mental states, along with a finer grained distinction between different kinds of memory.[19]

Williams's ideas have been interpreted and incorporated in different ways in subsequent theories of personal identity. For instance, Parfit's and Shoemaker's discussions on the appropriate causal conditions that quasi-memory should satisfy to ground the relation of personal identity seem to include a condition to the effect that proper memories must have the right sort of causal connections (Chapter 4). Jeff McMahan's embodied mind account of our nature emphasises that the right sort of causal connection – continuity of the same brain – plays a crucial role in defining what we are and how we persist (Chapter 8). So, one contribution of the previous arguments to the current debate is also that of making a case in favour of one way in which some of the mental states employed in psychological theories should be specified. Admittedly, in certain cases (e.g., McMahan's theory), it is hard to classify a theory as belonging either to the psychological or to the physical approach. However, I think that it is reasonable to classify certain approaches as psychological when the physical or bodily connections (e.g., brain continuity) are introduced as necessary conditions in the theory because they sustain psychological capacities or because physical connections are regarded as relevant in virtue of the fact that they sustain appropriate psychological connections.[20]

4 Our physical nature: animalism

Several supporters of the psychological approach have presupposed or endorsed these claims: (1) We are (essentially) persons, and (2) an entity that is now a person is essentially a person.[21] However, some contemporary advocates of the theory of our nature called animalism, e.g., William R. Carter, Paul Snowdon, David DeGrazia, and Eric Olson, have questioned these claims. Both Snowdon and Olson have provided extensive defences of animalism, but in what follows I focus mostly on Olson's account. In an early work (1997), he characterises the 'Biological Approach' as including two claims: (1) you and I are human animals – what is nowadays considered as the characterising thesis of animalism – and (2) psychological continuity is neither necessary nor sufficient for *us, qua* human animals, to persist through time. On this view, an entity that is a person at this moment may persist without thereby always being a person. In fact, Olson holds that our nature and persistence conditions are determined entirely by the natural kind 'human animal'. In other words, he maintains that this kind specifies the essential features of those entities to which the personal pronouns 'I', 'you', 'we', etc. (and, arguably, proper names) refer.

With respect to their commitment to our modal properties, there are at least two versions of animalism. According to non-modal/non-essentialist animalism, we are (human) animals. According to essentialist animalism, we are essentially (human) animals. This latter version holds that so long as we exist, we cannot but be human animals. In other words, our nature is such that our continuity through time is always and cannot but be the continuity through time of a human animal. Essentialist animalists usually identify the natural kind under which we fall with the kind *human animal*. In turn, animalists generally understand this natural kind as relevantly equivalent to the kind *living human organism*. In short, the form of essentialist animalism under consideration here claims that we are essentially living human organisms and that our identity conditions over time are specified by the identity conditions over time of a human organism – the identity conditions of which are further specified in terms of sameness of life (see section 2). There are versions of animalism according to which our identity conditions over time are not the identity conditions of a *living* human organism. For instance, some (e.g., David Mackie) have claimed that, on the supposition that we are animals, we can persist as, e.g., *dead* animals or corpses. Imagine that you are witnessing an unpleasant event such as the death of a human animal. When the human animal finally dies, you do not seem to experience the sudden disappearance of the entity in front of you. Rather, when the human animal dies, it looks as if the entity in front of you simply changes its state or phase: a living human organism is becoming a dead human organism. Supporters of this form of animalism claim that we may persist at least until the dead animals we may become maintain certain basic structural properties. This last condition, if properly specified, may allow us to avoid identifying human organisms with decomposed corpses – although individuating a cut-off point in the process of decomposition will seem arbitrary to many. On this version of animalism, there is a sense in which the expression 'a dead man' is not equivocal or paradoxical: I am a human organism and, *qua* human organism, I will not necessarily cease to exist when I cease to function as an organised whole.

A non-modal version of animalism simply implies that even though we are animals now, we may not always be animals.[22] This second version of animalism is less popular, one of the reasons being that most contemporary animalists believe that we essentially fall under the natural kind that characterises our nature. Using David Wiggins's terminology, the natural kind 'human animal' (or 'human organism') is referred to by using a **substance-sortal**.[23] In general, a sortal is a concept that may correspond to a natural kind or way in which we identify, classify, and count things. Wiggins maintains that a kind counts as a sortal only if it provides an answer to the question 'what is it?' – that is, sortal concepts should provide the conditions of identity of the entities that fall under them. Substance-sortals are not the only type of sortals; in fact, Wiggins distinguishes *substance*-sortals – that is, those sortals that an individual must fall under so long as it exists – from **phase-sortals** – that is, those sortals under which an individual may not always fall. Now, if *human animal* is a substance-sortal, then a human animal is essentially a substance of this kind – that is, its conditions of identity are determined by this sortal – and would go out of existence in case it undergoes a number of changes such that it did not fall anymore under the same substance-sortal. On the supposition that *human animal* is a substance-sortal, an entity that is a human animal at t_1 could not persist through time as the same entity that at t_2 is not a human animal. An example of a phase-sortal is *human child*, as this sortal may be specific enough to identify an entity but does not require that the entity that is a child at t_1 ceases to exist when and if it does not fall any longer under the same phase-sortal at t_2. In fact, we normally think that a human animal that is a child at t_1 can become a human adult at t_2 without thereby going out of existence. A version of animalism that includes the idea that 'human animal' is a substance-sortal entails essentialist animalism: (1) I am a human animal, (2) *human animal* is a substance-sortal – what is a human animal cannot fail to be a human animal, (3) so it is not possible for me to exist and not be a human animal, which is one way of saying that I am essentially an animal – where the modalities at issue here are metaphysical.

Now, what are the identity conditions of human animals? Several animalists, including Olson in some of his early works, specified the conditions of identity of human animals as including, as a necessary condition, the continuity of the animals' brainstem. The reason behind this choice was that the brainstem was taken to be essential to the life of a human organism. However, animalism is not tied to this condition, the plausibility of which is based on empirical findings. Olson has recently specified the more general identity conditions of human animals as follows: "if x is an animal at a time t and something y exists at t*, then x=y iff the event that is x's life at t is the event that is y's life at t*."[24] As already discussed in section 2 of this chapter, the idea is that a human animal is a human organism, and a human organism is a living human organism – hence the reference to 'life'. On this view, it follows that we were foetuses: after all, the life of a developed/developing foetus seems to be the same as the life of the corresponding adult human organism that is one of us. The idea is that a developed foetus and the causally related adult human organism seem to be stages of the same human organism. So, if I am identical to the human animal that is longing to finish this book, this same human animal was once a foetus devoid of those biological structures biologically necessary to want to finish this book. The implications of this approach for the morality of abortion are explored in Chapter 8, section 2.

5 The thinking animal argument, the embodied mind view, and constitutionalism

Is animalism (in either form) a plausible theory of our nature? One argument in favour of this theory is called the 'Thinking Animal argument', which can be summarised as follows:[25]

1   There is a human animal sitting in your chair right now – or wherever you are now (L).
2   The human animal in L now is thinking.
3   You are the thinking being in the spatio-temporal location L.
4   Therefore, the human animal in L is you.

Premise (1) can be hardly denied – perhaps a mereological nihilist or a supporter of some other form of revisionary metaphysics (see Chapter 2) may find ways of denying it. Premise (2) seems plausible too: the human animal in L has a functioning brain and, let us suppose, all that is (biologically) required for thinking so we would need good reasons to deny that such an animal is thinking. Denying premise (3) seems to imply that, if you are not the thinking animal in L, then there are at least two thinking things co-located in the same spatio-temporal region – you and the human animal. Probably one thinking thing too many – call this the 'Too Many Thinkers problem'. More specifically, if you deny (3), Stephan Blatti distinguishes these kinds of questions:[26]

A   Practical questions (e.g., which thinker is going on holiday in a week – the thinking thing that is *not* the animal or the animal sitting in your chair?).
B   Epistemic questions (e.g., how can you tell whether you are the animal or the thinking thing, since they both seem to think the same thoughts – at least judging from their behaviour?).
C   Linguistic questions (e.g., what are the referents of personal pronouns such as 'we', 'I', 'you'? The thinking thing(s) or the animal(s)?).
D   Ontological questions (e.g., what is the nature of the relationship between the animal and the thinking thing both in L?).

Some of these questions, e.g., the ontological questions, are reminiscent of some of the doubts raised against Cartesian and certain soul-based views of our nature (see Chapter 1). In particular, one version of the too many thinkers problem can be used against certain versions of the soul approach. For instance, we may argue that if you are a compound of your soul and your body, and your soul thinks, it seems that there are two things thinking your thoughts – the compound of soul and body (that is, you) and your soul. Again, one thinking thing too many. Now, animalists claim that their theory provides a straightforward and simple answer to the question regarding the relationship between the thinking thing and the co-located animal: identity. In other words, the animalist's solution is that the animal and the thinking thing are one and the same entity.[27]

Animalism, however, has its problems. In particular, one of the most serious troubles that animalists face is the way they seem to have to describe the outcomes of certain thought experiments. More specifically, they seem to have problems with the description that follows from the application of their theory to the outcomes of some brain-transplant scenarios. One version of this problematic thought experiment, which is a modern re-interpretation of some of Locke's thought experiments, runs as follows. Suppose that a surgeon removes the upper part of the brain contained in the human animal A, the animal associated with person PA before the operation. After having removed the upper part of another animal's (B) brain, the surgeon then plugs the upper part of the brain previously in A into animal B, which is an animal that was previously associated with person PB. The surgeon then connects B's previous upper brain to A. Suppose that both the upper brains thus transplanted are enough to generate those higher cognitive capacities and mental content generally associated with personhood – say, a significant number of memories, character traits, desires, etc. In addition, suppose that the surgeon has performed such operations in a way that did not interrupt the lives of A and B.[28] As a result, animal A now remembers everything (or a great part of what) PB used to remember, behaves as PB would have behaved, and A seems to show interest in those projects that were previously associated with PB. For instance, if PB was previously interested in writing a book on atheism and remembered a holiday in Amsterdam in 2002, now these features are encountered when interacting with animal A. Similarly, if PA before the operation used to remember a holiday in Osaka in 2015 and was previously interested in writing a book on Japanese horror, now these psychological features are displayed by B. (Suppose also that PA was not interested in writing a book on atheism and did not remember a holiday in Amsterdam and that PB was not interested in writing a book on Japanese horror and did not remember a holiday in Osaka.) How should we describe the outcome of these operations? In particular, where are PA and PB? The trouble for animalism is generated in two steps. The first one is that many people, or so it is generally assumed, would say that PA is now associated with B – now PA goes where B goes – and that PB is now associated with A. The second and crucial step is the identification of one of us with either PA or PB, e.g., *you* are PA and *I* am PB. Given these two assumptions, if an operation is performed such that what is responsible for *my* memories, character, desires, etc. – say, the upper part of the brain – is transplanted into *your* body, then whichever metaphysical entity is me after the operation seems to be what is associated with your body after the operation. However, animalists would have to describe the outcome of the operations differently; namely, they would have to say that you, your human organism, is still *you*, despite its having all of my relevant psychological features and my upper brain. In other words, the animalist would have to say that you have just received a new cerebrum. However, many would claim that this is the wrong way of describing the outcome – or, at least, not the way in which users of terms such as 'I' and 'you' would describe the outcome of the operations. Since animalism implies the wrong description in this case and since the case can be generalised, animalism does seem to misrepresent the correct use of some of the basic concepts and terms we use to think about our nature.[29]

5.1 The embodied mind view and constitutionalism

The previously stated problem for animalism becomes more pressing if the supporters of rival views can provide convincing replies to the thinking animal argument. In particular, Jeff McMahan and, more recently, Derek Parfit (2012) have endorsed versions of the embodied part view, of which the embodied mind view is one version. According to them, we are the conscious, thinking, controlling parts of human beings. On this view, premise (2) of the thinking animal argument ("The human animal in L now is thinking") is not, strictly speaking, true or, at least, it needs to be specified as follows. What is doing the thinking in L is the thinking part of the animal located where you are now, and the human animal where you are now thinks by having a part that does the thinking. This view would also solve the too many thinkers problem because it denies that there are two entities that think in the same sense. More specifically, on what Parfit calls the best version of the embodied part theory, human animals think by having a conscious thinking part, which is a person in the Lockean sense.[30] So, the human animal can still be described as thinking, although in a *derivative* sense, that is, in a sense similar to when we say that a human animal digests food by having a digestive system. In the case of the digestive system we don't say that there are two entities that digest the food ingested by the animal, namely, the animal and the digestive system, rather we say that the human animal digests food by having a digestive system, which is one of its proper parts.

Another way of replying to the thinking animal argument is (1) to deny that a human animal can think and (2) to claim that the relation between the relevant human animals and us is not identity but constitution. In one version of this strategy, Sydney Shoemaker claims that the nature of mental properties, e.g., beliefs, is such that they can only belong to entities having certain psychological persistence conditions. In other words, only entities that have identity conditions involving psychological features are the proper subjects of ascriptions of mental properties. The reason is that mental states are characterised and individuated by their functional and causal roles, which essentially refer to certain conditions that are both physical *and* psychological. For instance, the state of being in pain is a state that can be caused by bodily damage of some kind and may dispose the one who is in pain to avoid this feeling. Shoemaker's point is that such states are essentially characterised by a structure that involves psychological continuity, so an entity that is not characterised by psychological conditions – as for instance a human organism – is not the proper subject of mental states. So, strictly speaking, it is human *persons*, not human organisms, that are the kind of entities that think. The problem of specifying the relationship between the relevant human animal and the thinking person is addressed by claiming that a human animal *constitutes* a person without thereby being identical with it. In other words, each of us is constituted by a biological organism, and given that constitution is not identity, we are not human organisms, although we are spatially coincident with at least one of these organisms. As a piece of marble constitutes a statue without thereby being identical with it, so our human organisms constitute us without thereby being us. McMahan's embodied mind view and Baker's version of constitutionalism are further discussed in relation to their consequences for the debate on abortion in Chapter 8.

6 Summary

Let us review some of the key points of this chapter. We began with the Stoic understanding of the notions of body and soul. Their conception of a corporeal soul was taken up by some Christian thinkers (e.g., Tertullian) who, in elaborating certain Biblical metaphors, proposed various accounts of resurrection – and thus of persistence through time – that include physical criteria. The upshot is that, on their views, some form of physical or causal continuity is essential for our persistence through time. There are many ways of making these ideas more precise, for instance, in terms of identity of matter, bodily continuity, or by referring to sameness of a human organism's life.

Not many contemporary philosophers hold that the conditions of *personal* identity are merely physical, in the sense that they may not include any reference to memory, character traits, desires, and so on. However, a stronger case has been made to believe that some considerations regarding physical or causal continuity provide at least a necessary condition for personal/our identity over time. We explored some of the reasons in favour of this belief in our discussion of Williams's reduplication argument. In particular, I argued that one of the main points of Williams's reasoning is that the distinction between memory-continuity (and/or identity of memory and/or proper remembering) and similarity of memories is metaphysically possible only in terms of causal or physical continuity. This suggestion seems to have been implemented into some contemporary versions of the psychological approach – for instance, into those theories holding that brain continuity is a necessary condition of personal identity. Other accounts of the metaphysical individuation of mental states may prescribe different and/or additional criteria.

One theory that employs solely physical criteria as persistence conditions over time is animalism, which is *not* a theory of personal identity but a theory of our nature. On this view, *we* are not essentially psychological entities; rather, we are human organisms – in the most popular version of the theory, we are essentially living human organisms. One of the main arguments in favour of this view is the thinking animal argument. A concise version of the argument goes as follows. (1) There is a human animal where you are now. (2) That human animal is thinking. (3) You are that thinking being. (4) Therefore, that human animal is you. The conclusion is supposed to generalise (i.e., from 'you' to 'we'). Negating one or more of the premises of the argument is theoretically problematic, or so the animalist says. However, animalism seems to have problems with how it describes the outcomes of some brain-transplant scenarios, that is, thought experiments designed to elicit a series of intuitions regarding our identity. In particular, animalism seems to describe some of these outcomes in a way that many find problematic. What these thought experiments are sometimes taken to reveal is that theories of personal identity and our nature can hardly be completely disjointed from considerations regarding some of our central psychological features. In the next chapter, we will explore more in detail some of the psychological features that we may want to associate with our persistence through time, as individuals and/or as persons.

The final part of this chapter also introduced two theories of our nature that seem to provide acceptable (although disputed) replies to the thinking animal argument. In particular, the embodied mind or part view retains a crucial insight of the physical approach, namely, the idea that, although psychological connections are fundamental for our own identity, they should be sustained by *normal* causal connections, that is, those responsible for brain continuity. The main idea of this theory is that we are essentially psychological entities, in particular, the thinking parts of a human organism. The constitutionalist theory advances a different way of understanding our relation to our bodies. In particular, this view holds that we are not identical with our bodies; rather, we are essentially psychological or mental entities, and our human organisms constitute us (without thereby being identical to us).

Notes

1 Identity theories in philosophy of mind according to which physical properties and mental properties are identical (or, better, conscious states and brain states are identical), unless the kind of physical continuity is otherwise specified, seem to imply a collapse of the distinction between the two kinds of theories of personal identity. See Heil (2013), Chapter 5 for identity theories and Thomson (1997) for a bodily theory of personal identity.

2 The main text is based on Long (1996).

3 An extremely informative paper on the complexity of the debate in philosophy of biology on biological individuality – which is not the same as organic individuality – is Pradeu (2016).

4 This list is taken from Olson (1997), pp. 126–131. Olson elaborates a proposal originally formulated in Van Inwagen (1990).

5 Van Inwagen (1990), pp. 148–149.

6 This claim is controversial. Some theories of our consciousness emphasise the essential role played by the body. However, the point made in the main text can be easily modified so as to include these different theories (e.g., by including all of those parts of a human organism that are responsible for our consciousness or psychological properties).

7 Shewmon (2001).

8 What if God reassembles P's body minus one eye – perhaps because it was particularly sinful? Would the resulting body meet the material continuity condition? Tertullian may hold that a rather broad (and hardly plausible) degree of physical variation can still meet the material continuity condition, since he also maintains that the resurrected bodies will be purified and modified in many significant aspects. (For instance, he claims that we will have teeth, but we will not have to

eat – apparently, God would keep our teeth for aesthetic reasons. Similarly, our mouths will be used only to sing praises to God.)

9   See Williams (1956/73). The discussion of his argument is a slightly revised version of Sauchelli (2017a).
10 For instance, one version of the reduplication argument was proposed by Samuel Clarke (1675–1729) in his attack on Locke's theory of personal identity. See Uzgalis (2011).
11 Among Williams's precursors, A. J. Ayer (1910–1989) held that, if we understand the self as a logical construction out of sense-experiences, (1) it is a necessary and sufficient condition for two sense-experiences to belong to the same self-structure that these experiences be organic sense-contents that are elements of the same body and that (2) it is logically impossible for any organic sense-content to belong to more than one body.
12 Sauchelli (2017a).
13 Sauchelli (2017a), p. 332.
14 Sauchelli (2017a), p. 334.
15 Williams (1956/73), p. 5.
16 The argument in the main text is a revised version of my reconstruction of the same argument in Sauchelli (2017a).
17 Sauchelli (2017a), p. 334.
18 The reader familiar with the literature on externalism about mental content may understand Williams's argument as a case in favour of externalism about the content of memory. See Lau & Deutsch (2014) for an introduction to the topic.
19 See Bernecker (2008), Lawlor (2009), and Michaelian and John Sutton (2017). Also, a case can be made that further progress in the formulation of psychological theories *requires* such finer grained distinctions among kinds of memory (e.g., between procedural memory, the kind of memory we display when we perform certain skilled actions, and episodic memory, the kind of memory described by expressions such as 'I remember driving my car last night').
20 In another influential paper, Williams argues that physical continuity seems to track not just some of our intuitions about personal identity but also our intuitions about the rationality of our concern for some future states (e.g., fear for something that may happen to us in the future). I discuss these issues in Chapter 7. See Williams (1970) for his argument on the topic.
21 The discussion of animalism is based on Sauchelli (2017b).
22 Olson (2016).
23 This section contains a slightly revised version of parts of Sauchelli (2017b).
24 Olson (2016), p. 292.
25 This version of the argument relies on Blatti (2014), in particular 3.1.
26 Blatti (2014).
27 The alleged theoretical superiority of animalism with respect to the previous questions has been disputed. See Yang (2015) for discussion.
28 This version of the thought-experiment differs from Shoemaker's classic discussion of the topic in a way that takes into account the recent developments of animalism and the debate on our nature. In the literature on the thought-experiments involving brain transplants, it is generally assumed that the brainstem is exclusively responsible for the regulation of certain functional aspects of our organisms. However, this seems to be a gross oversimplification. See Shewmon (2001) for discussion.
29 Animalists have proposed various answers to the reasoning in the main text. See the bibliography on animalism at the end of this chapter.
30 Parfit (2012).

Suggested further readings

Stoics and early Christians

Bynum, Caroline Walker, *The Resurrection of the Body in Western Christianity, 200–1336* (New York: Columbia University Press, 1995).

Gill, Christopher, *The Structured Self in Hellenistic and Roman Thought* (Oxford: Oxford University Press, 2006).

Long, Anthony A., 'Stoic Philosophers on Persons, Property-Ownership, and Community', in Anthony Long (ed.) *From Epicurus to Epictetus* (Oxford: Clarendon Press, 1997/2006), pp. 335–360.

Long, Anthony A., 'Soul and Body in Stoicism', in Anthony Long (ed.) *Stoic Studies* (Berkeley: University of California Press, 1982/1996), pp. 224–249.

Physical criteria of identity

Carter, William, 'Will I Be a Dead Person?', *Philosophy and Phenomenological Research*, 54 (1999), pp. 16–71.

Feldman, Fred, 'The Termination Thesis', *Midwest Studies in Philosophy*, 24 (2000), pp. 98–115.

Guay, Alexandre and Thomas Pradeu (eds.) *Individuals Across the Sciences* (Oxford: Oxford University Press, 2016).

Heil, John, *Philosophy of Mind*, Third Edition (New York and London: Routledge, 2013).

Hershenov, David, 'Do Dead Bodies Pose a Problem for Biological Approaches to Personal Identity?', *Mind*, 114, 453 (2005), pp. 31–59.

Hull, David, 'Individual', in Evelyn Fox Keller and Elisabeth Lloyd (eds.) *Keywords in Evolutionary Biology* (Cambridge, MA: Harvard University Press, 1992).

Nagel, Thomas, *The View From Nowhere* (Oxford: Oxford University Press, 1986).

Olson, Eric, 'Is There a Bodily Criterion of Personal Identity?', in Fraser MacBride (ed.) *Identity and Modality* (Oxford: Clarendon Press, 2006), pp. 242–260.

Pradeu, Thomas, 'The Many Faces of Biological Individuality', *Biology & Philosophy*, 31, 6 (2016), pp. 761–773.

Shewmon, Alan, 'The Brain and Somatic Integration', *Journal of Medicine and Philosophy*, 26, 5 (2001), pp. 457–478.

Thomson, Judith Jarvis, 'Persons and Their Bodies', in Jonathan Dancy (ed.) *Reading Parfit* (Oxford: Blackwell, 1997), pp. 202–219.

Wilson, Robert A. and Matthew Barker, 'The Biological Notion of Individual', in *Stanford Encyclopedia of Philosophy* (2013). https://plato.stanford.edu/entries/biology-individual/

Reduplication thought-experiment and personal identity

Bernecker, Sven, *The Metaphysics of Memory* (Dordrecht: Springer, 2008).

Lau, Joe and Max Deutsch, 'Externalism About Mental Content', in *Stanford Encyclopedia of Philosophy* (2014). https://plato.stanford.edu/entries/content-externalism/

Lawlor, Krista, 'Memory', in Ansgar Beckermann, Brian P. McLaughlin, and Sven Walter (eds.) *The Oxford Handbook of Philosophy of Mind* (Oxford: Oxford University Press, 2009), pp. 663–678.

Michaelian, Kourken and John Sutton, 'Memory', in *Stanford Encyclopedia of Philosophy* (2017). https://plato.stanford.edu/entries/memory/

Sauchelli, Andrea, 'The Early Reception of Bernard Williams' Reduplication Argument (1956–1962)', *Archiv für Geschichte der Philosophie*, 99, 3 (2017a), pp. 326–345.

Uzgalis, William (ed.) *The Correspondence of Samuel Clarke and Anthony Collins, 1707–1708* (Ontario, CA: Broadview Press, 2011).

Van Inwagen, Peter, *Material Beings* (Ithaca: Cornell University Press, 1990).

Williams, Bernard, 'Personal Identity and Individuation', in Bernard Williams (ed.) *Problems of the Self* (Cambridge: Cambridge University Press, 1956/1973), pp. 1–18.

Williams, Bernard, 'Imagination and the Self', in Bernard Williams (ed.) *Problems of the Self* (Cambridge: Cambridge University Press, 1960/1973), pp. 26–45.

Williams, Bernard, 'The Self and the Future', in Bernard Williams (ed.) *Problems of the Self* (Cambridge: Cambridge University Press, 1970/1973), pp. 46–63.

Animalism

Bailey, Andrew, 'Animalism', *Philosophy Compass*, 10, 12 (2015), pp. 867–883.

Blatti, Stephan, 'Animalism', in *Stanford Encyclopedia of Philosophy* (2014). https://plato.stanford.edu/entries/animalism/

Olson, Eric, *The Human Animal* (Oxford: Oxford University Press, 1997).

Olson, Eric, 'The Person and the Corpse', in Ben Bradley, Fred Feldman and Jens Johansson (eds.), *The Oxford Handbook of Philosophy of Death* (Oxford: Oxford University Press, 2013).

Olson, Eric, 'The Role of Brainstem in Personal Identity', in Andreas Blank (ed.) *Animals: New Essays* (Munich: Philosophia, 2016), pp. 291–302.

Pradeu, Thomas, 'What Is An Organism? An Immunological Answer', *History and Philosophy of the Life Sciences* 32 (2010), pp. 247–267.

Sauchelli, Andrea, 'The Animal, the Corpse, and the Remnant-Person', *Philosophical Studies* 174, 1 (2017b), pp. 205–218.

Snowdon, Paul, 'Persons, Animals, and Ourselves', in C. Gill (ed.) *The Person and the Human Mind* (Oxford: Clarendon Press, 1990), pp. 83–107.

Snowdon, Paul, *Persons, Animals, Ourselves* (Oxford: Oxford University Press, 2014).

Wiggins, David, *Sameness and Substance Renewed* (Cambridge: Cambridge University Press, 2001).

Yang, Eric, 'Unrestricted Animalism and the Too Many Candidates Problem', *Philosophical Studies*, 172 (2015), pp. 635–652.

Embodied mind and constitutionalism

Baker, Lynne Rudder, *Persons and Bodies: A Constitution View* (Cambridge: Cambridge University Press, 2000).

McMahan, Jeff, *The Ethics of Killing* (Oxford: Oxford University Press, 2002).

Parfit, Derek, 'We Are Not Human Beings', *Philosophy*, 87 (2012), pp. 5–28.

Shoemaker, Sydney, 'Persons, Animals, and Identity', *Synthese*, 163 (2008), pp. 313–324.

Shoemaker, Sydney, 'On What We Are', in S. Gallagher (ed.) *The Oxford Handbook of the Self* (Oxford: Oxford University Press, 2011).

6 Practical and narrative approaches

1	Familiarisation, assenting, and *prohairesis* in the Stoic tradition	147
2	Frankfurt on personhood	150
	2.1 Volitions, the will, and personal identity	153
3	Practical unity and the self-constitution view	154
	3.1 What is a self-constituting self?	156
	3.2 Agency and personal identity	157
4	Self-constituting narrative view	158
	4.1 Narrative identity and personal identity	160
5	Summary	162

> If you have your 'why?' in life, you can get along with almost any 'how?'. People don't strive for happiness, only the English do.
>
> —Friedrich Nietzsche, *The Twilight of the Idols*, 1889

Psychological theories of personal identity of the kind discussed in Chapters 4 and 5 do not generally specify any particular structural conditions on the relevant psychological connections that are taken to sustain the relation of personal identity. The few conditions included in the most influential psychological theories of personal identity are frequently spelled out solely by referring to the *right kind* of psychological connections or continuity that these theories should incorporate – where 'the right kind of connections' is then understood in terms of the physical/causal connections explored in the previous chapter, e.g., a psychological connection of the right kind is a psychological connection that is caused by the continuity of the same brain. However, many contemporary philosophers have suggested that the supposed relevance of personal identity for a variety of questions in our everyday life is insufficiently explained solely by such generic psychological theories. Better at this are practical and narrative theories. Although these theories of personal identity are sometimes proposed as rivals to the aforementioned psychological approach, some of the practical and narrative theories can be seen as ways of further specifying the generic psychological theories discussed in Chapter 4 (and criticised in Chapter 5). In fact, one of the main principles behind, e.g., practical and self-constitution narrative views is that what we are and how we persist depend also on the structure of the psychological connections we identify ourselves with. For instance, certain versions of the practical approach hold that only psychological connections of the right kind – those that compose a certain agential unity – are what is relevant for personal identity. In turn, practical and narrative theories are supposed to provide better accounts or explanations of the relevance of personal identity for everyday life.

In the first section of this chapter, I discuss some of the main principles of the Stoic philosophy of mind. In particular, I provide an introduction to the concepts of familiarisation, appropriation, and ***prohairesis*** (or moral character). All these notions describe certain mental processes whereby we internalise some of our desires or representations, processes through which we identify certain aspects of our minds as our own. In particular, according to certain Stoics, our true self – what we may understand as the entity essential to our identity through time – is individuated by our moral character and by what we choose to be.

In the contemporary debate, the relationship between our capacity to assume a certain attitude towards some of those desires and other mental states that motivate us to act and the notion of a person has been influentially explored by Harry Frankfurt (b. 1929). In particular, Frankfurt claims that a necessary condition for being a person is that of being able to have and regulate a specific kind of desires. How this is supposed to work and its connection to personal identity is explained later. Along similar lines and from a broadly Kantian perspective, Christine Korsgaard (b. 1952) also argues that the structure of agency is intimately related to the process of self-constitution. According to her, the self is an entity that creates itself at the moment of action, and the conditions for its proper constitution include the formal requirements already specified by Immanuel Kant in his discussions of moral agency. The process of self-constitution may seem puzzling because it is not clear how to make sense of the idea that an entity constitutes itself. In this regard, Daniel Dennett (b. 1942) has suggested that we are akin to fictional characters created by our brains, that is, we are a way of coping with the environment. On this account, the entity that creates the narrative or story of the fictional character in question does not have to represent itself as part of the narrative. On the other hand, J. David Velleman (b. 1952) believes that part of what constitutes being an agent is also the capacity to act for reasons; in particular, also those reasons that are used to create a coherent narrative of our own selves. Our behaviour can be modified in virtue of the representational content of the narrative that we create, and the entity that creates the narrative may figure as the protagonist of the narrative content. A further possible clarification of this idea of self-creation through narrative is explored by Marya Schechtman (b. 1960). According to her narrative theory, the personal identity debate should also discuss under what conditions an event in an individual's life becomes part of her identity as a person, not solely (or not at all) the metaphysics of personal identity.[1] In particular, Schechtman holds that (at least part of) the study of personal identity should be based on the notion of a **self-/ person-constituting narrative**. A self- or person-constituting narrative is a narrative in which a self spins a story that properly connects various parts of her life. One of the relevant features of her theory is that it is not focused on what Schechtman calls the re-identification question – to a first approximation, the metaphysical task of specifying the synchronic and diachronic metaphysical conditions of personal identity – but rather on the characterisation question. In turn, the characterisation question addresses our biographical identity – the kind of question psychologists or intrusive in-laws may ask, e.g., who are you? Still, an answer to the characterisation question may offer one way of addressing the metaphysics of personal identity: a specification of the conditions under which a series of psychological connections structures the biographical identity of an individual or person may also provide us with those thicker structural conditions that generic psychological theories usually lack.

An important preliminary point is that an astounding number of contemporary scholars with different aims and perspectives have developed a great variety of versions of the narrative approach. In addition, the concept of narrativity has been applied to fields ranging from psychology to media studies.[2] Recent philosophers discussed the narrative approach starting from the work of some 'continental' philosophers (e.g., Wilhelm Schapp, Jean-Paul Sartre, Paul Ricouer, or John Davenport and Anthony Rudd in relation to Søren Kierkegaard). Others debated the idea of the narrative subject and the ethics of identity with regard to a variety of other topics in moral and political philosophy (e.g., Alasdair MacIntyre, Charles Taylor, and Anthony Appiah). Other narrative accounts have been fruitfully developed by feminist philosophers (e.g., Hilde Lindemann, discussed in the next chapter), and criticised by aestheticians and philosophers of art (e.g., Gregory Currie, Peter Lamarque, and Paisley Livingston). Not all of these discussions have been explicitly related to the kind of metaphysical concerns that are the main focus of this book. Now, certain so-called narrative identity theories may provide colourful accounts of the ways in which people fashion their own lives and arrange episodes that happened to them. These projects may presuppose one form of psychological continuity but do not seem to address directly a metaphysical concern: a further and specific argument would be required to claim that a narrative identity (say, national identity narratives) are themselves also ways of specifying constraints on some of the various psychological views discussed in the previous chapters. In short, we should not confuse what people think of as essential to their sense of who they are with claims about the metaphysical basis for their identities through time. This connection may hold, but a further argument is required for believing that it does.

1 Familiarisation, assenting, and *prohairesis* in the Stoic tradition

An important concept for many Stoic philosophers, especially those in the Roman tradition, is that of *oikeiosis*, sometimes translated with the terms 'appropriation' or 'familiarisation'. Some of the ways in which such a concept is characterised may be helpful in understanding at least part of the process of identification discussed by contemporary philosophers such as Frankfurt. Julia Annas characterises *oikeiosis* in the Stoic tradition as a relation at the core of discussions regarding impartiality and the proper extension of our ethical and practical concerns.[3] In particular, Annas claims that *oikeiosis* is a three-place relation having the following formal structure: X familiarises Y with Z. In turn, this structure is instantiated in two ways: first, nature familiarises us with ourselves and then, afterwards, nature familiarises us with others. The Stoic Chrysippus is reported to have claimed that every animal is familiarised by nature with its own constitution, where this is supposed to explain our natural impulse to preserve and care about ourselves. On this view, *oikeiosis* is not self-love; rather it is the condition for developing it. Annas describes the developmental story proposed by certain Stoics as a progress from an initial and primitive concern for ourselves in childhood to a familiarisation with more stable dispositions to perform certain actions guided by rational principles (second stage). The third stage in this progression is that of the agent's familiarisation with the capacity to appreciate the value of virtue. Annas also suggests that this last stage of the familiarisation process culminates in the realisation that we may have reasons to act that do not coincide with self-interested reasons. Cicero in *De Finibus*, which contains an exposition of certain tenets of Stoic thinking, claims that self-love is our first principle of action. When this principle of action directed at self-preservation is discovered, we become familiar with it. However, Cicero maintains that once an individual acquires an understanding of nature and of its order and harmony, this individual begins to value such an understanding more than anything else. Annas also distinguishes a second, social kind of *oikeiosis* in the Stoic thought, which was discussed by the same Chrysippus. This second kind of *oikeiosis* is again described following a developmental model, this time applied to the development of our caring for others. More specifically, on this model, our concern for others starts from our care for the members of our own family, and then expands so as to include all our fellow human beings.[4] Annas holds that the Stoics did not see ethical reasons for limiting the expansion of our concern to friends and family. The Stoic sage will eventually perceive as his own those ethical desires that result from a complete process of *oikeiosis*. Virtuous action is familiar to the Stoic wise person, as such an action does not derive from an alienated (e.g., foreign) desire. The Stoic Hierocles uses the image of a series of concentric circles to describe the structure of our concern for others. The first centre is the one drawn around our own mind and body, followed by the circle of our familiar affects. Other circles include our fellow-citizens and so on until we reach the largest circle, which is supposed to include all humanity. Hierocles claims that people should strive to draw all these circles closer to their centre. One strategy for drawing people closer to our inner circles of concern is that of calling those in the exterior circles in ways similar to how we call those in the more internal circles.

The previously stated process of familiarisation and appropriation through different stages was developed in conformity with a specific theory of mind. In particular, Anthony Long proposes the following reconstruction of the Stoics' understanding of the mind.[5] The *hēgemonikon* (see Chapter 5.1), the commanding part of the soul, is constantly informed by *phantasiai* (representations), which derive from the faculty called *phantasia* and by *hormē*, a faculty we may call 'impulse'. *Phantasia* – the term used to refer to this faculty may also stand for the representations themselves – is a faculty that encompasses all objects of awareness and always involves a form of self-perception in all the representations that inform the *hēgemonikon*. Long claims that, according to the Stoic, a *phantasia* or representation can be a feeling, a recollection, or any other mental state we may be in. A representation always has a reflexive aspect, a point that Long clarifies by saying that, on the Stoic account, an animal that has *phantasiai* must thereby have "some sense of itself as the subject of its own experience". A representation informs us of what happens in the world (and not only), but may also not be veridical and thus mislead us. Whether veridical or not, however, representations always present something to the commanding part. The way in which a representation is presented to our minds depends on the conceptual and linguistic faculties available to us at the moment of perception. Long emphasises that, according to the Stoics, the mind is a unity, which implies that the subject having *phantasia* is also the subject having impulses. The mind is something to which things appear (as representations) and that responds to such representations with desire or aversion. *Phantasia* and *hormē*, however, do not reside in two different and separable parts of the soul that may potentially conflict with each other. Rather, the Stoics maintain that the *hēgemonikon* is actively engaged, hence the unity, in all of the various aspects of our experience. The general idea is that the central rational activity of the mind is always active and forms a rational unity with *phantasia* and the volitional aspect of the mind.

A further crucial point for our discussion is this: in addition to the faculties just mentioned, the Stoics generally recognise a third faculty, that is, the power of giving or withholding assent to certain representations. This faculty (*synkatathesis*) also plays the role of mediating between impulses/volitions and representations. For example, seeing a nice tie in a shop generates in us (at least in me) a representation of the tie as a well-made object that deserves the price it is sold for, which may inform our impulse to buy it. Our mind, however, has the capacity to withhold assent to such a representation that has claimed our attention.[6] According to the Stoics, a representation that affects our mind does not impel us to immediately follow it; in fact, the impulse to act upon it depends on whether we have previously given our assent to the representation. As Long describes this process, a representation may be part of my experience, but "I can make it *mine* – my outlook, or belief, or commitment – or *not mine*, by giving or withholding assent." Also, the faculty of assenting to representations does not generate representations; rather it has a judgmental, interpretive, and volitional role in our mental architecture. Some of the contemporary discussions of the structure of our agency and of how agency is related to personal identity crucially depend on the recognition of a faculty significantly similar to the one just described.

The connection between the faculty of assenting, our own nature, and the moral life is discussed by, among the others, Epictetus (55–135). In particular, he explicitly associates the correct use of representations to the ethical life because, according to him, the ethical life is characterised by the correct use of the assenting faculty in accepting representations. More specifically, Epictetus claims that our *prohairesis* – our moral character, that is, the faculty that regulates which representations we should assent to or withhold, and that also judges their value – is our essential self, what we really are. In some passages of the *Discourses*, Epictetus seems to make such an explicit identification: we are our own capacity to assent to certain representations (*Discourses* III.1.40). Long further elaborates Epictetus's position by claiming that it is our own "individual's autonomy and responsibility" we should identify ourselves with, not the whole and more general faculty of reason. The faculty by which we give our assent to the representations and volitions concerning entities we familiarise with is, according to Epictetus, what we should care about and what we really are. Call the view according to which we are this faculty, the *prohairesis* theory of our own nature. More specifically, we can describe a *prohairesis* or moral character theory of what we are as follows. We are entities that essentially have the faculty of regulating their own representations in the form of assenting or not to them. Our *prohairesis* is what we are, but this does not mean that it should be understood as a pure (or featureless) Cartesian ego or as a minimal subject. In fact, Long claims that such a faculty is the result of our personal histories and that *prohairesis* should not been seen as striving to distinguish itself from nature. Quite the contrary, the Stoics believed that the ethical way of life should be that in accordance with nature. Epictetus's emphasis on a continuous and thorough examination of our representations is perspicuously characterised by Michel Foucault as a kind of permanent self-examination. To sum up, on this view – and integrating certain aspects of the psychological approach – we are essentially psychological entities of a certain kind, namely, psychological entities with a certain moral character. In addition, the continuity of such a character, through appropriate psychological connections, is what grounds our identity through time as persons.

The idea that we are entities capable of appropriating, identifying, or accepting certain aspects of our mental lives has played an important role in contemporary theories of the nature of personhood and agency. One of the most influential of these theories is Frankfurt's, the main points of which are discussed in the next section.

2 Frankfurt on personhood

In his paper 'Freedom of the Will and the Concept of a Person' (1971), Frankfurt claims that it is entities having a certain kind of second-order desires that can be properly classified as persons. A second-order desire is a desire about one or more of our basic desires. For example, we may want – Frankfurt uses the verbs 'to desire' and 'to want' almost interchangeably – to kill somebody (a first-order desire) and we may also want not to have such a desire (a second-order desire). A physician may want to experience the energy and drive related to the desire of consuming certain drugs without thereby wanting to consume any drug. From the fact that somebody wants to want to do X, it does not follow that this person also wants to do X, and vice versa. Frankfurt maintains that when a desire is such that someone wants that a desire also move her to action – that is, the agent desires that one specific desire be effective and motivating – then such a desire is (part of) her will. These motivating second-order desires are called 'volitions' and, according to Frankfurt, having volitions is a necessary and sufficient condition for being a person. The idea is that an individual that has these second-order desires cares about which of her desires prevail, and such *desired desires* become part of the agent's will. To the degree that such volitions are internalised and properly recognised as belonging to an agent, they may constitute not just the agent's will but also contribute to the identification and persistence over time of the agent *as the same person*. This volitional criterion for being a person, although useful to highlight the connection between our being persons and being agents responsible for our actions and desires, may be problematic. In particular, as Frankfurt himself points out, there are entities that we may want to classify as persons but that, according to his criterion, would not count as persons. For instance, those individuals Frankfurt calls the 'wantons'. A wanton is an entity that does not have second-order volitions. Probably non-human animals, children, and possibly certain human adults – e.g., certain drug addicts – may be wantons. Such entities do not care about the desirability of some of their desires, never question them, but may still have rational capacities and consciousness such that there may be contexts in which classifying them as persons does not seem a misuse of the concept 'person'. Frankfurt admits that a simple volitional criterion for personhood may be too strict, and claims that, although this criterion may not capture all of our intuitions about personhood, it is useful for some specific theoretical purposes; for instance, to improve on our understanding of the connection between the will and identity.

Frankfurt claims that freedom of will involves being free to want what one wants. In other words, an entity that has free will is free to want its own will, which is also what makes such an entity a person. Our capacity to want our own will plays an important role also in another paper, 'Identification and Externality' (1976), in which Frankfurt further discusses the old problem of providing an account of the distinction between actions and non-actions, i.e., the distinction between actions that can be *properly* attributed to a person and events that are still associated with a person but that are, say, mere bodily spasms. More specifically, muscular spasms may be associated with our body, but we seldom consider them as our own doings. Frankfurt claims that a distinction similar to that between *internal* and *external* actions is appropriate also in the case of certain thoughts we may happen to entertain. As not all physical events related to our bodies are to be attributed to us, we should not be identified with all of the thoughts in our minds either.[7] The point seems to be that only certain thoughts determine our identity as persons – the underlying idea being that only those actions and thoughts that are expressions of ourselves determine what we are.

When is a mental event such as a passion external to a person's identity – and thus, a passion the absence of which should not count as a reason to believe that a person is not the same through time? To begin with, a passion seems to be external to us when it is induced by certain means such as drugs and hypnosis. Frankfurt also claims that some emotional outbursts may be sincerely or properly recognised as completely extraneous to one's own person, as if an external agent had violated the internal or inner core of a person's will. Phenomenologically, the occurrence of an undesired passion may give us a feeling that such an episode does not show what we really are. It is also plausible that, if such a passion is recognised as extraneous, we do not want it to motivate us to act. On the other hand, an authentic or identity-defining passion is a passion we want to motivate us to act. One general principle underlying these considerations could be that a passion is to be properly recognised as part of ourselves *qua* persons when we want it to be part of what we feel or desire. However, Frankfurt claims, the distinction between an internal and an external desire cannot be drawn exclusively on the ground of an ideal self-image, where this last concept stands for an idealised will that a person desires herself to be/have. In fact, the attitude that a person has towards her desires may not be sufficient to distinguish internal from external desires. After all, a person may reluctantly accept that certain undesirable passions are her own, if only as an unwelcome part of her will.

Gary Watson, in his 'Free Agency' (1975), criticises Frankfurt's use of higher-order mental states to explain the process of identification of desires and actions as our own. More specifically, Watson's concern is articulated by referring to what he calls 'higher-order wantons': maybe there are entities who have second-order volitions but are also wanton about them, that is, there are entities who do not care about their second-order volitions. The problem seems to be that having higher-order volitions does not explain, by itself, the distinction between internal and external desires, as also certain higher-order desires may not count as desires that belong to a person – as exemplified by the case of second-order wantons. Perhaps, Watson claims, something more basic explains why some higher-order volitions are our own.

In a series of later papers published after Watson's criticism, Frankfurt seems to rely on the idea that the process of identification – the process through which we identify certain mental states as our own – should be understood also as a form of decision process. According to this view, agent A truly identifies herself with a desire to X in case A's higher-order desires favour X *and* A has decided in favour of that desire. This account has been developed by a number of other recent philosophers of action. For example, Michael Bratman has further elaborated on the conditions of appropriateness that a decision is supposed to have in order to count as an instance of identification. In particular, he claims that an identification-involving decision may have to be accompanied by a sense of satisfaction – I decide to act upon a certain desire *and* I am also satisfied with such a decision – and/or such a decision may also have to involve treating a desire as reason-giving. A desire is taken as reason-giving in case an agent "treats it as setting an end that can to some extent justify means and/or preliminary steps."[8]

These theories can be used to characterise a more specific psychological approach to personal identity; in particular, the ideas regarding the process of identification may be translated into criteria to discern which psychological connections are relevant for our personal identity through time. I specify the details of the resulting theories in the next section.

2.1 Volitions, the will, and personal identity

Frankfurt seems to endorse, perhaps implicitly, the view that we are essentially persons and psychological entities. We can describe a first version of a volitional theory of what we are as follows. We are essentially entities that have the faculty of regulating their own representations in the form of assenting to them, that is, we are essentially volitional entities. For an entity to have the kind of volitions described previously, the possession of certain psychological states is clearly required. Another version of the volitional theory maintains that we are essentially entities that can identify with some of their desires (in the sense of familiarising ourselves with such desires). These two theories – which belong to the practical approach – can be further developed into different accounts of personal identity:

(Higher-order Desire Theory of the Metaphysical Foundation of Personal Identity)

For all t, P at t_1 is one and the same person as Q at t_2 iff Q's volitions (and/or the mental faculties responsible for their persistence and development) at t_2 are part or an evolution of the same mental structure responsible for those desires that P at t_1 identified as part of P's will.

(Decision and Higher-Order Desire Theory of the Metaphysical Foundation of Personal Identity)

For all t, P at t_1 is one and the same person as Q at t_2 iff (1) Q's volitions (and/or the mental faculties responsible for their persistence and development) at t_2 are part or an evolution of the same mental structure responsible for those desires that P at t_1 identified as part of P's will; and (2) P and Q have decided (in an appropriate way) to follow the higher-order desires connected to the mental structure referred to in the previous clause.

A different formulation may simply rely on the notion of the will:

(Sameness of Will Theory of the Metaphysical Foundation of Personal Identity)

For all t, P at t_1 is one and the same person as Q at t_2 iff Q at t_2 has the same will as P's will at t_1.

Two mental states correctly classified as instances or parts of the same will at different times should be properly related. In turn, this connection can be understood in terms of a relation that may involve certain degrees of change, e.g., under the form of development and/or evolution. More specifically, we may argue that the content of Q's will should be the proper development and/or evolution of the content of P's will. As a consequence, Q's will may be the same will as P's will also in case Q's will and P's will do not include exactly the same volitions. In turn, these conditions can be seen as specifications of the structure that psychological connections of the right kind should have to sustain personal identity – that is, as characterising a more specific version of the psychological approach.

One possible problem of these definitions is circularity: if a desire's belonging to P's will depends on whether such a desire is identified with or by P, then what distinguishes relevant from non-relevant volitions is the fact that the relevant volitions already belong to a person. If this is the case, volitions are defined and identified in terms of the identity of P as a person – given Frankfurt's definition of a person in terms of its capacity to have volitions. One of the consequences would be that there may not be an independent way of knowing whether a relevant volition is part of a person's will without already knowing the conditions of identity of the person in question. A specification of the conditions that make some volitions and decisions relevant to the identification of a person should not rely on the identity of the person, if we want these conditions to figure in a non-circular theory of personal identity.

3 Practical unity and the self-constitution view

Korsgaard criticises Parfit's theory of personal identity from a broadly Kantian perspective. In her 'Personal Identity and the Unity of Agency' (1989), she argues that at any given time we do consider ourselves as a single unitary individual over time for practical rather than metaphysical reasons. So, to understand ourselves as synchronically and diachronically individuated persons – the concepts of a self and of a person are not always clearly distinguished in her article – we should start from the concept of agency. In particular, Korsgaard claims that what grounds our synchronic practical unity – or, at least, our sense of being such a unitary kind of entity – is the necessity of eliminating internal conflicts within us. Although we may have conflicting desires, our doing any action at all depends on our having previously resolved (at least temporarily and/or partially) various internal conflicts. At any given time, in fact, we have to act as a single unified entity if we are to act at all. The second element of our synchronic practical unity – a unity we experience irremediably at the same moment in which we act as proper agents – is the seemingly independent standpoint from which we make our choices. In particular, Korsgaard argues that it is as if there were a single entity over and above our conflicting desires that chooses the specific course of action that we subsequently follow. In addition, this process of choice implies that we take ourselves to have reasons for and against following one desire rather than another. Korsgaard also claims that, when we choose one specific course of action, there is some principle that underlies such a choice and that we regard as expressive of ourselves. Such a principle or law, Korsgaard says, can become what we identify ourselves with. Using a Kantian terminology, she maintains that identifying yourself with such a principle is to be "a law to yourself" and, for these reasons, the synchronic unity of a subject is provided to us on practical rather than metaphysical grounds.

Korsgaard proposes a similar view in relation to our diachronic unity. In particular, she maintains that actions, e.g., significant actions such as carrying out a rational life plan, presuppose that our identity as practical agents be extended over time. Such an identity, she clarifies, is both presupposed and constructed formally: identity is constituted at least at the moment of action since it is presupposed in our practical agency (that is, for being proper agents). The point is that the holding of the relation of personal identity over time is a requirement for us to be rational agents. It is a matter of practical necessity, a fact dictated by the structure of our practical agency, that we think of ourselves as continuing entities, each having a (hopefully sufficiently long) life to lead. Korsgaard also claims that when a person is seen as an agent, it cannot be seen as a merely non-extended or momentary self. In fact, the basic unit from which our agency is exercised is a human body extended in time, at least given the state of our present technology. So, if she is right, we are agents composed of a group of psychological functions and states appropriately related to a body, and both aspects must operate as a unified agent to function properly. Authorial psychological connectedness, as Korsgaard calls the relevant psychological relation that connects the various psychological aspects of a single person, is compatible with drastic changes. In particular, the relation of authorial psychological connectedness can hold to the degree that these changes are the result of actions of which the person herself is reasonably taken to be responsible.

Throughout her career, Korsgaard has articulated at great length her ideas on the relationship between practical unity and identity and, in some recent works, she has emphasised some of the constructivist aspects of her theory.[9] On her view, our distinctive feature *qua* human beings (or, as we called them, 'human *persons*') is reason, where this is the capacity for normative self-government, that is, the capacity to decide what to count as a reason for belief and/or action. Korsgaard claims that whenever we choose to perform an action, we are thereby constituting ourselves as the authors of such actions. Insofar as we are responsible for our actions, we constitute ourselves as the persons we are – one of the functions of action is thus nothing less than self-constitution. The way in which we can properly constitute ourselves is Kantian: the laws or principles with which we identify should be in accordance with universal principles which we can will as laws for every rational being – an explicit reference to one of Kant's formulations of the categorical imperative. Korsgaard also maintains that the actions which we identify as our own are those actions that better unify us as self-constituted agents.

The important points for our discussion to be remembered from this brief introduction to Korsgaard's complex theory are:

- Our diachronic and synchronic identity is better understood by studying the structure of our agency rather than by starting from the metaphysics of identity. The main reason is that being an agent essentially involves individuation and continuity. If we recognise ourselves as agents, as Korsgaard thinks we should, we cannot but ascribe to ourselves some of the features discussed previously. Metaphysical considerations such as those advanced by Parfit do not play a foundational role in this process of recognition.

- Human agency is constructivist in character, that is, an agent (and thus a person) constitutes itself at the moment of acting upon certain principles. Korsgaard further adds that our nature – understood in a broadly Aristotelian teleological way – is such that a criterion for proper actions is moral and involves the constitution of a practical unity over time.

One problem of this approach is that it is not clear how to understand the process of creation of the self (or person) in question. In particular, Korsgaard seems to believe that the self is constituted at the moment of acting-for-a-reason because acting formally unifies our various internal aspects. However, we still do not have a clear account of what is responsible for this constituting act and of its features. Fortunately, several other philosophers have discussed a process of self-creation similar to the one proposed here. In the next sub-section, I introduce some of their views.

3.1 What is a self-constituting self?

Is there an underlying entity responsible for the process of self-constitution? What is the result of this creative process, a self, a person, or a fiction? According to Dennett, the self – again, selves and persons are not always properly distinguished – is a centre of narrative gravity, a useful abstraction created by our brains.[10] So, a self is the creation of an entity that does not have to be itself a self. Rather, the resulting self or person is a fiction through which we deal with the social and natural environment. In general, having a self is not essential for coping with the environment; after all, many living entities seem to survive without being equipped with anything so complex. However, the self happens to be one of the specific tools used by human beings to survive. In particular, Dennett claims that the brain produces a self in the sense that it represents such an entity to exist as part of our peculiar strategy to direct some of those activities conducive to our survival. On his view, the brain produces strings of narrative as if they were originated from a single source, whereas in reality there is no physical centre or point to which such a centre corresponds.

Velleman understands Dennett as making the claim that it is a mistake to regard the protagonist of our narratives as also being necessarily their author: the brain, as the author of our autobiography, is not also its main character.[11] In other words, we do not spin our stories, our brain does it for us. Velleman proposes a different approach – certainly more in tune with Korsgaard's theory. In particular, he claims that the fictional self is itself capable of enacting and modifying its own story on the basis of the representations of which the story is made. A self-narrator takes part in the process of determining the behaviour of an agent also in virtue of its capacity to follow or modify the content of the self-representation. Velleman, referring to studies in social psychology, also claims that the self (or person) tends to refer and act in accordance with the person's autobiography or the person's self-conception. The point is that a person's behaviour is or can be affected by the kind of self-representation that is generated. For example, when certain people make explicit predictions concerning their character or future behaviour, they are more likely to act according to such predictions. What Velleman calls 'the narrative module' is that part of our cognitive architecture responsible for generating internally and externally coherent narratives or self-representations. This implies that the protagonist of our autobiographies can modify the content of her autobiography (and act following some of the descriptions contained in it).

3.2 Agency and personal identity

A metaphysical account of personal identity based on the previous considerations can be summarised as follows:

(Agent Theory of the Metaphysical Foundation of Personal Identity)

For all t, P at t_1 is one and the same person as Q at t_2 iff Q at t_2 is the same agent as P at t_1.

In turn, being the same agent through time may involve a specific form of psychological continuity – for instance, a continuity determined by strong chains of *authorial* psychological connections. Again, these relations can be understood as determining the proper structure of psychological connections required to sustain personal identity.

An account of personal identity may also be given in terms of the identity of a self-representation or in terms of the identity of the narrative module responsible for our self-constitution:

(Self-representation Theory of the Metaphysical Foundation of Personal Identity)

For all t, P at t_1 is one and the same person as Q at t_2 iff Q at t_2 is the same self-representation as P at t_1.

(Narrative Module Theory of the Metaphysical Foundation of Personal Identity)

For all t, P at t_1 is one and the same person as Q at t_2 iff Q's narrative module at t_2 is the same module as P's narrative module at t_1.

A more nuanced account of the structure of what should count as a proper identity-sustaining narrative, that is, a narrative capable of sustaining the relation of personal identity, is proposed by Schechtman, whose theory is discussed in the next section.

4 Self-constituting narrative view

An explicit criterion for the success of Schechtman's narrative view of personal identity is the capacity to provide an explanation and a justification of the connection between personal identity and certain aspects of our practical and moral lives. According to Schechtman, one reason for the alleged inadequacy of many theories of personal identity based on (generic) psychological connections is their inability to explain, in their attempts to formulate criteria for numerical identity over time, the importance of identity to matters of survival, moral responsibility, future concerns, and compensation.

In the early part of her career, Schechtman proposed a widely cited person-/self-constituting narrative theory that operates at two different levels, the level of the self and that of the person.[12] In particular, she maintains that the self is the inner mental entity responsible for our thinking, while a person is, if anything, an entity that can persist an entire lifetime. According to her, we should provide an account of at least two types of narratives, one *self*-constituting narrative and one *person*-constituting narrative. A person-constituting narrative is a story that is supposed to address the practical importance of being the same – numerically – over relative long periods of time. On the other hand, a *self*-constituting narrative is a story that affects a qualitative change in its subject's present experiences. This qualitative change in the phenomenological character of the experience of the present moment takes place because the various past episodes of the self-constituting narrative are connected to the present experiencing self by what Schechtman calls 'empathic access'. A self-constituting narrative is thus a story that informs the subjective aspects of an individual subject of experience. More precisely, the self-constituting narrative provides an ordering of the individual's memories and concerns for certain future states by ordering past experiences and expectations from a first-person perspective characterised by an empathic attitude towards them. As a result of this empathic access, current psychological states modified by affectively connected parts of the self-constituting story are phenomenologically different from how they would be experienced had they lacked such a connection. In other words, experiencing an event under the perspective of a connected narrative modifies the way we perceive this event. Schechtman claims that the narratively constituted self recognises as her own not just memories but also mental states such as desires and beliefs, and influences the course of her actions and the ways through which reality is perceived. The role of a person-constituting narrative is broader in that it also inscribes this individual self in the relevant social and moral landscape.

Not all narratives are acceptable as proper self- or person-constituting. More specifically, a proper identity-sustaining narrative, according to Schechtman, must adhere to a *reality* constraint, be intelligible, and sufficiently explain the actual mental states of the person-narrator. In addition, the story in question must be told by an individual about herself, using the structure of a conventional linear narrative. Schechtman claims that an adequate explanation of the importance of identity for our survival must include the persistence of "a single, experiencing subject, and such persistence is necessary to make sense of the attitudes and practices surrounding these features." This theory seems to suggest that we can be identified as self- or person-constituting narrative tellers. Our nature is that of individuals capable of making proper narratives out of the various events happening to them (Self-/person-constituting Narrative view of our own nature). In what follows, I do not further distinguish between self- and person-constituting narrative, and use 'self-constituting narrative' or 'person-sustaining narrative' to refer to an identity-sustaining narrative that can operate at various levels.

Galen Strawson has advanced several poignant criticisms against the narrative view.[13] For instance, he claims that we do not necessarily experience our lives in the way stories and/or narratives are structured. Intended as a descriptive or psychological claim about our experience of ourselves as temporally extended subjects, G. Strawson argues that the narrative view is wrong, at least in his own case. In addition, he maintains that narrative theories seldom specify what a narrative is. In fact, in many cases the terms 'narrative' and 'stories' seem to have been used just for rhetorical effect – that is, claims according to which we are our own stories/narratives would be simply trendy catchphrases. More sympathetically to the narrative approach, these criticisms can be intended as requests to better specify what a narrative is. In reply, we may argue that the creation of a person-sustaining narrative can be the result of: (1) a general tendency to *form-finding*, that is, some sort of tendency to recognise and conceptualise large scale coherence-seeking, pattern-seeking tendencies – this idea seems to be what Velleman has in mind; (2) a *story-telling* tendency, whereby we constitute our lives along the lines of some recognised literary genre. As writers of our own autobiography, we decide which parts to include in our own story, with a mild preoccupation to steer away from utter imaginary fabrications; (3) a special *quest-for-the-good* tendency, that is, a refined and morally driven form of story-telling whereby we recognise or inscribe our lives into a broader moral context which, in turn, gives meaning to our narratives, that is, meaning to our lives. Grandiose religious narratives of conversions come to mind as examples (e.g., Augustine's *Confessions*).

There are other requirements that can be imposed on what a *proper* identity-sustaining narrative is. For instance, a proper narrative may have to be more or less coherent and/or capable of providing an account of a significant number of episodes in the life of its narrator. A proper narrative may also have to be (1) available to one's own consciousness, (2) kept into account when certain decisions are made, (3) embodied – e.g., be from the point of view of an essentially bodily narrator.[14]

Schechtman claims that having an identity-sustaining narrative story may just amount to having a certain understanding of how some of the events that have happened to us hang together. Such an understanding may be the result of a process that can be largely automatic but that can, in principle, be retrieved and used to operate in the social context in which we live. In addition, Schechtman holds that a self-constituting narrative has a social dimension because most of the elements of our stories derive from the particular environment in which we happen to live – e.g., our language(s), people we interact with, family.

What are some of the consequences of having a narrative? Arguably, some Buddhist philosophers and nihilists would claim that having a narrative would just add another layer of unnecessary deception. Having a narrative may even cause one individual to become more attached to her own life and thus increase her existential anxiety – especially when confronted with the possibility that such a narrative may come to an end. So, from a Buddhist perspective, lacking a narrative may actually be liberating (or even illuminating). G. Strawson also argues that an episodic self, a self that does not experience itself as part of a narrative, may be or feel free to partake in certain forms of life (e.g., the happy-go-merry free spirit who does not think about what will happen tomorrow) that are not available to a supporter of the self-constituting narrative approach. However, many subjects lacking the capacity to narrate their own life story, or even incapable of retrieving and updating an existing one, do not seem to live enviable lives. For instance, the neurologist Oliver Sacks has vividly described several pathological cases of people who have lost the capacity to retrieve or form their life-stories due to certain neurological diseases.[15] One of these patients, who suffered from an acute form of Korsakov's syndrome, is described as incapable of forming new stable memories, recognising people, and giving an order to the various mental states generated by his brain. Sacks portrays the life of this patient as devoid of stable and significant human interactions, if only because the patient is not capable of appropriately recognising and contextualising people whom he had already met. Sacks also reports the case of a man who continually confabulates random personal stories patching together several memories. Interacting with this individual gives a sense of interacting with someone who has lost the capacity to form certain emotional attachments based on reality that we seem to regard essential to a valuable life.

4.1 Narrative identity and personal identity

A metaphysical theory of personal identity based on the previous version of the narrative approach can be formulated as follows:

> (Self-constituting Narrative View of the Metaphysical Foundation of Personal Identity)
>
> For all t, P at t_1 is one and the same person as Q at t_2 iff P at t_1 and Q at t_2 are the same protagonist/narrator in the same ongoing and proper identity-sustaining narrative. A proper identity-sustaining narrative is a narrative that is produced and developed through time by a self or narrator *internal* to the narrative, that is, by a person-constituting narrator that is also the protagonist of the identity-sustaining narrative, and such that the qualitative content of her experiences is modified by the content of the narrative. The structure of this narrative can involve various degrees of complexity and structure, a complexity that, in certain cases, may resemble that of a character in a work of literature.

It is important to notice that, according to this version of the self-constituting narrative approach, the subject or self that is spinning the constituting narrative is telling her own story. The creator is also, so to speak, what is created by the narrative. As emphasised in the introduction to this chapter, Schechtman's early version of the narrative approach was *not* meant to specify a series of metaphysical conditions for the re-identification of persons over time. Rather, her main objective was that of re-directing the debate on personal identity from being focused on re-identification questions (e.g., what am I? How do I [metaphysically] persist through time as the same person?) to characterisation questions (e.g., who am I? What actions can be properly described as my own actions?). In this section, I have described one way in which an answer to the characterisation questions may offer also an answer to the metaphysical/re-identification question.

One of the reasons in support of this approach is that generic versions of the psychological approach may not contain conditions on the structure of the psychological connections that sustain personal identity that are rich enough to satisfy some of our beliefs about our identity over time – for instance, the idea that not all of our psychological connections are equally relevant or important for us to persist over time. This idea, in turn, can be translated into the requirement that an account of personal identity should properly explain why not all psychological connections seem equally relevant to the constitution of what we are and/or in sustaining the identity of a person over time. The self-constituting narrative view may provide such an explanation: certain psychological connections (e.g., memories, character traits) are more important than others because they form part of a person-constituting narrative. In particular, if a person-sustaining narrative is such that the protagonist interprets herself as having developed, say, certain character traits, then the persistence over time of these character traits will be considered by the narrator as being fundamental to her identity.

Some philosophers, for example Alasdair MacIntyre, argue that having an identity-sustaining narrative is essential to leading a virtuous life. In particular, MacIntyre maintains that a moral action is intelligible only in the context of a life considered as a narrative. The reason is that, according to him, a correct characterisation of a human action is possible only after an action is included and inscribed in at least one narrative story.[16] Such an inclusion provides the means for understanding the exclusively human motives behind an action, in contrast to a purely biological or mechanic agitation of molecules. MacIntyre claims that the narrative form of telling stories is essential to characterising human actions and, *a fortiori*, to characterising the morality of such actions. This view on the connection between morality and narrative is not endorsed by all those who support the narrative approach.

Another version of the narrative approach, explored more in detail in Chapter 8, rejects the idea that the self-constituting self, the entity that produces the narrative, must itself create the story and/or already exist in order to be the future referent of its own identity-sustaining narrative. In particular, a *non*-self-constituting narrative approach can hold that it is not a necessary condition for being a proper identity-sustaining narrative that the narrative be produced by the subject the narrative is mainly about.

One problem of the narrative approach is that it seems to prescribe a too-demanding condition on personhood and on the holding of the relation of personal identity. Although it may provide an explanation of why we deem certain psychological connections more important than others, it seems that even weak forms of narrativity – e.g., form-finding – are not manifested by certain individuals that we may still want to consider as persons. In fact, certain people do not seem to have any significant tendency to seek for or conceptualise themselves as having narratives with long-term coherent patterns. In addition, the approach seems to imply that we would be justified in regarding cases of total amnesia as cases in which persons have literally gone out of existence. Although some may welcome such a consequence, others may think that not all cases of amnesia amount to the death of a person.

5 Summary

This chapter explored two approaches to personal identity that are motivated by similar considerations. In particular, I introduced the practical and narrative approaches as ways of articulating the point that, although psychological connections of the right kind (e.g., appropriately causally connected) may be essential to our identity, not all such psychological connections are equally essential to our persistence (as individuals and/or as persons). More specifically, the practical approach relies on the intuition that those psychological faculties responsible for our capacity to make choices are what sustain the relation of personal identity. For instance, Epictetus claims that our *prohairesis* (moral character), which depends on giving or withholding assent to some of our representations (including feelings), is what we are essentially. In this chapter, I also outlined a series of metaphysical theories of personal identity based on Frankfurt's work on personhood and the will. The main point is that persons' persistence over time depends on the continuity of some of those faculties responsible for our acting for reasons, that is, of those faculties essential to our being practical agents. As practical agents, we have the capacity to plan and structure our actions on the basis of intentions that may persist over a significant amount of time. Korsgaard develops these points and claims that identity over time is thus strictly connected to what we take agents to be.

The other approach discussed in this chapter articulates the idea that not all psychological connections are equally relevant to identity over time by using the notion of a narrative. In particular, narrative theories generally hold that we are entities identified, synchronically and diachronically, by a narrative or a story (an identity-sustaining narrative). Some versions of this approach (e.g., Schechtman's) maintain that the relevant identity-sustaining narrative is a narrative told by the narrating individual itself – a person is at the same time both the narrator and the entity that is self-constituted by the narrative. Various conditions may then apply to what counts as a proper identity-sustaining narrative (e.g., the reality constraint). One of the problems of this approach is that having a narrative may be sufficient, but does not seem necessary to be a person: there are cases of individuals that we may want to classify as persons, but that do not seem (or claim) to be (self-) narrators at all.

Notes

1 Schechtman has recently published a book (2014), that defends ideas similar but also relevantly different from those I ascribe to her in this chapter. So, when I write "Schechtman claims that [...]", or "Schechtman holds that [...]" these expressions should be understood as being about her views prior to the publication of the book in 2014.

2 Even a partial bibliography of such studies would occupy a whole book.

3 See Annas (1993), p. 262.

4 The idea of a gradual expansion of our ethical concern is present also in certain models of self-cultivation in the Confucian tradition; see Chapter 3.

5 Long's characterization of the Stoic account draws from various sources, e.g., Hierocles, Origen, and Plutarch. See Long (1991/1996).

6 I am not here claiming that the Stoics were the only philosophers who discussed a mental faculty such as the one outlined in the main text – e.g., also Locke employs a similar notion, in particular, the notion of suspension (*Essays*, 2.21).

7 Frankfurt is not using 'identification' in either of the senses described in the introduction. Rather, he has in mind a psychological process through which we recognise certain mental states as our own. More details in the main text.

8 Bratman (1996), p. 198.

9 Korsgaard (2009).

10 See Dennett (1991).

11 Velleman (2005/6).

12 Schechtman (1996), (2001), and (2007).

13 Strawson (2004).

14 See Menary (2008) and MacKenzie (2009).

15 Sacks (1970).

16 See in this regard, the work of Gilbert Ryle on thin and thick description in his *Collected Papers, Volume II* (London and New York: Routledge, 2009), and Clifford Geertz's *The Interpretation of Cultures* (New York: Basic Books, 1973), in particular Chapter 1.

Suggested further readings

Familiarisation, appropriation, and Stoicism

Primary sources

Epictetus, *The Handbook of Epictetus*, translated by Nicholas P. White (Indianapolis: Hackett, 1983).

Epictetus, *The Discourses of Epictetus*, revised translation by Robin Hard, with an introduction by Christopher Gill (London: Everyman, 1995).

The Hellenistic Philosophers, Volume I, translations by Anthony A. Long and David Sedley (Cambridge: Cambridge University Press, 1987).

Hellenistic Philosophy: Introductory Readings, translations by Brad Inwood and Lloyd P. Gerson (Indianapolis: Hackett, 1998).

Secondary literature

Annas, Julia, *The Morality of Happiness* (Oxford: Oxford University Press, 1993).

Foucault, Michel, *The Hermeneutics of the Subject* (New York: Palgrave Macmillan, 2005).

Gill, Christopher, *The Structured Self in Hellenistic and Roman Thought* (Oxford: Oxford University Press, 2006).

Hadot, Pierre, *Philosophy as a Way of Life* (Oxford: Wiley-Blackwell, 1995).

Inwood, Brad, *Ethics and Human Action in Early Stoicism* (Oxford: Clarendon Press, 1985).

Long, Anthony A., 'Representation and the Self in Stoicism', reprinted in his *Stoic Studies* (Berkeley: University of California, 1991/1996), pp. 264–285.

Sedley, David (ed.) *Cambridge Companion to Greek and Roman Philosophy* (Cambridge: Cambridge University Press, 2003).

Second-order desires, agency, and personhood

Bratman, Michael, 'Identification, Decision, and Treating as a Reason', reprinted in his *Faces of Intention* (Cambridge: Cambridge University Press, 1996/1999), pp. 185–208.

Bratman, Michael, 'Reflection, Planning, and Temporally Extended Agency', *Philosophical Review*, 109 (2000), pp. 35–61.

Frankfurt, Harry, 'Freedom of the Will and the Concept of a Person', reprinted in his *The Importance of What We Care About* (Cambridge: Cambridge University Press, 1971/88), pp. 11–25.

Frankfurt, Harry, 'Identification and Externality', reprinted in his *The Importance of What We Care About* (Cambridge: Cambridge University Press, 1976/88), pp. 58–68.

Moran, Richard, 'Frankfurt on Identification', in Sarah Buss and Lee Overton (eds.) *Contours of Agency* (Cambridge, MA: MIT Press, 2002).

Watson, Gary, 'Free Agency', *Journal of Philosophy*, 72 (1975), pp. 205–220. Reprinted in John Christman (ed.) *The Inner Citadel* (Oxford: Oxford University Press, 1989), pp. 109–122.

Self-constitution

Dennett, Daniel, *Consciousness Explained* (Boston: Little Brown and Company, 1991), in particular Chapter 13.

Korsgaard, Christine, 'Personal Identity and the Unity of Agency', reprinted in her *Creating the Kingdom of Ends* (Cambridge: Cambridge University Press, 1996), pp. 363–397.

Korsgaard, Christine, 'Self-Constitution in the Ethics of Plato and Kant', *Journal of Ethics*, 3 (1999), pp. 1–29.

Korsgaard, Christine, *Self-Constitution: Agency, Identity, and Integrity* (Oxford: Oxford University Press, 2009).

Velleman, J. David, 'The Self as Narrator', reprinted in his *Self to Self* (Cambridge: Cambridge University Press, 2005/2006), pp. 203–223.

Self-constituting narrative view

Lamarque, Peter, 'On Not Expecting Too Much From Narrative', *Mind and Language*, 19, 4 (2004), pp. 393–408.

Lindemann, Hilde, *Holding and Letting Go* (Oxford: Oxford University Press, 2014).

Livingston, Paisley, 'Narrativity and Knowledge', *Journal of Aesthetics and Art Criticism*, 67, 1 (2009), pp. 25–36.

MacIntyre, Alasdair, *After Virtue, Third Edition* (Notre Dame: The University of Notre Dame Press, 1981/2007).

MacKenzie, Catriona, 'Personal Identity, Narrative Integration, and Embodiment', in Sue Campbell, Letitia Meynell, and Susan Sherwin (eds.) *Embodiment and Agency* (University Park, PA: Pennsylvania State University Press, 2009), pp. 100–125.

Menary, Richard, 'Embodied Narratives', *Journal of Consciousness Studies*, 15, 6 (2008), pp. 63–84.

Rudd, Anthony, 'In Defense of Narrativity', *European Journal of Philosophy*, 17,1 (2007), pp. 60–75.

Sacks, Oliver, *The Man Who Mistook His Wife for a Hat* (New York: Simon & Schuster, 1970).

Schechtman, Marya, *The Constitution of Selves* (Ithaca and London: Cornell University Press, 1996).

Schechtman, Marya, 'Empathic Access: The Missing Ingredient in Personal Identity,' *Philosophical Explorations, 4, 2* (2001), pp. 95–111, reprinted in Raymond Martin and John Barresi (eds.) *Personal Identity* (Oxford: Blackwell Publishing, 2003), pp. 238–259.

Schechtman, Marya, 'Stories, Lives, and Basic Survival', in Daniel Hutto (ed.) *Narrative and Understanding Persons* (Cambridge: Cambridge University Press, 2007), pp. 155–178.

Schechtman, Marya, *Staying Alive* (Oxford: Oxford University Press, 2014).

Strawson, Galen, 'Against Narrativity', *Ratio*, 17 (2004), pp. 428–452.

Strawson, Galen, 'Episodic Ethics', *Royal Institute of Philosophy Supplement*, 82, 60 (2007), pp. 85–115.

7 What matters in survival and life-extending technologies

1	Self-concern and survival: Butler and Hazlitt	168
2	The psychological approach and what matters in survival	171
3	Lewis, survival, and cohabitation	176
4	Survival and the other approaches to personal identity	178
	4.1 The simple-soul approach	178
	4.2 Buddhist no-self approach and nihilism	179
	4.3 Relational approach and Confucian role-person	180
	4.4 The physical approach and animalism	181
	4.5 Practical and narrative approaches	182
5	Life-extending technologies, our nature, and personal identity	184
6	Cryonics and mental uploading	185
	6.1 The simple-soul approach	188
	6.2 Buddhist no-self approach and nihilism	188
	6.3 Relational approach and Confucian role-person	189
	6.4 The psychological approach	190
	6.5 The physical approach and animalism	191
	6.6 Practical and narrative approaches	191
7	Summary	192

Hunted by scavengers . . . Haunted by those I could not protect. So I exist in this wasteland . . . a man, reduced to a single instinct: Survive.

—Max Rockatansky, *Mad Max: Fury Road*, 2015

One of the most, if not perhaps the most, practical of our concerns is the concern for our own survival. Concern for our own survival is an attitude that generally involves expecting that certain future events will be related to our present self in a particularly intimate way. Expecting certain future events in an intimate way does not imply that our survival is all we value or that we are essentially selfish; rather, it is one phenomenological aspect of the attitude, call it 'self-concern', we generally have towards certain expected future states or events involving ourselves as subjects. Expecting to experience an event in a specific way is not the only sense of self-concern discussed in the current literature. In fact, sometimes self-concern, also called 'special concern', is understood as being one particular way in which we are concerned, in the sense of being interested or preoccupied, about certain future states. In what follows these two aspects are discussed together.

Now, self-concern and similar attitudes have been frequently assumed to be a crucial aspect of how we regard our identity over time. In particular, it has been claimed that if the relation of personal identity does not hold between A and B, where A and B exist at different times, A may not have, or it is rational for A not to have, a special concern for what happens to B. The reason would be that B's persistence through time does not preserve what matters in A's survival in case B is not the same person and/or individual as A. If a future entity is not you, it is rational for you not to have a special concern for that person, even though such a person may be psychologically connected to you. Some may claim that the holding of the relation of personal identity is a sufficient and/or necessary condition for the rationality of our concern for our own survival – that is, some claim that the relation of personal identity is an essential part of what is valuable in survival. However, some authors, notably Derek Parfit, have argued that personal identity is not what matters in survival – in the terminology I will adopt here (with one exception later on), Parfit questions whether personal identity is always a necessary condition for determining whether the general survival relation holds between A at t_1 and B at t_2. The holding of this relation is valuable, in particular, valuable in virtue of what we regard/ought to regard as valuable in our persistence as such. If the relation of survival holds between A and B, then what is valuable in survival is preserved. Take the relation *X personally survives as Y* (or, *personal survival*, for short) to be a relation the holding of which requires that two successive entities stand in the relation of X survives as Y (or, the survival relation) *and* in the relation of personal identity. Parfit claims that, all things being equal, the fact that two entities are not in the one-to-one relation of personal identity does not make the relation of survival between them as bad as death (or at least it does not make it not valuable). So, it may well be the case that, although certain kinds of social and practical considerations may count against the desirability of forms of non-personal survival, other considerations may even suggest that, in certain contexts, non-personal survival is better than personal survival. There is a sense in which you may survive – what matters in survival persists – even though you are not identical as a person to any future entity (that is, even though you do not personally survive). Philosophers who object to this view can be seen as claiming that personal survival is the sole form of survival (or that any valuable form of survival should at least be personal).

The first part of this chapter focuses on the debate over survival and related notions. In particular, I discuss Joseph Butler's (1692–1752) view as representative of the many philosophers who assumed that our special concern for survival requires the holding of the relation of personal identity. William Hazlitt (1778–1830) has been singled out by recent scholars as one of the first who questioned such an assumption. After introducing an interpretation of Parfit's view on what matters in survival, I discuss in section 3 one reply offered by David Lewis to the claim that personal identity is not essential for survival to matter in a special way.

In section 4, I explore how other approaches to personal identity and our nature can be applied to the debate on what matters in survival.

In the second part of the chapter, starting from section 5, I discuss these questions: if some forms of survival are valuable, to what extent are some life-extending technologies and enhancements desirable/rational to pursue? What contributions can the theoretical discussion on personal identity make to the debate on life-extending technologies? These technologies give rise to a variety of different theoretical and practical issues, which include an assessment of their expected cost-benefit balance, the feasibility of certain lines of research, the overall desirability of such technologies given their intended scopes, and so on. For example, a lifespan extension in a given population can be the result of a continuous process of improvement in the standards of living that, in turn, may involve simply the prevention of certain diseases. Life-extending technologies are sometimes discussed in relation to and as forms of human enhancements, both biomedical and non-biomedical. The debate on the connection between theories of personal identity, what matters in survival, and life-extending technologies is in its infancy, and there are not many studies in which such topics are discussed together – despite their obvious connections. Section 5 is an introduction to how some of these connections can be drawn, with particular emphasis on two life-extending technologies, mental uploading and cryonics. One of the main points of the discussion is that the relation between debates on life-extending technologies and personal identity does not have to be thought of as being unidirectional – moving, say, from general abstract philosophical theories to their practical applications – but rather as mutually influencing each other, e.g., some life-extending technologies can be seen as providing thought experiments to test the plausibility of some theories of personal identity. The technologies discussed in this chapter, that is, mental uploading and cryonics, are highly speculative, and this speculative character makes them particularly apt to play both roles.

I Self-concern and survival: Butler and Hazlitt

Among others, Butler discusses the importance of identity for our future- or past-directed concerns. In the context of a criticism directed against some Lockeans (probably including Anthony Collins), Butler claims that their approach to personal identity would imply that a person would be just fictional, that is, a non-substantial aggregate of successive acts of consciousness or mental states (call these more or less cohesive aggregates 'separate selves'). If this view were true, then, Butler claims:

> it is a fallacy upon ourselves to charge our present selves with any thing we did, or to imagine our present selves interested in any thing which befell us yesterday; or that our present self will be interested in what will befall us tomorrow; since our present self is not, in reality, the same with the self of yesterday, but another like self or person coming in its room, and mistaken for it; to which another self will

succeed tomorrow. This, I say, must follow: for if the self or person of today, and that of tomorrow, are not the same, but only like persons, the person of today is really no more interested in what will befall the person of tomorrow than in what will befall any other person.[1]

One way of re-phrasing this reasoning is: if (or given that) separate selves do not compose a person (in the sense of a persisting substance), and this is known by such selves, each single self will not have the same type of concern for the other members of the series as it has for itself. In turn, the conclusion of the previous reasoning was taken to be a problem for Locke's theory of personal identity. In particular, according to Butler, since Locke's theory implies that the unity of all these selves is fictitious or fictional – since no substance is responsible for such a unity – then his theory cannot accommodate our intuitions about self-concern. These intuitions cannot be explained or justified because each single separate self is not identical to the next in the series so, strictly speaking, the relation of identity does not hold between them. Although Butler did not use the expression 'intuitions about our self-concern', his reasoning seems to be based on the presupposition that the (known) holding of the relation of personal identity is a necessary condition for our special concern towards certain future entities. In other words, personal identity seems to be one of the necessary conditions for our concern for what matters in survival: it is a relation the instantiation of which between A and a successive B contains something that matters for A's self-concern and/or A's survival over time. One way of putting the main point at issue is to say that survival should be *personal* survival to be the proper object of our special concern for survival.

According to Raymond Martin and John Barresi, in the second part of the 17th century a substantial number of works on the nature of personal identity anticipated some of the developments that would have to wait until the second half of the 20th century to be further investigated by influential philosophers. In particular, the works of Joseph Priestley (1733–1804) and of his student William Hazlitt (1778–1830) showed that, at least conceptually, philosophers started to distinguish between the question of whether we are the same through time and the question of whether and to what degree personal identity should matter for the rationality of our special concern towards some of our later stages.

Hazlitt claims that, although we are mechanically or biologically connected to our past selves, it is only by an imaginative act that we project ourselves into the future – if only because future selves do not already exist the moment in which we imagine them. The impulse that seems to justify our special attitude towards our future-directed states is based, according to Hazlitt, on a kind of habituation of the mind that feeds certain future-directed personal attitudes that, in turn, do not have a metaphysical basis. In short, the connection with our past is real, while the connection with future selves is merely imaginary.[2] One of the consequences of this point for our future-directed attitudes is that, according to Hazlitt, in respect to the special care you may have, it makes no difference whether you pursue an imaginary future self-welfare: such a welfare would be yours only in the imagination. To sum up, Hazlitt argues against the possibility of having rational self-interest for an alleged future self along the following lines:

1   Our concern or care ("personal interest") for anything must have as its intentional object: (1) the object that generated a current impression in us (and such an impression cannot be generated if the object does not exist), or (2) an impression of a past object with which we have been connected "mechanically".
2   We cannot rationally have concern or care for future impressions. If such a concern arises, it is only because of our anticipation of certain states "with greater warmth of present imagination."

The first premise would certainly be questioned by supporters of certain versions of the narrative approach (and not only them). In particular, they would claim that, although it may be true that future selves do not exist, we can be justified in being concerned about the product of certain imaginative acts, more specifically, those imaginative acts responsible for tying together certain expected future events to our current mental states as parts of the development of an ongoing narrative.

Hazlitt also clearly distinguishes between questions of personal identity in cases of reduplication from questions regarding the rationality of self-concern. In particular, while discussing a scenario in which a deity transmits the same consciousness to more than one entity (and assuming that consciousness grounds personal identity), he asks:

> Am I to regard all these [other future entities psychologically connected to me] as equally myself? Am I equally interested in the fate of all? Or if I must fixate upon some one of them in particular as my representative and other self, how am I to be determined in my choice?
>
> (Hazlitt 1805: 136)

Hazlitt then seems to suggest that, given the possibility of fission, reduplication, and other fantastic scenarios, the continuity of consciousness that grounds personal identity does not seem to ground "the least alteration in my present being" in regard to the concern shown for these imagined various future existences. According to Hazlitt, the reasons for being more concerned about one future self as opposed to any other one is not personal identity but the degree of anticipation and warmth with which such a self is imagined. In a sense, Hazlitt does seem to claim that personal identity is not what grounds self-concern, but only because it cannot hold between an existing self and a future self, since the latter does not exist. Our concern for the future – for instance, for personal survival – may be rather grounded in an imaginary or projected relation of qualitatively significant psychological connections. This reasoning anticipates some of the debates on self-concern, survival, and personal identity in the 1960s; however, Hazlitt does not seem to have explicitly claimed that an imaginary/psychological connection with two or more fictitious future selves can preserve what (if anything) matters in our self-concern for just a single future self. The importance of this last claim will be evident in the next section in relation to Parfit's discussion of a fission scenario.

2 The psychological approach and what matters in survival

Parfit has famously argued that identity is not what matters in survival. His argument for this conclusion is based on one version of the psychological theory of personal identity (see Chapter 4). The reader may want to keep in mind the following version:

> (Parfit's Normal Cause Theory of the Metaphysical Foundation of Personal Identity)
>
> For all t, P at t_1 is the same person as Q at t_2, provided a definition of psychological continuity in terms of overlapping chains of strong connectedness, iff (1) P is psychologically continuous with Q (relation R holds), (2) psychological connectedness and/or continuity have the *normal kind* of causes, and (3) they have not taken a branching form (uniqueness condition).

Drawing from the literature on brain bisection (e.g., R. W. Sperry's work on the topic), Parfit holds that it is metaphysically and even biologically possible to sever a brain into two parts called 'cerebral hemispheres' (this kind of procedure has been carried out in critical and severe cases of epilepsy). Another relevant fact regarding our brains is that, although our normal development is such that certain functions and mental contents (e.g., memories) are distributed across different and specific areas (e.g., our speech capacity in the left hemisphere), our brains are rather plastic and adaptable; for example, people who have had a stroke in their left hemisphere may regain speech with time.[3] In general, there are actual cases in which half of the brain is considered as sufficient for personal survival – after all, it is perfectly normal to say that someone has survived a stroke that destroyed half of her brain. Parfit also claims that, although technologically impossible at the moment, brain transplants are at least conceivable, in the weak sense of it not being incoherent to imagine them. In the next step of his argument, Parfit proposes the following imaginary scenario. Suppose that brain transplants are now technologically possible and that your brain is successfully transplanted into a new body. According to Parfit, the best description of the outcome of the operation is that you have acquired a new body. More specifically, you are the recipient of a new body and you have thus survived the operation. (The plausibility of this description also depends on the assumption that psychological continuity has been maintained through normal [or almost normal] causal means, that is, by brain continuity.) Presumably, the new body would have to be similar to the one you once had in order to preserve long-term psychological connectedness and/or avoid some form of mental disorder. For instance, if you are an adult bodybuilder who values his physical achievements and you receive the body of a six-year-old child, the consequences for your character and psychology may be unpredictable – e.g., psychological connectedness and/or continuity may become compromised. However, suppose that the body you receive is that of your (well-trained) twin, or that your brain is implanted into a brainless updated clone of yours. Although Parfit does not use the term 'personal survival', he would maintain that cases satisfying these conditions are cases of *personal* survival – you would survive and be the same person. Now, if it is true that the persistence of half of the brain is sufficient for survival – as we normally claim it to be, since we normally believe that a person can personally survive a stroke, even though with severe problems and traumas – then a transplant of only half of your brain into a new body would be sufficient for your personal survival as well. After all, the relevant condition for your personal survival, the persistence of your brain and of a sufficient number of psychological connections, is met in both situations – in the stroke and the half-brain transplant cases. Now, Parfit asks: what would happen if, instead of transplanting only half of your brain, also the other half were successfully transplanted into a numerically different (but qualitatively similar) body from the one into which the other half has been transplanted? Let us call the two resulting entities, each containing one half of your brain, A and B. Suppose that each hemisphere has an equal or highly similar degree of psychological connectedness with you and that the operations have been successful. Let us describe the situation by using solely the term 'survival' as it is commonly used (thus forgetting for a moment the technical specifications of the concept, e.g., the distinction between survival and personal survival). Now, ask yourself, would you 'survive' the operation?[4] There are four possibilities:

1   You do not survive.
2   You survive as one of the two people, say, A.
3   You survive as B.
4   You survive as both.

Parfit argues against (1) in this way: you would survive if your brain were successfully transplanted into a new body and you would survive with only half of your brain. So, if half of your brain were transplanted, you would survive. Also, if the other half of your brain were destroyed, you would survive. Now, if both are successfully transplanted, how could you fail to *survive* at all? How could a double success be a failure, i.e., a case in which no survival occurs? Against (2) and (3), Parfit claims that, given sufficient or equal psychological connectedness between (i) you and A, and (ii) you and B, there is no fact that would make you A instead of B or the other way round. In other words, there would not be a fact of the matter determining that A's continuing to exist instead of B's continuing to exist constitutes the only case in which you survive (and vice versa). Holding (4), Parfit claims, would imply a great distortion in our concept of a person, on the supposition that 'survive', in this context, implies that the relation of personal identity holds. To see the problem, imagine that after some time, A and B move to different parts of the world and have their own lives. One day they meet again and play tennis against each other. Would that be a situation in which one person plays against herself? But then how could one person win and another one lose? Parfit maintains that it is unlikely that one person can be properly said to be identical, as *a* person, to two other spatio-temporally distinct individuals with completely independent centres of consciousness. If this reasoning is correct, then it is not clear how it can be said that you survive as both. So, (4) is not very plausible, although it does not imply a contradiction. (Remember that in the original discussion, Parfit does not distinguish between survival and personal survival and uses only the term 'survival'.)

Parfit's solution to this conundrum is that, on his reductionist view, there is a sense in which the problem disappears. According to him, the four possibilities are really just four descriptions of the same outcome; in particular, the outcome that after the two operations there will be two people, each of whom has a body similar to yours and who is sufficiently psychologically connected with you – that is, a degree of psychological connectedness such that, if only one had survived, you would identify yourself with such a person. (We are working here with the assumption that person essentialism and psychological essentialism are true.) Although Parfit claims that the best description of the outcome of the operation is that neither of the resulting people would be you at the same time (so, according to the best description you do not personally survive), he also maintains that this does not imply that such a description must also be true: in a reductionist framework, it is possible to claim that certain answers to the question whether you are the same through time can be *indeterminate*.[5] In particular, certain outcomes of the fission scenario described previously can be indeterminate. So, it may be indeterminate whether in the previous scenario you personally survive. The important question, according to Parfit, is rather how you should regard this outcome – or, in general, cases in which it is indeterminate whether you personally survive. In particular, if enough psychological connections hold between you and the two resulting individuals, is this outcome as bad as death? Or, using again our distinction between 'survival' and 'personal survival' (see the introduction to this chapter), should it rather count as a case of survival – maybe not as a case of *personal* survival but still something good enough? Are all cases of indeterminate or non-personal survival – for our present purposes I will not distinguish between them – as bad as death, as when we do not survive at all? If these outcomes were as bad as death, then it would be misleading to distinguish between survival and personal survival: they are one and the same thing. However, Parfit claims that we ought to hold certain outcomes of cases involving fission – as the one described previously – to be as good as personal survival, or, at least, as preserving what matters in normal cases of personal survival.

The recent literature is replete with discussions about how precisely we should understand Parfit's account and the nature of the relation that is supposed to ground value judgments about survival, which is called relation R or the R-relation (see 4.5). This relation has been generally understood as the relation that grounds personal identity *minus* the non-branching condition. However, even in Parfit's own writings, it is not always clear whether relation R is: (1) only psychological continuity, (2) psychological continuity *and/or* psychological connectedness, or (3) psychological continuity *and* connectedness. These differences may be crucial in assessing whether what matters in survival – other than identity – has been preserved: there can be cases that involve unconventionally (for a normal human lifespan) long periods of time, in which psychological continuity, but no psychological connections, may hold between P and Q. For example, take the fictional story of Methuselah. If relation R is specified in terms of (3), then some form of psychological connection (e.g., connectedness of memories, desires, intentions, character traits) is supposed to hold between Methuselah at 30 and Methuselah at 200 to claim that Methuselah at 200 is in a relation that matters in survival with Methuselah at 30. If Methuselah at 200 does not remember anything of what happened to Methuselah at 30 or he has a different character, and is devoid of even a single desire or intention among those displayed by Methuselah at 30, psychological continuity may still hold despite a lack of psychological connections between Methuselah at 30 and Methuselah at 200. If this situation is possible, and what matters in survival requires that certain direct psychological connections hold, then Methuselah at 200 may not be regarded as an entity in a relation that matters in survival with Methuselah at 30. Parfit seems to hold that some degree of connectedness is required or, at least, that, in this context, psychological connectedness is more important than continuity. Still, even if relation R is understood as (3) (that is, in terms of psychological continuity *and* connectedness), in the previous case of fission involving brain splitting, the relations of psychological continuity and connectedness between you and A and the relation between you and B would not fail to contain what matters in survival. One way of framing the discussion is this: it is generally assumed that a case of survival is essentially a case of personal survival – if A survives, then A must thereby personally survive. However, our previous example seems to have shown that not all cases of survival – not all descriptions of a situation in which an entity can be properly said to survive – are thereby cases of personal survival.

In discussing versions of the fission case described previously, Parfit does not use the distinction between personal survival and survival; rather, he claims that it would be indeterminate whether you survive (i.e., it is indeterminate whether personal identity holds). Although it is indeterminate whether personal identity holds, the point is still that (a satisfactory description of) the outcome of a fission case akin to the one previously discussed is sufficient to show that identity is not necessarily what matters in survival, since certain cases of brain splitting are not as bad as death, where death is understood as implying non-survival (i.e., as not preserving what matters in survival).

To sum up, when relation R is spelled out in terms of psychological continuity and/or psychologically connectedness with the normal kind of cause, Parfit claims that it is R's holding between *at least* two persons existing at different times that matters in survival, not that R holds *at most* between two persons that exist at different times. If R also takes a one-to-one form, we say that personal identity holds – and thus that a person personally survives. Parfit further claims that the lack of uniqueness in the holding of R between two different entities – uniqueness is a feature that R has when it relates only two persons that exist at different times – does not make a great difference in the value of R's survival. Given that uniqueness does not greatly increase or does not constitute the value of R's survival, R must be what fundamentally matters, or so Parfit claims. (Even if uniqueness had value, it would be irrational to regard the outcome of the fission scenario as a double failure.)

If relation R is specified in terms of a relation the holding of which can be sustained by any kind of cause (*widest* relation R), survival can occur also in cases in which we may intuitively think that it does not.[6] Take a tele-transportation case in which a replica P is generated on Mars on the basis of the information provided by a scanner on Earth that records the exact psycho-physical configuration of a person Q. In one variation of such a scenario it is also imagined that the original entity on Earth is destroyed after the tele-transportation. In case the replica on Mars is created out of the exact psycho-physical configuration of Q, the widest version of relation R would hold between P and Q and so the scenario may count as a case of survival – even personal survival. Although you may be rationally concerned about preserving your original body as opposed to its replica on Mars, this would be a desire similar to your preferring the original watch that your father gave you for your 18th birthday instead of a qualitatively identical watch: the former may have solely sentimental value. The point is that, so long as tele-transportation sustains relation R through a causal chain between different persons at different times – when R is supposed to hold given any causal connection – R may have all that matters in survival. As we have seen in Chapter 4, Parfit distinguishes other ways in which relation R can be connected to causal conditions: for instance, through a reliable cause (e.g., a stable functioning tele-transportation device or through brain-continuity). In discussing a different type of case, Parfit also proposes that the value we may ascribe to the survival of a certain individual P who is R-connected to us may not simply depend on the degree of psychological connectedness between us and P, but also on how we value some of the features that the resulting R-connected person may happen to have. For instance, in a case of non-symmetric fission of A into B and C, if some of A's unwanted features – or, at least, some of the features that A did not completely recognise as her own (see Chapter 6.1, 6.2) – are transmitted only to B but not to C, it may be rational for A to have a special concern for C.

Parfit also says that, once we abandon the ideas that personal survival is the only kind of valuable survival and that personal identity depends on some persisting Cartesian ego, we can experience an attitude to certain existential worries similar to that described by the Buddhist (see Chapter 2):

> When I believed that my existence was such a fact, I seemed imprisoned in myself. My life seemed like a glass tunnel, through which I was moving fast every year, and at the end of which there was darkness. When I changed my view, the walls of my glass tunnel disappeared. I now live in the open air. There is still a difference between my life and the lives of other people. But the difference is less. Other

people are closer. I am less concerned about the rest of my own life, and more concerned about the lives of others.

Parfit maintains that his view of death and the connection between himself and other people is different once he sees his personal identity in terms of psychological continuity and connectedness. The idea seems to be that re-describing the events connected to our own demise impersonally and/or in terms of psychological connections may have a psychologically beneficial effect. Instead of saying 'I shall be dead', we can re-describe our death as a series of events in which our psychological states are no more connected to any entity in the future – that is, no further selves will be connected to us now. Although it is true that the way in which we describe and conceptualise the events of our lives affects our emotional reactions to them – and, in general, how such events are organised within the context of one's life – Parfit recognises that a positive psychological response to an impersonal re-description of our own death may not be a universal human psychological feature.

Some of Parfit's formulations of the philosophical consequences of his discussion seem to make a stronger claim: identity is not what matters in survival and/or identity should not matter in survival. However, these claims may be unnecessarily strong. As Raymond Martin argues in his study on self-concern, making a normative case against the rationality of our concerns for personal survival is likely to be challenged given a series of other considerations relative to the specific agent in question.[7] For example, given a specific series of interests, it may not always be rational for an individual to see his fission as a case of survival and/or as being valuable. More specifically, in cases in which your future interest in survival is also dictated by considerations related to the uniqueness of certain interpersonal relationships (say, traditional marriage), if survival is not personal survival, then you may regard such a fate as harming you as much as a case in which you do not exist any longer.[8]

3 Lewis, survival, and cohabitation

Lewis agrees with Parfit that what matters in survival is (at least) psychological continuity and connectedness. More specifically, Lewis claims that what matters is that our mental states have appropriate future successors. These successors should have a certain degree of similarity and, if changes occur, such changes should be gradual rather than sudden. Also, the connections between mental states should be regulated by a lawful causal dependence. The objection, or rather, the observation that Lewis advances is that we do not have to disagree with Parfit's claim that psychological continuity and connectedness are what matters in survival, if we also believe that personal identify is what matters in survival. In this section, Lewis's claim that what matters in survival is identity is understood as the claim that what matters in survival *qua* survival is identity, or that identity is the (or, at least one of the) specific component(s) giving value to our survival as such. Lewis articulates his point by using the notion of 'momentary person-stage', i.e., a proper part of a continuant or persisting person. It may be useful to imagine a continuant person as a spatio-temporal extended worm, an entity extended in space *and* time. Each section or slice of this space-time worm has a momentary duration and is connected to another temporally different section in virtue of the relation of psychological continuity and/or connectedness. Each section of a continuant person is a person-stage. On this framework, when you wonder whether you will survive tomorrow's battle, you are wondering whether there is a person-stage after the battle to which your current person-stage will be/is connected. The relation that holds between several stages of a *single* continuant person is called the I-relation – a non-branching R-relation. A continuant person is an aggregate of person-stages each I-related to the others. The idea proposed by Lewis as an objection to Parfit's theses on identity and survival is that a maximally extensive R-related aggregate of stages cannot differ from a maximally extensive I-related aggregate of the same stages.

Lewis's reply to Parfit is based on the idea that it is possible for one or more person-stages to be a stage of two or more different continuant persons – although in normal, non-fission, non-fusion cases this does not happen. In addition, Lewis maintains that the I-relation does not have to be transitive, as in cases in which there is partial overlap between continuant persons – otherwise we would have to claim that the two post-fission persons are the same. Lewis describes the outcome of Parfit's brain-transplant scenario by saying that it is possible to have a pre-fission stage – e.g., before having the brain transplant operation – that is R-related simultaneously to two post-fission stages that are not R-related to each other. On Lewis's account, cases of fission can then be described as cases in which different continuant persons share certain stages. Imagine a path, A, that forks into two different paths, B and C. When did B and C begin? One way of answering is this: B and C began at the same time, that is, when A began. They are different paths, since they go in different directions after A forks, but they share a part in common, that is, A. B is the totality of A and the trait that goes from where A forks to the end of B – similarly for C. *Mutatis mutandis*, a similar strategy is applied to the description of Parfit's fission scenario. Adopting an a-temporal way of counting and identifying persons – a way of counting that can take into account the whole spatio-temporal extension of continuant persons – we can say that there are two post-fission persons who have existed even *before* the fission took place, since they both had at least a person-stage before the fission event and several afterwards. In other words, when we discuss the destiny of continuant persons involved in alleged cases of fission, we are considering the destiny of two people who existed even before the event that allegedly separated them. The two people simply cohabitated in the same spatio-temporal region for a certain amount of time and space.

Temporal stage: a temporal stage is a proper temporal part of a persisting entity. The existence of temporal stages is controversial and is often related to particular theories of the nature of time. Those who include these entities into their ontology employ temporal stages to explain various puzzles related to time and change. David Lewis maintains that objects persist through time by having temporal parts or stages. On this view, a persisting object is an object that is extended in time, not solely in space. How long do temporal parts or stages last? Some philosophers claim that they are instantaneous, while others hold that the temporal extension of temporal parts is variable: for instance, one of your temporal parts is you-during-the-whole-2015. As suggested by Willard V. O. Quine, when we adopt such a framework we have to be careful about how we understand the reference of terms such as proper names and other indexicals. For example, if someone claims today that, in a strict sense, mum is identical to how she was yesterday, this claim is likely to be false: living organisms generally acquire and lose nutrients throughout a day (we are here assuming animalism for simplicity). However, if we understand the referential term 'mum' as applied to the sum of all of her temporal stages, and we claim that mum is identical to herself, then the claim is trivially true – as all claims of self-identity are supposed to be. For we are claiming that a temporally extended worm is identical to itself. So, we have to distinguish reference to mum-today and mum-yesterday from reference to mum as the sum of all mum's temporal stages. What Lewis calls "counting from the standpoint of no definite time", is counting sums of temporal stages that (at least apparently) compose spatio-temporally extended persons. So, although mum can have a number of temporal stages at least as numerous as time can be divided in discrete moments (if at all), from the standpoint of no definite time, there is only one person – on the assumption that mum does not undergo fission.

The point of Lewis's reply relevant for our discussion is that the crucial fission cases that motivated Parfit's idea that identity is not what matters in survival can be re-described in a way that is compatible with the view that personal survival and survival *de facto* never differ. In fact, Lewis's point is that we do not have to think that personal identity and what matters diverge in cases of fission: the R-relation and the I-relation do not actually diverge extensionally. If we count from the standpoint of no definite time, Lewis's answer to the question of how many people were involved in an alleged episode of fission is two – hence the name *cohabitation* view – and both of them personally survive the fission. When A and B meet again after their fission from you (and after having played tennis), they may reminisce about the good time they had when they were one.

4 Survival and the other approaches to personal identity

4.1 The simple-soul approach

According to versions of the simple-soul approach such that an indivisible and immortal soul is associated with a particular consciousness, there may always be a fact of the matter that settles whether A survives as either B or C – even in cases of fission. Whether a soul continues to exist in/as A rather than B in a case of fission may never be known by beings like us, but there can be a metaphysical fact such that an answer may be known by, say, an omniscient knower. One of the features of certain versions of the soul approach (say, one version according to which we are souls$_{mind}$), is that, whether we want it or not, we always personally survive – on the assumption that souls are immortal. As we have seen, it is not necessary to believe that if we have a soul, we thereby also have to believe that it is immortal or that a soul is always associated with a specific consciousness or mind. However, certain soul-based theories are held also because some philosophers believe that only these theories can provide an explanation of or a justification for the belief that (part of) what matters in personal survival can be preserved also after our bodily demise.

Some accounts of soul$_{mind}$ emphasise the tight connection between a soul and a body. For instance, some of these theories hold that for a soul to function properly – that is, to generate consciousness – the soul must inform a brain and/or be embodied. So, on these accounts, X personally survives only if X's soul is embodied. A soul may have the capacity to preserve our identity through time, but such a capacity can be actualised only when embodied. Resurrection was supposed to be one way in which we could personally survive, so early arguments against the Lockean theory of personal identity were meant to prove that his account could not explain personal resurrection and personal survival. According to some Christians, for instance, only an immaterial soul could guarantee personal resurrection, so, given their conviction that God will resurrect us, the only acceptable theories of personal identity would be those based on a belief in the existence of an immaterial soul.

4.2 Buddhist no-self approach and nihilism

Those who believe that personal resurrection is a desirable good may be likely to object to the Buddhist approach to survival. The reason is that a declared aim of many Buddhist schools is precisely that of putting an end to the cycle of continuous reincarnations. Moreover, a belief or faith in a personal rebirth or personal survival through rebirth is grounded on the illusion that there is such a thing as an enduring self. It seems that *Karmic/transmigrational* **survival**, i.e., the survival of an individual through a series of causal connections that spans through different cycles of death and rebirth, is not regarded by various Buddhist schools as rationally desirable – given that existence is essentially connected to suffering.

Nihilist views of our nature may imply the following reasoning: we do not exist; if we do not exist, then we never survive; so, we never survive. This may be just one among the many counterintuitive consequences of nihilism about our own nature. However, there can be ways of making sense of some of the claims regarding our own survival along the lines already discussed in 2.5 – if these counterintuitive consequences are taken to imply that the theory at issue is implausible. For instance, we can say that, although strictly or literally speaking, we do not exist, it is conventionally true that we exist. So, to the degree that there are certain conventions such that a certain number of particles arranged person-wise can be described as composing an entity that persists through time, then a person can be said to personally survive under such conventions. Once statements about persons or us have been thus reformulated following one theory of personal identity or our nature – intended as nothing more than a set of conventional rules regarding how we use concepts such as 'person' or 'ourselves' – nihilist theories become parasitic on those other theories on which we base our paraphrases. For example, if we claim that the relevant conventions regulating the notion of a person are those established by Parfit's psychological theory, then, in judging statements about survival, one should apply the considerations examined previously.

4.3 Relational approach and Confucian role-person

As discussed in Chapter 3, the relational approach includes theories according to which it is a necessary condition for an entity to be a person and persist through time as the same person that such an entity maintain a specific network of relations with certain other entities. A consequence of this view is that A's personal survival depends not only on A's intrinsic properties but also on the entities relevantly connected to A. If these entities form a social context, then also this particular social context may be essential to A's personal survival. A role-person approach may stipulate even stricter conditions for our personal survival, e.g., A may also have to keep her particular role in a specific relational structure to persist through time – so, the persistence of the relational structure to which A belongs may not be the only necessary condition. A *Confucian* role-person approach may include even more detailed conditions on what is an appropriate relational or social structure for a person to survive – e.g., those conditions suggested in the Confucian rites.

If personal identity depended only on role continuity and if what matters in survival is personal identity, then the consequences of certain social reforms (or even of being fired) may result in the literal end of one or more persons. Similar claims would apply to ourselves as individuals, on the assumption that we are essentially an instance of one or more roles. Such a result may appear counterintuitive: when someone is no longer playing her specific role in a society, it does not seem that such an individual and/or a person has thereby gone out of existence. One reply to this problem is that *role-person* is not a substance-sortal, but rather a phase-sortal, or a way in which an entity or individual non-essentially is. (See 5.4 for the notions of substance- and phase-sortal.) The idea is that being a person who plays a specific role may be a mode in which an entity can be. It may be true that when someone does not play a specific role any longer there is a sense in which a specific kind of person is no more exemplified; however, this may simply mean that a substance or person is no more also a person of a certain type. This change need not be seen as a case in which an entity or a substance literally goes out of existence.

Another possible line of thought that connects survival (and what matters) with the relational approach is provided by the emphasis that relational and/or role-based accounts of personhood may put on the ways in which a person may survive in a specific social structure. More specifically, if a person is identified with, say, a specific multiply exemplifiable role and such a role is subsequently played by another individual, we may claim that, to the degree that the first entity identifies herself with her role, what matters in her survival can be preserved by the fact that some other entity plays the same role. In other words, what matters in survival for P may be that some entity have P's role in the future. Call this form of survival 'role-survival'. Alternatively, one supporter of a general version of the relational or the role-person approaches may claim that a person can survive to the degree that the relevant social structure, say, a nation or a more specific group, persists. Whilst this may not be a case of personal survival, someone may argue that what matters in survival is preserved to the degree that what grounded the status of personhood for P is what matters for P's survival. Whether relational, role, or other similar forms of survival still have what we think matters in survival is certainly a matter of dispute.

4.4 The physical approach and animalism

Physical continuity, intended as a necessary condition for personal identity, may be considered as crucial for various forms of survival, e.g., a person can personally survive only if her/his body survives. Much of what this requirement amounts to depends on the specific account of what constitutes physical continuity. Bernard Williams famously argued that certain future-oriented attitudes (e.g., fear) seem to be determined or grounded on certain forms of physical continuity, for example, bodily continuity. Imagine that you were told that a sadistic scientist was going to torture you, but not before he had removed all of your memories and character traits – and somehow reproduced them into your worst enemy's brain. Williams argues that losing your memories and your character would not make your concern for the future torture any less pressing. In addition, the copying of your psychological states into someone else's brain is likely to have little effect on mitigating your actual concern.[9] So, despite the future lack of psychological connection, you would still be afraid – although the only relation you have with the entity that is going to be tortured is physical continuity.

An interesting consequence of animalism for our discussion of survival is the following. Suppose we do not believe that what matters in survival is just the persistence of a human animal (and/or our persistence as human organisms). However, according to animalism, we are human animals. So, although our persistence conditions coincide with the persistence conditions of a human animal, these conditions do not seem to determine or gauge what matters in our survival. Paul Snowdon claims, in his *Persons, Animals, Ourselves*, that some of Parfit's ideas about survival are compatible with animalism. To prove this point, Snowdon proposes a scenario, reminiscent of David Wiggins's amoeba cases discussed in the '60s, that is consistent with animalism and that is similar to the case of fission discussed before. In particular, Snowdon asks us to imagine that an animal can be perfectly cut in half in a way we would describe as a case of survival. If the human animal is cut in half and both sides continue to live, then neither can be the original animal – Italo

Calvino describes a similar case in his *Il Visconte Dimezzato* ('The Cloven Viscount', 1952). In this tale, the viscount is split in two by a Turkish cannonball and the two halves miraculously survive. Certainly, this thought experiment may seem irrelevant to our thinking about living organisms. Still, we may appeal to some usual (and abused) imaginary 'marvellous future scientific discovery' and suppose that it may be technologically difficult but not biologically impossible to have a splitting scenario involving a symmetrical division of a human animal in which both halves remain alive. Such a scenario, Snowdon argues, may support certain intuitions similar to those used by Parfit to claim that what matters in survival would be preserved in this case of physical-fission survival – a kind of survival that involves a physical organism divided into two living entities both equally standing in the relevant physical connections with the original physical organism. Although it may be indeterminate whether the original animal survives, what matters in (animal?) survival is preserved in this case of survival: it would be irrational to consider physical-fission survival to be as bad as death. So, our unique persistence may not be what matters in survival on this approach either.

4.5 Practical and narrative approaches

One of the characteristic claims of a narrative approach such as Schechtman's is that perceiving our life as a structured narrative confers meaning and significance to our experiences. For instance, Schechtman argues that we can recognise and experience ourselves as significant in a special way because we think of ourselves as a persisting, structured being with plans, projects, and temporally extended desires – that is, as having a narrative. However, critics have pointed out that there are significant differences between our understanding of narrative elements such as fictional characters and our understanding of the real unfolding of our mental lives, which is usually characterised by random and unconnected episodes. In addition, it may be argued that in order to explain the significance that some of our experiences have, the notion of a narrative may not be necessary. Still, Schechtman maintains that generic psychological accounts of personal identity – psychological accounts that do not prescribe specific structural requirements on the psychological connections that compose a person – fail to account for certain important aspects of our practical lives as persons. In particular, she claims that a proper account of personal identity should explain (not explain away) some of the reasons why, for instance, we care about our personal survival. According to her, and *contra* Parfit, having a narrative, that is, seeing the events of one's own life as having a narrative structure, would explain why we care about our personal survival. Schechtman's argument to the effect that the narrative approach – or, at least, her self-constituting view – is superior to other non-narrative psychological accounts can be reconstructed as follows:

1   On one version of the narrative approach, the relation of personal identity is defined in terms of connections between certain parts of a self-constituting narrative.

2   The interruption of a self-constituting narrative puts an end to the type of experiences and interactions enjoyed by the individual who narrated the story.

3   Thus, the experiencing individual, to keep on living the type of life she is experiencing, has an interest in preserving her self-constituting narrative, that is, her identity.

4   Criteria of personal identity couched exclusively in terms of generic psychological connections and/or continuity are ultimately unable to explain why identity matters in survival (see Parfit's arguments to this effect).

5   There are independent reasons not to give up identity as part of what matters in survival.

6   Therefore, given that the self-constituting narrative view is better at explaining the idea that identity is part of what matters in survival, and given that a theory of personal identity is superior also in case it is able to explain why identity matters in survival, the self-constituting narrative view is superior to other non-narrative psychological approaches.

A problem for Schechtman's reasoning is that having a narrative *in itself* may not always be what explains or justifies our interest in personal survival or in other practical concerns. In particular, having a self-constituting narrative does not seem a necessary condition for explaining self-concerns related to personal survival: for instance, certain individuals may simply be so motivated for biological natural causes. Besides, having a self-constituting narrative, in itself, is not even a sufficient condition for displaying concern for our personal survival. In fact, there are many different types of self- or person-constituting narratives that do not seem to be conducive to an interest in personal survival or that may provide an explanation of why it may matter to us. Literary examples, such as *Romeo and Juliet*, *Die Leiden des Jungen Werthers*, *Le Ultime Lettere di Jacopo Ortis*, 瘋癲老人日記 (*Diary of a mad old man*), codes of honour such as the 武士道 (*Bushidō*), Buddhist edifying stories, and narratives of self-martyrdom provide influential conceptual resources and narrative stereotypes for particular self-destructive or self-denying narratives. Given that there are many linear, reality-constrained, and self-constituting narratives that are explicitly self-destructive or self-denying, or that at least lead to a kind of behaviour that negates the importance of identity, having a narrative of this type may reduce our concern for personal survival. In short, the self-constituting narrative view is equally compatible with: (1) self-constituting narratives that can explain or justify our concern for personal survival, and (2) self-constituting narratives that explain or justify a non-personal concern for survival, as well as (3) self-constituting narratives that explain or justify a lack of concern for survival and even an active interest in non-survival. In other words, unless differently specified, the self-constituting narrative view is logically neutral with regard to our concern for personal survival. This neutrality extends to the case of morality: for instance, Velleman maintains that certain narratives may even lead to consistently immoral behaviour; in particular, when an individual strives for coherence with an immoral self-image (e.g., the Jihadist narrative). Similarly, general versions of the practical approach seem to be neutral with respect to self-concern and survival, to the degree that certain forms of agency (and/or planned actions) are maintained (or carried out), for example, those involving self-destruction.

5 Life-extending technologies, our nature, and personal identity

What is a life-extending technology? The following characterisation of life-extending technologies builds on the notion of lifespan extension. Now, there are at least three kinds of lifespan extensions.[10]

1 **Strong lifespan extensions**: extensions resulting from technologies that increase both average and maximum lifespan.
2 **Weak lifespan extensions**: extensions that result from an incremental surge in life expectancy obtained through improvements in the treatment and prevention of disease. The causes at the basis of weak lifespan extensions include a better access to appropriate treatments and the promotion of a healthier lifestyle – e.g., healthy diet, physical activity, social engagement, and active mental functioning.
3 **Deep lifespan extensions**: extensions the ultimate aim of which is the elimination or interruption of the process of ageing. Such extensions are *deep* because, in principle, they can be endless.

In general, life-extending technologies can then be classified as those technologies aimed at producing one or more of the previous types of extensions. Given this broad (and circular) definition, it follows that life-extending technologies are a highly heterogeneous category – which may include the introduction of certain substances in our diet, social cooperation, physical exercise, reduction of calories, genetic manipulation, and various forms of enhancements. A subset of these life-extending technologies, that is, life-extending *enhancement* technologies, include education, vaccines, and, when available, genetic manipulations. The conceptual difference between an enhancement and a treatment is problematic, but to a first approximation we can understand an enhancement as an intervention to improve human beings for reasons not directly connected to medical needs – where medical needs are those needs that derive from disease, impairment/illness, or as departures from some kind of optimal functioning. Against this distinction, many contemporary bioethicists have pointed out that an enhancement may count as a treatment depending on the context under scrutiny.[11] Sadly, it seems that medical interventions aimed at some forms of strong or deep lifespan extensions are unlikely to be available in the near future. People alive now are more likely to witness weak lifespan extensions, at least according to Jayne C. Lucke and Wayne Hall (1996). In particular, they maintain that, in certain industrialised countries, we may register an increase in the average lifespan in the coming twenty to thirty years. However, it is not probable that people living now will live longer than, say, 130 years.

Spectacular revolutions of the available life-extending technologies do not seem to be forthcoming, or, at least, it is not foreseeable that new technologies will be widely available to the greater part of the world population in the proximate future.

The ethical debate on life-extending technologies and the metaphysics of personal identity can be connected in several ways. For example, given a set of life-extending technologies, we may assess the compatibility of the results of such technologies with various theories of personal identity and of what matters in survival. More specifically, if what matters in survival is, say, the R-relation, we may assess whether certain technologies are rational to pursue, *qua* life-extending technologies. However, despite the apparently fertile field of research that these considerations may disclose, contemporary philosophers have been more interested in issues such as the desirability of immortality, the badness of death, or population ethics. Not all of these debates have focused on the role of different theories of personal identity in the topics discussed, and not all of them are directly relevant to life-extending technologies. For not all life-extending technologies are intended or conceived of as means to achieve immortality – besides, successful deep lifespan extensions would not ensure *invulnerability*. More specifically, and as John Harris has clearly pointed out, immortality as non-ageing is not immortality understood as never dying: unexpected events such as wars, new diseases, or accidents, the heat death of the universe, and other cosmological scenarios may still kill non-ageing people. If immortality as non-ageing is for us still a remote possibility, invulnerability seems to be even less probable.

As the variety of life-extending technologies is such that we may doubt the possibility of saying anything general enough that can be applied to all of these technologies, it can be methodologically more interesting to see how certain theories of personal identity and survival fare in respect to some specific technological research projects. In the next section, I discuss two technologies that are still at a highly speculative and/or experimental level: cryonics and mental uploading.

6 Cryonics and mental uploading

The basic idea behind cryonics is that of extending our lives by preserving our living or dead bodies at extremely low temperatures. The details of how this freezing procedure would be achieved are still not clear, although it seems that it is both nomologically and technologically possible to freeze and indefinitely interrupt the process of biological deterioration. It may be objected that this procedure should not count as a form of life-extending technology: so far, cryonic procedures have been applied to the dead bodies of people and animals, so, strictly speaking, their lives have not been actually extended. (This point is related to how death is defined. See the next chapter for discussion.) However, the hope of those interested in this technology is not that of remaining indefinitely frozen; rather, they wish to be resurrected or reactivated by some future and technologically advanced benefactors. Some of these ideas have circulated in various more or less academic and literary contexts – for instance, in Neil R. Jones's sci-fi work 'The Jameson

Satellite' (1931) and other related stories – and even put into practice by some cryonic agencies. There is an uncanny similarity between these ideas/hopes and some
passages of the Bible cited in Chapter 5 – a mortal and dying individual leaving a
seed – the frozen body – that will later be resurrected by a powerful god – a future
and hyper-technologically advanced civilisation – which will (hopefully) transform our mortal flesh into an unperishable body. Transhumanists, modern thinkers
characterised by a common desire to promote the improvement of the human condition through the use of increasingly sophisticated technologies, consider cryonics
as one possible means of time-travel. In particular, cryonics is a means to extend
our lives to a time in which technological advancements will have reached a level
sufficient to realise what is necessary for an everlasting life (or something close
enough). For our purposes, we can understand a successful cryonic procedure as
involving: (1) the preservation of a specific amount of bodily parts (which may
include brain, heart, lungs, or the whole body) for an indefinite (but finite) amount
of time; and (2) such a procedure should be in principle reversible in the sense that
the preservation of the frozen bodily parts should be such that a significant functionality of these bodily parts can be retrieved in the future. For instance, if a brain
is frozen successfully, then such a brain should have the capacity to be reactivated
after a finite amount of time. Cryonics may not be solely a means to deliver our
bodies to some future benefactors, but also a complementary technology to space
exploration: given the astronomical amount of time required to travel to other parts
of the universe, we may need to significantly extend the lifespans of those astro-
nauts who will be eventually exploring the universe.

The other life-extending technology discussed in this chapter is mental uploading, "the process of migration from brain to computer".[12] One of the presuppositions of this technology is that our minds can, in principle, be replicated in a variety
of material supports (e.g., biological, synthetic). In support of this presupposition,
some philosophers have argued that being made of biological parts is not essential for being conscious. According to these philosophers, mental states – including those responsible for our personal identity – can in principle be replicated in
non-biological systems, for example, in a silicon computational system. Mental
uploading would involve a process of identification and reproduction of the relevant structures responsible for our consciousness and/or other specific psychological features (e.g., memories). Data regarding these relevant structures would
then be readable, replicable, and apt for being subsequently loaded into a computer
capable of running an accurate simulation of the neural behaviour and dynamics of
the brain from which the information has been extracted – what David Chalmers
calls "a functional isomorph of the brain". More specifically, according to Chalmers, the process of uploading can involve the following: (1) a gradual replacement
of brain parts with parts not-necessarily organic, and/or (2) an instant scanning and
activation, and/or (3) a scanning followed by later activation. These procedures can
then lead to at least two kinds of mental uploading working in different ways. For
example, a functional isomorph of the brain that runs *into* a computer; or a functional isomorph of the brain that runs in the skull (or something close enough) of an

entity that before was only biological. The latter would be a case of *embodied* mental upload, provided that sufficient connections are established between the new mind-support and the rest of the body. It may not be so obvious that if an individual that has undergone the second procedure (embodied mental upload) can be thought of as having consciousness, then also a simulation in a computer can be properly said to be conscious as well. For instance, some may claim that consciousness as we know it must be embodied in one way or another.

Similar to Parfit's tele-transportation thought experiment, a mental uploading of the second kind may involve either a subsequent destruction or preservation of the original biological brain – the latter case can be motivated by a desire to keep a blueprint to utilise in case of necessity. After all, mental uploading scenarios can be seen as variations on the tele-transportation thought experiments. The different forms in which such an uploading may take place are, again, a matter of speculation and debate – and some of these forms may appear to be more literary devices in a sci-fi story than serious case studies in an academic philosophical context. For example, among the various possible imagined marvellous future technologies, Chalmers alludes to the possibility of nanotechnological devices that, once inserted into the brain, may learn how to emulate the behaviour of each single neurone. Once this behaviour is well modelled, the nanorobot may take the place of the neurone and/or can send the relevant information of the neurone's behaviour to a computer. This second procedure would be what is properly called a mental *upload*, in the current sense of the term. In what follows, I will restrict our discussion to (imagined) mental uploading scenarios that involve a process of copying and transmitting some relevant information from a brain to some device, say, a sophisticated computer, capable of displaying those functional traits that characterise our mental states.

What is the relationship between mental uploading and life-extending technologies? Mental uploading seems to involve a radical transformation of the current material support of our consciousness (what is sometimes called "the neural correlate of our consciousness"), from carbon-based neurones and/or those other bodily parts that are taken to be relevant for our psychological features into something inorganic and eventually more durable. Mental uploading can be seen as a life-extending technology to the degree that this new material support is indeed of a more durable nature compared to our current biological substratum. The rationale behind this technology may not be only that of extending our lifespan. For example, we may want to have a back-up of ourselves in case of unexpected accidents, or improve our mental and/or computational capacities, or cure dementia, and so on. Some of the theoretical presuppositions underlying mental uploading – for instance, a specific view of the nature of the mind such that its biological support is not nomologically necessary for its persistence – will not be disputed here.

How can theories of personal identity and survival bear on the debate over cryonics and mental uploading? Even if these technologies are ultimately figments of fervid imaginations, they can be seen at least as interesting complications of those thought experiments that have already played a crucial role in the formulation of many theories of personal identity and of what matters in survival. So, if Locke's prince and the cobbler or Williams's reduplication thought experiments are taken to be important for the debate in personal identity, then the previously described technologies can also have a similar cognitive value.

6.1 The simple-soul approach

The main versions of the simple-soul approach to personal identity are not, in themselves, incompatible with a desire to extend our earthly lives in one of the two ways described previously, although there is a sense in which these procedures can be seen as unnecessary: if we are immortal souls, then, strictly speaking, our existence will not be prolonged by life-extending technologies (provided that souls cannot be destroyed). Perhaps someone convinced by Plato's *Phaedo* that our mortal bodies hinder a pure intellectual acquaintance with the Forms may desire not to prolong her earthly life indefinitely, as in the case of a Christian who believes that, when death comes, she will go to Heaven or to some other miraculous place and finally obtain some kind of acquaintance or communion with God. Although simple soul theories of personal identity can be logically separated from these religious or other supernatural beliefs, they are usually parts of a system of beliefs (e.g., one specific Christian denomination) that are generally taken to support each other. For example, some theists may believe that we are immortal souls and that the time of our departure from this earthly life is something providentially established by one or more divine entities. Following this reasoning, some may conclude that deep life-extending technologies would tamper with this providential plan and thus be illicit. However, it will then be difficult for those motivated by these beliefs to justify the use of certain medicines or therapies, which are supposed to prolong their stay on Earth, such as aspirin, organ transplants, antibiotics, etc., whilst rejecting deep life-extending technologies, especially in case radical extensions would be the result of the only available therapies to cure some illnesses. For instance, imagine that a brain tumour is such that a person may only save her life by undergoing a mental upload. This may have the side effect of prolonging the life of such a person indefinitely – and thus of delaying her eventual ascension to Heaven. Would a committed and conservative Catholic refuse such a treatment or regard it as immoral/irrational?

To sum up, the claims that we are souls and/or that our identity as persons depends on the continuous existence of a soul do not seem to entail that a desire to extend our lives indefinitely is irrational. However, these claims are generally associated with certain religious worldviews that may prescribe different attitudes towards these technologies. In addition, on the view that our persistence depends on the identity of soul, life-extending technologies may be regarded as unnecessary as means of prolonging our existence.

6.2 Buddhist no-self approach and nihilism

Views such as those supported by Vasubandhu (e.g., Buddhist no-self view#1) may suggest the following reasoning: although longevity is positively regarded in Buddhism, certain deep life-extending technologies miss the point because, in reality, personal identity or survival are a kind of illusion or conceptual construct. Besides, since existence is intimately connected with certain forms of suffering, the unnecessary extension of our existence does not seem to be particularly appealing and/or meaningful. Different schools of Buddhism may have different views on these matters. A nihilist view of our nature, in itself, may prescribe different attitudes towards cryonics and mental uploading. For instance, if such a view is combined with a psychological theory of personal identity (e.g., a supporter of this stance may claim that, literally speaking, we do not exist or persist, but it is true according to the fiction of Parfit's normal cause theory of personal identity that we exist and that our practical choices should be based on considerations combining nihilism and Parfit's theory), we may regard the rationality/desirability of life-extending technologies along the lines of the latter (see 6.4 below).

It is worth remembering that suicide or ending our life prematurely – "out of a craving of annihilation" – is not generally seen positively by many Buddhist traditions. Peter Harvey narrates the story of the monk Maha-Kassapa who, asked by a materialist the reasons why morally good people such as some monks do not kill themselves to gain immediately the Karmic goods accumulated, replies with a parable the main point of which is that it is bad "to hasten the ripening of that which is not yet ripe".[13] The monk suggests that hastening the Karmic process would be acting like a pregnant mother who cuts open her belly because she cannot wait to know the sex of her child – with the result that both she and the child die.

In general, the idea that we should not rush the *right time*, either because it has been decided by a supernatural intentional entity or because it violates the hidden causal mechanisms of Karma (although a common interpretation in Buddhism holds that the length of life is indeterminate), may be appealing to the general religious public, but it faces overwhelming problems. For instance, how can we determine whether using one specific technology rather than another is God's will or not? For example, a successful neurological intervention to remove a brain tumour is sometimes considered as a sign of God's goodness or as a miracle, but what about a mental uploading that can have the same result – saving a patient from an otherwise incurable illness?

6.3 Relational approach and Confucian role-person

Relational and/or role-person theories, especially when interpreted as involving the claim that certain relations or roles are essential for our personal identity and/or our survival, may have interesting consequences for both cryonics and mental uploading. In particular, and perhaps rightly so, the main point these theories may raise is that non-relational survival – a kind of survival that does not involve the continuity of at least some of the crucial relational features that characterise our lives – may not contain all that matters in survival. We do not have to support a strict Confucian role-person theory to appreciate this point. Suppose that you have successfully hibernated and been re-activated after three thousand years. The environment you were familiar with throughout your pre-hibernated life is gone: nobody speaks your native language anymore, all of the people you loved have passed away, the cities you liked have so radically changed that you cannot recognise any of them. Perhaps the customs and habits of the benefactors who reactivated you have become so radically different from what you have so far identified yourself with (e.g., a certain set of values and beliefs) that contemporary cases of culture shock would pale in comparison to what you will experience. The problem highlighted by this line of reasoning – a problem of what we may call spatio-temporal or Zeitgeist alienation – can be understood as making a psychological and/or an ontological point. In the former sense, the point is that, given the loss of a number of relations that partially constitute what matters in survival and/or our diachronic identity, some forms of life-extending technologies may be less appealing to those who value certain attachments to their environment. This does not mean that deep life-extending technologies are not rational: rather, the previous reasoning can be used to justify a prescription for the development of deep life-extending technologies that appropriately address the previous worries. In particular, certain forms of deep life-extending technologies may need to deal also with possible dramatic cases of psychological alienation in order to be appealing. The lack of concern for these aspects emerges also in Chalmers's discussion of mental uploading. In particular, he seems to presuppose that what matters in survival is determined solely by the intrinsic mental features of the uploaded individual. Supporters of the relational approach would certainly disagree. The ontological point that supporters of a relational approach may make is that it would not be sufficient to hibernate our bodies or upload some of our mental capacities to ensure the persistence of what sustains our identity as persons (or as individuals) through time. On the view according to which our role in a social context is essential to our identity as persons, our identity through time requires not only the continuity of a functional isomorph of our brain but also the continuity of those social structures that ground our current identity.

6.4 The psychological approach

A psychological approach to personal identity compatible with the claim that relation-R is what matters in survival and according to which *any* cause can be responsible for the holding of relation-R may suggest the following line of reasoning. A process of mental uploading into a computer, provided that it is possible to, so to speak, *translate* consciousness and other mental features or their neural correlates into transferrable and reproducible pieces of information, can be one form of survival. If R assumes the form of a one-to-one relation, then an episode of mental uploading may even count as a case of personal survival. If the procedure requires multiple copies of those relevant psychological features that are responsible for your identity, the resulting individuals will not be personally identical with you – as the non-branching condition would be violated. However, we may argue that this outcome is not as bad as death. If the causal process behind the mental uploading is a kind of procedure compatible with what is considered as the right causal connection for what matters in survival and for the identity of mental states through time, then mental uploading can count as a form of survival. On certain views of the nature of the mind and its content, it is not necessary to preserve also our brains to survive: after the copying of the relevant information in my brain is completed and successfully transferred to the designated computational device, I do not also need to undergo a cryonic procedure in order to maintain what matters in survival. However, if what matters in survival is the holding of relation-R sustained by its *normal* cause (brain continuity), then, all things being equal, cryonics, and not mental uploading, would have to be prioritised as a research project to be publicly financed, along with those regenerative technologies that would make it possible to subsequently re-activate the brain.

6.5 The physical approach and animalism

On an account of personal identity, our nature, and/or what matters in survival according to which physical continuity is a necessary condition, only those life-extending technologies that preserve or facilitate such a continuity are valuable or rational to pursue, all things being equal. In addition (or alternatively), we may argue that considerations related to appropriate bodily continuity should dictate the priority among those research projects publicly funded to develop deep life-extending technologies. Suppose that a specification of the physical continuity at issue is in terms of the brain-part condition (for all t, a necessary condition for P at t_1 to be the same person/organism as Q at t_2 is that the relevant parts of Q's brain responsible for some relevant higher forms of cognition [awareness, character, planning, etc.] at t_2 be part of the same brain-life in which the relevant part of P's brain is/was partaking at t_1) and that brain continuity is a necessary condition for personal identity and/or for what matters in survival. On this view, cryonics is, on a par, a form of life-extending technology to be privileged over mental uploading (or similar technologies), unless mental uploading is devised to maintain brain continuity as well (is the brain essentially biological?). It is clear that, if investments in cryonics are to be effective, then a whole range of other technologies have to be developed as well – e.g., devices that can repair those damaged frozen tissues that sustain brain-continuity.

According to an essentialist version of animalism, we cannot survive unless we are human animals. The process of mental uploading and migration to a computer would not be a way of persisting through time for us. In other words, uploading our minds to a computer would not count as a case in which we ensure our individual survival, given that a necessary condition for us to exist is that of being human animals. Still, under the supposition that our own nature does not necessarily determine what matters to us, animalism can be compatible with the view that mental-uploading survival may not be as bad as death.

6.6 Practical and narrative approaches

Practical and narrative approaches, at least in their basic forms, seem to be compatible both with the claim that it is rational/desirable to pursue mental uploading and/or cryonics and with the claim that pursuing them is not rational/desirable. An example of the second case is that of a person-constituting narrative informed by elements belonging to a specific religious narrative that may require that the final chapter of a proper identity-sustaining narrative must contain an alleged reconciliation or acquaintance with a divinity. In turn, this reconciliation can be postulated as possible only by embracing our mortality. (It can be argued that such a narrative violates the reality constraint, but this is an issue I will not discuss here.)

Given an understanding of both approaches as more refined forms of the psychological approach, practical and narrative theories may have consequences regarding their conceptual connections to certain life-extending technologies similar to those encountered in the case of generic psychological theories. For instance, the self-constituting narrative view may simply suggest that, so long as a self-constituting narrator is functionally active, mental uploading can be sufficient to sustain personal identity and/or maintain what matters in survival. Unless certain constraints are applied to the content of the identity-sustaining narrative, mental uploading may thus constitute a form of narrative and/or personal survival. Versions of the practical approach to personal identity, unless further specified, seem to have similar consequences. Unless the content of the projects and/or intentions considered as fundamental for the identity over time of the same person are specified in a way that precludes the rationality of the life-extending technologies in question, mental uploading may constitute a form of (practical) survival. Cryonics may count as a form of survival under both approaches to the degree that the relevant psychological capacities can be restored at a later time.

7 Summary

This chapter explored two related series of ethical and philosophical problems, namely, (1) the connection between survival/personal survival and theories of personal identity (and our nature); and (2) the connections between theories of personal identity (and our nature) and the ethics and rationality of two life-extending technologies, that is, cryonics and mental uploading. With regard to the first series of issues, great emphasis has been put on Parfit's famous thesis that personal identity is not what matters in survival. More specifically, Parfit argues that survival and personal survival are distinct and that the former is not as bad as death: to the degree that there are relevant psychological connections of the right kind between A and at least one future entity, it is not necessary that such connections hold at most with only one future entity for A's fate to be rationally regarded as not as bad as death. We can survive but not personally survive, e.g., if we are (psychologically) connected in the right way to more than one future individual. Different theories of personal identity and of our nature, however, may question this conclusion. For example, some Buddhist schools hold that personal survival is always an illusion and that rebirths – arguably, a form of non-personal survival – are not rationally desirable, the main reason being that existence is essentially connected to suffering. Soul-based theories do not imply that we should be exclusively interested in personal survival, although some of their supporters (e.g., Butler) believe that an argument in favour of these theories is that they can best provide an explanation of the rationality of our concern for personal survival. In other words, these supporters of soul-based theories argue that we have one additional reason to believe these theories because they alone (or better) explain the rationality of our concern for personal survival – or, at least, they (better) explain the idea that personal identity is a necessary condition for the rationality of our concern for survival. On their view, the only rational concern for our future survival should be for those forms of survival that include personal identity. The relational approach may contribute to the debate by providing other conditions on our concern for survival to be rational. For instance, supporters of this approach may claim that, since we are essentially also role-persons, for us to persist through time and/or for us to be rationally concerned about our future, we should also be concerned for the persistence of the social context that sustains our identity-sustaining roles. For example, it can be argued that also the social context we are essentially part of should persist for us to survive – and thus for us to be rationally concerned about survival we should be concerned for the persistence of the social context in question. The physical approach may prescribe physical conditions on what counts as personal or individual survival – e.g., continuity of the same brain. However, some have maintained that physical theories of our nature such as animalism are not necessarily connected to theories of what matters in (personal) survival. Some cases analogous to Parfit's brain-split scenario can be imagined to the effect that an individual thinking organism may not regard its future physical fission as a fate as bad as death. As a consequence, animalism can be compatible with the view that a case of fission-organism survival may not be as bad as death. Practical and narrative approaches vary significantly with regard to the kind of narrative that is considered as a proper identity-sustaining narrative. I also argued that Schechtman's claim that the self-constituting narrative view in itself better explains our concern for personal survival is false, or, at least, the defence of such a claim is underspecified. My point was that there are narratives equally supportive of the rationality of personal survival as there are narratives that are not. So, a narrative theory as such seems to be neutral with respect to the rationality of personal survival.

The second part of the chapter addressed the conceptual connections between some life-extending technologies and theories of personal identity. From our discussion it emerged that, in general, the debates on life-extending technologies and on personal identity can be connected in one or more of the following ways:

1   There is a set of life-extending technologies and considerations regarding personal identity that may help us distinguish which of these *existing* technologies are rational to pursue further, privately or as publicly funded research projects. In other words, we should choose among the existing life-extending technologies those compatible and/or in accordance with our best theories of what matters in survival and personal identity.

2   Considerations regarding personal identity and what matters in survival may help us discern which forms of life-extending should be developed in the

future. For instance, certain lines of research may be irrational to pursue *qua* researches on life-extension, given our best theory of what matters in survival. The life-extending technologies that fall into this category are not yet developed or are in their infancy (e.g., cryonics). More specifically, we have seen that, on certain versions of the psychological approach – those theories according to which psychological connections and/or continuity may hold in virtue of any causal connections – certain forms of mental uploading may count as forms of survival, even personal survival. However, physical theories – and other theories that include physical conditions to their analysis of the relation of personal identity – may suggest that cryonics is, all things being equal, a better form of life-extending technology.

3   Life-extending technologies may offer, whether they exist or not, hypothetical thought experiments useful to test our theories of personal identity and of what matters in survival and eventually thus provide a series of case-studies to help us rethink some of the key concepts used in the debate.

Survival, personal survival, and life-extending technologies all have to do with avoiding death and a desire to persist through time. A natural question may arise at this point: according to the theories investigated so far, what is death? In addition, we may argue that, if we understand what our end is, we may also understand when we began to exist. Knowing the metaphysical conditions of our beginning, in turn, can shed some light on a series of ethical issues such as the morality of abortion. I outline some of these conceptual connections in the next and final chapter.

Notes

1 Butler (1736), pp. 320–321.
2 The plausibility of Hazlitt's view depends also on specific theories on the nature of time and of persistence.
3 The situation is more complex than what it is appropriate to discuss for the case at issue. In fact, the ability of our brain to heal itself with respect to the severity of a stroke varies greatly from case to case.
4 Suppose that you are a person and a psychological entity.
5 "(1) My relation to each of the two resulting people would contain what matters. Either (A) It is not determinately true that this relation is identity, or (B) It is determinately true that this relation is not identity. Therefore (3) Identity cannot be what matters" Parfit (1993), p. 29. See Johansson (2010) for discussion.
6 In a note added in 1985, Parfit says that he has withdrawn his support to the Wide Psychological Criterion, the version of the psychological theory according to which psychological continuity can have *any* cause as he claims that we do not need to choose between different criteria. See Parfit (1984/6/7), p. X.
7 Martin (1998).
8 I take this to be the main point of a line of criticisms advanced by, among the others, Susan Wolf in Wolf (1986).
9 See Williams (1970). Even knowing that your enemy's mental states will be reproduced in your brain will not eliminate your special concern for what is going to happen to you – for example, you may think that your fate is particularly bad as you will go mad (because you will lose your memory and character and become similar to your worst enemy) and then be tortured.

10 The first two kinds are discussed in Lucke and Hall (2006).
11 See Bostrom and Savulescu (2009), Douglas (2013), and Harris (2007).
12 My discussion is based almost exclusively on Chalmers (2010).
13 Quoted in Harvey (2000), p. 287.

Suggested readings

Historical overviews

Butler, Joseph, 'Of Personal Identity', in John Perry (ed.) *Personal Identity* (Berkeley, CA: University of California Press, 1975), originally published in his *The Analogy of Religion* (1736).

Cooper, John, *Body, Soul, and Life Everlasting* (Grand Rapids, MI: Eerdmans, 2000).

Hazlitt, William, *An Essay on the Principles of Human Action* (London: J. Johnson, 1805).

Martin, Raymond and John Barresi, *The Naturalisation of the Soul* (London and New York: Routledge, 2000).

Martin, Raymond and John Barresi, 'Hazlitt on the Future of the Self', *Journal of the History of Ideas*, 56, 3 (1995), pp. 463–481.

Parfit and what matters

Brueckner, Anthony L., 'Parfit on What Matters in Survival', *Philosophical Studies*, 70, 1 (1993), pp. 1–22.

Ehring, Douglas, 'Survival and Trivial Facts', *Analysis*, 47 (1987), pp. 50–54.

Ehring, Douglas, 'Why Parfit Did Not Go Far Enough', *Philosophical Studies*, 165, 1 (2013), pp. 133–149.

Johansson, Jens, 'Parfit on Fission', *Philosophical Studies*, 150 (2010), pp. 21–35.

Parfit, Derek, *Reasons and Persons* (Oxford: Oxford University Press, 1984/6/7).

Parfit, Derek, 'The Indeterminacy of Identity: A Reply to Brueckner', *Philosophical Studies*, 70, 1 (1993), pp. 23–33.

Parfit, Derek, 'The Unimportance of Identity', reprinted in Raymond Martin and John Barresi (eds.), *Personal Identity* (Oxford: Blackwell Publishing, 1995/2003), pp. 292–317.

Sperry, Roger W., 'Brain Bisection and Mechanisms of Consciousness', in John Eccles (ed.) *Brain and Conscious Experience* (Berlin: Springer Verlag, 1965), pp. 298–313.

Identity and what matters in survival

Harvey, Peter, *An Introduction to Buddhist Ethics* (Cambridge: Cambridge University Press, 2000).

Hawley, Katherine, 'David Lewis on Persistence', in Barry Loewer and Jonathan Schaffer (eds.), *A Companion to David Lewis* (Oxford: Blackwell-John Wiley & Sons, 2015), pp. 237–249.

Johnston, Mark, 'Human Concerns Without Superlative Selves', in Jonathan Dancy (ed.) *Reading Parfit* (Oxford: Blackwell, 1997), pp. 149–179.

Johnston, Mark, *Surviving Death* (Princeton: Princeton University Press, 2011).

Lewis, David, 'Survival and Identity', reprinted with Postscripts in David Lewis, *Philosophical Papers, Volume 1* (Oxford: Oxford University Press, 1976/1983), pp. 55–77.

Lewis, David, *On the Plurality of Worlds* (Oxford: Blackwell, 1986).

Martin, Raymond, *Self-Concern* (Cambridge: Cambridge University Press, 1998).

Perry, John, 'The Importance of Being Identical', in Amelie O. Rorty (ed.) *The Identities of Persons* (Berkeley, CA: University of California Press, 1976), pp. 67–90.

Shoemaker, David, 'Personal Identity and Practical Concern', *Mind*, 116, 462 (2007), pp. 317–357.

Sosa, Ernest, 'Surviving Matters', *Noûs*, 24, 2 (1990), pp.297–322.

Unger, Peter, *Identity, Consciousness, and Value* (Oxford: Oxford University Press, 1990).

Whiting, Jennifer, 'Personal Identity: The Non-Branching Form of "What Matters"', in Richard Gale (ed.) *The Blackwell Guide to Metaphysics* (Oxford: Blackwell Publishers, 2002).

Williams, Bernard, 'The Self and the Future', reprinted in his *Problems of the Self* (Cambridge: Cambridge University Press, 1970/73), pp. 46–63.

Wolf, Susan, 'Self-Interest and Interest in Selves', *Ethics*, 96 (1986), pp. 704–720.

Life-extending technologies

Bostrom, Nick, and Julian Savulescu (eds.) *Human Enhancement* (Oxford: Oxford University Press, 2009).

Douglas, Thomas, 'Enhancement, Biomedical', in H. LaFollette (ed.) *International Encyclopaedia of Ethics* (Malden, MA: Wiley-Blackwell, 2013).

Harris, John, *Enhancing Evolution* (Princeton: Princeton University Press, 2007).

Lucke, Jayne C. and Wayne Hall, 'Strong and Weak Lifespan Extension: What Is Most Feasible and Likely?', *Australasian Journal of Ageing*, 25, 2 (2006), pp. 58–62.

Partridge, Brad, Mair Underwood, Jayne Lucke, Helen Bartlett, Wayne Hall, 'Ethical Concerns in the Community About Technologies to Extend Human Life Span', *The American Journal of Bioethics*, 9, 12 (2009), pp. 68–76.

Wareham, Christopher, 'Life Extension and Mental Ageing', *Philosophical Papers*, 41, 3 (2012), pp. 455–477.

Cryonics and mental uploading

Chalmers, David, 'The Singularity: A Philosophical Analysis', *Journal of Consciousness Studies*, 17, 9–10 (2010), pp. 7–65.

Chalmers, David, 'Uploading: A Philosophical Analysis', in Russell Blackford and Damien Broderick (eds.) *Intelligence Unbound* (Malden, MA: Wiley-Blackwell, 2014), pp. 102–118.

Corabi, Joseph and Susan Schneider, 'If You Upload, Will You Survive?', in Russell Blackford and Damien Broderick (eds.) *Intelligence Unbound* (Malden, MA: Wiley-Blackwell, 2014), pp. 131–45.

More, Max and Natasha Vita-More (eds.) *The Transhumanist Reader* (Malden, MA: Wiley-Blackwell, 2013).

Pigliucci, Massimo, 'Mind Uploading: A Philosophical Counter-Analysis', in Russell Blackford and Damien Broderick (eds.) *Intelligence Unbound* (Malden, MA: Wiley-Blackwell, 2014), pp. 119–130.

Sandberg, Anders and Nick Bostrom, 'Whole Brain Emulation: A roadmap', Technical Report 2008-3, Future for Humanity Institute, Oxford University. http://www.fhi.ox.ac.uk/brain-emulation-roadmap-report.pdf

Shaw, David, 'Cryoethics: Seeking Life After Death', *Bioethics*, 23, 9 (2009), pp. 515–521.

8 The beginning and the end

I	Our beginning	199
2	The physical approach, animalism, and abortion	200
3	The soul approach and abortion	205
	3.1 Aquinas's hylomorphism and the Catholic view on abortion	206
4	The psychological approach and abortion	208
	4.1 Embodied mind and abortion	210
	4.2 The constitution view and abortion	212
5	Self-constituting narrative and practical approaches, and abortion	213
6	Relational-narrative entities and abortion	214
7	Buddhist no-self and abortion	216
8	Our death	217
	8.1 Defining 'death'	218
	8.2 Why 'death' matters	222
9	Summary	223

Mais où sont les neiges d'antan? [But where are the snows of yester-year?]
—François Villon, *Le Testament*, 1461

The beginning of a human organism and the beginning of the person (normally) associated with it may not coincide. Similarly, the end of a human organism and the end of the person associated with it may not be the same event. These possibilities have important conceptual consequences for some of the arguments regarding the morality of abortion and of other issues at the margins of life (e.g., organ transplantation). Conceptual clarity in matters related to our beginning and death are thus of crucial importance not just for shedding light on the understanding of what we are, but also for matters of vital importance. This chapter clarifies how metaphysical theories of our nature and of personal identity are connected to some debates in practical/applied ethics; in particular, debates on abortion, moral status (see the appendix), and some issues related to the definition of death.

One of the most important divergences in contemporary non-religious debates on when *we* begin to exist (and die) is between psychological (e.g., psychological essentialism) and physical theories (e.g., animalism) of our own nature. For expository reasons, I group together various theories according to which we are essentially psychological entities and certain versions of the relational account. With regard to physical theories, I focus mostly on animalism. However, some of the accounts explored here do not clearly or univocally belong to either category. For instance, Jeff McMahan's embodied mind view (see Chapter 5) holds that we are essentially embodied minds (psychological entities) but also that the (non-branching) continuity of certain parts of our brains is a necessary condition for our continued existence. Besides, on some naturalistic or physicalist accounts of our mental states, the previous way of dividing the field may even be conceptually misleading. With regard to the other approaches discussed in the book, one of the main points is that soul-based theories in themselves do not prescribe a conservative approach to the topic of abortion. Another important distinction to keep in mind is that between what a no-self or nihilist approach to our identity may imply and what Buddhism, intended as a wider set of beliefs, rules of conduct, and other practices may prescribe on the topic of abortion. For instance, a Buddhist school may prescribe a particularly restrictive attitude towards abortion, whilst a no-self theory may be compatible with a more liberal stance.

The first part of this chapter contains a brief summary of various recent findings in biology concerning the beginning of human organisms. Some of these biological facts are of significant metaphysical and, consequently, practical interest. For instance, given a definition of our continuity in terms of the life of an organism, it is important to understand the relevant biological facts about the beginning of biological organisms. In the subsequent sections, I discuss how the various metaphysical theories introduced in the previous chapters can determine the soundness of certain arguments in favour of and against the morality of abortion. Particular emphasis is put on what is considered one of the best non-religious arguments against abortion, namely, Don Marquis's **future-like-ours argument**. While discussing some soul-based theories, I also introduce one new theory of our nature, that is, one version of the hylomorphic view. This theory is also discussed in relation to one of the strictest stances on abortion – i.e., the stance adopted by the Catholic Church. Another theory analysed in this chapter is the relational-constituting narrative view proposed by Hilde Lindemann. In particular, this theory holds that we are individuated by certain narratives, and that such narratives may be solely relational.

Accounts of our beginning and end are, in certain cases, mirror images of each other. Theories of our nature and persistence, as already discussed in the previous chapters, may determine specific positions regarding when we do not survive, and thus when we die. In turn, the definition of death is of relevance for a series of practical issues such as: (1) The desirability and/or rationality of continuing certain medical treatments. In particular, there are cases in which, all things being equal, it seems morally permissible to discontinue certain treatments depending on whether a patient is dead. (2) The rationality and/or morality of performing or delaying certain operations aimed at removing organs for transplantation. Given the current technological resources, **organ procurement** should be performed in the shortest possible time after or before cardiac arrest in order to improve chances of success.

However, such operations cause, at least in cases involving some vital organs removed before complete cardio-pulmonary failure, the death of the organism from which they are taken. So, different definitions of when we die may influence the morality of the temporal framework of organ procurement – since performing operations that would kill one of us is illegal and presumably immoral. Other issues at the end of life relevant to accounts of when we die and personal identity are euthanasia, advance directives, a series of debates on persistent vegetative states, the rationality of certain attitudes towards death (e.g., fear), and deep coma.

1 Our beginning

Not all philosophers use the same terminology to refer to the various early stages of human development. For example, some use 'embryo' to refer to the phase or stage of an entity that goes from fertilization up until after about nine weeks – after this period, the term 'foetus' is generally used. However, others use the term 'foetal' to refer to all the stages of human development up until birth. Also, many key terms – e.g., 'human being', 'human life', 'human individual', are not used consistently by the participants to the debate over the legality and morality of abortion. (The use of emotionally charged terms such as 'baby' is to be avoided.)

Knowing some relevant information about the early stages of our biological development is crucial to assess how some of the theories about our nature and persistence can be applied to the debates discussed in this chapter. First of all, biological forms of life undergo changes that seem to form a continuum. As a consequence, there are situations in which it is not clear how to apply to certain biological entities some of those everyday concepts that seem to require well-defined boundaries. Although sometimes it may be clear whether molecules or corpuscles are in existence, some other biological entities are hard to straightforwardly classify as members of one specific and identity-determining sortal. The beginning of *our* biological individuality – as human beings, human animals, or human organisms – is also not easily or straightforwardly identifiable with the moment of conception. In particular, the zygote, or fertilised egg, does not seem to reach a stage of internal stability and organisation sufficient to individuate a unified and teleological entity until around two weeks after fertilisation – some even claim that the required period to achieve such an individuality is sixteen days. Before this time, the fertilised egg reproduces itself through division and, a few days after fertilisation, it is still possible to separate each single product of such a division in a way that can generate several different biological individuals – as in the case of monozygotic twins. For these reasons – lack of significant structural organisation between the cells that would allegedly form a new organism and the possibility of divisions that can generate different individuals – some philosophers and researchers think that it is hard to maintain that conception is an event in which a new human individual like us, P, is brought into existence such that P is numerically identical to the entity that comes into this world around nine months later. Although different interpretations of these data have been proposed, even certain conservative scholars seem inclined to believe that the individual entity that will develop into a mature human organism begins only fourteen to sixteen days after fertilization.

Another important point is that, prior to the latter part of the second trimester, human foetuses lack those neurological structures that are responsible for relatively complex mental states and/or for the capacity to feel pain – e.g., Mary Anne Warren reports that it is "almost certain" that at early stages foetuses have not yet developed the structures biologically necessary for mental states. Although these early foetuses may show some neurological activity, their brains cannot have a subjective point of view with the same complexity as ours.[1] The majority of abortions in the U.S. are reported to happen significantly before the early foetus develops a more complex brain.

An important distinction is between having the actual capacity to do something and having the potential of having the capacity to do something. Having the first implies that the structural properties, whether physical or of whatever other nature, responsible for something are already in place. The same may not be true in the other case – that is, having the potential of having a capacity. This distinction has consequences for the debate on abortion because, according to some interpreters, what morally matters is having the actual capacity to have consciousness, not also the potentiality to develop into something that will have/has the capacity to have consciousness. For instance, an early foetus may have the potential to develop into an entity that has the capacity to have consciousness, without thereby having already the capacity to have certain mental states.

2 The physical approach, animalism, and abortion

One argument against abortion, summarised, but not endorsed, by David Boonin, goes as follows:[2]

1   I am the same individual being as the zygote from which I developed.
2   I am essentially a person.
3   If an individual living being has an **essential property** at one point in time, then it has that property at every point in which it exists.
4   Given (1), (2), and (3), it follows that the zygote from which I developed was a person.
5   Since I am not different from anyone else in this respect, all human zygotes are persons.
6   We all believe that, all things being equal, killing a person is wrong.
7   Abortion is one way of killing a person – and such a person has not committed any crime.
8   Hence, abortion is wrong.

Premise (1) may seem one way of applying animalism to the abortion debate. However, as we have already pointed out, it is not an analytic truth that 'individual being', in this context, is synonymous with 'individual human animal'. For the purpose of discussing this argument, let us assume that it is. There are versions of animalism according to which the identity condition of a human animal are the identity conditions of a *living* human organism, and there are versions according to which the identity condition of a human animal are simply the identity conditions of a human organism. So, premise (1) may be questioned on the basis that it does not seem that a persisting biological individual, an individual that will persist longer than fourteen days, begins before the second week after conception. However, premise (1) and (5) can be amended:

1* I am the same individual being as the embryo that has existed since about the second week after fertilization.

Even after amending the argument, the advocate of the claim that abortion is morally wrong cannot have it both ways in applying animalism to her case: even if a certain understanding of animalism can support premise (1) the same theory is generally understood as denying (2) the claim that we are essentially persons – given an understanding of the notion of a person as that of an entity that has at least the actual capacity to have mental states. In addition, the identity conditions of a psychological entity of this kind do not coincide with the identity conditions of a human organism, or so a supporter of animalism generally claims. Hence, it may be true that an animal is not always a person and, as a consequence, (2) would be false. Supporters of the view that we are essentially persons and that persons essentially have at least the capacity to have some mental features (as psychological and self-narrative views of personal identity seem to hold), can deny premise (1): in fact, if we are essentially persons, and if persons essentially have mental properties – or the actual capacity to have mental properties – then we did not begin to exist until our organisms started to have a certain number of appropriate mental properties or, at least, until certain relevant structures that can support such properties have developed.

Another argument against abortion that, under certain formulations, is influenced by animalism, is the popular future-like-ours argument. Don Marquis devised the original version of this argument and subsequently modified it several times. The main points of the argument can be restated as follows:

1 Assume one version of the deprivational account of the badness of death/killing (i.e., killing/death is wrong/bad because it deprives the victim/individual of something valuable): if one of us has a valuable future, killing one of *us* (or someone like us) is wrong because it deprives one of us (or someone like us) of a future of value;

2 Since *we* have futures of value, a foetus has a future of value (or, in most cases, it is likely to have a future of value);

3 Abortion deprives a foetus of a future of value;

4 Given that depriving an individual of a future of value is immoral, it follows that abortion is immoral, because it deprives a foetus of a future of value.

It is not always clear whether Marquis thinks that (i) for a future to be valuable, it must also be valued by the individual's actual standards or (ii) for a future to be valuable it must be valued by the standards that the individual or an ideal agent will and/or would have, although in later formulations of his argument he specifies that what he has in mind is the conditional version of (ii). In what follows, let us assume that an individual's future is valuable to the individual in question in case she or an ideal agent would value it. Some variations of this account include the idea that the future is valuable if an ideal agent in those future circumstances would value it. (There are other subtle variations on the same idea and on how to disentangle the details of the account.)

One crucial element of the future-like-ours argument – namely, the point that the foetus *has* a future like ours – was not explicitly discussed in Marquis's original formulation of the argument (in the 1989 version), but rather simply assumed. In fact, Marquis seems to take it as obvious that when/if a foetus develops, it becomes one of us in the same sense in which we say that a child becomes an adult, that is, without going out of existence. In one of the most recent discussions of his argument, Marquis explicitly draws the connection between his argument and animalism. In fact, he claims that: "we know that foetuses have futures of value because we were all foetuses once and their futures of value are the goods of our past lives, our present lives, and our future lives. (I am assuming that we are biological organisms.)".[3] Assuming animalism thus helps the argument because, among other things, it provides a justification to the claim that a foetus *has* a future like ours: if the foetus is a human organism, then it is already one of us. If you were a foetus, the *same* individual you are now started as a foetus and is now (presumably) an adult with a future of value.[4]

Marquis also seems to support the idea that an individual must exist for that individual to have a future like ours (and thus a future of value).[5] This is an important dialectical point in relation to the contraception/abstinence objection to his argument. More specifically, Marquis does not believe that contraception or abstinence are morally wrong. However, an unwelcomed consequence of the future-like-ours argument would be that, if it is wrong to deprive an entity of a future like ours, then it can be argued that we are acting immorally, e.g., when we do not fecundate all of the eggs available in the world (or, at least, those eggs it is in our actual capacity to fecundate). In other words, we are doing something wrong when we deprive individuals of a future like ours, more specifically, all those possible individuals who can be actualised by continuous sexual intercourse or by an industrial process of artificial insemination. I take this consequence to lead to a possible *reductio ad absurdum* of the argument. Now, Marquis concurs that contraception and abstinence are not morally wrong and believes that sperm and eggs do not have a future like ours. The theoretical basis for these claims is that before the process of individuation of the relevant organism (say, after fourteen or sixteen days), there isn't an individual with the property of having a future like ours. Or maybe there is an individual – for example, the fertilised egg – but that individual is not the same individual that will have a future like ours. The entity that has a future like ours does not exist before fourteen or sixteen days after fertilisation. Eric Olson, David DeGrazia, and others seem to agree that a single-cell zygote is not metaphysically individuated, at least not in the way we are. Although a single-cell human zygote may be considered as a biological individual with human DNA, DeGrazia claims that it is not the same organism of the kind you and I are. It is only when the relevant cells start to function as a single integrated unit that we may identify this new organism with someone/something like us. It is important to emphasise again that it is difficult to determine clear-cut ontological boundaries for human organisms at this early stage of development. Still, according to DeGrazia, what can be plausibly defended with some confidence are these two claims: (1) before the sixteen-cell stage, we do not exist, and (2) by the time the parts of the embryo are differentiated and twinning is no longer possible, an entity of a kind similar to us has come into being.[6]

As discussed in 5.4, the criteria of identity for entities like us proposed by Olson are spelled out in terms of sameness of life, which in turn involves the continuity of an organism. ("[I]f x is an animal at a time t and something y exists at t*, then x=y iff the event that is x's life at t is the event that is y's life at t*.") These identity conditions must be compatible with the view that we were foetuses, as one of the reasons Olson gave to prefer animalism over other views is the alleged theoretical advantage of implying that you and I were once foetuses.[7] Why is this an advantage? Olson proposes the following reasoning. Assume that we are essentially psychological entities. According to embryology, until at least between twenty-five and twenty-six weeks after fertilisation the cerebral cortex still does not seem to have the capacity to sustain appropriate mental functions. From these two premises, it follows that we did not come into existence when a foetus did. Since two entities cannot be the same if they didn't have the same beginning, we were never foetuses. Now, the conclusion that we were never foetuses, Olson maintains, is problematic. First of all, we would not have a straightforward account of apparently unproblematic expressions such as "the normal foetus is a potential person", or "the foetus is an entity that will develop into a person". The problem is that, according to Olson, the straightforward and best account of these expressions is this: the notions of potentiality and development involved in the previous expressions imply that one entity – a foetus – becomes or can become an entity like us at a later stage. In other words, it is one and the same entity that changes and acquires mental capacities, not a different entity. Similarly, you were once an adolescent and now you are an adult, but you are still the same individual – assuming that no adolescents, but only entities that developed from adolescents, are reading this book. Olson also argues that if you do not believe that you were once a foetus, then you may incur some metaphysical troubles. In particular, suppose that you were not a foetus. Then, what happened to the foetus relevantly connected to you? You may reply that (1) the foetus ceased to exist, or (2) the foetus continued to exist, but did not become a person – given that you are a person but you were not a foetus. Olson claims that the first option is hard to believe because it implies that a normal foetus never becomes a normal adult human being. In Olson's words "why, we should want to know, should a fetus [sic] perish simply because, in the course of carrying out the program encoded in its genes, it (or rather its successor) came to be able to think?".[8] The second option – the foetus continues to exist and eventually develops into an adult human organism – would be equally problematic. Now, one reason to believe this option is that you do not believe that you are identical to a human animal, given that you do not believe that you were a foetus. However, denying that you were a foetus provides an ideal starting point for the thinking animal argument (see 5.6). In particular, suppose that a foetus develops into an adult human organism. This human being has a nervous system, so it can probably think. This animal is where you are now. So, you are this animal. Now the problem is clear: if this argument is sound, the reason you had to hold option (2) does not stand any more. The conclusion seems to be that, after all, you would better believe that you were a foetus.

The claim that we were foetuses has important consequences for how classical arguments in favour of abortion have been formulated. For instance, certain arguments to the effect that we do not harm anybody *like us* in performing an abortion because the foetus – at least at an early stage – is not a psychological entity and thus not a person, may not be sound. All things considered, it may seem that adopting (some versions of) animalism may simplify (or make more convincing) certain arguments against the morality of abortion. It has to be emphasised that (some versions of) animalism does not entail that abortion is morally wrong; rather, it *facilitates* certain arguments against abortion. In fact, given other assumptions, an animalist may consistently believe that, in certain circumstances, abortion is moral. An example of an animalist who supports a liberal stance on abortion is DeGrazia. His argument against the FLO argument starts by questioning Marquis's presupposition that, in evaluating the future of value of someone like us, we should assume a whole-lifetime perspective. In particular, the deprivational account of the badness of death on which Marquis bases this idea states that the badness of X's death at any time is a simple function of the total goods X is thereby deprived of. However, this would imply, according to DeGrazia, the implausible consequence that a pre-sentient foetus would be more harmed by death than a ten- or twenty-five-year-old (or, why not, even a thirty-six-year-old) human being.[9] If the badness of death is simply proportional to the a-temporal total value of the goods an entity is deprived of, then, all things being equal, it seems that we take away more future of value from a foetus than from a growing up adolescent. According to DeGrazia, this does not seem to capture our intuitions about the harm or badness of death. In particular, some claim that it is significantly worse when (or for) an adolescent dies than when a miscarriage happens. DeGrazia – drawing from McMahan's work – argues that there is a better account of the badness of death that takes into account this intuition: the **time-relative interest account (TRIA)**. According to this view, the badness of X's death is a function also of X's time-relative interest in continuing to live at the moment of death. DeGrazia clarifies this point by claiming that the harm of death is not just a function of lost opportunity for valuable life, but also a function of the degree of psychological connectedness with one's possible future life. In turn, the structure of the relevant psychological connections is specified by referring to some principles of the narrative approach. His point here is that the psychological connections spelled out along the lines of the narrative identity theory discussed in Chapter 6 may ground the special concern for one's own future and/or for what is valuable in someone's life. So, the persistence of someone like us, the conditions of which are specified by the identity conditions of a human animal, is not the only element that it is rational to factor in when it comes to prudential concerns for our own future and/or for evaluating what matters in our lives – and thus to determine the harm of losing it. In fact, some form of psychological structure also matters. In particular, DeGrazia claims that, following McMahan, the degree of psychological unity is a function of:

> (1) The amount of internal reference between earlier and later mental states (e.g., memories of past experiences, anticipations of future experiences), (2) the proportion of the subject's mental life that is sustained over the stretch of time in question, and (3) the richness of the subject's mental life.[10]

These conditions are significantly similar to the conditions that supporters of the narrative approach would recognise as weak forms of narrativity. The TRIA, applied to the case of the pre-sentient (but individuated) foetus, would imply that its death would not harm it, since there is no degree of psychological connectedness with future stages of its life, given that the foetus does not have any mental properties yet. This evaluation would change in case the foetus started to develop certain mental faculties, and depending on the degree in which some of these mental states become parts of the psychological development of the foetus itself (or of the resulting person).

DeGrazia also argues that the TRIA is to be preferred to certain versions of the desire-based approach to the harm of death. A simple desire-based account of the badness of death states that death harms us because we do not obtain what we want: staying alive. Some also claim that a necessary condition for having interests is that of having psychological states. Now, the TRIA better explains why killing infants is significantly wrong, despite their lack of a cognitive structure sufficient to have a desire to be alive: all things being equal, the TRIA claims that killing an infant is bad, significantly worse than destroying a pre-sentient foetus because an infant is supposed to have a psychological development such that it will result in an entity that has psychological unity. The same result could not be obtained on *simple* versions of the desire-based view.[11]

3 The soul approach and abortion

We have already considered several theories regarding the origin of the soul in Chapter 1, section 5. If we are souls, then, depending on which theory of the soul's origin we adopt, we may have different answers to the questions concerning when we begin and the morality of abortion. Plato's account in the *Phaedo* is compatible with different theories of the origin of our souls – for all he said, our souls may have always existed and keep on reincarnating. If we believe that we are souls$_{mind}$, and that souls$_{mind}$ are essentially thinking entities, then we may argue that we began when we started to think or have the actual capacity to think. If this is the case, and you believe that having a brain is necessary for your soul$_{mind}$ to have mental states, then you may also believe that you came into existence (or started to function again) when a relevant foetus developed some relevant physical structures. This idea can have consequences for the debate on when we begin. For instance, Descartes suggested that consciousness is essential to the soul$_{mind}$ and he took this to imply that the human soul, even inside the mother's womb, is conscious and always thinking, although it does not remember this afterwards. Other accounts, such as Swinburne's, hold that the soul$_{mind}$ has as its essence only the *capacity* for experience and action. So, according to this second approach, we began when we first started to have the capacity for them.

To sum up, some of those theories according to which our conditions of identity and of our nature coincide with those of a soul$_{mind}$ can be compatible with a belief in the morality of abortion. It is interesting to notice that, strictly speaking, if someone believes that we are immortal simple souls, then abortion is not an event that brings about the destruction of someone like us. After all, if we are immortal souls, we cannot be destroyed – at least not by an abortion. Perhaps only some miraculous divine intervention could destroy a soul – something well beyond the powers of authorised doctors. The alleged immorality of abortion would have to be due to something other than the annihilation of someone like us.

In general, it is hard to apply theories according to which we are immaterial souls to the debate on abortion. In fact, in the absence of evidential criteria for determining when a soul informs a body, it is indeed hard to understand what can count as a methodologically sound criterion for determining whether a theory of our beginning is more plausible than another – in absence of dogma, faith, or alleged divine revelation. A possible reply to this worry is contained in hylomorphic theories of the soul, as discussed in the next sub-section.

3.1 Aquinas's hylomorphism and the Catholic view on abortion

Explicit theorising focused on establishing when souls are allegedly created and/or connected to our bodies has been done with a certain degree of complexity in the context of hylomorphic theories of the soul. One of the main characterising points of these theories is that the soul is associated or identified with the form of the body. There are various versions of this idea and, according to one of them, the process of ensoulment is gradual, given the gradual development of the corresponding body. Accounts of this kind, for instance those inspired by Aristotle's theory of the soul, have played a significant role in the history of the debate on our beginning and on the doctrine of abortion. In particular, part of the contemporary Catholic approach to abortion is based on the work of the extremely influential Christian philosopher St. Thomas Aquinas (1225–1274). Aquinas, elaborating on Aristotle's metaphysical and biological works, maintained that the male semen contains 'the active power' (the efficient cause of generation) that begins the various generational processes, whilst the 'material' (the material cause) of the foetus is provided by the impregnated woman. The male semen carries the active power that ingenerates the vegetative- and the sense-soul (forms of the body that are devoted to basic functional activities we have in common with plants and animals), which in turn accrues the material cause. (The details of these speculations are mostly of historical interest.)

Aquinas claims that the intellective soul, what characterises us as human beings, is generated by God when the developmental stages ingenerated by the male semen have come to the right point – that is, when the right organs are at least formed. This point is controversial, as some thinkers have claimed that, since our intellectual capacities cannot be generated from configurations of matter alone, the intellective soul cannot be generated from the 'potentiality of matter' alone, that is, only from what is already part of the developing embryo. So, in order for certain structures to be further organised so as to accommodate our intellect, we need a divine intervention to generate the relevant intellective soul-form. Interestingly, Aquinas seems to claim that, after conception, there is a continuous process of 'comings-into-being and dissolutions' in which several entities succeed each other in tight succession. The entity that results from this process of incremental and gradual accumulation inherits its positive powers from the previous entities. Apparently, Aquinas also maintains that the creation of a human rational soul happens at different times for males and females – males are ensouled in forty days, while females in ninety.[12]

Some have ascribed to Aquinas the view that human beings ('man'), or *we*, are a compound of body and matter. This may seem a form of compound dualism (see Chapter 1); however, some scholars have claimed that classifying this view as simply a form of *compound* dualism would miss the Aristotelian emphasis on the unity of matter and form. In addition, scholars such as John O'Callaghan attribute to Aquinas the view according to which a specific human soul is a constitutive part of a human substance, incomplete in itself when it does not inform a human body. On this view, a soul is not a substance in its own right, although it is capable of outliving the matter it informs. Call this view 'Aquinas's hylomorphic dualism', or simply, *hylomorphic dualism*. As further evidence in favour of this interpretation of Aquinas, we can add his distinction between us and (intellectual) souls. In fact, according to Aquinas, Socrates (one of us) had a series of vital activities that were properly classified as his activities, and such activities were akin to those of a living animal. In turn, some of these activities cannot be identified with the activities of the intellectual soul that informed the soul-body compound called 'Socrates'. So, Socrates and his soul were not identical. If Socrates was not a soul, we are not either.

John Haldane and Patrick Lee maintain that, throughout the Middle Ages and beyond, the metaphysics of ensoulment determined the criteria of punishment to be applied in cases of abortion and how this practice may differ from homicide. To the degree that the process of ensoulment was at an early stage, penances related to the voluntary or involuntary destruction of the foetus were supposed to be less severe than in cases involving foetuses in later stages of ensoulment – also called late hominization. The Catholic Church seems to have shifted from holding the doctrine of late hominization to an approach according to which ensoulment takes place at conception. Writing from a Catholic perspective, Norman Ford claims that "[t]he Catholic Church in particular, not finding any positive answers to this question in the Bible [when does a human being, complete with a rational soul, begin?], over the centuries has always adopted the commonly accepted well-informed opinion of the day."[13] A similar point is at least implied in the 1974 'Declaration on Procured Abortion': the Declaration claims that abortion is illicit at any stage, and that in the Middle Ages, although it was believed that the soul was not present after conception, abortion was still considered illicit – although possibly a sin of less gravity. In the document *Donum Vitae* (1987), the Congregation for the Doctrine of the Faith states that "from the moment the zygote has formed, [it] demands the unconditional respect that is morally due to the human being in his bodily and spiritual totality. The human being is to be respected and treated as a person from the moment of conception [. . .]". This change of perspective is allegedly justified on the basis of scientific findings. In the same document, the Congregation also 'recalls' the teaching according to which from the time an ovum is fertilised, a new life has begun. Such a life is different from that of the father or the mother, and is the life of a new human being. As we have seen in the previous section, this idea is highly controversial – and, according to many bioethicists and biologists, wrong if 'a new human being' is taken to refer to an ontologically identified individual that is numerically identical with a properly causally connected future human organism that, on some accounts, is one of us or that, on other theories, will constitute us.

4 The psychological approach and abortion

The general inclination of advocates of psychology-based theories is to attribute to the early foetus at best the potential to develop into a person. On this approach, being a person – someone like us – is generally taken to have a special moral value (in virtue of the features that make us persons). Since the early foetus is not a person – given that it does not have the relevant actual psychological capacities that a person has – abortion does not amount to the killing of a person, or of one of us. It may be wrong to destroy a foetus for some other reasons, but not because it is one of us or because it is a person (that is, not because of some intrinsic features that would make it valuable). This general reasoning has been specified in various ways. For instance, Michael Tooley associated the notion of personhood with that of having rights, in particular, the right to life. Since the early foetus does not have interests, it does not have a right to life, on the assumption that a pre-condition for having a right to life is that of having interests (and more specifically, an interest in staying alive).[14] Now, consider psychological essentialism and the any-cause Parfit's theory of the metaphysical foundation of personal identity (For all t, P at t_1 is the same person as Q at t_2, provided a definition of psychological continuity in terms of overlapping chains of strong connectedness, iff [1] P is psychologically continuous with Q, [2] psychological connectedness and/or continuity are sustained by *any* cause, and [3] they have not taken a branching form). What are the consequences of these views for the question concerning our beginning and abortion? McMahan suggests an interesting way of approaching these problems. Assume the previous psychological theories and consider how you would describe the successive stages of increased dementia at the end of someone's life. If A is a person and also a victim of Alzheimer's disease (AD), then the slow degeneration of A's brain will result in a gradual loss of mental contents and/or functions. At an early stage t_1 of the degenerative process, we may find a series of psychological connections such that the relation of psychological continuity still holds between A at t_1 and A at any other prior time at which A existed. However, with the progression of the disease, an increasing number of connections will fade away, until a human organism reaches a point t_2 where it is no longer plausible to claim that psychological continuity holds between A at t_1 and the individual previously associated with A at a time earlier than t_2. According to the psychological theories at issue, the best description of this scenario goes as follows. There are clear cases in which A persists through time (say, at t_1); however, there are cases in between t_1 and t_2 when it is indeterminate whether the relation of personal identity holds between A at t_1 and the relevant entity that exists at these times. At t_2 the relation of psychological continuity does not hold any longer, so A does not exist anymore. Perhaps the organism previously associated with A at t_1 still persists even after t_2, but not A, the person. How is this discussion on the end of life related to the question concerning when we begin? The psychological theories at issue would hold that coming into being is the reverse process of the previously described case of fading into nonexistence. In particular, we begin when we start to form several psychological connections that sustain a non-branching relation of psychological continuity. However, there are time intervals in which it is indeterminate whether the same person exists through them. This indeterminacy is not a problem for the theory at issue, at least not for Parfit's versions of it. Rather, it is a foreseeable consequence: given that the process of development of the structures responsible for our mental states seems to form a continuum, it is only to be expected that there are cases in which it is indeterminate whether we exist. According to McMahan, this psychological account implies that we begin to exist sometime in early childhood. Some may even claim that, since the psychological connections of a newborn infant are so sparse and fragmented, some versions of the psychological approach may even imply that an infant P at t_1 and an infant Q at t_2, where t_2 is one day after t_1, are not even sufficiently psychologically connected to sustain personal identity between P and Q. If this reasoning is correct, then, by generalising the case, the previous account may be compatible with the view that we come into existence at a time significantly later than the latest time we generally think (e.g., right after birth).

The psychological theories discussed previously may claim that (1) there is a dimly conscious subject that exists before the relevant physical structures have developed to the degree that significant psychological connectedness and/or continuity hold; however, this entity is not one like us, a person; (2) such a *sub-person* or *pre*-person begins to exist only when the organism acquires the capacity to support the relevant psychological connections, and ceases to exist when a full-blown person comes into being. An advocate of this way of describing the initial stages of our existence may provide a similar description of cases of Alzheimer: when the psychological connections and, in general, most of A's other mental faculties have significantly deteriorated, a new post-person – a rudimentary subject of experience that is not the same person as A before the illness became too severe – comes into existence; however, such post-person may not be a person like us due to its limited psychological capacities. To sum up, some versions of the psychological approach are compatible with (but do not entail) the view that in the blurred periods of our beginning and end, certain entities (a pre-person and a post-person) with diminished mental faculties – compared to persons like us – come into being. These entities are not the same kinds of persons as us, given their lack of the capacity to form and maintain significant mental connections. The point of suggesting the existence of these entities is that of making sense of the claim that, although an organism may not always have those faculties that sustain personal identity, an organism may sustain some forms of unitary and significant mental life. This rudimentary mental life is different and arguably less desirable than ours, but still not completely negligible. In evaluating this suggestion, McMahan claims that recognising the existence of these pre- and post-person entities is metaphysically suspicious at best, and does not really solve the problem of borderline cases, e.g., when would we be justified in drawing a line between the mental faculties of one like us and those of a pre- or post-person? In addition, McMahan maintains that the distinction between us and pre- and post-persons does not track what we seem to care about in, for example, the Alzheimer case. More specifically, before her disease, person A may still care about what happens to her related post-person, even though A and the related post-person may not be the same person. The reason is that A's egoistic concern may be based solely on a residual thin degree of psychological connectedness, not on the strong chains of psychological connections that generally sustain personal identity. McMahan also claims that an account of our concerns based on psychological connections and/or continuity would imply that, when there are no more psychological connections, say, at a later stage of the illness, the early patient would have no more reasons for being egoistically concerned. The problem is that, according to McMahan, many would say that it is still reasonable to care about the post-person in an egoistic way. For instance, we may be self-concerned about the ordeal the post-person related to us will have to go through in the final days of her life.[15] McMahan thus argues that a different approach is required, the main features of which are discussed in the next section.

4.1 Embodied mind and abortion

McMahan proposes to revise the accounts of our future concern and of our identity by introducing new terminology.[16] In particular, he defines *broad* psychological continuity as a relation of overlapping chains of psychological connectedness of any degree, weak or strong. In turn, a *weak* psychological connection holds when there are fewer connections than half the number of psychological connections that hold every day in the life of a normal adult. McMahan's revised theory is:

(Broad Psychological Continuity Theory of the Metaphysical Foundation of Personal Identity)

For all t, P at t_1 is the same person as Q at t_2 iff, provided a definition of broad psychological continuity in terms of overlapping chains of psychological connectedness, (1) P is broadly psychologically continuous with Q, (2) psychological connectedness and/or continuity are sustained by the same relevant areas of the brain, and (3) the connections have not taken a branching form.

A related account of our egoistic concern may hold that what matters is (any degree of) psychological connectedness and/or broad psychological continuity. Some of the motivations supporting the previously stated theories are mostly based on an analysis of our intuitions regarding several scenarios, such as variations on the tele-transportation and the brain-fission cases. In particular, McMahan claims that we tend to think that in those cases of fission involving the separation of A's two brain hemispheres A survives. He also argues that a tele-transportation case involving the destruction of the original brain and body is not a case in which the scanned person survives. If we combine these intuitions with the further point that egoistic concern for our survival generally follows or tracks intuitions about when we personally survive, then psychological connectedness and continuity make a difference with respect to the holding of personal identity when they are grounded in the non-branching continued existence of the same relevant areas of the brain (i.e., those areas of the brain responsible for the relevant psychological relations). In short, McMahan's point is that we tend to judge that we persist through time when some degree of our psychological connections is sustained by the same brain life. There are various ways in which sameness of brain can be specified (see Chapter 6), whether in terms of continuity of its constitutive matter, or in terms of its functional structure or organisation. McMahan claims that enough physical and *functional* continuity of the areas of the brain in which consciousness is realised in a non-branching form is a necessary and sufficient condition for personal identity. Functional continuity is a relation that holds in case the same brain retains its basic psychological capacities over time. An organisational continuity involves the retention of the content of mental states over time. These conditions of personal identity form the core of the embodied mind account of our nature. McMahan further claims that the embodied mind account, the point of which is that a mind is individuated in virtue of its physical non-branching embodiment, is compatible with different theories about the metaphysical relationship between mind and brain. However, the relationship between ourselves – intended as embodied minds – and our organisms is that of a proper part and its whole. So, on this account, you are not identical to your own organism; rather, you are a separable part of it: you are an embodied mind.

The implications of this account for the debate on when we begin and abortion are: (1) we do not begin to exist until our organisms develop the actual capacity to generate consciousness. Although there is no general consensus on the precise timing, McMahan claims that it is unlikely that our brains generate consciousness until around the sixth month of pregnancy. So, (2) there is not someone like us to be harmed in early abortions, that is, in abortions procured before the actual capacity for consciousness has significantly developed. Early abortions would simply prevent something from becoming someone in a way that is relevantly similar to contraception and abstinence. Since contraception and abstinence are not morally wrong, early abortions in themselves are not morally wrong either.

4.2 The constitution view and abortion

Lynne Rudder Baker offers an answer to the question of our beginning – when do we begin? – that can be classified as another application of the psychological approach.[17] In particular, she believes that we are fundamentally and essentially people constituted by human organisms. In addition, she claims that constitution is not identity and thus that people may come into existence at a time different from when the organisms that constitute us do. Baker claims that 'person' is a primary kind, similar to 'organism', so that an instance of these kinds essentially belongs to them (recall the notion of substance-sortal in Chapter 5). The characterising feature of persons is the possession of the mental property having-a-first-person-perspective. Adult persons have this property when they are able to think of themselves without the use of any proper names, descriptions, or demonstratives: having a first-person perspective is the ability to think of oneself from the inside as a continuing entity, an ability we may manifest even in cases of total amnesia. For example, if A has total and irreversible amnesia, and thus could not remember any description about herself, A may still wonder how *she*, the entity having that particular first-person perspective, ended up in that situation or what her future will be. Being conscious does not imply having a first-person perspective, as in the case of certain conscious nonhuman primates. Such creatures probably have certain psychological states, but are not aware of their having such states (but see later for a qualification of this claim).

To better clarify the notion of a first-person perspective, Baker distinguishes between a robust and a rudimentary first-person perspective. In particular, she maintains that a *robust* first-person perspective is the basis of rational agency and other higher forms of consciousness. Having a point of view does not imply being capable of *conceiving* of oneself as a subject of experience. Baker also claims that having this kind of first-person perspective is sufficient for personhood, independently of the particular material substrate in which such a perspective is realised. A *rudimentary* first-person perspective is a faculty that X has iff "(i) X is a conscious, sentient being; (ii) X has a capacity to imitate; (iii) its behaviour is explainable only by attribution of beliefs, desires, and intentions."[18] Baker then claims that human infants and certain nonhuman mammals have a rudimentary first-order perspective. The development of a robust first-person perspective is an inherently social process, and the potentiality to develop one distinguishes, according to Baker, a person from a non-person. So, an infant is a person in virtue of its actual capacity to have a robust first-person perspective, whilst a dog, which has only a rudimentary first-person perspective and cannot develop a robust one, is not a person. So, "a being with a rudimentary first-person perspective is a person only if it is a kind that normally develops robust first-person perspectives." According to Baker, her view implies that a human person comes into existence near birth.[19]

The consequences of this version of the constitution view (or constitutionalism) for the debate on abortion are spelled out by Baker in these terms: "Any premise that implies that abortion before development of a rudimentary first-person perspective is the killing of an innocent person is false."[20] Baker also adds that her view implies that neither mere human organisms nor pre-rudimentary first-person perspective foetuses have the same ontological/moral status as we do.

5 Self-constituting narrative and practical approaches, and abortion

Self-constituting narrative and practical approaches have implications for the debate on abortion similar to those of the previous psychological accounts. Since a foetus and/or an infant are not capable of generating a self- or person-constituting narrative, and/or if we are essentially self-narrative entities, then we did not exist at such early stages of our biological lives. So, in early pregnancies, an entity like us still does not exist and abortion does not amount to the killing of a person. Similarly, advocates of the practical approach may argue that, since foetuses or embryos are not actually capable of agency in the way we are, at least early abortions are not events in which someone like us is destroyed.

Narrativists may follow different strategies for replying to the previous reasoning, if they so desire. For instance, they may claim that, even though it is true that foetuses are not persons, the self-narrative process may work backward and connect each of us to a foetus by establishing a narrative link between our current mental states and the earlier stages of our biological lives. In other words, a self-constituting narrative entity may later identify or familiarise herself with a certain entity in the past and establish an appropriate narrative connection between herself and the infant or early foetus to which she is relevantly biologically connected. So, abortion would prevent this (retroactively constituted) future series of meaningful narrative connections and, if we believe that narrative psychological connections matter, is therefore wrong. An objection against drawing such backward connections so far in the past is that such backward connections could not have the empathic access that Schechtman thought of as being crucial in characterising our experience as narrative entities. In particular, it seems difficult to familiarise and/

or have a sympathetic affection towards certain biological processes so remote and possibly completely inaccessible to us.

Some narrative theories drop the requirement that our identity must be constituted by a *self*-narrating agent and instead claim that our narrative identity can be told not only by the self-constituting agent that is also the protagonist of the narrative but also by others. This option and its ethical consequences are explored in the next section.

6 Relational-narrative entities and abortion

In this section, I introduce Hilde Lindemann's narrative theory – a narrative account that includes elements of the relational approach. In particular, she holds that four elements constitute personhood:

1   "A human being has or will have sufficient mental activity to constitute a personality (among other things, feelings, thoughts, desires, and intentions).
2   This personality is expressed bodily.
3   Other persons recognise such an expression.
4   These other persons respond to such an expression."[21]

Why is Lindemann's theory one version of the narrative approach? Because she describes the social response to the bodily expression of P as articulated/articulable in a web of stories, that is, an identity-sustaining narrative. This social-narrative practice is relational in the sense we discussed in Chapter 3 and, more importantly, does not have as a necessary requirement for P to be a person that P be also her own self-constituting narrator. In other words, the identity-sustaining narrative may be the result of extrinsic social/relational processes. Lindemann's theory can be seen as one version of the relational necessity theory as she maintains that social practices are crucially important in creating and maintaining personal identity. She also claims that such practices provide the link between personhood and morality: given that personal identity is essentially constituted by social practices and that significant social practices have a moral character, our identities are infused with a moral dimension. What kind of identity-sustaining practices does Lindemann have in mind? One example is that of a "one-sided practice" that may take place in certain "structures of intimacy" (e.g., families) in which certain people take care of a severely disabled individual – a practice through which an individual, the disabled, is "held in personhood". So, although a disabled person may not spin a self-constituting narrative, others can do it on his or her behalf – provided that the disabled individual is somehow capable of expressing at least minimal forms of personality. Again, some (most) supporters of the narrative approach do not understand their views as specifying metaphysical conditions of identity. Rather, they tend to see their theories as addressing some of the characterisation questions – e.g., when is a certain action properly attributed to me? Who am I? These questions are about our biographical identity and do not necessarily have a metaphysical or ontological significance. As explained in Chapter 6, however, we can understand narrative theories, including Lindemann's, as prescribing structural conditions on the psychological connections that sustain our continuity through time.

Lindemann claims that the process of identity formation begins in infancy and often even earlier, especially in the context of the family. Similar to the Confucian understanding of the role of the family, this theory also emphasises that the process of identity formation begins in that context.[22] The role of the external reality – what is outside of the person's body – is not simply that of constraining the constituting narrative, what Schechtman calls 'the reality constraint'. Rather, on this narrative/relational view, certain aspects of this external reality can play a more active role in shaping and maintaining personal identity. Still, Lindemann claims that other kinds of reality constraints apply – she maintains that members of the identity-constituting community may get certain things about an individual wrong.

Lindemann's relational account shares certain features with the psychological approach as well. In fact, she understands the notion of a self as the socially shaped "locus of idiosyncratic causation, sensation, and experience." Later foetuses, Lindemann argues, would not be persons because they cannot yet be part of the practice of bodily recognition that is allegedly essential to being a person. It may be argued that being inside the womb and thus hidden from sight seems a bizarre condition for determining whether someone is a person or whether an individual can be the object and subject of an identity-sustaining narrative. Lindemann seems to avoid some of the most implausible consequences of her view by claiming that the mother of the foetus can enact the necessary social practice of recognition of the foetus inside her, at least when/if the pregnancy is welcomed.

What are the consequences of this hybrid view for abortion? If the pregnancy is wanted and the mother begins to develop a significant narrative about the growing foetus, Lindemann claims that the mother is "calling the foetus" into personhood. In less metaphysically obscure terms, the point seems to be that a new person's narrative may begin also when an individual does not have actual mental capacities and is hidden, in the sense that her bodily expression is not part of a public social context. In particular, Lindemann claims that, at first, such a new narrative may be told exclusively by the mother, and then it will slowly develop into a rather more comprehensive story that is dependent on and integrated with the narratives of the relevant social entities that will surround the new individual's existence. If the pregnancy is not wanted, the foetus may not be 'called into personhood', or, if it is, it will not be seen as an integrated member of the mother's social context. Rather, it will likely be classified as an entity intruding in the woman's body. This account may provide an explanation, which is not explicitly endorsed by Lindemann, as to why we have the intuition that we wrong a woman if we forcibly remove a foetus from her womb when she has expressed her desire to continue the pregnancy: there is already a person that has been called into existence – at least when and to the degree that such a foetus is capable of reacting and being known to the mother. Voluntary (early) abortions would not count as cases of murder, as the narrative process of relational identity has not yet brought anyone into existence. Although this account is intriguing, one possible problem is that it is not clear how it can resolve cases of conflicting voices that seem to contribute to just one narrative. For instance, it is certainly possible that our self-constituting narrative diverge from the narratives that others tell of ourselves – and both can meet some versions of the reality constraint. In this case, it is not clear whether the account implies that there are two different persons and/or one person to which conflicting descriptions are applied. But if the constituting narratives are taken to be ontologically relevant, then it seems that the account implies that there are as many entities as constituting narratives. A too-many-narratives problem, similar to the too-many-thinkers problem, seems to loom over this account.

7 Buddhist no-self and abortion

Doctrines such as the Buddhist no-self view#1 can be applied to cases of practical ethics in different ways. However, as a preliminary point, it is important to distinguish Buddhist theories of no-self and their consequences from what certain Buddhist schools prescribe or regard as morally correct. For instance, Damien Keown and Peter Harvey, in reporting certain attitudes towards abortion in some forms of Buddhism (e.g., those inspired by the *Theravādin Vinaya*), hold that there is a general convergence in forbidding monks and nuns from the facilitation (or performance) of abortions. Harvey claims that abortion is generally seen in this tradition as always wrong, the main reasons given being that human life begins at conception and that such a life is full of potential in terms of Karma and rebirth. Harvey reports passages from Buddhist texts according to which being aborted may anger a foetus and thereby cause it to have a bad rebirth. However, as we have previously seen, early foetuses do not have mental states and do not seem to have the actual capacity to be angry. Only certain (dubious) religious or speculative beliefs – such as the belief that an early foetus can get angry – may support this argument against abortion. When certain supernatural beliefs (e.g., in Karma and rebirth) are left aside, Buddhist no-self view#1 and Buddhist no-self view#2 can have different consequences for the debate on the morality of abortion. For instance, one of the main moral principles of these views is that, under certain circumstances, ownerless altruism and compassion are good. More specifically, these views tend to support the idea that, since pain is always morally bad and that there is no my or your pain but simply painful events, all pains matter. If this is the case, we could have the philosophical basis for claiming that we should avoid harming an entity that may feel pain – so, it may be morally wrong to remove a foetus when (and only if) it can feel pain, if they do at all.

The practical consequences of accepting certain forms of personal nihilism are, again, hard to assess. As already discussed in Chapter 2 and in relation to the debate on what matters in survival (Chapter 7), the plausibility of this approach depends also on how it accommodates or makes sense of certain everyday practices and beliefs. So, although certain forms of nihilism imply that, literally, we never even begin to exist, they may hold that, according to a series of social conventions, we begin to exist at a certain time. In turn, the series of conventions that regulate these existential claims may be identified with the content of other accounts of our beginning. So, also in this case, the advocate of nihilism may implement into her view one (or more) of the other approaches to our beginning.

8 Our death

There are various accounts of what death is and when it occurs. Among the most popular definitions – as it is standard in the literature, 'definition' refers to a conceptual analysis or account – of death we can include: (1) the **cardiopulmonary definition**, (2) the **whole brain definition**, and (3) the **higher brain definition**. Another definition of death, based on the soul approach, states that our (earthly) death is the departure or separation of our soul from the body. However, since it is not clear how to judge when a soul leaves the body, this soul-body separation criterion generally relies on one of the other accounts to define what is/constitutes evidence for human death. So, a supporter of the soul-body separation account may claim that our earthly death is the separation of the soul from the body and maintain that evidence of such a separation having taken place is provided by one of the other approaches (e.g., whole brain death).

Since at least two of the stated definitions refer to the brain, it is useful to recall here some basic information about its functioning. In the current literature, it is generally taken for granted that the brain has a higher part, which includes the cerebrum and the cerebellum, that is responsible for consciousness and the coordination of action. The lower part of the brain, sometimes identified with the brainstem (and which is divided in other sub-systems and parts), is taken to be responsible for, among other things, the control of certain basic functional activities (e.g., spontaneous respiration) and as containing an area that functions as an activating centre for consciousness. Such an area, if damaged, does not seem to affect the content of our mind, but solely the possibility of accessing such a content. When a patient has a substantial degree of damage in his higher brain, she may fall in a *permanent vegetative state* (PVS). In such a state the brainstem may still function and, although consciousness may never be restored, the patient is capable of spontaneous breathing and seems to be awake. Patients in a permanent coma generally do not even appear to be awake – although heartbeat and spontaneous breathing are present. Patients in this unfortunate state generally pass away in a relatively shorter time than do those in PVS.

According to some recent studies, the role played by the brain (in both of its parts) is slightly different from what has been assumed by supporters of the whole brain definition of death. In particular, Alan Shewmon argues that certain regulative processes, which were assumed to be essentially connected to the brain, can take place, to a lesser degree of functionality, even in brain-dead patients (Chapter 5). Among these processes, some researchers include the assimilation of nutrients, the detoxification of certain cells, wound healing, and the cardiovascular and hormonal responses to inflicted wounds. Shewmon also suggests that the brain, in certain cases, can be understood as having the function of enhancing rather than enabling certain regulatory systems. In his own words,

> each part of the body, especially the brain, contributes to the stability, robustness, and richness of the body's vitality and unity, but no one part or even combination of parts constitutes that vitality or unity. The main functions of the heart can be accomplished by a mechanical pump and the body will be just as alive as before (although more precariously so than with a healthy heart). Most brains cannot be artificially substituted (at least presently, and perhaps even intrinsically), but their irreplaceability has nothing to do with whether a brain-destroyed body possesses integrative unity. The relatively few brain functions necessary for maintaining (an already given) somatic integrative unity in the wild are indeed replaceable in both theory and present practice.[23]

8.1 Defining 'death'

Since the soul-body separation account of death is popular primarily in religious contexts and/or is parasitic on the accounts favoured by other theories of personal identity, the discussion immediately following is focused on the relation between the three current main definitions of death and the other approaches to personal identity and our nature.

1   Cardiopulmonary definition: human death is the irreversible cessation of cardiopulmonary function.

Theories of our nature according to which we are animals, in the sense of living human organisms, seem to provide reasons to believe that we die when our cardiopulmonary system stops functioning. The reason is that, since cardiopulmonary cessation results in the death of a living organism – and, according to (one version of) animalism, we are living human organisms – our death is the cessation of cardiopulmonary function. Since our brains may not be essential for keeping our organism alive, our death is not the cessation of brain function. A contemporary modification of this approach is the circulatory-respiratory standard: death is the irreversible cessation of *circulatory-respiratory* function. The advantage of this definition is that it emphasises the correct reason of the collapse of cell functioning, that is, the disruption of the circulatory-respiratory system. This means that it is not the disruption of a specific organ (e.g., the heart) that determines the death of an organism – as its function can be carried out vicariously – but the collapse of a specific system. Contemporary animalists have frequently assumed that what is essential to the maintenance of the unity of the organism is the brainstem. However, even if this (empirical) belief turns out to be false, it does not substantially hinder animalism. In fact, the main point of animalism in this regard is simply that our death is an event caused by the cessation of the continuous functioning of a human organism and of its teleological unity. It is an empirical question which organs, systems, or events are responsible for the death of a human organism, so, in principle, animalism *qua* animalism is compatible also with, e.g., the whole brain definition. Still, animalists would deny that the destruction of the higher brain can be identified with the biological fact that puts an end to the life of a human organism, as there is plenty of evidence for the belief that human organisms can survive even when they have lost their cortex.

Not all forms of animalism would support the previously stated reasoning. For instance, David Mackie, in discussing Locke, proposes that "the persistence of biological organisms depends on their retaining (enough of) the organisation of parts that is the product of their natural biological development, and that makes them apt for life, while stopping short of saying that life itself is necessary."[24] According to this version of animalism, we do not cease to exist when the organisms we are die. Rather, we persist as corpses, at least until the organisation of those parts that once had the function of keeping us alive deteriorates substantially – on this view, a dead animal is still an existing animal.[25]

Psychological approaches to our nature and identity through time – whether having the form of relational, generic psychological, practical, or self-constituting narrative views – tend to regard the circulatory-respiratory definition as wrong. Although this definition may provide a satisfactory criterion of when our *organism* dies, it is not a satisfying account of when *we*, psychological entities, die. Still, all that psychological theories may be committed to is simply the claim that our death occurs when our psychological functions cease irreversibly. Which organs or structures are or can be responsible for our psychological life is an empirical question, not to be specifically addressed by any versions of the psychological approach.

Certain relational-narrative accounts of our nature and personal identity may have different consequences for the circulatory-respiratory definition. For instance, given that relational-narrative theories do not involve as a necessary condition the existence of a self-constituting narrative, advocates of such accounts may argue that it is possible for us to persist through time – and thus not die – if our personal narratives are properly carried out even by someone else (this form of persistence is also called 'role-survival').[26] If appropriate narrative links are established between our proper relational-constituting narrative and those who survive our bodily death, we may literally not die. (This view is not compatible with Lindemann's: according to her, some psychological activities expressing a personality should be present for the related person to exist.) One radical version of this approach may also provide a rational foundation to those beliefs and desires that certain people have to be remembered by future generations. In fact, on some (radical) relational theories, it can be literally true that we keep on living in the minds of those who remember us. Tombs, graveyards, the remembering of stories about certain historical individuals – not to mention the practice of writing autobiographies, possibly that of keeping online blogs and diaries, social media profiles – may literally be a way in which we do not die. Whether this romantic way of survival may provide some kind of genuine psychological solace to certain people is disputable. In any case, this hybrid relational-narrative theory seems to favour the view according to which our persistence involves other people's willingness to keep us alive when we are no more capable of constituting our own narrative, say, because our brain is no more functioning. There are two possible ways of specifying a conception of death under these assumptions: (i) human death is the irreversible cessation of relational-constituting narrative updating, e.g., when nobody adds anything to our narratives; or (ii) human death is the irreversible cessation of the accessibility to relational-constituting narratives, e.g., if nobody remembers or has (proper) access to our constituting narratives.

2   Whole brain definition: human death is the irreversible cessation of functioning of the whole brain.

Physical- and psychological-based theories of personal identity may both provide reasons to support this definition. As discussed in Chapter 5, in fact, some of these theories include certain forms of the bodily continuity condition for personal identity. This point may translate into specific conditions internal to the psychological approach, in particular, to the specification of the kind of causal connections among psychological connections essential for our persistence through time as persons. However, the death of the whole brain does not seem to be a biologically necessary condition for a person to die: if our identity through time as persons is determined by psychological connectedness, then it is not necessary for the whole brain to stop functioning for persons to stop existing. For example, our consciousness may be irremediably lost whilst the brainstem can continue functioning. A generic psychological theory of our nature and personal identity can thus be compatible with the claim that the irreversible destruction of the whole brain is not necessary for us, *qua* psychological entities, to die. On one reading of Locke's account of personal identity, what we may properly call *our own* death would occur, e.g., in case God decides not to resurrect us when the time comes, that is, in case our psychological connections are irremediably interrupted, thus well after the destruction of our brain. On this account, our death is the irremediable interruption of psychological connections, and brain death is one way in which this may happen, but the latter is not, in itself, what our death is.

The specific details of the animalist stance towards the whole brain definition depend, again, on empirical facts regarding what is responsible for the continuity of the life that is supposed to provide the identity conditions of the organisms we are. If the brainstem turns out to be essential for the life of a living organism, then whole brain death is sufficient for our death. However, it may not be necessary; e.g., if the brainstem is essential to the integrated functioning of our organism, then it is not necessary for the whole brain to stop functioning for the organism to die. Views according to which we are essentially human organisms – not necessarily *living* human organisms – may hold that, supposing the essential role of the brainstem for maintaining the unity of the organism, it is true that an organism dies when the brainstem does. However, such an approach to our nature would also hold that we may continue to exist as dead organisms: the death of an organism is not our death. One problem of associating animalism with the whole brain death definition is that, according to certain forms of animalism, we were foetuses even before we developed a brain. If this is true, and given that certain early foetuses die, the cessation of the functioning of a whole brain is not a necessary condition for a developing human organism to die.

Despite its many problems, the whole brain definition of death is still the theoretical basis for many legal definitions of death around the world and regulates several legislations on organ donation and transplantation.[27]

3 Higher brain definition: human death is the irreversible cessation of the functioning of the higher part of the brain (or of those parts responsible for our consciousness).

Not all of the psychological theories may hold that the destruction of the higher brain is a necessary condition for our death. For instance, if we adopt a self-constitutive narrative approach to our synchronic and diachronic identity, there is a sense in which, when the self-constituting narrative is irremediably interrupted and/or forgotten, one specific self-constituting entity has ceased to exist. This may happen to an individual even though such an individual has not lost the upper part of her brain. More specifically, certain cases of irretrievable amnesia or mental illness that do not involve the destruction of the upper part of the brain may be regarded as coinciding with the end of someone like us. Similar considerations apply to practical identity theories, generic psychological theories, and relational accounts that include also certain forms of mental functioning as a necessary condition for personal identity. Still, excluding the possibility of resurrections, posthumous mental uploading, and other related scenarios, on these psychology-based accounts the destruction of the higher brain is a sufficient condition for our death – although, again, on these accounts, the irreversible cessation of higher brain function is not what our death is.

Most of the discussed physical-based accounts do not seem to support this definition of death, for reasons similar to those discussed before in relation to brain death: if we are, say, human animals, and we identify a human animal with a living human organism, it seems that a living human organism can, in a relevant sense, stay alive even deprived of the higher part of its brain. So, on this view, we do not die in case our cortex stops functioning.

No-self and nihilistic approaches to our own identity are compatible, in themselves, with different approaches to death. A supporter of a conventionalist form of nihilism may claim that we do not exist, we have never come into existence and, consequently, we do not die. Still, certain propositions, e.g., that Socrates is dead, can be regarded as true (solely) in a conventional or fictional context. So, a nihilist may maintain that there is a sense in which a certain number of particles arranged person-wise (or Socrates-wise) may no longer be parts of a causal chain of events that holds them together in a way that social conventions – e.g., those captured by psychology-based theories – find sufficient to classify as composing one of us. To sum up, no-self and nihilistic approaches, to the degree that they are supposed to accommodate (and not dispense with) everyday practice, are parasitic upon other accounts in determining the best definition of death. It is clear that this derivative way of describing reality may seem unnecessarily clumsy, counterintuitive, and confusing. However, this is not necessarily an argument against the plausibility of a theory. As the scientific understanding of subatomic particles has provided us with a bewildering account of reality at that scale, we may argue that general metaphysical theories may equally provide counterintuitive accounts of reality without thereby being implausible. Even if we believe that certain parts of contemporary science are not (or should not be understood as) aiming at providing a description of the deep structure of reality, we can still claim that the conceptual instruments they provide us for understanding and predicting physical phenomena are frequently very different from the concepts that most of us use to understand and describe our everyday life. However, we do not think that their eventual incongruence is a reason not to believe in scientific theories. So, why should it be a reason not to believe nihilism?

8.2 Why 'death' matters

In addition to the intrinsic interest of understanding what our death is, there are several practical matters of extreme moral importance that are conceptually connected to the definition of death. In fact, to different definitions correspond different evaluations of public health policies and legal practices. Consider the so-called **dead donor rule**, that is, the principle according to which donors must be declared dead prior to any procedure aimed at transplanting their organs. Certainly, people may voluntarily donate some of their organs, but when this procedure would take their lives, the principle is generally applied. In addition, since the main source of organs for transplantation comes from cadaveric donors and given the perishability of certain organs, different criteria of death may determine a radically different availability of organs for transplantation. As a consequence, many lives are at stake because of the way in which death is defined, in particular, the lives of the many people waiting for a transplant. For example, holding the dead donor rule along with a version of animalism according to which we are living organisms may have significant repercussions. As we have seen, animalism seems to favour an account of our death according to which brain death is neither necessary nor sufficient. If certain accounts (e.g., Shewmon's) of how somatic and integrative functionality and unity of our organisms are correct, then the whole brain definition is not correct. In turn, animalism may also imply that brain-dead patients whose hearts are still beating should not be considered dead: after all, they are still living organisms like us. If the dead donor rule upholds, organ transplantation does not seem to be justified in these cases. In turn, this would amount to a drastic reduction in the availability of organs for transplantation, not to mention the reduction of the success rate of these operations – since organs rapidly deteriorate after the disruption of the circulatory-respiratory system. In order to legally remove certain organs, doctors would have to wait for the disruption of the circulatory-respiratory system, with the result that many of them will deteriorate to the point of not being useful any longer.

It is worth mentioning that it is not necessary for an animalist to hold that it is always forbidden to operate on someone like us before her death. For instance, an animalist may hold an account of what matters in survival in terms of self-constitutive narrative unity or psychological connectedness – remember DeGrazia's TRIA. On these views, a brain-dead patient would have already lost what matters and gives value to her life, e.g., the capacity to have meaningful and structured psychological connections. So, although one of us may still be alive (i.e., one human organism may still be alive) transplanting organs from such an organism permanently incapable of having any mental state may not harm this individual and thus be justified.

On the other hand, psychology-based accounts of our nature and identity through time tend to imply that our death occurs when certain meaningful psychological connections are irremediably severed – or, possibly, take a branching form. Hybrid views such as the embodied mind approach imply that when our higher brain is irremediably deprived of the capacity to generate consciousness, we die. One of the consequences of these approaches is that organ transplantation may be allowed in cases in which consciousness is irremediably lost, unless other moral restrictions apply. Taking certain organs from a mindless – in a literal sense – organism does not constitute the murder of anybody like us. Obviously, there may be other moral reasons for refraining from the operation, but violating the dead donor rule would not be one of them.

9 Summary

One of the main upshots of this chapter is that, in general, psychology-based theories of personal identity and our nature (e.g., McMahan's and Baker's) tend to favour a more liberal stance in the debate on abortion. On the other hand, physical approaches – in particular certain forms of animalism – seem to support some arguments against the morality of abortion – for example, Marquis's future-like-ours argument. However, animalists such as David DeGrazia have argued that, in certain cases, abortion is morally right on the basis of a divergence between (1) our conditions of identity over time, (2) what is valuable in our lives, and (3) an appropriate account of the harm or badness of death. Although according to some of the main versions of animalism we begin to exist fourteen or sixteen days after conception, it does not follow that harming or destroying a developing foetus is always morally wrong and/or that it is as wrong as harming an adult. What matters in our lives is not directly determined by the natural kind to which we belong. Psychological theories, on the other hand, generally do not hold or imply that we came into existence when a foetus relevantly connected to our organisms began to exist. Rather, according to these theories, we began to exist when our organisms – or our brains – started to have the actual capacity to be conscious or have significantly structured mental states (e.g., practical agency or narrativity). So, if early abortions are wrong, they are not wrong because they destroy a person or someone like us.

Soul-based approaches can be interpreted in various ways depending on their additional views on the nature of the soul and mind. If the soul is eternal, then maybe we have always existed and have forgotten our past lives. Hence, when an abortion is performed, we are merely preventing one soul from informing one body. On other accounts, our souls are essentially psychological entities, and evidence of their activity should be found in the body they inform – e.g., by looking at the structure of the brain. Supporters of soul-based theories generally apply a broader religious framework that may impose restrictions to the permissibility of abortion. To the degree that nihilistic theories do not embrace an eliminativist strategy with respect to our everyday practice of talking about our beginning, these theories seem to rely on other approaches to account for our beginning and the morality of abortion. In particular, nihilists may prescribe the use of paraphrases of our talk about our beginning that derive from other theories – e.g., they may claim that, although literally speaking we do not exist, according to such-and-such a convention or fiction (e.g., a generic psychological theory, intended as a fiction), we begin to exist when our brains start to have certain features. Relational theories may imply that we begin when we start to be embedded into certain social structures – a narrative version of this approach holds that members of the community to which we belong may even spin our identity-sustaining narrative on our behalf. On Lindemann's view, abortion can be justified in cases in which the foetus is not brought into personhood by the mother.

Defining 'death' is as important for other debates in applied ethics as knowing when we began for debates on the morality of abortion. In particular, we saw that policies related to human organ transplantation are connected to principles that include specific reference to the time of our death. Psychological theories seem to favour those definitions of death that take into account the idea that we are essentially psychologically entities. On these views, our death coincides with the irreversible cessation of those structures that sustain our mental states. More specific psychological theories may imply that our death and/or the death of persons depend not just on the existence of certain psychological connections but also on how such psychological connections are sustained or structured (e.g., moral agency, narrativity). Self-constituting narrative theories, for instance, may imply that X's death is the irreversible loss of X's self-constituting narrative – so, although higher brain death may be sufficient for such a loss, it is not a necessary condition for a person to die. On the other hand, popular forms of animalism would have the consequence that, although persons may die as a consequence of the irreversible cessation of their brain functions, *we* do not die until our organisms stop functioning. In turn, this conclusion may provide reasons for restricting certain policies regarding organ procurement.

Notes

1 See Steinbock (2011), pp. 42–50 for a survey of recent stances on the beginning of the psychological capacities of embryos and foetuses. In particular, it is there reported that "in the first 12 weeks of pregnancy, […] none of the spinal pathways and cortical connections necessary for pain perception are present, and experts agree that the foetus is not sentient."

2 Boonin (2003).

3 Marquis (2007), p. 399.

4 The crucial role of animalism in supporting Marquis's argument is not fully recognised in the current literature on the topic.

5 See Marquis (1997/2013), p. 408.

6 DeGrazia (2005), pp. 249–252.

7 Olson (1997a) and (1997b).

8 Olson (1997a), p. 101.

9 This line of reasoning was elaborated by McMahan in relation to Marquis's argument.

10 DeGrazia (2012), p. 32.

11 Boonin and Steinbock discuss more refined versions of the desire-based approach. See their works in the bibliography at the end of this chapter. Also, Boonin developed a sophisticated version of the desire-approach that has a way of replying to DeGrazia's previous claim; see Boonin (2003), Chapter 2.

12 Aquinas discusses various issues concerning human nature and ensoulment in his *Summa Theologiae* Ia 75–89. Many works have been devoted to the study of what is nowadays called 'immediate vs. delayed hominization' in Catholic circles. See Haldane & Lee (2002), note 5, for an extensive bibliography on the subject and Pasnau (2001) for a recent interpretation of Aquinas on human nature.

13 Ford (1988), p. xv.

14 Tooley (1983).

15 The intuition behind this claim is similar to that related to a situation described by Bernard Williams in his 'The Self and the Future' (1970).

16 McMahan (2002).

17 Baker (2005).

18 Baker (2005), p. 30.

19 Baker's notion of a rudimentary first-person perspective is similar, although relevantly different, to Tom Regan's notion of a subject-of-a-life (Regan 1983). In the context of arguing for a criterion of inherent value stricter than Peter Singer's sentience principle but broad enough to encompass certain animal species, Regan defines various mental capacities that subjects-of-a-life have. For instance, they have beliefs, desires, perception, memory, a sense of the future, an emotional life, preferences, an ability to initiate action, and a psychophysical identity over time.

20 Baker (2005).

21 Lindemann (2014), p. ix.

22 An emphasis on the importance of the family is not the only relevant feature of the Confucian approach. Ivanhoe claims that, in Confucian societies, there is broad latitude with respect to the way in which the general reverence for life, another characteristic of Confucianism, is weighted against concerns for the welfare of women. Ivanhoe proposes that public policies based on Confucian principles may include a review process for those women who decide to undergo abortion, a means to prevent unnecessary measures. See Ivanhoe (2010) for discussion and Olberding (2015) for criticism.

23 Shewmon (2001), p. 473.

24 This passage from Mackie (1999), 236.

25 Feldman is a contemporary defender of this view – see Feldman (1992).

26 Chapter 8, 4.3.

27 See Bernat (2006).

Suggested readings

Our beginning

Baker, Lynne Rudder, 'When Does a Person Being?', *Social Philosophy and Policy*, 22, 2 (2005), pp. 25–48.

Davies, Jamie A., *Life Unfolding* (Oxford: Oxford University Press, 2014).

DeGrazia, David, *Human Identity and Bioethics* (Cambridge: Cambridge University Press, 2005).
Ford, Norman, *When Did I Begin?* (Cambridge: Cambridge University Press, 1988).
McMahan, Jeff, *The Ethics of Killing* (Oxford: Oxford University Press, 2002), Chapter 1.
Olson, Eric, 'Was I Ever a Fetus?', *Philosophy and Phenomenological Research*, 57, 1 (1997a), pp. 95–110.
Olson, Eric, *The Human Animal* (Oxford: Oxford University Press, 1997b).
Sadler, Thomas W., *Langman's Medical Embryology, Thirteenth Edition* (Philadelphia: Wolters Kluwer, 2015).
Van Inwagen, Peter, *Material Beings* (Ithaca: Cornell University Press, 1990).
Wilson, Robert A. and Matthew Barker, 'The Biological Notion of Individual', in *Stanford Encyclopedia of Philosophy* (2013). https://plato.stanford.edu/entries/biology-individual/

Abortion: general discussions

Boonin, David, *A Defense of Abortion* (Cambridge: Cambridge University Press, 2003).
DeGrazia, David, *Creation Ethics* (Oxford: Oxford University Press, 2012).
Little, Margaret Olivia, 'Abortion', in Raymond G. Frey and Christopher Heath Wellman (eds.) *A Companion to Applied Ethics* (Malden, MA: Blackwell Publishing, 2005), pp. 313–325.
Marquis, Don, 'An Argument That Abortion Is Wrong', in Hugh LaFollette (ed.) *Ethics in Practice* (Oxford: Blackwell, 1997), pp. 91–102. Reprinted in Russ Shafer-Landau (ed.) *Ethical Theory: An Anthology* (Malden, MA: John Wiley & Sons, 2013), pp. 400–409.
Marquis, Don, 'Abortion Revisited', in Bonnie Steinbock (ed.) *The Oxford Handbook of Bioethics* (Oxford: Oxford University Press, 2007), pp. 395–415.
Steinbock, Bonnie, *Life Before Birth, Second Edition* (Oxford: Oxford University Press, 1992/2011).
Warren, Mary Anne, 'Abortion', in Peter Singer and Helga Kuhse (eds.) *A Companion to Bioethics* (Malden, MA: Wiley-Blackwell, 2009), pp. 140–148.

Souls and abortion

Haldane, John and Patrick Lee, 'Aquinas on Human Ensoulment, Abortion, and the Value of Life', *Philosophy*, 78, 2 (2003), pp. 255–278.
Martin, Christopher, *The Philosophy of Thomas Aquinas: Introductory Readings* (London: Routledge Kegan & Paul, 1988).
Pasnau, Robert, *Thomas Aquinas on Human Nature* (Cambridge: Cambridge University Press, 2001).
Stump, Eleonore, *Aquinas* (London: Routledge, 2003).

Psychological and relational theories and abortion

Ivanhoe, Philip J., 'A Confucian Perspective on Abortion', *Dao*, 9 (2010), pp. 37–51.
Lindemann Nelson, Hilde, 'What Child Is This?', *The Hastings Center Report*, 32, 6 (2002), pp. 29–38.
Lindemann, Hilde, *Holding and Letting Go* (Oxford: Oxford University Press, 2014).
McMahan, Jeff, *The Ethics of Killing* (Oxford: Oxford University Press, 2002), Chapter 4.
Nie, Jing-Bao, *Medical Ethics in China* (London and New York: Routledge, 2011).
Olberding, Amy, 'A Sensible Confucian Perspective on Abortion,' *Dao: A Journal of Comparative Philosophy* 14, 2 (2015), pp. 235–253.

Schechtman, Marya, *Staying Alive* (Oxford: Oxford University Press, 2014).

Tooley, Michael, *Abortion and Infanticide* (Oxford: Clarendon Press, 1983).

Death

Bernat, James, 'The Whole-Brain Concept of Death Remains Optimum Public Policy', *Journal of Law, Medicine & Ethics*, 34, 1 (2006), pp. 35–43.

Blatti, Stephen, 'Animalism', in *Stanford Encyclopedia of Philosophy* (2014). https://plato.stanford.edu/entries/animalism/

DeGrazia, David, 'The Definition of Death', in *Stanford Encyclopedia of Philosophy* (2016). https://plato.stanford.edu/entries/death-definition/

Feldman, Fred, *Confrontations with the Reaper* (New York: Oxford University Press, 1992).

Fisher, John Martin (ed.) *The Metaphysics of Death* (Stanford: Stanford University Press, 1993).

Gilmore, Cody, 'When Do Things Die?' in Ben Bradley, Jens Johansson, and Fred Feldman (eds.) *The Handbook of Philosophy and Death* (Oxford: Oxford University Press, 2012).

Mackie, David, 'Personal Identity and Dead People', *Philosophical Studies*, 95 (1999), pp. 219–242.

Nagel, Thomas, 'Death', *Noûs* 4, 1 (1970), pp. 73–80.

Robertson, John A., 'The Dead Donor Rule', *The Hastings Center Report*, 29, 6 (1999), pp. 6–14.

Shewmon, D. Alan, 'Chronic "Brain Death": Meta-analysis and Conceptual Consequences', *Neurology*, 51 (1998), pp. 1538–1545.

Shewmon, D. Alan, 'The Brain and Somatic Integration: Insights Into the Standard Biological Rationale for Equating "Brain Death" With Death', *Journal of Medicine and Philosophy*, 26, 5 (2001), pp. 457–478.

Veatch, Robert, *Death, Dying, and the Biological Revolution* (New Haven, CT: Yale University Press, 1976).

Moral status

Feinberg, Joel, 'Abortion', in Tom Regan (ed.) *Matters of Life and Death* (Philadelphia: Temple University Press, 1980), pp. 183–217.

Jaworska, Agnieszka, 'Caring and Full Moral Standing', *Ethics*, 117 (2007), pp. 460–497.

Regan, Tom, *The Case for Animal Rights* (Berkeley and Los Angeles: University of California Press, 1983).

Singer, Peter, 'Speciesism and Moral Status', *Metaphilosophy*, 40, 3–4 (2009), pp. 567–581.

Warren, Mary Anne, *Moral Status* (Oxford: Oxford University Press, 1997).

Tooley, Michael, 'Abortion and Infanticide', *Philosophy and Public Affairs*, 2 (1972), pp. 37–65.

Appendix

Personhood and moral status

The notion of moral status is frequently discussed or associated with that of personhood. For instance, some claim that X's being a person is sufficient for X's having moral status. In this appendix, I discuss the connection between these two notions and introduce Mary Anne Warren's account of moral status.

You may wrong your neighbour by inflicting pain on him not just because by hurting him you would sadden his wife, but also because you would violate something valuable for its own sake. An individual that has moral status can be wronged in virtue of violating something that matters for its own sake. All other things being equal, individuals like us have moral status and are valuable in themselves. However, it has been disputed whether being a person is also a necessary condition for having moral status. For instance, certain non-persons may deserve at least some degree of moral recognition – that is, even entities that are not persons may have moral status. Some philosophers draw the distinction between entities that have *full* moral status and entities that have it to lesser *degree*. So, full-grown human beings in possession of their cognitive capacities may have full moral status, whilst certain animals with some high cognitive skills (e.g., dolphins or great apes) may have some degree of moral status, certainly more than mosquitos and/ or tables. Sometimes foetuses or embryos are taken to have a certain degree of moral status, although not the same degree that is ascribed to adult human persons. Alternatively, we may treat certain entities at the margin of personhood *as if* they had some degree of moral status. Treating an entity as if it had moral status is not equivalent to ascribing moral status to such an entity. For instance, we may propose that it is appropriate to treat certain animals that are not persons as if they had some degree of moral status because if we didn't we may cultivate certain attitudes that would influence how we treat human persons – think about inflicting gratuitous pain upon certain animals and the character traits this activity is said to foster in children.

With respect to the main focus of this book, it is worth noticing how, on certain accounts, what is taken to ground the metaphysical relation of personal identity – at least on certain psychology-based accounts – may be taken to influence not just whether an entity has moral status, but also its degree. Suppose that a certain level of mental capacity relevant to personhood is taken to determine moral status. It can be further argued that the level of such capacities determines an entity's *degree* of moral status as well. Kantian and practical approaches to personhood and morality (Chapter 6) generally consider sophisticated cognitive faculties (e.g., autonomy, practical reasoning, etc.) as deserving special moral standing. Other accounts take it as sufficient to have a perspective on the world, something akin to having a rudimentary first-person perspective, having interests, and so on.[1]

Mary Anne Warren has proposed an account of moral status that nicely summarises many of the lines of reasoning explored so far. She puts forward seven principles that determine moral status the use of which is best understood when they are related to each other. Warren maintains that each principle can be used as an independent criterion of moral status.

1 "The respect for life principle: living organisms are not to be killed or otherwise harmed, without good reasons that do not violate principles 2–7.

2 The anti-cruelty principle: sentient beings are not to be killed or subjected to pain or suffering, unless there is no other feasible way of furthering goals that are (1) consistent with principles 3–7; and (2) important to human beings, or other entities that have a stronger moral status than that based on sentience alone.

3 The Agent's Rights principle: moral agents have full and equal basic moral rights, including the rights to life and liberty.

4 The Human Rights principle: within the limits of their own capacities and of principle 3, human beings that are capable of sentience but not of moral agency have the same moral rights as actual moral agents.

5 The Ecological principle: living things that are not moral agents, but that are important to the ecosystems of which they are part, have, within the limits of principles 1–4, a stronger moral status than that based upon their intrinsic properties alone; ecologically important entities that are not themselves alive, such as species and habitats, may also legitimately be accorded a stronger moral status than their intrinsic properties would indicate.

6 The Interspecific principle: within the limits of principles 1–5, non-human members of mixed social communities have a stronger moral status than could be based upon their intrinsic properties alone.

7 The Transitivity of Respect principle: within the limits of principles 1–6, and to the extent that is feasible and morally permissible, moral agents should respect one another's attributions of moral status."[2]

To have a better understanding of how these principles work, let us apply them to the case of abortion. After having clarified that the morality of abortion may not have to be judged solely on the basis of the intrinsic properties of the foetus, Warren claims that early foetuses (first ten weeks of pregnancy) are not moral agents – thus they do not have moral status according to the Agent's Rights principle. In addition, early foetuses are likely to be not capable of sentience, so the Anti-cruelty and the Human Right principles do not confer moral status on them. However, they are alive (and thus the Respect for life principle applies) and are regarded by certain people as having (a certain degree of) moral status – a property that may ground the application of the Transitivity of Respect principle. However, given the formulation of the principles, the moral status of embryos is limited by the moral rights of women (see the Agent's Right principle). According to Warren, the reasons generally provided by thoughtful people in support of an abortion are thus sufficient to justify the destruction of a living entity that has only moderate moral status.

Notes

1 See Feinberg (1980), Tooley (1972). Jaworska (2007) also includes certain emotional capacities.
2 The list is taken from Warren (1997), Chapter 6.

Glossary

abortion The termination of pregnancy before childbirth. This termination can be induced, e.g., by a medical procedure, or occur more or less spontaneously (miscarriage).

animalism A theory of our nature. It comes in different versions, e.g., (1) we are essentially living human organisms (or living animals), (2) we are living human organisms (or living animals), (3) we are essentially human organism (or animals), etc.

approach to personal identity, an An approach to personal identity is a family of theories, theses, or views on personal identity having some key conceptual features in common.

ātman An enduring self, owner, and subject of experiences that can have a divine nature. Buddhists generally argue that such an entity does not literally exist (a thesis known as the doctrine of no-self or *anātman*).

biographical identity The kind of identity involved in questions such as 'who am I?', 'who are you?', etc. Our biographical identity can comprise other forms of identities but does not imply, as such, a metaphysics of personhood. However, as exemplified by the narrative approach to personal identity, considerations regarding the psychological connections that sustain our biographical identity can be implemented into generic psychological theories as further criteria of identity over time and thus be of metaphysical relevance.

brain-part condition, the A necessary condition for the continuity of organisms and/or persons over time. The main idea is that the relevant parts of the brain responsible for various relevant higher forms of cognition (awareness, character, planning, etc.) must persist through time for the relevant organism/person to persist as well.

Buddhist no-self theories Theories according to which there is no persisting self (*ātman*). Some of these theories hold that statements about persons or selves can be understood as being conventionally true, but not as ultimately true. Also, the relation of composition between parts and wholes does not hold and, on some of these theories, only simples exist. According to other Buddhist no-self theories, everything is empty, that is, everything is devoid of *svabhāva*.

cardiopulmonary definition of human death Human death is the irreversible cessation of cardiopulmonary functions.

circulatory-respiratory definition of human death   Human death is the irreversible cessation of circulatory-respiratory functions.

compound dualism   According to essentialist compound dualism, we are essentially a compound of body and soul. A non-essentialist version of this theory holds that we are a compound of body and soul.

conditions of personal identity   Those conditions or criteria that determine the synchronic and diachronic identity of persons.

Confucian role-person theories   According to these theories, a person is (at least) necessarily a relational entity, and this relationality should be understood in terms of the Confucian *lǐ* (or in terms of other basic concepts that belong to the Confucian tradition). There are weaker and stronger versions of these theories, some even implying that only a strictly Confucian upbringing can sustain personal identity.

constitution theory, the   A theory of our nature according to which we are people constituted by a human organism, but not identical with it.

cryonics   A life-extending technology the main aim of which is to preserve our living or dead bodies at extremely low temperatures.

dead donor rule, the   The principle according to which donors must be declared dead prior to any procedure aimed at removing or transplanting their organs that would cause death.

deep lifespan extensions   Extensions the ultimate aim of which is the elimination or interruption of the process of ageing. In principle, such extensions can be endless but do not amount to immortality or invulnerability.

dharma   In an ontological sense, an ultimate component of reality. *Dharmas* are sometimes described as particular (i.e., non-repeatable) and transient psycho-/physical simple entities.

diachronic conditions of personal identity   The conditions that an entity should satisfy to be the same persisting person over time.

duān (端)   According to Mengzi, these are the four inner moral dispositions characteristic of all human beings. This term is sometimes translated with 'sprouts' or 'beginnings'.

eliminativism about person-talk   A revisionist stance towards statements about persons. One of the main claims of this stance is that, since persons do not exist, we should refrain from making statements that appear to refer to them.

embodied mind theory, the   A theory of our nature according to which we are essentially the thinking part of an organism.

epistemicism and personal identity   In general, epistemicism is an approach to vagueness. Its application to personal identity implies that alleged borderline cases of personal identity are the result of our ignorance of the thresholds (or cut off points) of the concept at issue. In principle, there is always a determined answer to questions of existence involving persons.

essential property   A property that an individual cannot but have.

fission thought experiments   A thought experiment or scenario in which one entity seems to divide in at least two further entities, each individually having a sufficient number of features that, on some theory of personal identity/our nature, may justify the identification of such an entity with the original pre-fission entity.

future-like-ours argument, the One of the best non-religious arguments against the morality of abortion. The main points of the arguments are: a foetus has a future like ours, and since depriving an entity of a future like ours (which is valuable) is morally bad, abortion is morally bad.

generic psychological theories of personal identity Psychological theories that do not specify or impose particular structural constraints on the psychological connections that are supposed to ground personal identity – e.g., whether the identity-sustaining psychological connections should form a narrative structure.

hēgemonikon The commanding part of the soul.

higher brain definition of human death Human death is the irreversible cessation of the functioning of the higher part of the brain (or of those parts responsible for our consciousness).

identification/individuation (metaphysical) The conditions of metaphysical individuation (or identification) of an object are the general conditions that an entity has to satisfy to exist as a singular object. If an entity is metaphysically identified/individuated, then it is a particular object different in reality from other objects.

identification/individuation (epistemological/cognitive) An epistemological/cognitive act of individuation (or identification) consists in the mental recognition or isolation of one or more entities as individual objects of attention or thought.

identity-sustaining relation A relation that metaphysically grounds personal identity. For example, an identity-sustaining narrative is a narrative that, on certain narrative views, can sustain (or be) the relation of personal identity. Such a narrative can play this role because it is adequate with respect to a series of requirements, e.g., the reality constraint (in short, an appropriate identity-sustaining narrative should not be delusional and contain descriptions that are compatible with how reality is). Similarly, identity-sustaining psychological connections are those connections that allegedly sustain the relation of personal identity.

jūnzî (君子) The exemplary person. An ethical/aesthetical ideal in the Confucian tradition.

karmic/transmigrational **Survival** The alleged survival of an individual through a series of causal connections that spans through different cycles of death and rebirth regulated by the laws of Karma.

li (禮) Codified patterns of ritual behaviour.

Lockean theories of personal identity Theories according to which personal identity over time depends on the identity (or continuity) of consciousness. There are various and contrasting interpretations of what Locke means by 'consciousness'.

mental uploading   A life-extending technology described as the process of psychological migration from brain to computer, that is, a process through which our mental states are allegedly transferred or copied to a computer.

mereological nihilism   In mereology (the theory of part/whole or of parthood relations), the doctrine according to which nothing is (or can be) part of anything else. In other words, mereological nihilism holds that the relation of composition never holds/cannot hold.

minimal self   A minimal self is what provides (or is) the subjective point of view through/from which we know the external world or our inner mental lives. A minimal self is also sometimes described as being (almost) featureless, that is, as having essentially only the property of being conscious and a perspective.

moral status   An individual that has moral status can be wronged for her own sake. On some views, having moral status is a matter of degree.

nihilism about our nature   The theory according to which, literally speaking, we do not exist.

nirvana   An enlightened state or condition that involves the cessation of suffering (and which is thus desirable).

oikeiosis   A mental state/capacity sometimes also called 'appropriation' or 'familiarisation'.

one-to-one condition, the   This condition on the formal properties of personal identity holds that personal identity must be a one-to-one relation.

only-x-and-y principle or the intrinsic condition, the   The principle according to which in determining whether P and Q are the same person, we should take into account only the nature (intended as the sum of the intrinsic properties) of the related entities (P and Q).

organ procurement   A surgical procedure or medical practice to remove organs for eventual reuse.

organ transplantation   A surgical or medical procedure in which one or more organs are removed from one or more donors and implanted into one or more recipients.

organic (or biological) continuity condition, the   A condition that describes one necessary condition for personal identity over time. According to one of its formulations, a necessary condition for a person to persist through time is that her organism persist as well. There are theories that include a stronger form of this condition, i.e., one that describes organism continuity as a necessary *and* sufficient condition. However, such stronger versions are more frequently applied to *our* identity conditions (e.g., by animalists).

organism   In the current philosophical literature on personal ontology, organisms are generally taken to display at least: (1) a dynamic stability, i.e., organisms tend to maintain the same form and structure through continuous exchange of material; (2) teleological organisation, i.e., the proper parts of an organism are organised in an internal teleological manner; (3) internal organisation, i.e., the intricate internal structure of an organism is regulated by a complex set of basic operating instructions.

person essentialism   A theory of our nature according to which we are essentially persons.

personal ontology   An area of ontology that studies the basic ontological category or categories under which we should be classified; in other words, a sub-discipline of ontology that attempts to provide an answer to the question 'what are we?' based on the search for our ontological category or categories. Despite its name, personal ontology *as such* is not equivalent to the metaphysical study of personal identity.

personal survival   A form of survival that essentially involves personal identity.

phase-sortal   A sortal that provides an answer to the question 'what is it?' and under which an individual may not always fall without thereby ceasing to exist (e.g., human child).

physical approach, the   A family of theories of personal identity/our nature that emphasise the necessary role of certain forms of physical continuity.

place-time-kind principle, the   A principle ascribed to Locke and the interpretation of which is still controversial. On one reading, the principle implies that two existing things of the same kind cannot occupy the same place at the same time. This would be true because, according to Locke, a substance is identical to all and only those substances of the same kind that occupy its same spatio-temporal location.

practical approach, the   Theories of personal identity/our nature that employ as main explanatory concept the notion of practical/moral agency.

prince and the cobbler thought experiment, the   An imaginary scenario devised by Locke to argue in favour of the distinction between the persistence conditions of human beings and souls. This scenario is an early example of what we may call a body swap.

prohairesis   Our moral character, that is, the faculty that regulates which representations we assent or withhold to, and that also judges their value. Theories of our nature based on this notion hold that such a faculty is what we really are.

psychological connectedness   The holding of (a certain number of) particular direct psychological connections.

psychological connection   One entity is psychologically connected to another in case these entities have mental states in common and/or such mental states are properly connected. Psychological connections involve memory, character traits, desires, intentions, and so on.

psychological continuity   Psychological continuity is the holding of overlapping chains of strong psychological connectedness between individuals. Contrary to psychological connectedness, psychological continuity is a transitive relation.

psychological essentialism   A theory of our nature according to which we are essentially psychological entities. It comes in at least two versions: (1) we are essentially entities that have mental states, (2) we are essentially entities that have the actual capacity to have mental states.

prajñapti   Conceptualisation or projection into reality of a mental construction.

pudgala   Person or individual.

qì (氣)   An alleged constitutive force of the universe frequently called also 'vital energy'.

reduplication thought experiment   A thought experiment or scenario in which one entity appears to undergo a process of reduplication, that is, a process the result of which is that at least two entities are relevantly related to the original entity – relevantly related according to some theory of personal identity with respect to their identity. In turn, such a connection is not generally in terms of standard forms of physical continuity.

relational-necessity theories   Theories holding that it is a necessary and sufficient condition for a self or person to exist that they be relational entities – that is, entities that are in some specific kinds of relations with other entities. Weaker versions simply hold that a person can persist only as a relational entity (or only as a specific relational entity).

relational-origin theories   According to these theories, a person/self can come into existence only as the result of the interactions she has with (other) individuals or as the result of the interactions of certain relevantly connected individuals among them.

rén (仁)   The term referring to *rén* has been variously translated with 'benevolence', 'virtue' (in a general sense), and 'humaneness'.

role survival   An alleged form of survival in which an individual can be said to survive in case her (social) role is still played by at least one individual. Alternative or more detailed versions of this concept depend on the specification of the social role in question.

self-/person-constituting narrative theories   The main idea of these theories is that people/selves/ourselves are entities the identity-sustaining psychological connections of which are narratively structured by a narrator, which in turn is also the protagonist of the narrative.

simple dualism   A theory of our nature according to which we are (essentially) souls.

simple-soul approach, the   An approach to personal identity and our nature the main explanatory notion of which is that of a (mereologically) simple soul.

$soul_{mind}$ According to Descartes, the $soul_{mind}$ is a simple, immortal, and immaterial thinking thing. Sense, perception, intellect and will are its main functions.

$soul_{Platonic\text{-}Phaedo}$ Originally referred to by using the term '*psuchê*', the soul in Plato's *Phaedo* is divine, partless or incomposite, immaterial, invariant, indissoluble, and immortal. Also, $souls_{Platonic\text{-}Phaedo}$ exist before their embodiment, are capable of cognising the Forms, and are the principle of life.

$soul_{Platonic\text{-}Phaedo}$/$soul_{mind}$ Theories of Personal Identity   According to these theories, personal identity through time depends on the persistence of the same $soul_{Platonic\text{-}Phaedo}$/$soul_{mind}$.

strong lifespan extensions   Extensions of our lifespan resulting from technologies that increase both the average and the maximum lengths of our lives.

substance-sortal A sortal is a concept we use to identity, classify, and count things. Substance-sortals are those sortals that stand for kinds that specify the identity conditions of things that fall under them such that if one of these entities ceases to belong to the referred kind, it also ceases to exist.

sunyatta Emptiness, in the sense of absence of *svabhāva*.

svabhāva Depending on the Buddhist school and interpretation, the essence of an individual, the intrinsic nature of an entity, the real existence of an entity, or even a possibly misleading cognition.

synchronic conditions of personhood The conditions that an entity must satisfy to be a person at any time.

temporal stage A proper temporal part of a perduring object.

thinking animal argument, the One of the main arguments in favour of animalism. Its main structure is: (1) There is a human animal sitting in your chair right now – or wherever you are now (L). (2) The human animal in L now is thinking. (3) You are the thinking being in the spatio-temporal location L. (4) Therefore, the human animal in L is you.

time-relative interest account (TRIA) According to this account, the badness of X's death is a function also of X's time-relative interest in continuing to live and of X's psychological structure.

transitivity condition, the A formal condition that the relation of personal identity is supposed to satisfy; in particular, the condition holds that, since personal identity is a transitive relation, a relation in terms of which personal identity can be properly analysed should be transitive as well (e.g., psychological continuity).

volitional theories Volitional theories rely on the idea that personal identity depends on the continuity of our volitions or desires.

weak lifespan extensions Extensions that result from an incremental surge in life expectancy obtained through improvements in the treatment and prevention of disease. The causes at the basis of weak lifespan extensions include a better access to appropriate treatments and the promotion of a healthier lifestyle – e.g., healthy diet, physical activity, social engagement, and active mental functioning.

whole-brain condition, the A necessary condition for the continuity of organisms and/or persons. The main idea is that the whole brain must persist through time for the relevant person/organism to persist as well.

whole-brain definition of human death, the Human death is the irreversible cessation of functioning of the whole brain.

xin (心) In early Chinese thinking, the heart-mind, that is, the physical centre of our cognitive, affective, and conative capacities.

Index

Abhidharma tradition 53, 56–63, 64, 66
abortion 198; animalism and 200–205; Aquinas's hylomorphism and Catholic view on 206–208; Buddhist no-self view and 216–217; constitution view and 212–213; embodied mind and 210–212; personhood and moral status and 228–230; psychological approach and 208–213; relational-narrative entities and 214–216; self-constituting narrative and practical approaches and 213–214; soul approach and 205–208
agency and personal identity 157
Ames, Roger 80–81
Analects, The 76, 88
Anatta-lakkhana Sutta 59
animalism 13–14, 135–137, 198; abortion and 200–205; cardiopulmonary definition of death and 218–219; defined 124; essentialist animalism 18, 48, 102, 126, 135, 197; identity conditions in 136–137; life-extending technologies and 191; non-modal version of 136; survival and 181–182; whole brain death and 220–221
Annas, Julia 147–148
anti-criterialism 18
Appiah, Anthony 147
appropriations 108–109
Aquinas, Thomas 8, 11, 206–208
Aristotle 10, 32, 37, 206–207
assenting 147–153
Athenagoras 127
Ātman 54–56, 59, 65
Augustine 31, 48, 71; view on nature of the soul 37–38
Averroes 8

Baker, Lynne Rudder 212–213
beginning, our 199–200
beginning and the end, the *see* human development
biological approach 135

Bodhicaryāvatāra 69
bodies: lost 102–106; varieties of physical continuity of 128–131
Boethius 11
Book of Rites 86
brahman 55–56
brain-transplant scenarios 20–21
Bratman, Michael 152
Buddhist no-self approach 3, 4, 16, 22–23, 52–53, 72–73, 92–93; *Abhidharma, Skandhas,* and *Vasubandhu* 56–63; abortion and 216–217; compassion in 69–70; death and 221–222; emptiness of the self and Nāgārjuna in 63–66; ethics and 66–70; life-extending technologies and 188–189; nihilism and our nature in 70–72; survival and 179–180; teachings on suffering 53–56
Butler, Joseph 110, 167, 168–171
Bynum, Caroline Walker 126

Calvino, Italo 181–182
Campbell, Keith 57
cardiopulmonary definition of death 218–220
Carter, William R. 135
Catholic view on abortion 206–208
Chalmers, David 21, 41, 186, 187
Chappell, Vere 104
Christianity 123–124, 140; Augustine' view on nature of the soul 37–38; early views on the origin of the soul 38–40; God in 10–11; Medieval theologians 30–31; sin and resurrection in 124–128; varieties of physical continuity and 128–131
Chrysippus 124, 148
Cicero 10, 148
circularity objection 110–112
cohabitation 176–178
Collins, Anthony 168
compassion 69–70
composition as identity (CAI) 62
compound dualism 42–45

Confucian role-person 76–78; individuation, heart-mind and the Confucian self 78–80; and *Li* 83–87; life-extending technologies and 189–190; Mencius's four roots in 88–89; relational person and its origin 80–83; role-personhood and personal identity 87–88; self-cultivation and 89–91; survival and 180–181

Confucian tradition 9, 22–23, 76–78; relational-necessity approach 82–83; relational-origin approach 81–82; see *also* early Confucian tradition (ECT)

Connected Discourses of the Buddha,The 52

consciousness and personal identity 106–109, 118

constitutionalism/constitution view 137–140

constitution view and abortion 212–213

continuity of persons 16; varieties of 128–131

corporeal soul 125–128

Council of Alexandria 11

cryonics and mental uploading 21–22, 185–192

Currie, Gregory 147

Davenport, John 147

dead donor rule 222

De Anima 37

death 217–218; cardiopulmonary definition of 218–220; defining 218–222; higher brain definition of 221–222; intrinsic interest in 222–223; whole brain definition of 220–221

De Finibus 148

DeGrazia, David 135, 203, 204–205, 223

Dennett, Daniel 146, 156

Descartes, René 9, 31, 48, 71, 82, 101; dualism 46; on the soul$_{mind}$ 40–42; Swinburne's compound dualism and 42–45

descriptive metaphysics 79

developmental sense of relationality 81

dharmas 57–58, 72–73

Dick, Philip K. 97

Discourses 150

doctrine of double existence 104

Donum Vitae 208

Dr. Jekyll and Mr. Hyde 105

dualism: compound 42–45; hylomorphic 207; mind-body 40–42, 46; personal identity and 45–47

Duerlinger, James 62

early Confucian tradition (ECT) 77; heart-mind in 80; on our nature 88–89; self-cultivation in 89–91; on self-reflexive mental capacities 79–80; social relational-necessity approach 83–86; see *also* Confucian role-person

Egan, Greg 21

embodied mind view 137–140, 198; abortion and 210–212

emptiness of the self 63–66

Epictetus 149–150

episodic self 160

epistemicism 27

Essay Concerning Human Understanding,An 39, 97

eternalism 14–15

familiarisation 147–150

family of X-theories 4

Fight Club 105

Fincher, David 105

fission scenarios 20

Ford, Norman 31

form-finding 159

Foucault, Michel 92, 150

Frankfurt, Harry 146, 147; on personhood 150–154

"Freedom of the Will and the Concept of a Person" 150

"Fundamental Wisdom of the Middle Way, The" 65

Gallagher, Shaun 12–13

Ganeri, Jonardon, 54

Gasser, Georg 26

Gill, Christopher 10, 125

God, Christian 10–11, 127

Goodman, Charles 58, 69

Graham, A. C. 89

Greeks, ancient 30–31; Platonic-Phaedo soul and personal identity 35–37; *psuchê* 32–33; the soul in *Phaedo* (soul$_{Platonic-Phaedo}$) and 33–35

Haldane, John 207

Hall, Wayne 184

Harris, John 185

Harvey, Peter 189, 216

Hazlitt, William 167, 168–171

heart-mind 78–80

Hegel, Friedrich 77

higher brain definition of death 221–222

Hobbes, Thomas 100

Homer 32

human development 197–198, 223–224; death and 217–223; early stages of 199–200; personhood and moral status and 228–230; physical approach and 200–205; psychological approach and 208–213; soul approach and 205–208

Hume, David 65
hylomorphism 206–208

"Identification and Externality" 151
identification and individuality 7–9
Il Visconte Dimezzato (The Cloven Viscount) 182
individuation and the Confucian self 78–80
intra-personal ethics and no-self 66–68
intrinsic condition 113
invulnerability 185
Ivanhoe, P. J. 77, 90, 91

Jones, Neil R. 185–186

Kant, Immanuel 44
Karma 68, 189, 216
Keown, Damien 216
Kierkegaard, Søren 147
Korsakov's syndrome 160
Korsgaard, Christine 146, 154–156

Lamarque, Peter 147
Lee, Patrick 207
Leibniz, Gottfried W. 9
Le Testament 197
Leviathan 100
Lewis, David 167, 176–178
li 83–87
life-extending technologies 184–185, 192–194;
    Buddhist no-self approach and nihilism and
    188–189; cryonics and mental uploading as
    21–22, 185–192; lifespan extensions: strong,
    weak, deep 184–185; practical and narrative
    approaches to 191–192; relational approach
    and Confucian role-person and 189–190;
    simple-soul approach to 188
Lindemann, Hilde 84, 147, 198, 214–216, 219
Livingston, Paisley 147
Locke, John 9, 12, 21, 92, 97–98, 118–119; on
    circularity objection and quasi-memory
    110–112; on consciousness and personal
    identity 106–109; contemporary psycholog-
    ical theories and 112–118; death and 219,
    220; on lost souls and lost bodies 102–106;
    on pure substance 39; theories of identity
    and person 98–102
logical properties of identity 25
Lolordo, Antonia 104
Long, Anthony 124, 148–150
Lucke, Jayne C. 184

Mackie, David 219
MacIntyre, Alasdair 147, 161
Madhyamaka tradition 53, 63–66, 68–69, 70–71
Maha-Kassapa 189

Marquis, Don 198, 201–202
Martyr, Justin 126
Marxist philosophy 77
material soul 125–128
McMahan, Jeff 124, 139, 198, 205, 209–212
Meditations 41
Mengzi 77, 78, 89, 91, 94; and Mencius's four
    roots 88–89
mental uploading scenarios 21–22, 185–192
mereological nihilism 61
Metaphysical Foundation of Personal Identity 36
methodology of personal identity analyses
    19–23
Metzinger, Thomas 12
mind-body dualism 40–42, 46
moral accountability condition 114
moral character (*prohairesis*) 146, 147–150
moral status and personhood 228–230

Nāgārjuna 63–66, 72–73
narrative identity and personal identity *see*
    practical and narrative approaches
narrative module 157
narrative self 13
Nicomachean Ethics 10
Nietzsche, Friedrich 145
night- and day-man 105
nihilism 4; abortion and 216–217; death and
    221–222; and our nature 70–72; survival
    and 179–180
nirvana 54, 66
no-self theories *see* Buddhist no-self approach
non-branching condition 113, 173, 190
Nozick, Robert 117
numerical identity 8

oikeiosis 148
Olson, Eric 13, 26, 45, 135, 136, 203
one-to-one condition 113
only-x-and-y principle 113
*On the Free Choice of the Will
    (De Libero Arbitrio)* 38
On the Trinity 37
organism/organic continuity 21, 123, 129, 234

Palahniuk, Chuck 105
Pañcaskandhaka-prakana 58
Parfit, Derek 15, 19, 26, 27, 98, 124; embod-
    ied part view 139; psychological theory of
    personal identity 114–118, 208–209; on
    quasi-memory 111–112, 118–119, 134; on
    survival 167, 171–176, 181–182; tele-trans-
    portation thought experiment 187
Passions of the Soul (Les passions de l'âme), The 40
Perkins, Franklin 78

permanent vegetative state (PVS) 217
Permutation City 21
Perry, John 111
persistence and time 14–15, 17–18
personal identity: adequacy conditions for
contemporary psychological theories of
113–114; agency and 157; basic concepts of
7–16; basic logical properties of 25; Buddhist
traditions on (see Buddhist no-self approach);
Christian view on (see Christianity); circularity objection and quasi-memory 110–112;
concept of self and 1–2, 12–14; concepts
of personhood and persons in 9–12; Confucian view of (see Confucian role-person);
consciousness and 106–109; dimensions of
variation 17–19; dualism and 45–47; emphasis put on extrinsic or relational aspects of
18–19; essentialism and 18; identification
and individuality in 7–9; as illusion 63–66;
key questions in debate on our nature and 3;
life-extending technologies, our nature, and
184–185; Locke on person and 98–102; main
approaches to 3–7; methodological remarks
on analysis of 19–23; narrative identity and
160–162; Parfit's psychological theory of
114–118; persistence and time in 14–15,
17–18; physical approach in (see physical
approach); practical and narrative approaches
to (see practical and narrative approaches);
psychological approach to (see psychological
approach); relational-necessity theory of
82–83; relational-origin approach 81–82;
role-personhood and 87–88; self-cultivation
and 91; simple/complex, reductionism/nonre-
ductionism classifications of 26–28; simple
view of 31–32; soul and (see simple-soul
approach; soul(s)); specificity of definition
of sustaining conditions of 18; survival and
15–16, 178–184; theoretical aims of analy-
ses/conditions of 17; volitions, the will, and
153–154
"Personal Identity and the Unity
of Agency" 154
person essentialism 102, 126
personhood and persons 9–12, 86; Frankfurt on
150–154; Locke on 98–102; moral status and
228–230
Persons, Animals, Ourselves 181
Phaedo 30, 48, 54, 188; the soul in 33–35,
205–206
phantasia 148–149
physical approach 5–6, 123–124, 140–141;
abortion, animalism, and 200–205; animalism
and 13–14, 124, 135–137; consitutionalism
137–140; death and 220–221; embodied

mind view 137–140; life-extending technologies and 191; stoic body, Christian sin,
and resurrection in 124–128; survival and
181–182; thinking animal argument 137–140;
thought experiments and Bernard Williams's
reduplication argument 131–135; varieties of
physical continuity in 128–131
Plato 30, 32, 48, 188; on the soul, in *Phaedo*
33–35, 205–206; on soul$_{Platonic-Phaedo}$ and
personal identity 35–37
practical and narrative approaches 6, 145–147,
162; abortion and 213–214; death and 219;
familiarisation, asserting, and *prohairesis* in
the Stoic tradition 147–150; Frankfurt on
personhood in 150–154; life-extending technologies and 191–192; practical unity and
the self-constitution view 154–157; self-constructing narrative view 158–162; survival
and 182–184
practical unity 154–157
Priestley, Joseph 169
prohairesis 146, 147–150
psychological approach 5, 97–98; abortion and
208–213; on circularity objection and quasi-memory 110–112; on consciousness and
personal identity 106–109; contemporary
psychological theories and 112–118; death
and 219, 220–221; life-extending technologies
and 190–191; on lost souls and lost bodies
102–106; Parfit's 114–118; on pure substance
39; theories of identity and person 98–102;
and what matters in survival 171–176
psychological complexity condition 114
psychological continuity 26, 114–119
psychological connection 20, 145, 170, 174, 181,
211
psychological essentialism 102
pugdala 60
Pythagoras 32

qualitative identity 8
quasi-memory 110–112
quest-for-the-good tendency 159
Quine, Willard V. O. 19, 178

reactive attitudes condition 114
Reasons and Persons 116, 119
reductionism/non-reductionism 26–28, 116–117
reduplication experiments 20, 131–135
reflection 106–108
Reid, Thomas 110, 113
relational approach 5; abortion and 214–216;
compared to simple-soul and Buddhist
no-self approaches 92–93; Confucian
role-person and 76–94; death and 219;

life-extending technologies and 189–190; survival and 180–181
relational ethics and no-self 68–70
relational-necessity approach 82–83
relational-origin approach 81–82, 92
Republic 30, 35, 38
resurrection 124–128
Ricouer, Paul 147
Rodriguez-Pereyra, Gonzalo 46
role-person *see* Confucian role-person
Rosemont, Henry 83
Rudd, Anthony 147

Sacks, Oliver 22, 160
sameness of consciousness 108
Sankara 55
Sartre, Jean-Paul 147
Schapp, Wilhelm 147
Schechtman, Marya 146, 158, 161, 182–183, 213, 215
self: concept of 1–2, 12–14; Confucian 78–80; emptiness of 63–66; episodic 160
self-concern 166–167; survival and 168–171
self-consciousness 12–13
self-constitution view 154–157; abortion and 213–214; death and 219
self-constructing narrative view 158–162
self-cultivation in the ECT 89–91
Sergeant, John 110
Serveto, Miguel 10
Shantideva 68–69
Shewmon, Alan 217–218, 222
Shoemaker, Sydney 12, 111, 118–119, 139
Shun, Kwong-Loo 80
Siderits, Mark 28
simple/complex classification 26–28
simple-soul approach 4, 47–48; abortion and 205–208; Descartes on the soul$_{mind}$ 40–42; early Christian views on the nature of the soul 37–38; early Christian views on the origin of the soul 38–40; life-extending technologies and 188; in Plato's *Phaedo* 33–35; souls$_{Platonic-Phaedo}$ and personal identity in 35–37; survival and 178–179; Swinburne and compound dualism 42–45; wandering soul and *psuchê* 32–33
simple view 31–32
skandhas 56–63, 71
Snowdon, Paul 135, 181–182
social conception of the person 81
social relational-necessity approach 83–86
Socrates 30, 33–34
soul(s): corporeal or material 125–128; lost 102–106; *see also* simple-soul approach
special concern 167

Sperry, R. W. 171
Stefan, Matthias 26
Steinbock, Bonnie 224
Stevenson, Robert Louis 105
Stoic body 124–128
Stoics and *prohairesis* 146, 147–150
story-telling 159
Strawson, Galen 159, 160
Suarez, Francisco 9
substance 39–40, 46–47, 101
suffering, the Buddha on 53–56
Summa Theologiae 11
survival 15–16, 166–168, 192–194; Buddhist no-self approach and nihilism and 179–180; cryonics and mental uploading and 21–22, 185–192; Lewis on cohabitation and 176–178; life-extending technologies and 184–185; and the other approaches to personal identity 178–184; physical approach and nihilism and 181–182, 191; practical identity and narrative approaches and 182–184, 191–192; psychological approach and what matters in 171–176, 190–191; relational approach and Confucian role-person and 180–181; self-concern and 168–171; simple-soul approach and 178–179; Karmic/ transmigrational 179, 233
svabhāva 63–66
Swinburne, Richard 31–32, 48, 206; on compound dualism 42–45
symmetric identity 25

Taylor, Charles 147
tele-transportation scenarios 21–22, 187
temporal stage 177–178
Tertullian 10–11, 127–128
Theory of Forms 33–34
Thiel, Udo 11, 107–109
thinking animal argument 137–140
thought experiments 19–22, 104–106; reduplication argument and 131–135; tele-transportation 21–22, 187
Timaeus 30, 37
time and persistence 14–15, 17–18
Tooley, Michael 208
transitive identity 25
transitivity condition 113
Treatise on Human Nature 65
Treatise on the Soul, A 127
Twilight of the Idols, The 145

unity, practical 154–157
Upanishads 54–56

Valla, Lorenzo 10
Vasubandhu 56–63, 72
Velleman, J. David 146, 156–157
Villon, François 197
volitions 153–154

wandering souls and *psuchê* 32–33
Warren, Mary Anne 200, 228–230
Watson, Gary 152
Westerhoff, Jan 63, 70–71, 73
whole brain definition of
    death 220–221

Wiggins, David 11, 181
Wilkes, Kathleen 22
will, the 153–154
Williams, Bernard 98, 117, 123; reduplication
    argument 131–135
Williams, Donald C. 57–58
Wittgenstein, Ludwig 13
Wong, David 81

Xunzi 77, 78, 90–91

Yaffe, Gideon 99

37023210R00138

Printed in Great Britain
by Amazon